THE SUPERPOWERS

THE SUPERPOWERS

THE UNITED STATES AND
THE SOVIET UNION COMPARED

W. H. PARKER

M.A., B.Sc., D.Phil. (Oxon.)

Halsted Press Division
John Wiley & Sons, Inc.
New York

First published 1972 by
THE MACMILLAN PRESS LTD
London and Basingstoke
Associated companies in New York Toronto
Dublin Melbourne Johannesburg and Madras

Printed in Great Britain by
RICHARD CLAY (THE CHAUCER PRESS) LTD
Bungay, Suffolk

Published in the United States
by Halsted Press Division
John Wiley & Sons, Inc., New York

ISBN 0 470–66600–5

LC catalog card no. 72–3241

Contents

Preface

Comparison has long been recognised as an odious task: one of the parties compared is likely to take umbrage. In the course of making a very large number of comparisons it is fairly certain that an author, however objective he may strive to be, will incur the wrath of those on both sides. The favourable points he makes will be taken for granted but the unflattering contrasts will not be forgiven. He can, of course, confine the odium to one side by seeing that his comparisons uniformly favour the other, and such black-and-white studies of America and Russia have appeared in both countries. There are, fortunately, a few comparative works relating to the two superpowers which are admirably just in their appraisal. Paul Dukes's *The Emergence of the Super-Powers* and Brzezinski and Huntingdon's *Political Power: USA/USSR* are praiseworthy examples of well-balanced treatment, and there is much to be said for Paul Hollander's method – in his *American and Soviet Society* – of placing American and Soviet views on selected topics side by side. Such works, however, are not comprehensive comparisons of the two superpowers, but consider some special aspect of their development – historical political or social. The present writer has attempted a more general comparison in the belief that it may prove useful and convenient to have a wide range of information about the two countries presented and discussed within the compass of a small book.

Christ Church,
  Oxford,
30 *July* 1971

W. H. PARKER

Illustrations

Abbreviations

This list also gives the meaning of a few Russian words that have been used in the text.

ABM – anti-ballistic missile
Agrogorodok – small town built to house farm workers
Ala – Alabama
apparat – Soviet state or Party organisation
apparatchik – Soviet state or Party official
Ariz. – Arizona
art. – article
a.s.l. – above sea level
babushka – grandmother
bln – billion (i.e. 1,000,000,000)
b.s.l. – below sea level
c. – *circa* (approximately)
°C – degrees Celsius (centigrade)
Calif. – California
CENTO – Central Treaty Organisation
CIA – Central Intelligence Agency
COMECON – Council for Economic Mutual Assistance
CPSU – Communist Party of the Soviet Union
Dept – department
DC – direct current
D.C. – District of Columbia
druzhinnik – auxiliary policeman
°F – degrees Fahrenheit
Fla – Florida
ft – feet
Ga – Georgia
GNP – gross national product
GOSPLAN – State Planning Commission of the USSR
ha – hectares (one hectare = 2·4711 acres)
H.E.P. – hydro-electric power
Ill. – Illinois
Ind. – Indiana
kolkhoz – collective farm

kolkhoznik – collective farmer
km – kilometre(s) (one km = 0·6214 mile)
kw – kilowatt(s)
kwh – kilowatt-hour(s)
Ky – Kentucky
La – Louisiana
m – metres(s)
Mass. – Massachusetts
Md – Maryland
mi – mile(s) (one mile = 1·609 km)
Mich. – Michigan
Minn. – Minnesota
mln – million
mm – millimetre(s)
MRBM – medium-range ballistic missile
muzhik – peasant
n.a. – not available
Nar. Khoz. – *Narodnoye Khozyaystvo SSSR* ('The National Economy of
    the USSR', the Soviet annual statistical abstract)
n.d. – no data *or* no date
Nev. – Nevada
NORAD – North American Air Defence Command
N.J. – New Jersey
N.Y. – New York State
oblast – Russian administrative district
Pa – Pennsylvania
pop. – population
SALT – strategic arms limitation talks
SEATO – South-East Asia Treaty Organisation
Sib. – Siberia
SMA – standard metropolitan area
SLBM – submarine-launched ballistic missile
Stat. Abst. – *Statistical Abstract of the United States* (annual)
tayga – the forest, mostly coniferous, which covers much of the northern
    part of the USSR
Tex. – Texas
UAR – United Arab Republic
USSR – Union of Soviet Socialist Republics
Vnesh. Torg. – *Vneshnyaya Torgovlya SSSR* ('The Foreign Trade of the
    USSR' – an annual book of trade statistics)
Wash. – Washington
Wis. – Wisconsin
W. Va – West Virginia

General Note

Currency exchange rate. It is extremely difficult to relate the dollar to the rouble satisfactorily. At the official exchange rate one rouble is worth $1·11, but many American sovietologists consider a rate of between 40 cents and 50 cents per rouble more realistic. They have applied such a rate as a conversion factor for some years, despite the steadily declining value of the dollar and the relative stability of Soviet prices.*

Statistics. These present another difficulty, for there is disagreement among specialists as to the reliability of Soviet statistics. There is an excellent discussion of this question in *The Soviet Economy*, ed. H. G. Shaffer, pp. 3–26. The problem defies solution, and Soviet statistics have been given here because they are usually the only ones available. American statistics are invariably accepted without question, although private companies may be as liable to withhold or falsify information as Soviet officials and managers.

Comparative Table. A comparative table for ready reference to such facts as area, population, size of labour force, gross national product, etc., will be found at the end of the book (pages 329–34). Readers using it are advised to bear in mind the notes on exchange rates and statistics given on this page. The index may be used as a guide to further information and discussion.

* Since this note was written, the devaluation of the dollar has become likely and the figures given will need adjustment according to the amount of any such devaluation.

1 Global Position and International Relations

The fundamental contrast between the two superpowers derives from the disposition of land and sea over the surface of the globe. If Wegener's convincing hypothesis is true, the land originally formed a single mass, the outer parts of which have drifted away to form the separate continents.[1] They are still close enough together, however, for it to be possible to divide the globe into two halves in such a way that one half is covered almost entirely by sea, while the other contains most of the land. This land hemisphere consists of one large unbroken central area and a surrounding zone of peninsulas and islands, some small and some of continental size.

Over fifty years ago the British political geographer, Mackinder, argued that this massing together of the earth's land surface was the fundamental geographical reality, the implications of which had to be understood if a titanic struggle between land power and sea power were to be avoided. British sea power had long dominated the coasts of this 'world island'; but if a strong nation were to control and develop the 'incalculably great' natural resources of its 'heartland' – a region corresponding closely to the territories of the Russian empire and inaccessible to sea power – this new force would not be for ever content to remain confined within its natural fortress, suffering the constriction of encirclement and the humiliation of exclusion from the oceans.[2]

Because the USSR occupies a central position in the land hemisphere, its territory has difficult access to the open oceans and is, in turn, not easy to reach from them. Nowhere can its shores be approached or left without passing through seas or straits controlled by foreign powers or blocked, at least seasonally, by ice. The USA, on the other hand, lies astride the continent of North America, which trends away from the central land mass into the outer ocean. It has free access to the high seas from its open unimpeded Atlantic, Gulf and Pacific coasts. This difference between the two superpowers is further illustrated by the fact that, whereas the USA has only two immediate neighbours, the USSR has a common boundary with thirteen states and another seventeen lie, in whole or in part, within five hundred miles of its frontiers.

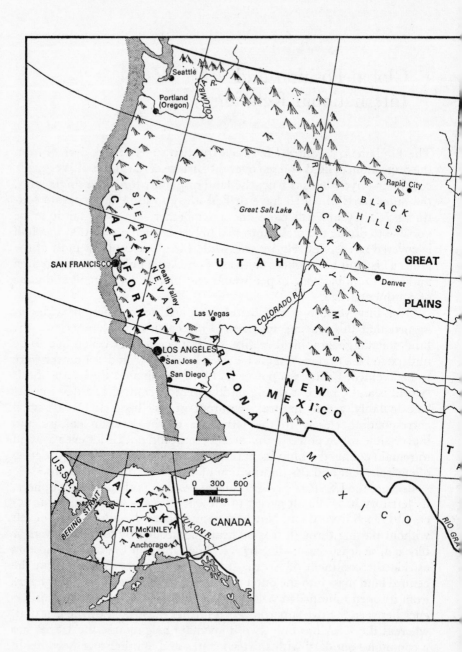

1. United States, general

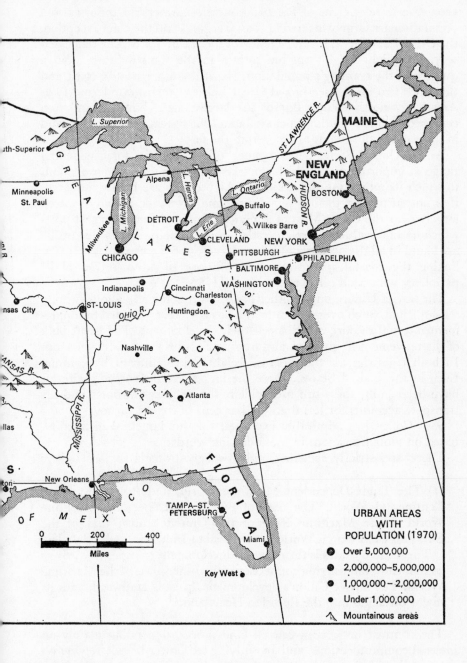

URBAN AREAS
WITH
POPULATION (1970)

- Over 5,000,000
- 2,000,000–5,000,000
- 1,000,000 – 2,000,000
- Under 1,000,000
- Mountainous areas

This contrast in global position has had a decisive effect upon the economic development of the two countries. American industry and population are largely located in coastal regions and the chief exception, the Great Lakes area, is connected with the sea by the St Lawrence seaway. The eight largest agglomerations in the United States hold a quarter of the country's population: six of them are on the coast and the other two on the sea-linked Great Lakes, sometimes referred to as America's 'north coast'. But of the largest eight Soviet population centres only one is on the sea coast and all the others are hundreds, and in some cases, thousands of miles from the sea.[3]

As the United States depends upon other countries for a widening range of imported materials, for markets, and for the immigrant skills to which its industrial and military achievements are highly indebted, it is not surprising to find population and economic activity located largely near the coast. Most of America's biggest cities are great ports which handle seaborne foreign trade. Ships participating in this traffic are found in all the oceans and seas that surround the central land mass, linking the coastal, peninsular and offshore island countries of its periphery with each other and with the USA.

The Soviet Union, on the other hand, is economically almost wholly self-sufficient. Such overseas trade as it has is merely intended to supplement internal resources and speed their development. The great bulk of the movement of goods to and from its industrial areas is over land. In both countries air transport of freight is insignificant by volume. Even in the United States, where the largest freight-carrying aircraft have been built, these are used chiefly for military purposes and air transport accounts for less than 0·2 per cent of freight turnover.

Saul Cohen has admirably expressed this fundamental distinction, based on global position, in the following words:

There are, strictly speaking, only two geostrategic regions today:

(1) The Trade-Dependent Maritime World, and (2) the Eurasian Continental World. The core of the Trade-Dependent Maritime World is the Maritime Ring of the United States; that of the Eurasian Continental World is the Russian Industrialised Triangle.

The United States is thrusting its development energies towards its coastal rims, intensifying connections with other parts of the Maritime World. The Soviet Union's development thrust is landward, with its major direction into the Eurasian Heartland.[4]

The contrast between a central land power, depending mainly on internal communications, and an outlying sea power largely relying on external links, is found also in the strategic and military sphere. Nothing illustrates the centre-periphery antithesis which the USSR and the USA present in their global position more clearly than a map showing the location of the allies and bases of the United States (Fig. 3). Before this ring was breached by the growth of Soviet influence in the Middle East, these formed almost a complete circle around the Soviet Union and China. India presented the only gap. On the other hand, the Soviet military presence is limited to a few countries along her western border, within the American ring. When she attempted to place a similar base of her own in Cuba, close to the United States, and well outside this containing American perimeter, she was compelled to abandon the scheme under threat of nuclear war.

It has often been argued that the development of air power and nuclear power have deprived global position and the distribution of land and sea of continuing significance, but nothing could be further from the truth. America's air and nuclear strength is increasingly borne by aircraft carriers and submarines which can move all round the central land mass and which, because they are mobile targets, are less vulnerable than fixed land bases. The fact that the United States has twenty great aircraft carriers, each carrying up to a hundred aircraft, and the USSR none, is eloquent testimony to the enduring nature of the sea power – land power antithesis.

In nuclear weapons, each superpower strives to maintain its 'second-strike capability', ensuring that, if struck first, it can still retaliate and achieve the enemy's total destruction. While such a balance is maintained, it may be fairly argued that all-out nuclear warfare is unlikely. This gives renewed life to conventional strategy which must take account, above all else, of the distribution of land and sea.

From the American point of view, there are two undesirable aspects of being compelled, by the balance of terror, to rely upon conventional arms. The first of these is the communist quantitative superiority in most branches of orthodox warfare. The second is the growing strategic advantage of land-based over sea-based power. The communist powers, entrenched within the central interior of the land hemisphere, by making themselves economically almost wholly self-sufficient have removed the greatest strategic danger of their land-locked position – vulnerability to blockade. They, and especially the USSR, are developing a system of overland communications, using rail, road, river, canal, pipe and power line, which although involving much greater cost and effort in its formation, and yielding less flexibility and accessibility compared with the free, open and continuous sea, has a vital advantage: it can be disrupted with any certainty of success only by nuclear-armed rockets which would precipitate the suicidal holocaust that it is assumed both sides must avoid. Soviet electronic equipment deployed in Egypt

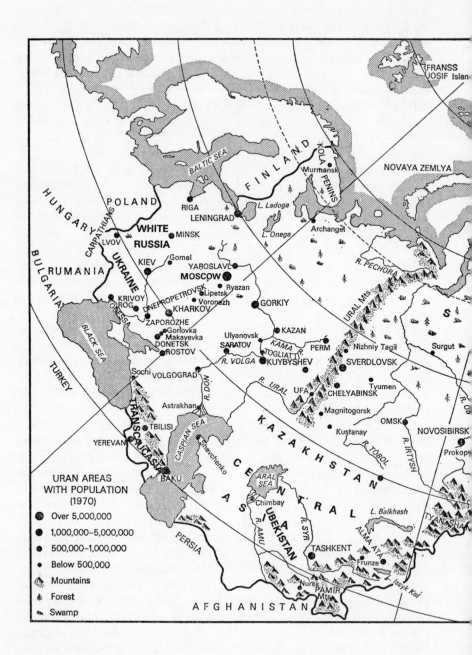

2. USSR, general

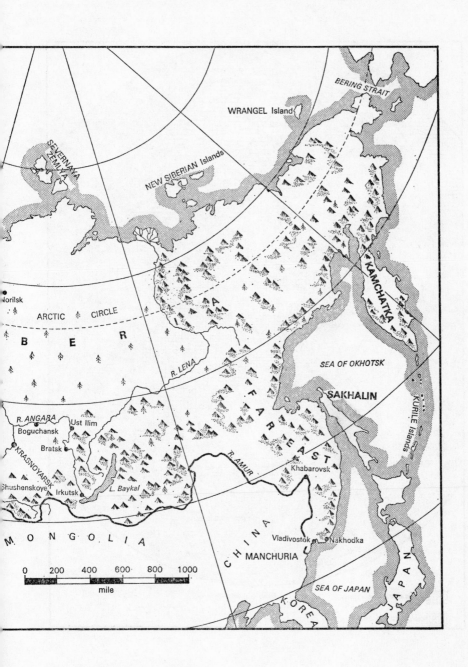

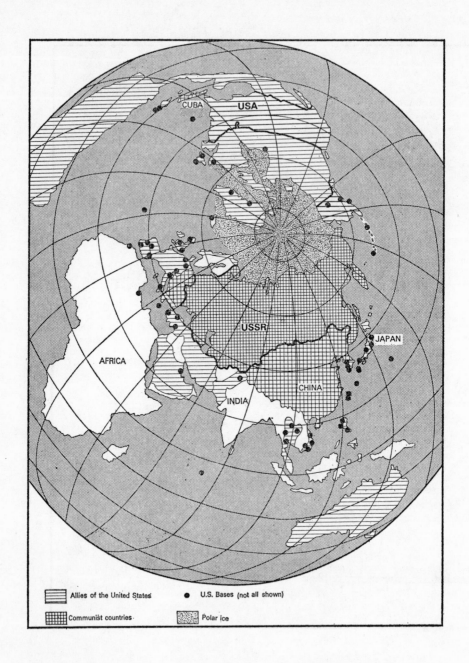

3. Allies, dependencies and overseas bases of the United States

has shown the unlikelihood of conventional aircraft being able to penetrate Soviet air defences.

The peripheral powers, on the other hand – those island and peninsular lands circumferential to the world island and dominated militarily and penetrated economically by America – must move their trade by sea. None of them, not even the United States, has anything approaching economic autarky, and such trade is vital to them. To protect this trade they must rely on naval power. But unlike the land over which Soviet internal trade moves, the sea is open to all. Communist naval forces are free to shadow the military and mercantile navies of the maritime nations as they please. They can crowd the water with submarines able, without warning, to sink and destroy the vessels upon which the peripheral states must rely, without departing from the rules of orthodox warfare. The maritime states cannot in the same way crowd communist territory with aircraft and tanks, nor use them to follow the movement of commercial goods and military supplies. In other words, using the jargon of the nuclear 'war game', the Soviet Union has a 'first-strike' conventional capability against the USA and its dependencies.

Maritime powers in the last two great wars have only just managed to escape defeat through submarine attacks on their commerce by developing successful anti-submarine methods of warfare. But the modern nuclear-powered submarine, gliding beneath the surface at sixty knots, is faster than surface vessels, whereas the old submarine was much slower. A Soviet admiral has written thus of the role of the modern submarine:

> The modern submarine is a most formidable weapon with a cruising range virtually without limit. Her atomic motive power permits high speeds to be maintained for as long as required.
>
> Atomic submarines . . . are equipped with the most modern means of navigation permitting the pin-pointing of position at any given moment. Other radio equipment permits them to 'see' the surrounding surface or underwater situation so as to effectively employ their weapons.
>
> Their communications system enables them to keep contact with their command headquarters and receive orders when submerged in any given part of the world.[5]

American submarines can be used against the Soviet Union only by discharging Polaris and Poseidon nuclear warheads. They are part of the 'mutual deterrence' assumption and therefore exist rather not to be used than for use. But Soviet submarines have a very different possible function: that of destroying oceanic commerce on the high seas without using nuclear weapons against the American mainland: 'the threat is therefore not the nuclear missile submarine but rather the conventional attack submarine used in its classic roles – to destroy merchant ships and naval vessels, to hunt and fight other submarines, to mine and scout in enemy waters.[6]

The following extract from the conversation reported to have taken place in Moscow in 1959 between Chairman Khrushchev and Vice-President Nixon, illustrates this difference of outlook:

Khrushchev – . . . navies are now obsolete. They are fit only to provide fodder for sharks. The USSR will build no more cruisers and aircraft carriers.

Nixon – What about submarines?

K – We are building as many submarines as we can.

N – Submarines are excellent for launching missiles and their usefulness in that regard would be greatly enhanced when solid fuel had been developed.

K – That is true, but Russian experts believe it is preferable to launch missiles from land than from the sea.

N – That depends on the strategic situation of the nation involved.

K – I want to reveal another secret. We will use submarines to destroy ports, military areas and the navy of the enemy. Destroying the enemy navy would paralyse his sea communications which is of great importance because the Soviet Union's potential enemy would be highly dependent on sea communications.[7]

Such dialogue goes far towards justifying Professor Hooson's assertion that 'the most fundamental of all the elements of national power is sheer location on the globe'.[8] Certainly, if the nuclear balance succeeds in restraining nuclear war, then global strategy must still reflect the inherent differences in land-based and sea-based power.

A comparison between the military equipment of the two superpowers provides a fitting conclusion to this brief strategic discussion (Table 1.1). Intercontinental ballistic missiles, being independent of the

TABLE 1.1 WARHEADS, BOMBERS, CARRIERS AND
SUBMARINES (ESTIMATED) 1970[9]

	USA	USSR
Land-based ICBM warheads	1,074	1,300
IRBM and MRBM warheads	0	700
Submarine-launched BM warheads	1,328	280
Long-range bombers	505	140
Medium-range bombers	35	800
Aircraft carriers	20	0
Helicopter carriers	157	2
Submarines	144	380

land–sea or centre–periphery antithesis, are comparable in quantity. But as the USA has few neighbours, and the USSR many, with several of them in the enemy camp, there is a striking contrast in the number of intermediate and medium-range ballistic missiles and of long-range and medium-range bombers. The great difference in the number of aircraft and helicopter carriers is also a strong confirmation of the geostrategic argument developed here.

CENTRAL POWER AND PERIPHERAL POWER

The contrast between the global position of the USA and the USSR thus has two aspects, both of which are founded in the world distribution of land and sea. One is that of land power versus sea power, and the other, that of central power versus peripheral power. History shows many examples of tension between centrally-located and outlying areas. The tension between the United States and the communist powers is new only in that it is on a global scale.

In the dark ages and early middle ages, when peoples perceived only their immediate geographical environment, this interplay of influence occurred on a local scale. Most European nation-states have a long history of conflict between their geographical 'cores' (which are not necessarily geometrically central) and their outer territories. The former sought to unite and centralise while the latter struggled to preserve a separate existence.

Lowland England won control of the outer highland zone to form a greater British realm, but the Irish problem and the vigorous existence today of Scottish and Welsh nationalism show that the resulting tensions have not been eliminated: there is even Cornish nationalism. Within three centuries the area around Paris, by uniting the peripheral regions, grew into the kingdom of France. But not without resistance: England attempted to sustain Gascony, just as France supported those in Scotland who resisted English control. And today the slogan 'Vive la Bretagne Libre' shows that Brittany has not been fully incorporated as part of France. Much of the history of Spain is explained by the tension resulting from the centralising efforts of Castile and the resistance of the surrounding regions, one of which – Portugal – maintained her separate identity with English help. In Russia, centrally placed Muscovy expanded in all directions to form a greater Russia.

Once the European nation-states had come into existence, the same principle began to operate on a continental scale. France found herself in a powerful central position in Europe, surrounded by individually weaker peripheral countries. Tension and conflict between her and them followed, and the peripheral areas formed encircling alliances, aided and abetted by the off-lying and navy-protected island of Great Britain, to resist aggression. By 1810, however, the whole periphery – Britain excepted – lay at Napoleon's feet. But France was too late in her attempt to unite Europe forcibly. By 1810 Russia had entered the European political and military system, a development which threw France off centre – she now lay too far to the west to be able to dominate Russia, as the catastrophic expedition to Moscow in 1812 showed. The French hegemony collapsed. It was Germany now who found herself central in the new and enlarged Europe and, as soon as she had become unified and strong, similar tensions developed between her and her surrounding neighbours. In 1942 Hitler, like Napoleon in 1810, was lord of a circumference of conquered or client states. But like Napoleon, he also was too late. For not only had the distant power of the United States arisen, a development he hoped Japan might neutralise, but Stalin's five-year plans had pushed Russian strength beyond the confines of Europe and beyond German reach.

Strategy, that had once been on a national scale and then on a continental scale, has now moved on to a global scale, as communications have improved and weapons have increased in range. In this new post-war global strategy the Soviet Union assumes the role of central power, and the United States that of the leading peripheral power: as such, she endeavours to unite the coastal, peninsular and island states and to strengthen their power and will to resist with military and economic aid. In so doing she has encircled the Soviet Union and China with a girdle of allies and bases often referred to as the American 'perimeter of defense'. She has organised military treaties with lesser peripheral powers, resulting in such organisations as NORAD, NATO, CENTO, SEATO and ANZUS. She has, besides, military pacts with 'rimland' states not included in such organisations, notably with Spain.

COMPETITION IN THE RIMLAND

Because the geographical positions of the USA and the USSR are so generically different, their interests do not directly impinge upon each other. It is around the edges of the central land mass (the 'rimland') that the tension between them exists and the incidents occur. It is here that competition for the allegiance of governments and for the goodwill of peoples is most intense. The reasons for keeping them out of the opposing camp vary. Because of their position close to and encircling the USSR they all offer desirable sites for American military bases. Most of them have been penetrated by branches and subsidiaries of the great American multi-national corporations. The countries of Europe are, for the most part, highly industrialised and their populations skilled, so that

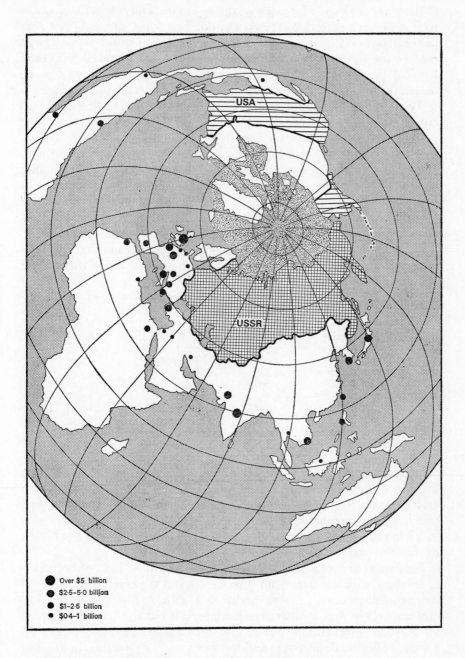

4. Principal recipients of American aid, 1945–69

they are able to make an important contribution to industrial and military technology. The same is true of Japan. The countries of south-west Asia have enormous reserves of oil. The states of south-east Asia not only possess vast quantities of manpower which could provide large markets for superpower surpluses but most of them are vital sources of tropical products or essential minerals. Indochina is thought to be underlain by one of the world's remaining large petroleum reserves.

The United States has so far been successful in holding back encroachment from the 'heartland' along most, but not all, sectors of the perimeter. Of the numerous countries surrounding the Soviet Union, only the six east European members of the Warsaw Pact, along with Mongolia, North Korea and North Vietnam are closely tied to that country. China, Yugoslavia and Albania have communist governments but act independently of the USSR. Of the rest, almost all are or have been linked in some way with the United States, the principal exceptions being Finland, Sweden, Austria, Switzerland, Burma and India. This success has only been achieved, however, at enormous cost, as may be seen from Table 1.2. To such expenditure must be added the colossal

TABLE 1.2   CHIEF RECIPIENTS OF AMERICAN AID 1945–69[10]
(*millions of dollars*)

India	7,788	Turkey	2,190
Great Britain	6,713	Yugoslavia	1,975
South Korea	4,684	Greece	1,673
France	4,150	Philippines	1,247
South Vietnam	4,117	Chile	1,129
Pakistan	3,632	Egypt	1,126
Italy	3,036	Austria	1,082
West Germany	2,865	Spain	1,039
Japan	2,475	Indonesia	1,037
Brazil	2,345	Israel	1,008
Formosa	2,231	Poland	963

sums spent at the two principal peripheral points where the United States has used armed force to prevent communist expansion – Korea and Vietnam. The sums given in Table 1.2, great though they are, pale into insignificance before expenditures directly attributable to the war in Vietnam, which ran at an annual total of between $20 and $30 billion during the period 1967–9.

Because of her smaller national income, the USSR has not been able to compete with the American scale of aid, but the emergence of newly independent countries, often permeated with strong anti-colonialist, anti-imperialist and anti-western feelings, created a favourable climate for Russian intervention. Soviet aid to backward countries began on a very modest scale in 1954, and has been not only smaller in amount but more selective than that from the United States (Table 1.3). In the period 1954–65, sixty per cent went to four countries: China, Cuba, India and the UAR.[11]

Soviet aid contrasts in three ways with that from the USA. In the first place, it is far more selective, concentrating – apart from the communist world – mainly on a few developing countries. Secondly, it is made almost wholly to the public sector of the recipient's economy, thereby strengthening its socialist character; and thirdly, it stimulates exports from the recipient country rather than swelling imports into it. Thus, whereas American aid often takes the form of shipping American goods to the developing country, Soviet aid usually involves educational and technical assistance in the exploitation of local resources and in the building of local plant – oil and gas wells, mines, steel works, power stations, pipelines and refineries, and the training of local personnel.

TABLE 1.3   CHIEF RECIPIENTS OF SOVIET AID 1954–65
(millions of dollars)

Cuba	1,100	Algeria	230
India	1,022	Turkey	210
United Arab Republic	1,011	Iraq	184
China	1,000*	Syria	150
East Germany	990*	Albania	141
Afghanistan	552	Argentina	115
Indonesia	372	Ethiopia	102
Bulgaria	370*	Rumania	95*
Hungary	338*	Pakistan	94
Persia	330	Yemen	92
Poland	300*	Ghana	89

* Data incomplete.

Between 1960 and 1965 the number of Soviet non-military technicians working abroad rose from 4000 to 9500.[12] For example, in 1969 there were 140 geologists in Algeria prospecting for water and oil, and nearly 400 lecturers, instructors and teachers. Payment for such services is rendered in the export staples of the recipient country or in resources developed as a result of the Soviet assistance – sugar from Cuba, cotton from Egypt, olives and fruit from Algeria, oil from Iraq, gas from Persia and Afghanistan. Soviet policy has, none the less, received many rebuffs from assisted countries, notably from China, Ghana and Indonesia. Indeed, it has been said – perhaps with some exaggeration – that 'every Soviet protégé except Nasser and Castro has either been deposed by his own people or has broken with Moscow'.[13] In Egypt, India and Indonesia the USSR has had to stomach persecution of the national communist parties. Often the presence of Soviet technicians has created as much ill will as the aid has gained goodwill.

Unlike the figures for American aid given in Table 1.2, the Soviet data in Table 1.3 do not include military aid. This amounted for the

period 1954–65 to $4 billion, bringing the total aid for those years to
$9 billion.[14] This figure has to be set against an American total of
$112 billion for the years 1945–67, of which $33 billion were for military
aid. Since 1965 the Soviet total will have been substantially increased
by massive military help given to the United Arab Republic and North
Vietnam.

American influence in the 'rimland' is increased not only by aid but
through capital investment and industrial penetration (Table 1.4).
This may take the form of gaining control of existing foreign companies
or of setting up overseas branches of American concerns. In western
Europe American corporations now control eighty-five per cent of the
electric computer industry and an even larger share of that yet more
recent technological innovation, the miniature integrated circuit, used
now in guided missiles and likely in the future to become vital to computer manufacture.[15] They are prominent in the automotive, chemical
and food-processing industries. Local firms can scarcely compete with

TABLE 1.4   USA: PRIVATE LONG-TERM INVESTMENT
ABROAD 1960–68[16]
(*billions of dollars*)

	1960	1968
Canada	11·2	19·5
Western Europe	6·7	19·4
Latin America	8·4	11·0
Asia	2·3	4·7
Africa	0·9	2·7
Australasia	1·0	2·6

the United States giants. These are supported by an immense home
market and backed by a more advanced technology, which has resulted
in part from lavish government assistance to industry and which has
been aided by the ability to attract – by offering high salaries and first-
class facilities – some of the best brains from Europe. The Soviet Union,
lacking the means of capitalist infiltration and without the necessary
technological lead, cannot compete in this aspect of 'rimland' domination, and is instead concerned to insulate her own empire in eastern
Europe from such an invasion.

Since the war, several changes have taken place in the attitude of the
states surrounding the 'heartland'. The most important was undoubtedly the transfer of power in China from the pro-American Chiang
Kai-shek's Nationalists to Mao Tse-tung's communists (1949). For
China, although holding on to a large share of 'heartland' territory, is
none the less fundamentally a peripheral or 'rimland' power, since most
of her population and economic development are concentrated in her
Pacific coastlands. But the period of Sino–Soviet friendship of the 1950s,

despite a great deal of Soviet aid, was succeeded by the recrimination and vituperation of the 1960s. Thus, although the United States suffered a setback here of the most serious kind, the corresponding Soviet gain has now been neutralised. In Greece and Malaya also, communist subversion imperilled the Western position, but here it was successfully thwarted.

More recently, the United States, and her chief ally Britain, have lost ground in the Middle East, having paid dearly for their support of Israel. Egypt, Syria and Iraq have been heavily dependent upon Soviet aid since the Arab defeat in the 1967 war. In 1969 Libya, after a revolution, left the American camp and ended her military co-operation with the West. Both Turkey and Persia, although still formally allied with the United States, have greatly improved their relations with the USSR. The CENTO sector of the American containing ring has been badly corroded. At the 1969 meeting of CENTO in Teheran the Persian foreign minister 'made it clear that the Iranian government no longer accepts the fundamental assumption of Soviet hostility'.[17] Symptomatic of the trend of growing Soviet influence in this sector was Pakistan's action (1968) in serving notice on the United States to remove its electronic espionage base near Peshawar.

Even Canada decided in 1969 to partially withdraw her European-based forces from NATO, while in the European sector France has ceased to participate in the activities of that alliance. General de Gaulle insisted that Europe should settle its own problems without outside interference. As, in his old-fashioned view, Europe extended to the Urals, and therefore included Russia, he was adopting the Soviet standpoint in this important matter.

An underlying difficulty for the Americans in western Europe and Japan stems from the fact that the United States and these industrialised countries are competitive economically rather than complementary. In the immediate post-war years the USA was prepared to strengthen their war-weakened economies by buying their manufactures in large quantities, even though she had surplus capacity and was well able to produce the goods at home. This pattern has persisted, but the American government is under great pressure from its own manufacturers to abate the import of foreign manufactured goods, especially as members of free-trade organisations like EEC and EFTA discriminate against the United States by favouring their own partners. Yet another anxiety is present in the recurrent financial crises and underlying doubts about the monetary system which threaten the complex nervous system of the capitalist world, and in the awful possibility of economic expansion giving way to recession.

The USSR has equally serious problems with the states of eastern

Europe, organised economically in COMECON and militarily in the Warsaw Pact. In some of these countries intense nationalistic feeling is accompanied by a long-standing dislike of the Russians which, as memories of German invasion and occupation recede, is becoming a political factor. East European communism in the 1940s and early 1950s stood for patriotism, resistance and victory. It has since become associated rather with Russian hegemony, and is therefore forced to insist on an independent and nationalist line so as not to forfeit all popular support. It may go even further: Nagy in Hungary in 1956 and Dubcek in Czechoslovakia in 1968 attempted to break loose from the bonds tying them exclusively to the USSR. Rumania, somewhat more cautiously, is also showing clear signs of political independence as the reception of President Nixon in 1969 showed.

Economic difficulties abound. Each east European country strives, like the USSR, for economic autarky but their resource bases are too narrow, their markets too small and, in some cases, their labour forces inadequate to achieve this without low standards and inefficiency. Ideally a real 'common market', with regional specialisation, is what they need, but steps in this direction prove difficult to make in the face of rising nationalist feeling and demands for more economic and political independence. Then there is the unsettling knowledge of the affluence and freedoms beyond the 'curtain' and the widespread belief that a reformed and liberal communism, if not a return to capitalism, would be necessary prerequisites for entry into a consumers' paradise.

The maintenance by the superpowers of their influence in the 'rimland' presents many difficulties. It is reassuring, however, to note that, in their international rivalry, there has been a clear determination on both sides to avoid the development of situations in which they themselves might be drawn into direct conflict. Much credit for this must go to Chairman Khrushchev and his propaganda in favour of 'peaceful coexistence', for which he brought down on his head the wrath of the Chinese. In the Arab–Israeli conflict of 1967, although their efforts were unsuccessful, both the USA and the USSR urged moderation and restraint upon the states dependent on them.

FOREIGN POLICY

The United States proclaims that its foreign policy is based upon the maintenance of 'freedom' and the defence of the 'free world'. 'Free' in this sense may mean possessing the liberty to elect governments within the multi-party system of parliamentary democracy, or it may signify nothing more than remaining non-communist. For those advanced countries where the parliamentary system operates and where the

Communist party is small, the American objective is clear: it is to protect this system from overthrow, whether from within or without. But in more backward countries the application of the democratic principle would present the United States with a serious dilemma. In most of these countries the majority of the population consists, not of prosperous industrial workers but of agricultural peasants and a hungry urban proletariat, who, if free to choose, would most likely elect a left-wing socialistic government. In these countries the classes opposed to socialism, and prepared to accept American intervention to protect the existing state of society – the landlord, business and professional classes – are in a minority. The United States is not, therefore, able to practise its democratic creed in such countries, but finds itself forced to support minority governments, whether dictatorial, monarchical, oligarchical or military. In Indochina the USA chose to intervene militarily rather than fulfil the Geneva arrangement by agreeing to free elections. American support for such governments takes the form of both economic and military assistance. Economic aid is intended to raise the general level of prosperity and so combat the propensity to revolution; but because of the nature of the social and economic system in these countries, it tends to stay with the propertied classes, rather than become diffused throughout society. It may thus widen the gap between rich and poor and fail in its objective. Military aid, even when primarily meant to enable the client state to resist aggression from without, is used inevitably to crush revolt at home.

The Soviet Union, for its part, maintains that its foreign policy rests upon the principles of self-determination and non-interference in the affairs of other countries, upon the protection of 'peace-loving' – i.e. socialist – states, and upon the support of national liberation movements in countries ruled by dictators, monarchs, capitalists or military juntas. In following this policy in practice, however, and in conformity with its own interests, the USSR faces a dilemma corresponding to that confronting America. In the more backward and poorer countries it may wholeheartedly and genuinely call for non-interference and for popular choice, since that would lead to the overthrow of tyrannies, monarchies and juntas, the expulsion of the Americans and the setting up of some form of socialist regime. But in the countries of eastern Europe the implementation of the principles proclaimed as basic to Soviet foreign policy would mean the overthrow of communist governments and the expulsion of the Russians. Soviet foreign policy then becomes no more than the unashamed defence of a dictated socialism, in the same way that, in south-east Asia, the democratic principles of American foreign policy degenerate into the defence of an unpopular capitalism.

In making this comparison one may, perhaps, add the impartial view of the Secretary-General to the United Nations. When U Thant urged a halt to the bombing of Vietnam in deference to 'the conscience of humanity' he was criticised by the Americans for not at the same time condemning the Russian occupation of Czechoslovakia. The Secretary-General replied: 'If the Russians were bombing and napalming the villages of Czechoslovakia, you wait and see what I have to say.'[18]

Because of their fundamentally different geographical positions and natural endowments, the attitude of the superpowers to non-alignment or neutralism varies. The United States, seeing as its main task the uniting of the peripheral rimland and outer ocean-trading world, i.e. the 'free world', in resistance to communist encroachment, looks to every non-communist state for participation and co-operation in a combined defensive system. This usually means expecting other countries to play host to American military installations. In what it would like to be seen as a contest between good and evil, between christianity and atheism, between freedom and slavery, it condemns neutrality as immoral. Furthermore, in order to protect its sources of raw materials and other essential products, to maintain free and open markets for its exports, and to safeguard the security of its investments and the operations of its international corporations, it is vital to America to be able to control or influence the government of other countries and their policies.

The Soviet Union, on the other hand, can be satisfied with neutrality. As a great centrally-located continental land power, she does not have the same need for foreign bases, and being self-sufficient economically she is not dependent on overseas sources for supplies and markets. Neutrality is also, in the case of most states in the inner and outer perimeters of the world island, a more realistic proposition for the USSR than their absorption in the communist world. With most countries, neutrality is the most that Russia could hope for; and in practical terms, their non-alignment denies much more to the United States than accession to the Soviet bloc would bring to the Soviet Union. A France expelling American forces from its territory or a Sweden sending medical supplies to North Vietnam are acting in the Soviet interest, without burdening the USSR with the problems that arise in a communist Czechoslovakia or a communist Poland.

Rivalry for influence in the countries surrounding the communist heartland inevitably involves the superpowers in the internal politics of those states. America supports established dictatorships, monarchies and oligarchies as well as constitutional parliamentary democracies, and gives them military aid and economic assistance. The Soviet Union supports left wing, popular, socialist and sometimes nationalistic revolutionary regimes.

Local oppositions to established government look to one or other superpower for aid in overthrowing their enemies in power. Lumumba in the Congo and Nkrumah were popularly-elected leaders on good terms with Moscow, who were overthrown by military juntas with the connivance of the Americans. The Greek parliamentary democracy, on the eve of an election in which a move to the left was confidently expected, was likewise overthrown (April 1967) by a military group with – according to democratic Greek politicians – American complicity. The United States was subsequently rewarded by the Greek colonels with a new base in Crete for the practice firing of missiles. The constant and vehement stream of propaganda poured into eastern Europe by the American wireless station 'Radio Free Europe' is credited on both sides of the Iron Curtain with some of the responsibility for the violent expressions of discontent in Hungary, Poland and East Germany in 1956, in Czechoslovakia in 1968 and in Poland in 1970. The Russians, for their part, have benefited by changes of government, often resulting from revolution, in Cuba, Algeria, Sudan, Libya, Aden and Iraq, while their encouragement of revolutionary groups in countries ruled by dictators or minorities, such as Spain, Greece and South Africa, is a constant irritant to the established governments. China, however, competes with Russia for the position of champion of the left-wing groups in the underdeveloped countries of the world.

Both superpowers have vied with each other in condemning 'colonialism' and in conniving at the expulsion of the European imperial powers. This they were able to do all the more enthusiastically since they had their own imperialisms safely consolidated into contiguous land empires. The United States in particular resented the discrimination that these empires practised in world trade. True independence, economic as well as political, has been hard to achieve, however, in a world dominated by superpowers. Many former colonies are now part of the American economic empire, though nominally sovereign states. One aspect of the evolution of newly-independent ex-colonial states works to the detriment of the USSR. Although they often begin life with democratic socialist governments, these régimes are likely sooner or later to be overthrown by the army and become military dictatorships. But army officers tend to be 'out of sympathy with Communists and the Left Wing'.[19]

The ability of the Soviet Union to build up a naval presence in the Indian Ocean is an example of how strategic benefits may be reaped from the establishment of friendly governments in some of the bordering states – notably Aden, Zanzibar and Mauritius. The growing Soviet

B

strategic strength in the area is likely to give heart to local revolutionary movements as well as making military support for them feasible. It could thus lead to the creation of additional friendly governments which would in turn make possible further strategic exploitation of the situation. The effect of this upon the United States is not merely to produce a strategic reaction – as with the decision to build an Indian Ocean naval base on the British island of Diego Garcia – but to make the administration more sensitive to the feelings of black African states bordering the ocean. Thus in the United Nations Assembly America usually follows a policy towards South African *apartheid*, white rule in Rhodesia and Portuguese colonialism that is acceptable to African leaders. These, because of superpower rivalry, are able to act as truculently as if their positions were backed with real military power. The United States has responded to black African aspirations with deeds as well as words. It has contributed $6 million towards the building of a road from Botswana to Zambia despite the urgent protest of the South African government that such a road would facilitate the movement of terrorists into its territory.

In some instances, however, a conflict of interests forces the superpowers to take an ambivalent attitude. Although anxious to placate black African opinion, so as to forestall Russian and Chinese influence, the USA would not welcome the breakdown of law and order in South Africa, nor even the end of white domination there, as this is a guarantee for the security of the considerable American business interest in that country. And the Soviet Union, once it has established cordial relations with a strong ruler, however reactionary, may not be too anxious to see him overthrown by a revolutionary movement.

2 Historical Development

Today's superpowers both at one time occupied relatively small and isolated 'cradle areas'. Here they developed the strength and nurtured the vitality which enabled them to expand their control over vast continental empires. In each instance the 'cradle area' was peopled by a migration of European peoples, although these migrations were widely separated in time.

Between the second and ninth centuries AD Slavs from the valleys of the Vistula and Danube colonised the forests of central Russia, sub-jugating the Finns and other non-European peoples. The Slavs were themselves conquered by Scandinavian raiders (Varangians or 'Russes') in the ninth and tenth centuries, but the resulting Viking–Slav state, extending from the Baltic to the Black Seas, did not last. Its concen-tration of settlement, commerce and wealth in the Dnieper valley, with capital at Kiev, was exposed to attack by nomadic hordes that period-ically swept across the steppes. Refugees abandoned this harried land for the central forested area.

In the thirteenth century the Kievan state was utterly destroyed by Mongol invaders (1238–40). But between the upper Volga and the tributary Oka, in a naturally-moated area, the princes of Moscow built up a highly-centralised and autocratic state which successfully resisted pressures from Swedes and Germans to the north-west, from Lithuani-ans and Poles to the west, and from Tartars to the south and south-east. It was this principality of Muscovy which took the offensive against the Mongol Tartars in the sixteenth century: in the reign of Ivan IV (The Terrible) the Muscovites emerged from their central forested refuge to march on the middle Volga, where they took Kazan in 1552, and then moved down the great river to seize Astrakhan (1556). During the same reign Russian Cossacks conquered western Siberia (1581–2).

Shortly after the Muscovites and Cossacks had begun to strike out from their 'cradle area', that of the future United States began to receive its first colonists. During the seventeenth century, the almost empty Atlantic coastlands between Spanish Florida and French Acadia were invaded by large numbers of English settlers, along with smaller contingents from other European countries. The primitive native inhabitants were exterminated or driven westwards. During the eighteenth century these first settlements had expanded greatly in wealth and population. In 1776, as a result of a concerted resistance to the British Crown, these 'thirteen colonies' became the United States. Their 'cradle area' also was an isolated one, being separated from Europe by the ocean, and surrounded on the landward side by unfriendly peoples – French, Spanish and native Indian.

Americans began to leave their Atlantic 'cradle area' to penetrate the continental West in the 1780s – two hundred years after the Russians had entered Siberia. They had been on the Atlantic seaboard less than two centuries, but their population already numbered one and a half million. The Muscovites had inhabited their larger 'cradle area' for a thousand years or more before their expansion outside of it began, and during this time their population had grown to a possible twelve million.

Not only hostile neighbours but physical obstacles helped to confine each people within its 'cradle area' until it had the necessary numbers to emerge effectively. Had this not been so, their strength might well have been dissipated over a wider but more thinly-held continental space, leading to vulnerable weakness and possible defeat at the hands of a rival power. But in each instance a belt of mountainous terrain and a broad river with steep bluffs impeded expansion. Eastwards of the Muscovites lay the Volga with its precipitous right-hand banks and its left-hand marshes, and beyond the Volga the forested Urals. These are by no means high and were easily crossed by fur traders, but in the harsh Russian climate even a small increase in altitude can convert a difficult environment for settlement into an almost impossible one. The Russians long knew them as the 'girdle of the earth'.[1]

Westwards of the American colonists lay the likewise forested Appalachians, similar in many ways to the Urals – not high or difficult to cross but by no means inviting to farmers in search of warm open fertile land, especially as they afforded refuge to ferocious Indians who made colonial penetration dangerous. Beyond the Appalachians lay the great Mississippi and its tributary the Ohio, and for the twenty years that preceded the Louisiana Purchase, the broad river formed the western boundary of the USA.

EXPANSION INTO CONTINENTAL EMPIRES

The Russians crossed the Urals in the 1580s; the Americans crossed the Appalachians in the 1780s. The immense distances between each mountain barrier and the Pacific Ocean were soon traversed by explorers and fur traders, using the rivers and portages. The Russians

(Moskvitin) reached the Pacific coast in 1639, the Americans (Lewis and Clark) in 1805. Agricultural settlement followed, but at a much slower rate and to a much more limited extent in the Russian empire

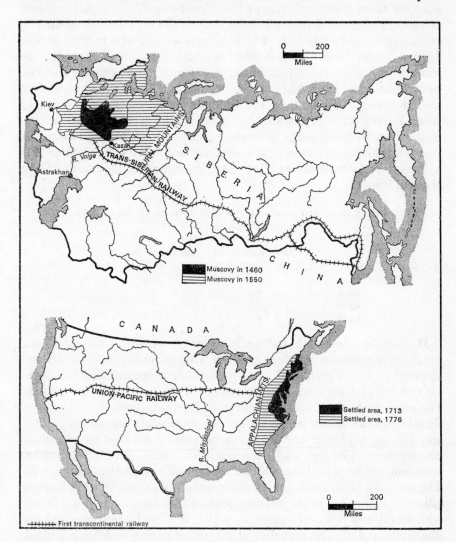

5. Cradle areas

than in America. Not only was most of the former physically hostile to farming, but Russian labour was immobilised by the system of serfdom and not free to migrate. On the other hand, Europeans poured into the United States throughout the nineteenth century and the early years of the twentieth, and they went west of the Appalachians in increasing numbers so that by 1920 the American West had double the population of the Russian East (Table 2.1). Widespread agricultural settlement over the more favourable parts of the American West led to improved communications and these, in turn, led to the exploitation of further resources, notably minerals. The first trans-continental railway in the United States – the Union-Pacific, completed in 1869 – preceded by some thirty years the Great Siberian railway. And whereas the rail network over the United States widened out and filled in to serve a fairly well distributed population, the Siberian railway remained a single track, linking together the long but narrow zone of Russian settlements in the east. In the absence of modern communications apart from this one great railway, it was impracticable and unprofitable to develop – on a similar scale to America – the even greater mineral wealth of the Russian empire.

TABLE 2.1   POPULATION OF THE AMERICAN WEST AND
THE RUSSIAN EAST 1800–1920[2]
(millions)

	United States west of the Appalachians	Russian Empire east of the Urals
1800	0·3	1·2
1850	9·9	2·9
1900	44·5	16·7
1920	62·1	30·0

During the nineteenth and early twentieth centuries the USA had many advantages, other than those of a more favourable natural environment, which promoted its more rapid development. English capital and Irish labour were available to speed the process of exploitation. Far away from the disturbing effect of European power politics and shielded by the British Navy, the rapidly-expanding supplies of capital and labour, skill and energy could be wholly devoted to economic development. The free and democratic structure of society favoured economic advance and the political system offered little to obstruct it. The situation of Russia was very different: she was entangled in foreign alliances, embroiled in one military conflict after another, and burdened with social and political structures which hindered enterprise and induced stagnation. This therefore was a period during which the United States rushed ahead while Russia progressed more slowly. Nevertheless, there was an impressive beginning of industrial advance in Russia between 1890 and 1914, considering the previous backwardness of the country. This, like the much greater American development, resulted from the investment of foreign capital, which came predominantly from France, Britain, Germany and Belgium. But Russian industrialisation before 1914 was in no way comparable in level of attainment to that of the United States. In 1913 production of mineral fuels was only eight per cent of America's, of electrical energy only nine per cent, of pig iron and steel only fifteen per cent and of cement only thirteen per cent – but her population was 168 per cent of America's.

Neither state was entirely unimpeded in the full flush of its expansion across its continent. Britain sustained Canada as a barrier to further American aggrandisement northwards, while China placed a limit to southward movement by the Russians. But it was an infinitely greater hardship for the Russians to be confined to the north than for the Americans to be excluded from it.

The growth of both powers was essentially imperialistic in nature. Because of their small size, their maritime position, and their insular or peninsular nature, the states of western Europe had ventured overseas to build empires which were discrete, being scattered over the surface of the earth and linked only by the slow process of sea communication. On the other hand, the United States and Russia found themselves each with a vast and compact territory close at hand and but thinly peopled by primitive peoples. The rapid improvements in land and air transport and in all forms of communication have aided the consolidation and unification of such land empires, while at the same time making more difficult the maintenance of dominion overseas. Improved land communications enabled overseas colonies to develop stronger links with their immediate land neighbours than with their distant motherlands. Situated in different parts of the world, each with its own climate and economy, its peculiar history, culture and race, its individual regional problems, all of which it shared with its immediate neighbours, colonies sought inevitably to loosen their ties with the metropolis. But in both superpower states it has been possible to weld peoples of different origin and culture into imperial nations. They have become conscious of a common allegiance as American or Soviet citizens living within one large but coherent continental area and subjected to common influences and pressures.

The United States has the advantage that it extends from ocean to ocean with clear-cut bounds, whereas the Soviet Union must for ever be preoccupied with the states which border upon it. But at the end of the nineteenth century both powers saw their interests threatened on the Pacific side by the rise of Japan. Owing to the greater proximity of the Land of the Rising Sun to Russia, it was the latter that first became involved in war – the Russo-Japanese war of 1904–5. But there was also a growing hostility between the United States and Japan, which worsened until the outbreak of hostilities in 1941. Fear of Japan did much to give America and Russia a common interest in the early twentieth century, and both found the Anglo-Japanese alliance of 1902 extremely distasteful.

There are certain similarities – and, of course, great differences – between the Russo-Japanese and American–Vietnamese wars. Each was a consequence of the arrival of people of European origin in the Pacific area and the determination of an Asiatic people to resist their encroachment. In each the non-Asiatic power was operating at a great distance from its industrial base. In each the Asiatic people was given support and encouragement by a great power hostile to the non-Asiatic belligerent. And in each, the non-Asiatic power was unable to achieve its military and political objectives. In both instances, this failure coincided with worsening social problems at home and contributed to their aggravation. Russia's Pacific war came some sixty years before America's: the latter had to await the time when United States power had crossed the wide ocean and been established on the far side.

The history of both Russian and American expansion can thus be viewed latitudinally – as aspects of the movements of peoples from either side of Europe around the globe in opposite directions, both eventually reaching the Pacific and coming into conflict with nations living close to the shores of that ocean. But the history of the two superpowers has been something more than a mere latitudinal or east–west movement. It was inevitably involved in what Mackinder termed the ultimate geographical reality: the distribution of land and sea, the concentration of most of the land in a world island, with the rest disposed around it in satellite continents, islands and peninsulas, the whole surrounded and penetrated by the oceans. Whereas the maritime peoples have been able to move easily by sea to occupy, colonise or exploit the shores of the land masses, building a series of overseas empires, the exploitation of the Russian empire followed much more slowly. For the 'heartland' position conferred many disabilities, arising mainly from its extreme continental climate. By unifying all effort in the power of a socialist state, by adopting the most modern technology, and by calling for sacrifices from the the people, the Soviets have partially overcome these disabilities so as to begin to realise the wealth of their land empire. So while the European empires have flourished and decayed, the Russian empire, more slowly but more surely, is merely beginning to mature.

In this contrast we have, on a world scale, a repetition of a somewhat similar evolution that took place in the early history of Europe, but on a continental scale. The many, favoured, coastal plains around the Mediterranean shores, isolated from each other by mountain ranges, but easily intercommunicable by sea, progressed rapidly as city-states, culminating in their association together in the great Roman empire. But the inhabitants of the transalpine countries, their energies devoted more to clearing forests and struggling with less genial climates, lagged behind in civilisation and were long thought of as barbarians. Yet once these 'continental' nations had mastered the geographical 'anti-resources' which had delayed their progress, and could use the greater potentialities their environment offered, they were able eventually to exceed the maritime peoples of the Mediterranean world in strength.

In such an analogy Greece stands for Europe and the early mastery of the seas and colonisation of the coasts. Rome stands for the United States, attempting the unification and domination of the seaward-looking ocean-communicating peoples. The Gauls and Germans stand for the USSR, long thought of as backward, but slowly uncovering the great resources of a continental land mass. The great difference is that in the episode of ancient times, which took place on a continental scale, the sea empire was surrounded by land and landsmen, whereas in today's global pattern, the land empire is surrounded by oceans and maritime peoples.

ALASKA

The history of Alaska, as the only territory to have been under the sovereignty of both superpowers, illustrates the effect of stagnation in Russia and dynamism in America. The original impetus of Russian fur-trading exploration and colonisation not only brought Russians in a remarkably short time to the Pacific coast but also across the Bering Strait and on to the north-western Pacific coast of North America. Had the full vigour of this westward movement not been sapped, Russians might well have penetrated the mountain barrier and emerged on to the Great Plains in the eighteenth century, contesting possession of the continent with Americans of west European origin. But the eastward human flow from Russia was diverted westwards to the battlefields of Europe and was stultified by the restrictions of serfdom; in consequence, Alaska, as a virile Russian colony, atrophied.

Today Alaska owes its importance to its development as an Arctic outpost close to Soviet territory and to its being a vital part of the American 'containing ring' forged around the communist world. Ironically it was given away almost for nothing to the United States in 1867 by the Russian tsar as a token of goodwill. The 1860s were a period of unparalleled Russian–American friendship. Tsar Alexander II saw in the growing strength of the United States a counterweight to chronically hostile Europe and in particular to Britain, for ever frustrating Russia's legitimate ambitions. He actively sympathised with the North in the Civil War, fearing that the break-up of the Republic would weaken it in this role of counterbalance, and Russian naval squadrons co-operated with the United States Navy. A Petersburg–Washington axis directed against London looked a distinct possibility.[3]

Despite the territory's obvious strategic value today, its purchase by the United States from Russia for $7,200,000 in 1867 was widely regarded at the time as a waste of money. But in 1959 Alaska became the forty-ninth State as a result of a rapid increase of population brought about by the military activities which now dominate its life. Its economy has recently become more broadly based with the discovery and exploitation of a large oilfield.

SLAVERY AND SERFDOM

In both countries slavery or serfdom became widespread during the seventeenth and eighteenth centuries and was abolished in the 1860s. There were obvious differences: slavery in America was confined to Negroes imported from Africa and their descendants, and was limited to the south-eastern regions of the country. Serfdom in the Russian empire involved the enslavement of Russians by Russians and was widespread over the whole of the long-settled parts of the country. Yet both economies relied upon this form of human exploitation for profitable exports of agricultural produce: cotton from America and livestock products and grain from Russia.

Abolition in the 1860s in each case followed and resulted from war. But in America the Civil War of 1861–5 was directly connected with the issue which its outcome decided. The link between the Crimean War and the abolition of serfdom in 1861 was more indirect. The Russian defeat exposed the crying need to modernise the country if she were ever to become strong enough to resist foreign pressures; and the ending of serfdom was one of a series of reforms undertaken to improve the efficiency of the Russian economy.

In neither case did liberation from the bonds of legal slavery entail full emancipation. In America the Negroes remained a caste apart, exploited and downtrodden; they were denied political rights and social equality. In Russia the ex-serfs' liberty continued to be restricted by compulsory attachment to their village communes. This notwithstanding, abolition eventually led to a greater mobility of labour which had momentous consequences. As Russia's industrial revolution gathered momentum in the early years of the twentieth century, the peasants were drawn into the towns, and their bitter resentment, previously diffused over the countryside, now became concentrated in city slums. This aggrieved urban proletariat listened readily to revolutionaries and agitators and produced the abortive revolution of 1905 as well as the successful one of 1917.

The transformation of the Russian ex-serf into an urban workman took place earlier than the similar change of status of the American Negro from rural sharecropper to city factory hand, because in Russia ex-serfs were the only large source of labour available. In America it was not until the 1941–5 war lifted the country out of economic depression and led to an unprecedented demand for labour, that Negroes were drawn from the southern countryside to the northern towns, a process that continued throughout the 1950s and 1960s. Here again the crowding of an aggrieved class – previously harmless because dispersed – into urban concentrations produced violent insurrection in the cities of the late 1960s.

THE AMERICAN AND RUSSIAN REVOLUTIONS

In the history of each superpower the opening up of the adjacent land empire was preceded by a rejection of Europe. By the American revolution of 1775 the thirteen colonies broke free from such control and restraint as Britain had been able to exercise. The mother country had discouraged the industrial development of her colonies, regarding them as potential markets for her own goods. The provisions of the Quebec Act of 1774, in which Britain placed obstacles in the way of westward expansion by the colonies, were powerful sources of dissatisfaction. The so-called American War of Independence was more a war for the possession and control of the West than for the independence of the colonies themselves. They were already virtually independent. The really significant consequence of the British defeat was that it was the new United States, and not Great Britain, which enjoyed the fruits of the British sacrifices and victories in the Seven Years War against France (1756–63).

The October revolution (7 November 1917, new style) severed the bonds that had increasingly tied Russia to Europe since the reign of Peter I the Great (died 1725). These bonds were dynastic, linguistic, social, political and increasingly economic. The royal family was German, the aristocracy spoke French, and together they perpetuated in Petersburg (now Leningrad) the brilliance of the court life of eighteenth-century France. The country was deeply implicated in the European political system and this involved it in the 1914 war. Important industries were dominated by foreign capital, and the direction of the economy was largely governed by the needs of foreigners. The country stood in a position of colonial status to Europe, sending to the West primary commodities such as grain and timber, and importing manufactured goods. In some respects its economy resembled that of the American colonies before their revolution.[4]

Both revolutions led to the idolisation and glorification of one man to whose leadership the successful overthrow of tyranny was largely ascribed: Washington in the USA and Lenin in Russia. Because Lenin-worship is still very much with us and adulation of George Washington is no longer fashionable, it is not easy to realise today that Washington came 'to occupy a place in the hearts of Americans in the nineteenth century no less great than Lenin in the hearts of Soviet citizens soon after the October 1917 Revolution'.[5]

Although comparison between the two successful revolutions which gave birth to new political structures in North America and Eurasia is the obvious one to make, it should not be forgotten that a great revolt took place in the Russian empire almost contemporaneously with the American War of Independence. If the latter is regarded as a revolt by subjects feeling themselves misgoverned from a distant metropolis, then it may indeed be compared with Pugachev's revolt in 1773–4. But it would be ridiculous to compare the legalistic grievances of the Americans with the real misery and suffering which drove the outlying subjects of Catherine the Great to insurrection. Pugachev, a Cossack, raised his rebellious bands among the serfs, the iron workers and the non-Russian peoples of the distant Ural region. Although for a while he was able to inflict a vast amount of material damage upon the eastern regions of Russia, his men, unlike the American revolutionaries, failed before the regular armies of the government.

Despite the strong influence which Europe inevitably had upon their cultures, there was a widespread feeling of superiority to Europe both in nineteenth-century America and in Russia.[6] In the United States it was a consciousness of social superiority: a belief that in the American democracy mankind had made a considerable advance on the monarchical and aristocratic institutions traditional in Europe. In the Russian empire it was the long-held conviction of moral superiority to a decadent society in which materialistic individualism had discarded the communal relationships that many Russians thought essential to mankind's happiness. Yet in both American and Russian society there was administrative corruption far worse than anything that existed in Europe.

The importance of the October revolution of 1917 and of the consolidation of Soviet power in the following decade, was that the country was now ruled by a dictatorship resolved to rely upon the country's internal resources, whatever the cost and sacrifice involved in developing them. The first five-year plan (1928–32) saw the beginning of an all-out Soviet attack upon the immense 'anti-resources' of its territory in order to exploit the resources, and Russia now began to experience an explosive development comparable in some ways to that which took place in North America half a century before. There are, however, some important differences. The Soviet expansion was based entirely upon home-produced capital and labour. It was interrupted by the destructive war of 1941–5, and retarded by the subsequent 'cold war' and arms race. The United States experienced no such handicaps.

In both countries the early upsurge in industrial development, transforming the economy from a primarily agricultural one to one mainly based on manufacturing, relied on coal as its principal source of energy. Table 2.2 shows the striking degree of similarity in the growth of coal

TABLE 2.2 PRODUCTION OF COAL
(*millions of short tons*)

USA		USSR	
1870	20	1910	23
1880	51	1920	9*
1890	111	1930	50
1900	212	1940	184
1910	417	1950	250*
1920	569	1960	567

* Amount depressed by after-effects of war.

production during the comparable half centuries of industrial revolution. But there were also important differences between the growth of the American economy before 1920 and of the Russian economy during the Soviet period. Thus, whereas advance in the United States pervaded all branches of production, in the USSR agriculture was sacrificed to industry. The collectivisation and mechanisation of agriculture that accompanied the first two five-year plans were designed to subject the independent peasant to state control and to set free a large portion of the rural labour force for the work of industrialising the country. But the effect of this was to interrupt, disrupt and slow down the growth of agricultural production.

After the Bolshevik revolution the energies of the country were directed eastwards and self-sufficiency was substituted for dependence upon overseas trade. For a thousand years the Russians had struggled for a place in the lucrative European commercial system based on maritime trade, but they had met frustration after frustration. When they secured a foothold on the shores of the only seas accessible to them, they found these to be merely the land-locked antechambers of the great oceans, barred by ice in winter, and controlled by potentially hostile powers at all times. In time of war they were painfully embarrassed and, on occasion, brought to their knees by their enemies' ability to deny them the overseas commerce upon which they had come to depend. There was little of advantage to show for this traditional policy. The country seemed relegated to a permanently inferior position as the backyard of Europe, unless it came to terms with its 'heartland' situation in the world island. In the nature of things these terms would be harsh. The new introspective policy had as its aim the transformation of Russia from a dependent colonial state on the eastern confines of Europe to a politically and economically independent world power fully exploiting its domination of the continental centre of the land hemisphere.

CIVIL WARS AND WORLD WARS

Both countries experienced a civil war, but the two conflicts differed greatly in nature. The American civil war of 1861–5 had its roots in the conflicting interests of two regions with differing economic and social structures derived from different climatic and other geographical conditions. The Russian conflict of 1917–21 was between two classes, the factory workers of the industrialised towns and the moneyed and propertied classes. The issue in the American war was whether the United States was to be divided into two separate countries or remain one union. In the Russian war it was whether the country was to be ruled by the Bolshevik revolutionaries or by some combination of the former ruling class. Foreign intervention in the American war was confined to sympathy for one or other side, while there was armed support from abroad for the Russian Whites against the Reds. Both wars cut off supplies to the world market of an important primary commodity: cotton from the American South and wheat from the Russian steppes.

Both countries were involved in the two 'world wars' of the twentieth century and on the same side. But in the first war the United States entered the struggle at about the same time that the Russians virtually abandoned it. The United States was the great supplier and the Russian empire the great receiver of war material. The United States was immune from invasion and counted her war dead in tens of thousands; Russia was invaded and her dead numbered millions. The consequences for the future superpowers were also very different. The United States emerged as the dominant victor power, with her wealth, strength and prestige all greatly enhanced. The Russian empire was plunged into defeat, disintegration, confusion, revolution and civil war. Yet in one respect this war had a similar consequence for both countries – they were freed from an immense load of foreign debt. In 1914 the USA had been a debtor nation to the tune of $6 billion while the Russian empire owed $4 billion.[7] The supply of arms to the allies from her enormous and expanding industrial base enabled the United States to move from the status of debtor nation to that of creditor, while the Soviets appropriated all foreign-owned industry and repudiated all foreign debts.

A curious by-product of the 1914–18 war was, in each country, the prohibition of the sale of intoxicating liquor. In Russia it was introduced at the outset of the war and by the tsar out of paternalistic concern for the welfare of a people at war.[8] In America it was enacted on a nation-wide scale (most States already restricted or forbade the sale of liquor) immediately after the war because of the pressure of the American matriarchy, which had been outraged by what they regarded as the debauchery of the American soldiery as a result of service in Europe. In the Russian case, because the government itself controlled the manu-facture, distribution and sale of liquor, the ban was effective, and the resulting loss of revenue contributed to the difficulties of the tsarist government. In America, where evasion was widespread and enforce-ment extremely difficult, prohibition contributed to widespread con-tempt for the law and the rapid increase of organised crime.

Neither country became directly involved in the second 'world war' until 1941, whereas the conflict had begun in 1939, and both were brought in as the result of a sudden enemy attack without declaration of war. The American homeland itself, however, was not assaulted, but the western regions of the Soviet Union were devastated. American industrial capacity was greatly expanded as a result of the conflict, whereas Soviet economic potential was crippled and took five years to reconstruct. American loss of life was about 300,000 compared with an unknown number of the Soviet military and civilian population, but estimates put the figure at about twenty-five million. Both powers found themselves, at the end of hostilities, in military occupation of a large area of Europe.

THE GREAT DEPRESSION

To Russia the two 'world wars' were incidents in a period charac-terised by a whole series of dramatic and traumatic calamities. To America they were primarily periods of feverishly accelerated economic growth. America's most traumatic experience came between the wars, in the great depression of 1929 onwards, which brought the country's capitalist system of production almost to a standstill and, in the absence of any organised 'welfare state', caused widespread poverty and deprivation. It also resulted in a sharp fall in the birth rate, so that today the age group born in the depression years is much smaller than it would normally have been.

The great depression in the United States corresponded closely in time to the first five-year plan in the Soviet Union, and Soviet industrial production began to grow sharply at the same time that American output was collapsing. This is exemplified by the following figures for the production of pig iron (millions of tons):

USA		USSR	
1929	46·5	1928	3·3
1932	9·8	1932	6·2

The capitalist depression and early Soviet development were, in fact, closely linked. The economic collapse in the West made many skilled engineers unemployed and destitute, and many of them accepted offers of work in the USSR, where they played a vital role in guiding the introduction of new industries.

In fact, as Paul Dukes writes, 'the year 1929 marks a watershed in the economic development of both powers'.[9] In the USSR it was the beginning of a great period of industrial expansion designed both to modernise the already settled areas and also to develop the rich resources of the hitherto untouched regions of the empire, to expand the frontiers of the 'ecumene'. In the USA it marked the end of a similar period of bursting economic expansion, which had begun about 1870 and which likewise had been called forth to satisfy a dual demand – that arising from the already developed parts of the country and from the newly developing areas created as the frontier advanced. By about 1910, however, there was no longer a geographical frontier and the larger of the two elements in demand lapsed. But productive capacity had continued to expand until 1928 as if this element in demand were still there. This it was able to do because the first great war in Europe (1914–18) and the post-war boom which wartime dislocations created, soaked up the excess production. As Roosevelt said in 1932: 'our industrial plant is built; the problem just now is whether under existing conditions it is not overbuilt. Our last frontier has long since been reached.'[10] Demand in the 1920s was also slowed down by a greatly reduced birth rate compared with previous decades and by the halting of immigration in the absence of new lands to open up. But industrial capacity continued to expand at a high rate until the depression began in 1929.

The first five-year plan inaugurated the fully-planned economy of the USSR, but the great depression also brought the state to play an important role in the American economy. With it the wholly free *laissez-faire* market economy ended and the intimate relationship between government and big business was born. Although its birth was passionately assailed as monstrous by business leaders at the time, it grew into an infant that was to be brought rapidly to maturity in the 1941–5 war. The corporations, for their part, soon came to realise the advantages of having government as a customer.

The state did not, however, always channel New Deal funds through the private corporations. The development of the Tennessee valley was, in planning and execution, a microcosm of what was now going on in the Soviet Union. There is, in fact, some evidence of a strong mutual influence between the two future superpowers in the 1930s. Not only were American models followed by Stalin in his development schemes but Americans actually participated in their fulfilment. On the other hand, many of America's leading intellectuals, some of whom were Roosevelt's associates and advisers, having become disillusioned with their private enterprise economy, had become interested in and in some cases enthusiastic over, the Soviet experiment: 'pragmatic economists, labour leaders, social workers, politicians and engineers all praised what they had seen during visits to the Soviet Union'.[11] The Soviet Union of the 1930s did not seem so bleak and repellent when looked at from the afflicted America of the Great Depression, with its bread lines and soup kitchens, its widespread misery and distress, as it does now in retrospect from a position of affluence. But the hostility to socialism among the influential conservative classes was so bitter, that any further dose of socialism in the USA had to be ruled out as politically impracticable. Despite its undisputed economic success, technological triumph and social benefit, there were no more Tennessee Valley Authorities, although several similar schemes had been planned.

THE PEOPLES

Russia was peopled by the easternmost and America by the westernmost of European races. The Russians not only found themselves left behind by the great westward migrations of history but became the constant victims of more warlike nations. No country has been invaded more times, conquered more times. As Stalin said:

> One feature of the history of old Russia was the continual beating she suffered . . . She was beaten by the Mongol khans. She was beaten by the Turkish beys. She was beaten by the Swedish feudal kings. She was beaten by the Polish and Lithuanian gentry. She was beaten by the British and French capitalists. She was beaten by the Japanese barons. All beat her . . .[12]

He might have mentioned also the many buffetings from the Goths, the Varangians and a whole succession of nomadic peoples which Russia received before the Mongol onslaught. Of course, at times in her later imperial and superpower history, Russian armies found themselves on the offensive. But the ordinary Russian has usually preferred peaceful colonisation to military conquest, and with a remarkable humility and lack of race-consciousness has taken his place alongside native peoples with surprisingly little conflict or friction. He has not seen himself as a superman destined to organise and enslave, nor as an avenging scourge to punish and exterminate, nor even as a missionary of religion or technology to uplift or civilise. He has remained remarkably natural and human. Few foreigners knew pre-revolutionary Russia so well as Sir Donald Mackenzie Wallace, who wrote of the ordinary Russian as follows:

> The Russian peasant is admirably fitted for the work of peaceful agricultural colonisation. Among uncivilised tribes he is good-natured, long-suffering, conciliatory, capable of bearing extreme hardships, and endowed with a marvellous power of adapting himself to circumstances.
>
> The haughty consciousness of personal and national superiority habitually displayed by Englishmen of all ranks when they are brought into contact with races which they look upon as lower in the scale of humanity than themselves, is entirely foreign to his character. He has no desire to rule, and no wish to make the natives hewers of wood and drawers of water. All he desires is a few acres of land which he and his family can cultivate; and so long as he is allowed to enjoy these, he is not likely to molest his neighbours.[13]

An earlier authority on Russia, Robert Lyall, wrote: 'We have heard much of the forbearance, kindness and toleration of Russia towards her conquered provinces, and she often deserves that praise.'[14] More recently these characteristics and their historical significance have been pointed out by Toynbee.

How different have been the antecedents of the American population! As the westernmost of Western peoples they are those who have come farthest from their primeval homes. They include therefore some of the most adventurous, the most acquisitive and the most aggressive elements culled from all the peoples of Europe. Even when they migrated because of persecution or poverty, it was they – in contrast to their fellows who stayed behind – who had the courage and the resolution to make a break and chance the hazards of the voyage and the dangers of a new and unknown land.

It is also not surprising that the Russians, content to play a passive role and inured to defeat, fell behind in material culture, whereas the new Americans, freed from the tradition and conservatism of Europe, readily grasped new ideas and applied new techniques, so that their inventiveness soon became a byword.

3 Geographical Background

The Soviet Union lies in the eastern hemisphere and forms the northern part of the Eurasian land mass, while the United States is in the western hemisphere where it makes up the bulk of the southern half of North America. This difference is expressed in terms of longitude and latitude in Table 3.1, from which it can be seen that the United States extends one-sixth the way round the globe in an east–west direction, the Soviet Union almost half-way (172 degrees of longitude). This contrast is not so great as it first appears because the circumference of the globe diminishes northwards from the equator.

TABLE 3.1 LINES OF LONGITUDE AND LATITUDE ENCLOSING THE CONTERMINOUS MAINLAND AREAS OF THE USA AND THE USSR

	USA	USSR
Longitude	125°W–66°W	19°E–169°W
Latitude	24°N –49°N	35°N–78°N

Alaska, a detached American state forming the north-westernmost part of the North American continent and stretching from latitude 54°N to 72°N, is more comparable in its position to the Soviet Union than the conterminous United States. It is separated from the Soviet Union only by the forty miles or so of sea – frozen in winter – which form the Bering Strait.

The Soviet Union is better endowed with off-lying islands. North of the mainland, in the Arctic Ocean, are several archipelagos extending to within the eightieth parallel: Frants Iosif Islands, Novaya Zemlya, Severnaya Zemlya, the New Siberian Islands and Wrangel Island. America's fiftieth State, Hawaii, consists of a group of volcanic islands situated just south of the Tropic of Cancer in mid-Pacific between 154° and 161°W, and 2,100 nautical miles south-west of San Francisco.

Traditional rectangular maps of the world show America in the north-western corner and Russia in the north-east, while maps often used in America, with the western hemisphere in the middle, split the Soviet Union into two parts, one on the extreme western and the other on the far eastern margins of the map. From neither type would it appear that the shortest distances between the two countries lie across

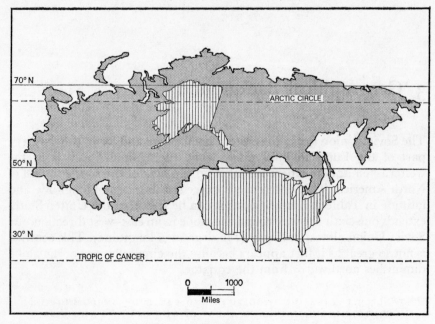

6. Latitudinal position of the USA relative to the USSR

7. Relative areas shown as squares

the polar ice or that, to take the most direct route between Moscow and Los Angeles, one would travel northwards.

SIZE AND SHAPE

The USSR is by far the largest country in the world. Its area of 8,650,000 square miles is double that of any other and amounts to about one-sixth of the land surface of the globe. The Soviet Union is about two and one-third times as large as the United States, which comes fourth in world order of size, China and Canada also being larger. There are considerable variations in the area of each superpower according to what is included (Table 3.2).

TABLE 3.2 AREAS

	USA	USSR	US area as percentage of Soviet
Gross area, including all territories and waters under jurisdiction	3,702,426 sq. mi 9,585,581 sq. km	8,649,490 sq. mi 22,402,200 sq. km	42·8%
Total area, including all territories but excluding coastal waters	3,628,062 sq. mi 9,393,053 sq. km	8,600,329 sq. mi 22,274,900 sq. km	42·2%
Total area, but the fifty States only for USA	3,615,123 sq. mi 9,363,179 sq. km	8,600,329 sq. mi 22,274,900 sq. km	42·0%
Land area (USA: fifty States only) excluding coastal and inland waters	3,540,938 sq. mi 9,167,489 sq. km	8,321,775 sq. mi 21,553,420 sq. km	42·6%
Conterminous area (USA: forty-eight States USSR: mainland only without islands) including inland waters	3,022,261 sq. mi 7,824,634 sq. km	8,530,459 sq. mi 22,093,200 sq. km	35·4%

The USSR is about twice as long as the USA east and west, but the difference in the north–south dimension is not so great (Table 3.3). In both countries there is considerable variation in the north–south width, the distance in the United States between Brownsville, Texas, and the point on the Canadian border due north being double that between the Gulf of Mexico coast near Tallahassee, Florida, and Lake Ontario. Likewise in the USSR the north–south distance between the southernmost point of the Pamir Mountains in the Tadzhik Republic and the northern coast of the Yamal peninsula is almost twice as far as the shortest distance across eastern Siberia between China and the Arctic Ocean.

In shape there is a certain similarity between the two countries in that they are both much longer east and west than north and south, but the configuration of all the boundaries of the USSR is much more

TABLE 3.3   APPROXIMATE MAXIMUM AND MINIMUM DIMENSIONS
OF THE CONTERMINOUS MAINSLANDS[1]
(*miles*)

	USA		USSR	
	Maximum	*Minimum*	*Maximum*	*Minimum*
East–west along parallel	2,800	2,200	5,700	4,600
North–south along meridian	1,600	800	2,500	1,400

irregular than those of the United States, offering nothing so uncom-
plicated as the forty-ninth parallel and the relatively unindented coastlines along the Pacific and Gulf of Mexico, and along the Atlantic south
of Cape Hatteras.

NEIGHBOURING STATES

The United States has common land frontiers with only two other
sovereign states, Canada and Mexico. A range of five hundred miles
from American territory brings in only four more countries: Cuba, the
Bahamas and Jamaica, and from Alaska, the Soviet Union. The
USSR, on the other hand, has a common land frontier with the
following thirteen countries:

Norway	Hungary	Afghanistan
Finland	Rumania	India
Poland	Turkey	China
Czechoslovakia	Persia	Mongolia
	North Korea	

and within five hundred miles of its territory lie seventeen more:

Sweden	Austria	Syria
Denmark	Yugoslavia	Iraq
East Germany	Albania	Pakistan
West Germany	Bulgaria	Nepal
Italy	Greece	Japan
South Korea	United States (Alaska)	

ADMINISTRATIVE DIVISIONS

The United States divides into fifty States, together with the District
of Colombia. In addition, there are the Commonwealth of Puerto Rico,
eight overseas possessions (Guam, Virgin Islands, Samoa, Midway
Islands, Wake Island, Canton and Enderbury Islands, Johnston and
Sand Islands, Swan Islands), and three outlying areas (Panama Canal

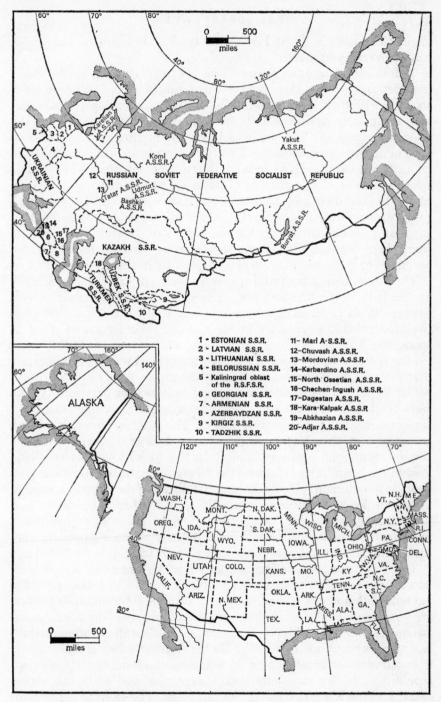

8. Major administrative divisions: Republics of the USSR and States of the USA (Hawaii omitted)

Zone, Corn Islands, Trust Territory of the Pacific Islands). The USSR has no overseas territories.

Within the American States there are metropolitan areas, cities, counties and towns. Metropolitan areas consist of one or more cities together with their suburbs and adjacent towns and villages; sometimes they are merely statistical units for assembling data pertaining to the urban areas as a whole, while in an increasing number of instances some kind of metropolitan council is formed. This may be just a consultative council or it may be given certain administrative powers, but in either case the independent structure of the constituent cities and towns remains. Several metropolitan areas cross State boundaries. Counties and towns exercise only minor administrative powers delegated to them by the States within which they lie, but cities have charters, also derived from their State, giving them much wider powers, including the authority to make laws within the scope of their charters.

The Soviet Union is administratively more complex than the United States. It is, in the first instance, divided into fifteen Republics which between them cover its whole area. These Republics are named after the predominant nationality at the time of their formation. One of them, the Russian, is much larger than all the rest combined, comprising seventy-six per cent of the total territory. The largest American State, Alaska, forms sixteen per cent of the total area of the USA. Most Soviet Republics are divided into *oblasts* (counties) or occasionally into *krays* (regions). The Russian Republic includes forty-nine *oblasts* or *krays* and sixteen autonomous republics. The latter are areas inhabited mainly by non-Russian peoples. They have their own governments and certain autonomous powers, mainly in the social and cultural field. Within the boundaries of some of the *oblasts* and *krays* there are areas set apart as autonomous *oblasts* and national districts: these again are areas inhabited by non-Russian nationalities, but which are either not numerous or else not developed enough to form autonomous republics: in them the administration is carried on in their own language, and their national customs and cohesion are respected.

The Ukrainian, White Russian and Kazakh republics are divided into twenty-five, six and sixteen *oblasts* respectively. The Uzbek republic has ten *oblasts* and one autonomous republic. The other union Republics are not systematically divided up into *oblasts*, and six of them – Estonia, Latvia, Lithuania, Moldavia, Armenia and Turkestan are administered as single, unpartitioned units. Within the Azerbaydzhan republic there is an autonomous republic and an autonomous *oblast*; in the Georgian republic there are two autonomous republics and an autonomous *oblast*; and the Kirghiz republic has one *oblast*. The closest approach to these formally organised autonomous national divisions in America are the lands under the jurisdiction of the Bureau of Indian Affairs. In 1967 these covered an area of 86,000 square miles distributed among twenty-five States.

In the USSR the *oblasts* (counties) and *krays* (regions), and those Republics which are not divided into *oblasts*, are further split up into *raions* (districts). Within these the further administrative subdivisions of *selsovety* (villages or village groups) and *poselki* (non-agricultural settlements) are distinguished. Large towns form distinct administrative units within their Republic and are themselves divided into *raions* (wards). Smaller towns are subordinate to the *oblast* or *raion* in which they are located, according to their size.

GEOLOGICAL STRUCTURE AND LANDFORMS

Both countries consist essentially of fairly stable parts of the earth's crust, which have not been greatly disturbed by the tectonic storms of geological history. The North American stable block continues southwards from Canada and occupies most of the area between the Rockies and the Appalachians, while that of the USSR extends for thousands of miles from the Carpathians in the west to the highlands of eastern Siberia. It is not a single feature as in America, but tripartite. In the west is the first part, the Russian platform, which has been elevated only slightly above sea level. It is separated from the second part, the West Siberian *plita* (slab) – scarcely raised at all – by a long and narrow zone of weakness along which the ridges of the Ural mountains have been elevated. The West Siberian *plita* is terminated in the east by another great rift, beyond which the third part, the central Siberian platform, has been strongly elevated.

The ancient crystalline rocks, such as granite and gneiss, which compose the resistant foundations of these stable areas, are for the most part concealed by later deposits, but in the United States they outcrop around the western end of Lake Superior; in the Soviet Union there are several such exposures or 'shields'. The 'shield' areas of both countries are distinguished by their metallic wealth. Over most of the stable area of each, the ancient basement rocks are covered by extensive formations of sedimentary rocks laid down at times when these continental expanses sank beneath the sea. Because of the fundamental stability of the crust beneath them, these great thicknesses of limestone, sandstone, shale and clay, with later additions of less consolidated alluvial material such as gravels and sands, lie relatively undisturbed in vast horizontal sheets, and contrast strongly, in both cases, with the highly contorted sedimentary beds of Europe. In both countries these sedimentary rocks hold massive accumulations of coal, petroleum and natural gas, fossil fuels derived from the decay of organic matter.

The stable platforms and 'slabs' are by no means flat, for they have

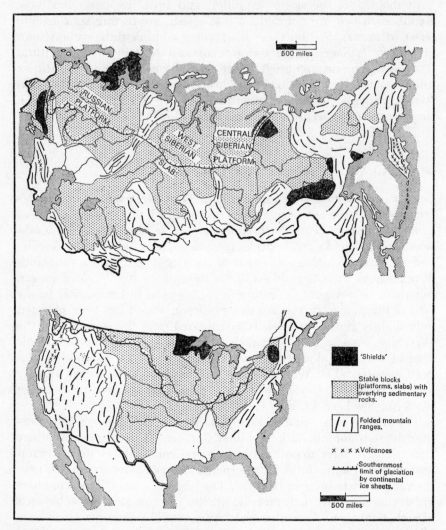

9. Geological structure (generalised)

not been entirely immune to the pressures and tensions that have transformed the build of adjacent parts of the world. They are warped upwards and downwards in places and, elsewhere, cracked or faulted, with portions rising and falling, between the fault lines. Such irregularities are in some instances too pronounced to be concealed by the overlying sedimentary mantle. They account for the existence of the Great Lakes in America, and of Lakes Ladoga and Onega in Russia. They have produced the Ozarks and the associated highlands that disturb the uniformity of lowland America, and they are responsible for the Donets Heights and other exceptions to the general flatness of the Russian plain.

In the Black Hills of Montana and South Dakota, and in the 'land of the little round hills' in Kazakhstan, molten subterranean magma has thrust up through the crust to affect the structure and relief of the surface. In the Black Hills the magma forms great domes or 'laccoliths' which culminate in such mountains as Harney Peak (7,242 ft a.s.l.); these rise up to 3,500 feet above the surrounding land. In Kazakhstan the granitic domes are smaller but more numerous, forming rounded hills rising a few hundred feet above the surrounding surface.

In each country the stable continental heartland is bordered by highly unstable zones which either have sagged, collecting immense deposits of sediment in deep seas, or have been thrust vigorously against the rigid central block, buckling up into mountain ranges. Such mountainous areas are found both to the west and to the east of the American interior stable area. The intricate mountain system of the west – the 'cordillera' – is geologically recent in formation (Tertiary) and possesses some lofty ranges as well as high plateaus and deep troughs. The eastern or Appalachian system is much narrower and, being much older (Palaeozoic), its once high relief has been well worn down. In the USSR, the main mountain masses have been pressed up against the southern and eastern sides of the central complex of stable platforms. Some of the resulting ranges are very recent and some are very old, with others of intermediate age, and they have therefore a wide range of elevation. In both countries the mountains have brought up, in their ancient cores of crystalline rock, rich metalliferous veins comparable to those found in the exposed 'shield' areas of the stable platforms. The western cordillera is America's chief source of gold, silver, copper, uranium, molybdenum, vanadium, tungsten and several other metals, and the southern ranges of the USSR are almost as important as sources of metallic wealth.

If the broad lineaments of the physique of each superpower have been determined by its basic geological structure, much of the detail has been etched in by the erosive work of ice, running water and wind. During the colder climates of the Pleistocene period, ice – both in the form of glaciers descending from mountain peaks and continental ice sheets advancing from the polar regions – was far more widespread than to-day. The mountain glaciers carved the summits and widened, deepened and rounded the valleys. The ice sheets scraped and polished the surface. They gouged out the softer rocks over which they rode and the resulting hollows are now filled with lakes. The harder rocks survive as great rounded humps. When the ice, whether of glacier or sheet, melted away, the rock debris which had been borne along on, in, and under it, was dropped and boulders, gravel, sands and clay were scattered over the surface in a haphazard mixture. These obstructions blocked up the normal drainage channels, creating lakes and swamps. The farther the ice had come, the more of this morainic material it carried, culminating in a maximum accumulation along its front. As a result, the farthest extent of the last ice sheet is marked by the deposition of a long line of terminal morainic hills.

In North America most of the glaciation is in Canada, but it extends into the United States in a broad belt some 400 miles wide around the Great Lakes. Its most widespread features here are terminal moraines and areas of 'drift' – eroded rock material spread out over the surface by the ice. The valleys of the western cordillera are also mostly filled with morainic material. In the USSR, because of its more northerly position, glaciation is far more widespread. In Russia itself the land glaciated at one time or other reaches southwards to within 160 miles of the Black Sea, while in Siberia it includes almost all the territory north of the sixtieth parallel. There are also extensive glaciated areas associated with the southern belt of mountains. The widespread glacial deposits in Russia, by masking the underlying sedimentary rocks over large areas, deprived Russians of access to building stone and road metal. This deprivation, not normally experienced in America, contributed to Russia's traditional reputation as a land of wooden buildings and bad roads.

However, the effects of the most recent glaciation – the Wisconsin in America and the Valday in Russia – are more comparable in effect and extent. The glaciated lands of Minnesota and Wisconsin – and to some extent those of northern New England – have some similarity in landscape and utilisation to those of north-western Russia. Both are forested morainic lakelands with the crystalline rocks scraped bare in places, with ill-assorted dumps of mixed material elsewhere, and with huge boulders strewn across the country. All are regions hostile to farming, but favourable to lumbering, and useful as retreats for recreation.

In both countries strong winds, blowing over the morainic zone during dry climatic conditions, carried off the finer and more fertile material and dropped it to the south of the glaciated regions. This rich and fine-grained deposit – löss – is widespread in both the USA and the USSR, but more so in the latter. It gives rise to a productive agriculture.

The effect of water running in rivers, streams and torrents has been to cut valleys back into the uplands which have consequently been dissected into complex groupings of hills and ridges. It has been particularly influential in areas that escaped recent glaciation – the western plateaus and most of the Appalachians in the USA, the central Russian uplands and Central Siberian plateau of the USSR. Here not only normal valleys but deep gorges, sculptured canyons and precipitous ravines gash the surface. The semi-arid conditions of much of the American West and of central Russia, along with the ill-advised removal of the natural vegetation by man, have led to the formation of several gullied 'badlands' in both. In the truly arid areas, sculpturing of the rocks into fantastic shapes by the wind has added its contribution to the landscape. But the breath-taking and awe-inspiring work of wind and water in Utah, Colorado and Arizona is matched neither in magnitude nor in magnificence in the Soviet deserts. Here erosion has more often demolished such natural monuments and reduced them to sand. Over wide stretches of the Soviet deserts the dune is the one ubiquitous and montonous feature. Sand dunes are relatively infrequent in the USA.

In porous and soluble rocks such as limestone, chemical action is added to the physical weathering of the rock to produce erosional and depositional features known collectively as *karst*, the name of a region in Yugoslavia where such phenomena abound. In typical limestone country there is, because of the porosity of the rock, a noticeable lack of surface water, even though rainfall may be high. The bare white rock breaks abruptly through the vegetation cover. Bare 'pavement' areas are exposed on level surfaces over which lumps of stone lie scattered. Sink holes and solution hollows pit the ground, which may be honeycombed by underground channels and caverns, with stalactite and stalagmite formation in the latter.

Because limestones form a much larger proportion of the exposed surface of the United States, karstic features are commoner there than in the USSR, and because the American territory is better populated and more easily accessible, the more remarkable examples have become widely known and developed as tourist attractions. A hundred years ago, John Watson, a visitor from Scotland, visited the Mammoth Caves of Kentucky as a tourist:

> After our arrival we drove at once to the hotel, and procuring tickets, as also a suit of over-alls, and a coloured guide to conduct us, we proceeded to the Mammoth Cave . . . and penetrating into the underground caverns for a distance of about two miles, we inspected the various parts . . .
>
> There is the *Church*, for instance, a wonderful piece of natural architecture; it is one immense apartment, 100 feet in diameter, with

a seamless rocky roof 63 feet over head, as also a space for an organ. Divine service, I was told, has been more than once performed in this so-called church . . .

It is said that visitors may, if they choose, travel for a distance of 200 miles in the various avenues and walks of the Mammoth Cave of Kentucky, which is certainly one of the most striking wonders of the New World.[2]

Even more renowned are the Carlsbad Caverns of New Mexico, where over thirty miles of subterranean channels and caves have been explored, with the deepest going down to 1,300 feet beneath the surface. The best-known karst topography in the USSR is found in the Caucasus mountains, particularly where the Alek range approaches the Black Sea near Sochi. Here the Nazarov cave, descending 1500 feet below the ground, is the deepest so far discovered in the Soviet Union. But the limestone areas of the USSR, although large, are usually in remote and sparsely peopled areas. They are only seldom visited and then mainly by geological and geographical scientists.

As both countries have Pacific coastlines, they possess volcanoes located in their respective sections of the circum-Pacific orogenic belt. The Soviet Union also has a share of the other great orogenic belt that runs from the Alps through southern Asia to the East Indies and New Zealand. The United States has twenty-two active or recently active volcanoes, 15 of them in Alaska and four in Hawaii. The Soviet Union has twenty-five in Kamchatka, thirty-nine in the Kurile Islands and one in Transcaucasia, sixty-five in all.[3] Some of these form high mountains. Geysers are associated with volcanic activity in both areas. Old Faithful in the Yellowstone National Park sends forth a four-minute jet of boiling water, enveloped in steam, every sixty-seven minutes on an average. Velikan in Kamchatka shoots up a hundred-foot jet of almost boiling water for four minutes every three hours. Earthquakes also afflict the mountainous zones of each superpower. In recent years the worst have been those which wreaked havoc in Anchorage, Alaska, in 1964 and destroyed large parts of Tashkent, Uzbekistan, in 1966.

RELIEF

Because of the basic similarity of geological structure, certain parallels can be drawn between the physiographical relief of the two superpowers. Inland from the Pacific coast of each is a zone of high folded mountain ranges, with high plateaus interspersed. In the United States this belt varies in width from 600 to 1,000 miles, and the highest peaks rise above 14,000 feet within the conterminous bounds, but in Alaska

Mt McKinley soars to over 20,000 feet. In the USSR the zone is between 400 and 1,600 miles wide, but the summits are lower, there being
few above 10,000 feet, other than the volcanoes of Kamchatka, the
highest cone of which reaches 15,585 feet in Mt Klyuchevskiy.

Beyond the Pacific mountain zone, in each country, come deeply
incised plateaus, several thousand feet above sea level: the Great Plains
of western America and the central Siberian plateau. But whereas the

TABLE 3.4 HIGHEST MOUNTAINS AND DEEPEST DEPRESSIONS

USA		USSR	
		Highest Summits	
Mt McKinley, Alaska	20,320 ft 6,194 m	Mt Communism, Pamir Mts	24,584 ft 7,495 m
North Peak, Alaska	19,470 ft 5,934 m	Mt Pobeda, Tyan Shan Mts	24,397 ft 7,439 m
Mt St Elias, Alaska	18,008 ft 5,488 m	Mt Lenin, Trans-Alai Mts	23,400 ft 7,134 m
Mt Foraker, Alaska	17,400 ft 5,304 m	Khan Tengri, Tyan Shan Mts	22,950 ft 6,995 m
Mt Bona, Alaska	16,500 ft 5,029 m	Mt Revolution, Pamir Mts	22,880 ft 6,974 m
Mt Blackburn, Alaska	16,390 ft 4,996 m	Mt Moskva, Pamir Mts	22,264 ft 6,785 m
Mt Sanford, Alaska	16,237 ft 4,949 m	Mt Karl Marx, Pamir Mts	22,067 ft 6,725 m
South Buttress, Alaska	15,885 ft 4,870 m	Mt Kurumdy, Trans-Alai Mts	21,688 ft 6,610 m
Mt Vancouver, Alaska	15,700 ft 4,785 m	Mt Gormo, Pamir Mts	21,633 ft 6,595 m
Mt Churchill, Alaska	15,638 ft 4,767 m	Mt Budor, Pamir Mts	20,118 ft 6,132 m
		Highest Volcano	
Mt Sanford, Alaska	16,237 ft 4,949 m	Mt Klyuchevskiy, Kamchatka	15,585 ft 4,750 m
		Deepest Depression	
Death Valley, California	−282 ft −86 m	Karagiye depression Kazakhstan	−433 ft −132 m

interfluvial stretches of the Great Plains have a true plateau nature,
with large expanses of level ground, rendered more striking by their
open treeless character, the Siberian upland has been so extensively
eroded by rivers that little plateau surface is left, the whole having been
cut up into a maze of ridges. Nor could there be a greater contrast between the high plains of the USA, with their open range country and
their vast wheat farms sweltering in the long, dry dusty summer, and
larch-clad ridges of central Siberia, one of the coldest parts of the earth
where the subsoil is permanently frozen and only the surface thaws in
the brief summer season.

Eastward of the Great Plains or high plateaus in the USA and westward of the central Siberian plateau in the USSR, come interior plains
of low elevation floored by sedimentary rocks. In America this plain
corresponds closely with the lower areas of the Mississippi basin, while
the interior plain of the Soviet Union – the west Siberian plain –
roughly corresponds to the basin of the Ob. It is remarkably level, the
largest and most uniform plain on the earth's surface. One of the several
features distinguishing the two plains is that the American slopes southwards down to the Gulf of Mexico, while the Siberian is inclined

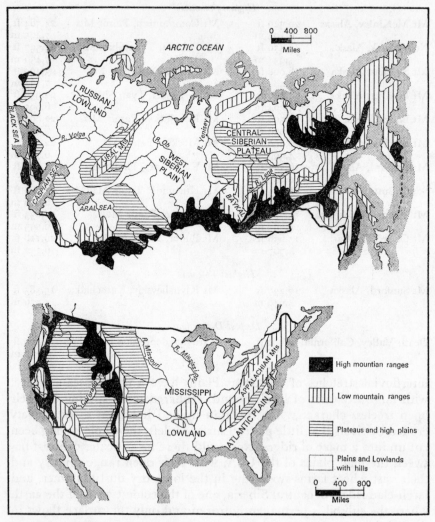

10. Major landforms (generalised)

northwards down to the Kara Sea in the Arctic Ocean. Here again, what similarity there is rests with the relief. The Mississippi lowland consists almost wholly of rich agricultural land, arranged, because of specialisation, into districts famous for some particular product: dairy produce, maize, cattle and pigs, tobacco, winter wheat, cotton or fruit. But the West Siberian plain is a great morass, with trees growing along the sandy ridges that emerge from the swamp, and the whole frozen for much of the year. The contrast is reflected in the population: 85 million Americans inhabit the interior lowlands of their country, but the West Siberian plain barely contains a million Russians.

Each plain is terminated – on the east in the USA, on the west in the USSR – by a system of relatively low, rounded, worn mountains elevated in the Hercynian age (about 200 million years ago). However, whereas the American Appalachians are made up of many parallel ridges, the Russian Urals consist, for most of their length, principally of one main range. The long narrow Ural chain is 1,800 miles long, and is continued for another 500 miles into the Arctic Ocean by the islands of Novaya Zemlya. The mountain belt, little more than fifty miles wide in its northern section, broadens southwards to a width of 300 miles, with parallel ranges comparable to the Appalachians. These latter are about 1,500 miles long and their complex of ridges, valleys and plateaus has an average width of about 200 miles. The summits of the two ranges are fairly comparable: the highest Appalachian mountain is Mt Mitchell, N.C., 6,684 feet a.s.l., the highest Uralian peak, Mt Narodnaya, 6,212 feet; the average height of the mountainous area is in each case between 2,000 and 3,000 feet a.s.l. There is no such low, clear and direct passage through the Urals as that offered by the Hudson–Mohawk gap through the Appalachians, but the south-central Urals, with summits of only 2,000 feet and valley bottoms well below 1,000 feet, form an easily crossed group of hills rather than a mountain range.

Both the Appalachians and the Urals have contributed to the economic development of their respective countries because of their remarkable mineral wealth. This contribution has been mainly in the sphere of metallurgy. Peter the Great established the first state ironworks in the Urals in 1699 and it began to produce pig in 1701. The industry expanded throughout the eighteenth century to become the leading source of iron in the world. After declining through obsolescence before the Revolution, the Ural iron and steel industry has been modernised during the Soviet period and in 1965 produced twenty-nine per cent of Soviet pig iron and thirty-three per cent of Soviet steel.[4] The Appalachian metallurgical industry dates from the end of the eighteenth century: a blast furnace began working in Pittsburgh in 1797, another

C

near Youngstown in 1808, and a rolling mill at Pittsburgh in 1812; but the district did not come to dominate the American iron and steel industry until the 1860s and after.[5] The Ural industry was based on iron ore, the Appalachian on coal. The Appalachian coalfield has long been the most productive coalfield in the world, and its high-grade coking coals feed the largest steel industry in the world. The Urals are the greatest single storehouse of minerals in the world, although they lack the greatest asset of the Appalachians – coking coal.

On the Atlantic side of the Appalachian and Ural systems there are plateaus into which Atlantic-flowing rivers in the USA, and tributaries of the Volga in the USSR, have sunk their valleys. In the United States the plateau is the Piedmont, distinguished by its hard old crystalline rocks and its sudden termination and drop to the coastal plain along the rectilinear 'fall line'. In the USSR, on the other hand, the sub-Uralian plateaus are built of horizontally disposed sedimentary rocks with Permian limestones on the surface. They slope gradually down to the plains to the west.

Beyond the American piedmont and the Russian sub-Uralian plateaus the analogy between the relief of the two countries becomes strained. Plains are found in both, but while America has only the narrow Atlantic coastal plain, which disappears altogether in the north, westward of the Ural plateaus stretches the broad Russian lowland: as far as Scandinavia in the north, into Poland in the centre, and to the Carpathians in the south. The American plain terminates in the sea, while that of Russia is but the widened eastward extension of the great European plain that begins in northern France.

High and geologically recently folded mountain ranges form the southernmost border regions of the USSR for almost the whole length of the country. These mountains hold the highest individual peaks and the longest glaciers to be found in either country, giving the USSR several mountains above twenty thousand feet in height above sea level. This southern wall of mountains has no parallel in the USA.

RIVERS

Both the USA and the USSR are countries of long rivers, but the USSR more so (Table 3.5). In the Soviet Union there are ten over 1,000 miles in length, four of which are over 2,000 miles long and two over 3,000. In the United States, there are six over 1,000 miles long, only one of which is over 2,000 miles long. But this is the Mississippi–Missouri, which with a length of 3,741 miles, exceeds that of the longest Soviet river. The Mississippi itself has four tributaries over 1,000 miles in length – the Arkansas, Ohio, Allegheny and Red, besides the

Missouri which, with its Red Rock headstream, measures 2,564 miles.

The Mississippi dominates the rivers of the United States. Its great drainage basin covers nearly half the country and includes nearly all the most productive farmland. It provides a magnificent waterway system which carries almost all the freight moved by river within the United States. It not only links the Great Lakes system and the corn belt in the north with the Gulf of Mexico and the cotton lands of the south, but its tributaries to the west reach up to the wheatfields, cattle

TABLE 3.5   LONGEST RIVERS
(those in the USA in roman type; those in the USSR in italics)

	length in	
	miles	*km*
Mississippi–Missouri–Red Rock	3,741	6,021
Yenisey–Selenga	3,584	5,767
Ob–Black Irtysh	3,342	5,378
Lena	2,562	4,123
Mississippi*	2,348	3,779
*Ob**	2,265	3,645
Volga	2,214	3,559
*Yenisey**	2,002	3,222
Rio Grande	1,885	3,034
Yukon (Alaska)	1,875	3,017
Amur	1,770	2,849
Ural	1,520	2,446
Colorado	1,450	2,334
Dnieper	1,371	2,207
Syr	1,284	2,066
Columbia	1,214	1,953
Brazos	1,210	1,947
Don	1,182	1,902
Pechora	1,074	1,728

* The named river only.

ranches and oilfields of the Plains, and those to the east into the coal-based industrial regions of the Appalachians. The Mississippi has no rival in the USA. The Rio Grande, America's second largest river, is nullified by forming the international boundary with Mexico; the third, the Yukon, is isolated away in Alaska, while the fourth, the Colorado, flows in a deep canyon through deserts.

The Volga is usually thought of as the foremost Russian river, and although the Ob, the Lena and the Yenisey are longer, the Volga holds first place in Russian hearts and is known affectionately as 'mother Volga'. This is not so easily understood, as it flows for most of its course through lands peopled by non-Slavonic races, and did not become wholly Russian until the sixteenth century. However, although this is relatively late in the context of Russian history, it antedates the absorption of the Mississippi basin into the United States by more than two centuries.

The Volga, like the Mississippi, is the most important river in the country's internal transport system, and like the American river, it links cool northern forested lands with warm and potentially productive southern ones. It also, with the help of its tributary the Kama, and linking canals such as the Volga–Baltic and the Volga–Don, serves most of the developed regions of Russia proper. But whereas the lower Mississippi flows through a region blessed with abundant rainfall, the lower Volga crosses a desert. Both rivers have built out deltas into the seas into which they flow, but the Caspian Sea, which receives the Russian river, is really a lake, for the Volga is part of a vast internal drainage system, unconnected (in its natural state) with the ocean. In fact all American rivers of any consequence have their outlets in the open ocean, but not a single Soviet river is so fortunate. They all flow either to landlocked seas or to frozen ocean. In each delta lies a famous port – New Orleans in that of the Mississippi and Astrakhan in that of the Volga. But New Orleans (pop. 1,064,000) is a large and flourishing centre of commerce, second only to New York in America, while Astrakhan's heyday was before New Orleans was even founded.

The Mississippi–Missouri, like all the long American rivers, rises in the high Rockies, but the Volga – along with several other important Russian rivers – has its source in a relatively low-lying swamp in the centre of Russia. But whereas the Mississippi is the central artery of a far-flung basin, the Volga, for the whole of its middle course, does not flow in a true river valley. Instead, it runs along the foot of a lofty escarpment, while the land on the opposite side stretches away imperceptibly into the misty distance. Such high banks (*yars*) on the right-hand or western side are characteristic of parts of the courses of other Russian rivers, notably the Dnieper and Don.

The Volga has a more irregular régime than the Mississippi. It freezes in winter, floods in spring and becomes very shallow in autumn. The Mississippi does not freeze but it has a long history of disastrous floods. These have been more destructive because lands alongside the great American river have been more densely populated and developed. The Volga has, however, been transformed in recent years. For much of its course it has become a staircase of hydro-electric and irrigation reservoirs and it runs through the country's most productive oilfield.

The Mississippi is supreme in the USA; the Volga is but one of several mighty rivers in the USSR, and four of them drain more extensive territories than it does. They are the four great rivers of Siberia and the Far East: Ob, Yenisey, Lena and Amur. But only the Ob drains a larger area than the Mississippi.

LAKES

Apart from her share of the Great Lakes and the Lake of the Woods, which constitute part of her northern frontier, the United States is remarkably lacking in large lakes. The Great Salt Lake is the only other lake whose area reaches a thousand square miles. Even smaller lakes are surprisingly few. In the Soviet Union, besides the huge Caspian Sea – also a frontier lake – there are several large natural water bodies with an area of over a thousand square miles, and smaller lakes are legion.

Both countries have salt lakes in their arid areas. Most famous is the Great Salt Lake of Utah which, apart from its salt-encrusted edges, contains four billion tons of dissolved mineral salts. These have attracted commercial exploitation on a large scale and the previously important

TABLE 3.6 LARGEST NATURAL LAKES
(*those in the USA in roman type; those in the USSR in italics*)

	sq. mi	sq. km
Caspian	141,840	367,392
Aral	23,924	61,963
Michigan	22,178	57,411
Superior*	21,118	54,396
Baykal	11,340	29,371
Huron*	8,975	23,245
Ladoga	6,624	17,206
Balkhash	6,000	15,540
Erie*	5,002	12,953
Onega	3,560	9,204
Issyk Kul	2,232	5,781

* Area is given only for that part of the lake which is
American territorial water.

touristic use has been harmed by pollution, aggravated by the presence close by of Salt Lake City and other urban centres. In the USSR there are also many salt lakes comparable to the Great Salt Lake in salinity, though not in size. Every summer evaporation from Lakes Elton and Baskunchak covers them with a pink or white salt crust. The waters of both the Caspian and Aral seas are salt, and the Karabogaz Gulf on the eastern shore of the Caspian contains commercially exploitable concentrations of sodium phosphate.

The Great Salt Lake in America and the Caspian and Aral seas in the USSR are all drying up. The chief cause is the diversion of water from the rivers that nourish these lakes. Water from the Bear, Jordan, Ogden and Weber rivers, which flow into the Great Salt Lake, is used increasingly for farm irrigation and urban water supply. Likewise, growing demands for irrigation water are being made on the Volga which supplies the Caspian, and on the Amu and Syr, which flow into the Aral. However, in 1970 the Soviet government decided to embark upon a grandiose scheme by which water from the Siberian Ob system will be brought southwards by canals into Central Asia. This project will save the Aral Sea from extinction. The area of the Great Salt Lake has shrunk during the past century from 2,250 square miles to 1,420 square miles.

The USSR has many interesting mountain lakes. Lake Baykal, occupying a remarkable fissure in the earth's surface, is the deepest lake in the world, descending in places over a mile. Lake Issyk Kul, 112 miles long and over 5,300 feet up among the Tyan Shan mountains, is fed by a hot spring and, in consequence, despite its altitude, does not freeze in winter. Farther up in this same range, at about 11,000 feet, is the 'disappearing lake', Mertzbaher, which, owing to glacier movement, loses its water for a period each summer. In the volcanic area of Kamchatka there are many crater lakes, notably the 400-foot-deep pool in the crater of Mt Kronoz. Against this wealth of Soviet mountain lakes, the USA can set its own Crater Lake in southern Oregon, which lies over 6,000 feet above sea level and is nearly 2,000 feet deep. In contrast to the deserted isolation of most Soviet lakes, however wonderful they may be as natural phenomena or curiosities, Crater Lake is a national park and is a well-frequented tourist attraction, with hotel, camp sites and vacation cottages. It receives half a million visitors a year. But things are now beginning to move in the same direction in the USSR, where resorts have been built alongside some of the beautiful mountain lakes in the Caucasus. Even Lake Baykal, in distant eastern Siberia, is to become a resort area. A large national park, with camp sites, hotels and hostels, is being developed around it, and already hydrofoils speed tourists across its waters in summer, just as lorries and cars use its frozen surface in winter.

4 Climate

The different global positions of the USA and the USSR, in regard both to latitude and to the distribution of land and sea, ensure that their climatic conditions vary widely. The more southerly latitude of the United States guarantees it more warmth from the sun and a lesser difference in length of day as between summer and winter. Thus, the northernmost parts of the USSR have a period of several weeks in winter when there is no daylight and in midsummer when there is no night. Such conditions occur nowhere in the USA except in northern Alaska.

The climate of a land area is governed to a considerable degree by the origin of the air masses and winds that move over it. In the USA in summer these have originated over the tropical and equatorial waters of the Atlantic (maritime tropical or mT air masses) and they bring warm humid weather to the eastern half of the country. But in winter the country becomes a battleground between this warm humid air pushing in from the south-east and drier, intensely cold, continental polar (cP) air masses coming in from Canada. The south-eastern quadrant of the country thus has warm humid air all the year round, although it is not unknown for the continental polar air from Canada to sweep south in winter, even into Florida. The north-eastern quadrant has the warm humid maritime tropical air in summer, while in winter it may have either this warm tropical air or cold polar air from the north, according to the position of the 'front' between these two air masses. This front is characterised by changeable and disturbed weather, associated with eastward-moving cyclonic 'depressions' and often accompanied by snowstorms in the north. The mountainous western States have more complex climates with great local variations, while the Pacific coast experiences warm dry summers and mild winters which become increasingly rainy towards the north.

The USSR is invaded in summer by air masses from all directions: from the west comes temperate air of cool moist maritime origin, but dried and warmed to some extent by its passage over Europe. From the Arctic Ocean cold polar air sweeps in over the northern areas and continental air invades from the south. In Central Asia this continental air is tropical in origin (cT) and hot and dry; farther east, where the continental air has come off the Mongolian plateaus, it is cooler but still dry. Storms develop over the heated interior and move generally eastwards, but they do not produce heavy precipitation because the moisture content of all the incoming air masses is usually quite low. Two exceptional areas are in the south-western and south-eastern

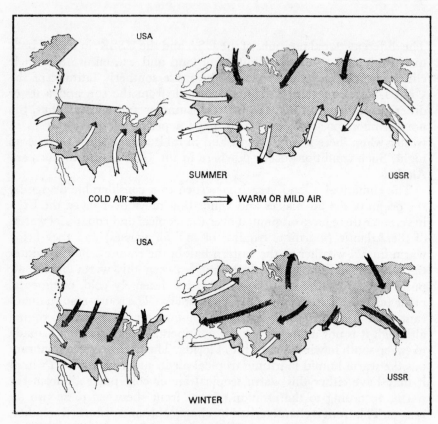

11. Movement of air masses (generalised)

corners of the country, into both of which maritime tropical air brings heavy precipitation. The south-western area covers a small strip in Transcaucasia extending inland from the Black Sea coast; the south-eastern area corresponds to the maritime district of the Soviet Far East, which has a monsoonal type of climate.

In winter over the USSR as a whole there is a predominance of cold polar air which often stagnates, becoming extremely cold and dry, and producing the lowest temperatures recorded on the earth outside of

Antarctica. Warm maritime air no longer blows into the south-eastern region from the Pacific, but the south-western, Transcaucasian area is more fortunate and continues to receive maritime tropical air by way of the Mediterranean and Black seas. From the west maritime temperate air, still retaining some of its original mildness and moisture, attempts – with varying success from winter to winter – to penetrate the great mass of cold air settled over the interior of the country. When it does so it too becomes increasingly cold and dry as it passes eastwards.

As a result of these differences in the kind of air masses influencing the climate, the USA is much warmer and much wetter than the USSR. The temperature contrast is greatest in winter, when virtually the whole of the USSR has a mean January temperature below 0°C (32°F), and

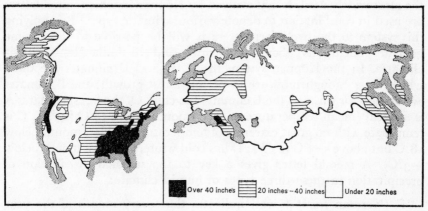

12. Average annual precipitation

when about half the country is below −20°C (−4°F). At this season only the northern and the more mountainous parts of the USA have a mean temperature below 0°C, while none of the country is below −20°C. In summer, however, the southern parts of the USSR enjoy temperatures comparable to those prevailing over much of the USA, but the vast Soviet northland is much cooler. In precipitation received only a very small area on the Soviet Black Sea coast gets as much rain as falls over the whole south-eastern quarter of America and along the Pacific north-western and the Atlantic north-eastern coasts of that country.

Nevertheless both countries may be said to have a continental climate over most of their territory, the characteristics of such a climate being that there is a large range of temperature between summer and winter, that temperatures climb quickly in a brief spring and fall rapidly in autumn, that there is more precipitation in summer than in winter and that summer rainfall comes mostly in the form of short sharp showers and winter precipitation as snow.

CLIMATIC TYPES

Any classification of climate into types for universal application is bound to be unsatisfactory. Local conditions of relief, aspect, drainage, etc., which profoundly affect climate and differ from place to place, cannot be allowed for. Averaged statistics, upon which such classifications are inevitably based, may or may not correspond to reality according to the degree of departure from the mean that is actually experienced. Perhaps the least unsatisfactory for middle and northern latitudes, and certainly the most widely used, is that evolved by Köppen in which initial letters are used in combination to denote various climatic types.[1] By applying this system to the two superpowers it will be possible to draw some general conclusions about similarities and dissimilarities in their climates. In the Köppen system the A, C and D climates are those which have enough moisture to permit forest growth; the B climates are too dry for this and the E climates too cold. Of the forest climates A is tropical (mean temperature of every month above 18°C (64°F); C is temperate with no great extremes of temperature (coldest month below 18°C but above —3°C (27°F); D has cold winters (coldest month below —3°C). A second letter gives a key to the seasonal distribution of precipitation in these three types of humid climate:

'f' (German *feucht* = wet) indicates that every month of the year receives a certain amount of moisture;
's' indicates a dry summer and 'w' a dry winter.

The C and D humid climates are further differentiated by a third letter to elaborate on their seasonal temperature distribution, thus:

'a' = warmest month over 22°C (72°F);
'b' = warmest month under 22°C but at least four months over 10°C (50°F);
'c' = less than four months with mean temperature over 10°C, but coldest month above —38°C (—36°F);
'd' = coldest month with mean temperature below —38°C.

Except for the southern tip of Florida and the very small area of the Hawaiian Islands, neither the United States nor the Soviet Union has any of the A (humid tropical) climate. As Fig. 13 shows, the United States has over a third of its territory with a C (humid temperate) climate and most of this belongs to the Cfa type, indicating rain all the year round, hot summers and mild winters. This is the most extensive single Köppen type in the USA with twenty-eight per cent of the country's area (thirty-four per cent without Alaska). Land with this type in the USSR is negligible in area, and the Soviet Union has a C climate in less than one per cent of its territory. D (humid continental)

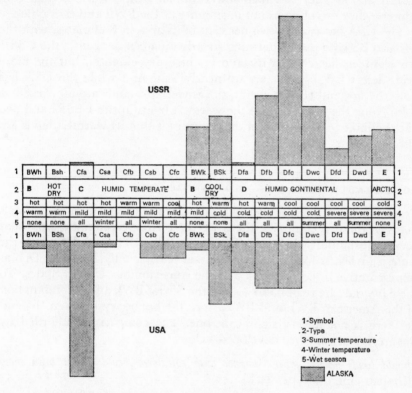

USSR

1	BWh	Bsh	Cfa	Csa	Cfb	Csb	Cfc	BWk	BSk	Dfa	Dfb	Dfc	Dwc	Dfd	Dwd	E	1
2	B	HOT DRY	C	HUMID TEMPERATE				B	COOL DRY	D	HUMID CONTINENTAL					ARCTIC	2
3	hot	hot	hot	hot	warm	warm	cool	hot	warm	hot	warm	cool	cool	cool	cool	cold	3
4	warm	warm	mild	mild	mild	mild	mild	mild	cold	cold	cold	cold	cold	severe	severe	severe	4
5	none	none	all	winter	all	winter	all	none	none	all	all	all	summer	all	summer	none	5
1	BWh	BSh	Cfa	Csa	Cfb	Csb	Cfc	BWk	BSk	Dfa	Dfb	Dfc	Dwc	Dfd	Dwd	E	1

USA

1-Symbol
2-Type
3-Summer temperature
4-Winter temperature
5-Wet season

ALASKA

13. Percentage distribution by area of the Köppen climatic types

climates cover sixty-nine per cent of the USSR, and its largest single type is Dfc, in which there is some precipitation all the year round, summers are cool and winters are cold. In addition to its large extent of Köppen D climate, the USSR has also nearly eight per cent of its land in the ET or Arctic Tundra climate in which there is no real summer, but – for two or three months – just sufficient warmth for a partial thaw of the ubiquitous snow and ice. The USA has no E climate except in Alaska.

Each country has land arid enough for it to come within the Köppen B (dry) group of climates, which are divided according to degree of aridity into BW (arid or desert: German *Wüste* = desert) and BS (semi-arid or steppe), and according to temperature into hot (BWh and BSh) and cold (BWk and BSk: German *kalt* = cold). The deserts and steppes designated as hot have an average mean annual temperature of over 18°C (64°F), those classified as cold, under 18°C. The cold deserts and steppes owe their lower annual temperature to their cold winters: they are often as hot in summer as the BWh and BSh types.

The USA has twenty-two per cent of its area in B climates, with the less arid BS type preponderating (nearly nineteen per cent); the USSR has eighteen per cent of its land in these dry climates, but the more arid, desert BW type makes up nearly half. And while the USA has both the hot and cold varieties, the Soviet arid lands are all classed as cold. None the less, they are the warmest lands in the USSR, and one of the climatic misfortunes of that country is that its warmest lands are also the driest.

COMPARABLE CLIMATES AND LANDSCAPES

From Fig. 14 it may be seen that, despite the great climatic contrasts between the two countries, there are three Köppen climatic types that occur substantially in each. These are BSk, Dfb and Dfc, but the American Dfc is found only in Alaska, leaving only BSk and Dfb as representative of both Russia and the conterminous United States. To these it would be reasonable to add the Soviet BWk and a combination of the American BWh and BWk, since the boundary between 'h' and 'k' here is not a very significant one. The comparisons afforded by these types are further developed below.

Humid lands having warm summer with rainstorms, cold winter with snow (Köppen climatic type: Dfb)
Area in USA: 350,000 sq. miles approx. or ten per cent of total area.
Area in USSR: 1,280,000 sq. miles approx. or fifteen per cent of total area.

This type in the USA forms a belt up to about three hundred miles wide which extends along the Canadian border from the upper Missouri to the Atlantic coast, and includes the Great Lakes region and northern New England. In the USSR it embraces a wide territory in the west, reaching from the Gulf of Finland and Leningrad in the north almost to the Black Sea in the south; thence it narrows eastwards, continuing in a thin strip almost half way across Siberia. In America it lies just south of the fiftieth parallel and in Russia, mainly to the north of it (Fig. 14).

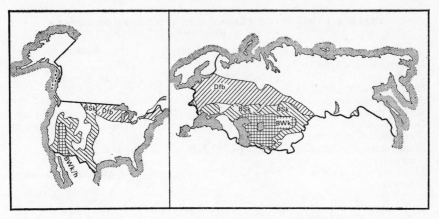

14. Köppen climatic types which are important in both countries

If any proof were needed that climatic classifications like Köppen's were not wholly satisfactory, it would be found in the fact that analogous conditions cannot be found in any two stations with the same type but located in different continents. If the temperature régime coincides, the precipitation pattern is different. If similar summer conditions are found, those of winter differ. The two examples given in Table 4.1 are chosen not because their climates are most coincident but because each is fairly centrally placed geographically in the type-region which it illustrates. Some of the differences reflect the differing nature of the two regions. The American region is penetrated and influenced by the Great Lakes water bodies, and Alpena, on the shore of Lake Huron, has the coldest period of winter delayed into February by this influence. The more continental position of Moscow is illustrated by its colder winter.

Both these regions have similar physical landscapes, since not only do they approximate climatically but both were glaciated by the ice sheets of the Quaternary glacial era. Hence besides the snow-covered ground in winter, a hummocky morainic relief, a liberal distribution of ice-age boulders and a mixed forest of both needle-leaved coniferous and broad-leaved deciduous trees are characteristic of both areas. Lakes and ill-drained land are also plentiful. The long harsh winters and the rather short summers combine with much poor leached and washed-out podzolic soil to make agriculture difficult. In the American region much of the land cleared and cultivated by pioneers has reverted to forest, and in the Russian area also, though to a smaller extent, there has been some decline in the cultivated area. Dairy products, potatoes and fruit form the typical farm output of the northern lakes region of the USA, while dairy products, rye, potatoes and flax are important in the Russian area.

TABLE 4.1   SELECTED CLIMATIC PARTICULARS OF ALPENA
AND MOSCOW[2]

Station	Alpena, Michigan	Moscow
Köppen climatic type	Dfb	Dfb
Position	45·04N, 83·33W	55·45N, 37·34E
Height above sea level	211 m (692 ft)	156 m (512 ft)
Annual precipitation	760 mm (29·9 in)	575 mm (22·6 in)
Wettest month	September: 92 mm (3·6 in)	August: 74 mm (2·9 in)
Driest month	February: 41 mm (1·6 in)	February: 28 mm (1·1 in)
Mean annual temperature	5·6°C (42°F)	4·4°C (40°F)
Mean temp. of warmest month	18·8°C (66°F) July	19·0°C (66°F) July
Mean temp. of coldest month	−7·4°C (18·5°F) February	−9·9°C (14°F) January

In the American zone the emphasis in economic exploitation has moved from farming to forestry and mining. Pulp and paper mills have proliferated and the great Lake Superior iron ore mines, rejuvenated by beneficiation processes which make the low-grade ore usable, are also within the region. Forest products are less important in the Russian Köppen Dfb area: it has been peopled for a thousand years or more and the pressure of a dense population over such a long time upon its forest resources has been severe. But like the American northern lakes region, it too contains a great iron ore field, that of the Kursk magnetic anomaly, about three hundred miles south of Moscow. This ore field is only in its infancy, its exploitation having been delayed by waterlogging, but it has vast reserves of rich hematite and magnetite as well as masses of low-grade quartzite. An output of 150 million tons of ore is envisaged for 1980. In 1966 the Lake Superior fields shipped 142 million tons of ore, eighty-eight per cent of which went to beneficiation plants.

There is one great and overwhelming point of contrast in the human geography of the two Dfb type regions. Whereas the American one forms a northerly margin, remarkable chiefly for its produce of farm, forest and mine, the Russian zone contains the historic heart of Russia, the ancient capital city of Moscow, and the most important industrial area in the USSR. As a result the Russian Köppen Dfb region has many more of the results of human habitation and transformation – not only farms but also numerous towns, villages, railways, roads, pipelines and electricity pylons.

Semi-arid lands having warm summer with rain showers, cold winter with snow (Köppen climatic type: BSk).

Area in USA: 465,000 sq. miles approx. or thirteen per cent of total area.

Area in USSR: 890,000 sq. miles or ten per cent of total area.

In the United States this type forms two north–south aligned belts on either side of the Rockies and merges southwards into the BSh type, as winters get warmer. In the USSR, however, it is oriented west–east and runs from the north shore of the Black Sea east–north-eastwards, passing to the north of the Caspian; in the region of Lake Balkash it swings south and then south-west, running along the piedmont zone of the Central Asian mountains, and enclosing the large desert (BWk) region of the USSR. The place chosen to represent this climate (Table 4.2) are Rapid City, in the northern part of the American Great Plains, and Kustanay, a town about 450 miles north of the Aral Sea in northern Kazakhstan. Once again the Soviet example, being located in the interior of the larger continental area and farther north, has temperatures well below the American in both summer and winter, but the average amount of precipitation is similar. In both instances it falls in rather infrequent summer rain showers and in light falls of snow during winter.

The natural vegetation of both these BSk areas was a steppe grassland, but much of this has since been converted into farmland either by dry farming techniques or by irrigation. However, not only is the average precipitation of about ten inches a year barely sufficient for cereal growing, even when dry farming techniques are used, but it is very unreliable, varying greatly from decade to decade rather than from year to year. The wetter 'good' years have encouraged farmers to plough up the steppe and grow wheat; then the drier 'bad' years have come, the grain has failed and the wind has played havoc with the bare ground, blowing off the soil in dark clouds of thick dust. In America the eastern farmers pushed into the Great Plains in the 1870s, attracted by the absence of trees and stones which had made the clearing of land so difficult in the forested glaciated areas. But in the late 1880s came droughts and ruin for the farmers. In the 1910s and 1920s wheat farming began again, but the droughts of the 1930s once more brought ruin.

A similar course of events has marked the recent history of northern

TABLE 4.2 SELECTED CLIMATIC PARTICULARS OF RAPID CITY
AND KUSTANAY

Station	Rapid City, South Dakota	Kustanay, northern Kazakhstan
Köppen climatic type	BSk	BSk
Position	44·03N, 103·04W	53·13N, 63·37E
Height above sea level	966 m (3,168 ft)	171 m (561 ft)
Annual precipitation	274 mm (10·8 in)	268 mm (10·6 in)
Wettest month	June: 78 mm (3·1 in)	July: 46 mm (1·8 in)
Driest month	December: 8 mm (0·3 in)	March: 9 mm (0·4 in)
Mean annual temperature	8·2°C (47°F)	5·9°C (42·5°F)
Mean temp. of warmest month	23·2°C (74°F) July	20·1°C (68°F) July
Mean temp. of coldest month	−5·6°C (22°F) January	−17·8°C (0°F) January

Kazakhstan. Here the steppe remained largely uncultivated until Khrushchev launched his 'virgin and idle lands campaign', in which these lands were to be ploughed up and sown to grain. Large state farms were created and new wooden villages built to house a vast influx of workers. The first few years were magnificently successful, adding tens of millions of tons to the annual grain harvest. Then drought struck and the years 1963, 1964 and 1965 were calamitous, with 'dust bowl' formation on a large scale. 1966, however, was a bumper year. In both the American and Russian Köppen BSk areas a degree of stability in grain production has now been reached, a result in part of the perfection of dry farming techniques, and in part of the substitution of livestock for wheat growing in some of the most marginal of the drought-threatened areas.

Ranching, dry farming and irrigated agriculture are not, however, the only uses to which the semi-arid lands of America are put. Oilfields and gasfields have been developed on both sides of the Rockies, especially on the Great Plains in Kansas, Oklahoma and Texas. Here it may be truly said that 'the landscape, with its grain elevators, vast open fields or ranches, its wind pumps, silos, livestock shelters, branding pens and dipping vats, and more recently its oil derricks, reflects, in the absence of prominent relief, human rather than physical geography'.[3]

In northern Kazakhstan the newly-ploughed-up steppe has been divided into large, fully mechanised state farms, each with its large village settlement, consisting of wooden houses, farm buildings, grain elevators, schools, clubs, hospitals and new roads. Large iron mines and copper mines are also found, while on the coking coalfield of Karaganda has sprung up, during the Soviet period, the large iron and steel centre of that name.

The southern limb of the Soviet semi-arid land, which coincides with the piedmont of the Central Asian mountains, has its precipitation mainly in spring, when the ground rapidly covers over with green grass and small flowering plants. But the long, hot, dry summer makes irrigation necessary for cultivation, and here, around Tashkent in Uzbekistan, most of Russia's cotton is grown. Irrigation in the piedmont zone of Soviet Central Asia goes back to prehistoric times and has given rise to a dense population and many historic towns, one of which, Tashkent, has grown – as capital of the Uzbek republic and as a large industrial city making textile machinery – to become the fourth largest city in the USSR (pop. 1,385,000 in 1970). The capitals of the Kirgiz and Kazakh republics, Frunze (431,000) and Alma Ata (730,000), also lie in this zone, while the famous city of Samarkand lies on the boundary of the arid desert lands which stretch away from the piedmont towards the north.

The American semi-arid lands have few large cities, except for marginal Denver (population of metropolitan area, 1,228,000 in 1970) at the foot of the Rockies, and the oil city of Oklahoma (641,000 in 1970). Other towns are relatively small and, for the most part, market, service and communications centres for their local agricultural districts. The newly-ploughed lands of northern Kazakhstan have towns of similar function, though rather bigger, and in this respect the two places chosen to illustrate the BSk climatic type, Rapid City and Kustanay, are also similar.

Arid lands having hot summers and warm winters (h) or hot summers and cold winters (k) (Köppen climatic types: BWh and BWk).
Area in USA: 120,000 sq. miles approx. or three per cent of total (BWh and BWk).
Area in USSR: 690,000 sq. miles or eight per cent of total (BWk only).

Both countries have land with a Köppen BW or desert climate. In the United States the deserts occupy an intermontane position between the Californian Sierra Nevada mountains and the Rockies. As they become warmer southwards, they pass from type BWk to type BWh, and continue thus into Mexico. The much larger desert area of the Soviet Union is bordered on the west by the Caspian lake, and on the south and east – beyond a narrow strip of semi-arid BSk type – by mountains. It encloses the Aral Sea.

The chief difference between the two examples shown in Table 4.3 is that, apart from the Russian station being cooler at all times, such precipitation as falls at Las Vegas comes very irregularly throughout the year, while at Chimbay, which lies just south of the Aral Sea, there is a pronounced winter–spring maximum. This greater reliability and regularity of the precipitation at Chimbay applies to the whole of the Soviet desert area, although farther north the period of maximum precipitation moves from spring to summer.

In both deserts, average annual precipitation is under seven inches, except on the higher ridges. In both, winter precipitation may come as snow but there is not normally much of it and it does not last long. However, there is more snow and it lasts longer in the colder Soviet deserts than in the milder American ones. The latter are well sheltered by mountains but the deserts of Turkestan, Uzbekistan and Kazakhstan are wide open to cold inroads of Siberian air. The deserts give both countries their highest absolute temperatures. The Death Valley of California has recorded 56·7°C (134°F) and up to 50°C (122°F) has been experienced in several places in Turkestan.[4] These are shade temperatures, however, and not very realistic because shade is rare in the desert.

All life out of doors not diminutive enough to shelter under stones or the low vegetation is exposed to the full force of the summer sun. Ground surfaces heat to 82°C (180°F) and will burn the bare foot. The air eddies up from the heated surface producing mirage effects, and strong hot winds periodically raise sand and dust storms that obscure the sun and produce a daytime dusk.[5]

There are some strong similarities between the landscapes of the American and Russian deserts. Long, narrow, erosion-etched and spine-like ranges of ancient and resistant rock rise from amidst a sea of sands, gravels and stones in both, although these ranges are much more numerous in the American intermontane area, usually known as the 'basin and range' province. In Soviet Central Asia, such ranges of hard old rock are fewer, but bolder; they strike out from the main mountain

TABLE 4.3 SELECTED CLIMATIC PARTICULARS OF LAS VEGAS AND CHIMBAY

Station	Las Vegas, Nevada	Chimbay, Uzbekistan
Köppen climatic type	BWh	BWk
Position	36·05N, 115·10W	42·57N, 59·49E
Height above sea level	461 m (1,512 ft)	66 m (217 ft)
Annual precipitation	99 mm (3·9 in)	89 mm (3·5 in)
Wettest month	July: 13 mm (0·5 in)	February: 14 mm (0·6 in)
Driest month	June: 1 mm (0·05 in)	August: 2 mm (0·1 in)
Mean annual temperature	18·9°C (66°F)	10·1°C (50°F)
Mean temp. of warmest month	32·3°C (90°F) July	26·2°C (79°F) July
Mean temp. of coldest month	6·4°C (43·5°F) January	−6·2°C (21°F) January

mass which forms the southern border of the USSR towards the Aral Sea.

Both areas have land below sea level, but whereas in America this is confined to the Death Valley, which reaches 282 feet below sea level, in Soviet Central Asia it forms a much larger zone around the Caspian Sea, and the bottom of one depression sinks to 433 feet below sea level. The Death Valley and the Salton Sea–Imperial Valley areas apart, the American deserts are more elevated than those of the USSR, lying mostly between a thousand and ten thousand feet above sea level, whereas the Soviet arid lands rise only exceptionally above a thousand feet. The higher American Köppen BW-type lands have a preponderance of rock desert, and this has been eroded to form deep canyons and flat-topped mesas, and many other fantastic landforms. Mesa-like formations are also found around the edge of the Ustyurt desert plateau in Soviet Central Asia. The Soviet deserts generally, however, have more sand-covered and baked-clay surfaces. Moving sand in the form

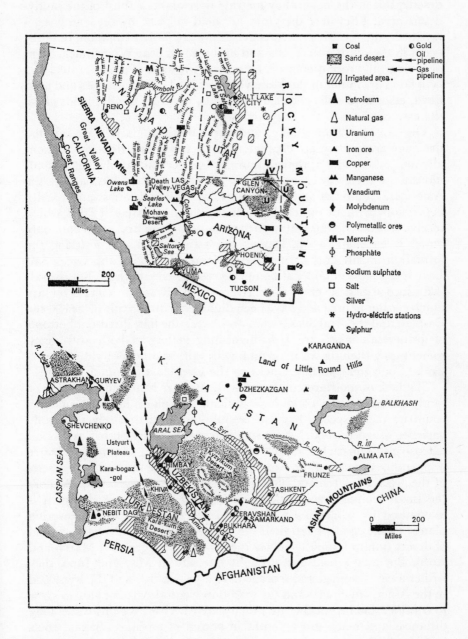

15. Arid regions of the USA and the USSR

of live dunes covers only five or six per cent of the southern Soviet sand deserts, but in the north they migrate over about a third of the sandy-desert area. Elsewhere the sands are held in place by the scanty vegetation. In the American deserts live dunes are far less common, but they occur in the south near Yuma and in the north near Winnemuca. Signs of geologically recent volcanic activity in the form of cones, craters and lava flows are found in the Mohave desert, and mud volcanoes and mud flows, associated with petroleum deposits, diversify the flat lands along the eastern shore of the Caspian.

The Soviet region wholly, and the American partly, are internal drainage areas. Both are characterised by rivers that flow only seasonally and others which, though more or less permanent, dry up ignominiously in their lower courses, or disappear into sinks, as do the American Humboldt and the Soviet Chu. The sinks are swampy, salty depressions without outlet. In both regions there are salt lakes which receive salt-laden water from the surrounding country but whose only outlet is by evaporation, leaving the salts behind and fostering the formation of salt crusts. In the American arid region the Great Salt Lake is the most notable, although there are several others. But the salt lakes into which several of the rivers of the Russian deserts flow are much greater in area and have been dignified with the title of 'sea' – the Caspian and the Aral Seas. *Playas* and *takyrs*, the flat, dried-out bottoms of former salt lakes, are a distinguishing feature of both arid zones, sometimes glistening white or pink with salt, at others revealing a network of polygonal surface cracks on the level clayey ground.

The lack of moisture combined with summer heat and the saline or sandy surface make conditions difficult for plant life, but in both countries many species have successfully adapted themselves, notably varieties of wormwood, whose small sparsely-spaced bushes are found extensively. The cactus, especially the giant *sahuaro*, adds to the bizarre appearance of parts of the American deserts, while the southern deserts of the USSR are remarkable for their ephemeral vegetation. Because the small annual precipitation comes fairly regularly in spring, it is maximised by coinciding with snow melt: a host of small flowering plants, able to go through their life cycle in six to eight weeks – a kind of desert tundra – rapidly covers the ground with green in March and April. But as the heat and drought intensify in May and June, they wither away, parched and scorched. The Joshua tree and the ironwood in the American deserts and the saxaul in Central Asia are able to grow to considerable heights because their extensive root systems travel long distances and reach great depths in search of moisture. Saxaul roots have been known to go down eighty feet. Both reflect the struggle for water in their chaotic and gnarled growth. Because of their adaptation to drought and salt, many plants in both arid regions have an unusual chemistry which reflects itself in peculiar odours and aromas, and sometimes in poisons.

The wild life is also generally similar. In both desert regions, small creatures, capable of sheltering from the sun under stones or of burrowing into sand, predominate: gophers, whistling mice, jumping rats, lizards and snakes. Both areas witness the phenomena of estivation – burrowing out of sight to sleep away the period of most intense summer heat and drought. The cool night rather than day is the time when the desert comes alive with the rustling, chirping, squeaking and whistling of its diminutive animal population. Among larger animals the camel is still seen in the Russian deserts.

Both arid areas remain remarkably alike in many ways because the natural landscape, largely a consequence of similar climates, has been only locally modified and diversified by man. Such modification and transformation have resulted, however, from the same kind of human activity: irrigation oases, towns, railways, roads, airfields, telegraph lines, electricity pylons and cables; pipelines; mining installations and settlements; and industrial and military establishments needing wide expanses of unpopulated land and a clear dry atmosphere. Large hydro-electric dams, however, such as are found on the Colorado river, are lacking in the Soviet arid region.

The differences result mainly from the fact that Soviet Central Asia is not only more densely peopled but has been settled by man for thousands of years and has witnessed the rise and fall, not only of empires, such as those of the Persian kings, Genghiz Khan and Tamberlaine, but of whole civilisations. These have left their mark in the Muslim palaces, mosques, minarets and madrasahs, in historical, commercial and industrial towns such as Khiva and Bukhara, in primitive irrigation installations and ancient earthworks, and also in the racial diversity of the inhabitants: Turkmen, Uzbeks, Karakalpaks, Kazakhs, Tartars and Russians, all with their distinctive dress and customs. This gives a richness of human and historic interest which is lacking from the more modern developments in the American deserts. In these it is the fantastic and weird natural phenomena rather than man's accomplishments that attract the tourist, although there is some tawdry exploitation of the remnants of Indian culture.

Differences also stem from the differing nature of the mineral wealth. In the United States the copper mines, with their awesome galleries, make the chief contribution, both in Arizona in the south and in Utah in the north. In the USSR, petroleum and natural gas are more important and oil derricks, refineries, gas wellheads and pipelines intrude upon the desert landscape in several areas. Two wide-diameter gas pipe lines leave the Gazli field, near Bukhara, for the Moscow region and another runs up to the Urals.

Many of the chief desert cities in both countries began as towns serving surrounding irrigated areas, with their intensive agriculture and dense farm populations, but whereas the history of centres in Soviet Central Asia such as Khiva and Bukhara goes back to distant antiquity, those of the American South West were creations of the nineteenth century. The American towns have, however, made more progress in acquiring other functions – industrial, residential, recreational, and have therefore grown to a larger size. The metropolitan area of Phoenix, Arizona, had a population in 1970 of 968,000, compared with 664,000 in 1960 and 332,000 in 1950. It felt the full effect of the intensification of military, industrial, resort and residential activity that characterised the economy of the American South-west in that decade. Its aircraft and electronics industries in particular have benefited from Defence Department contracts. Weapons manufacture has also been instrumental in the rapid growth of Tucson, another Arizona city. Farther north, Mormon associations lend interest to Salt Lake City (558,000 in 1970), founded in 1847, while the Nevada cities of Las Vegas and Reno have gained notoriety from the permissive State laws governing entertainment and divorce.

The principal city of Soviet Central Asia, Tashkent, and some other ancient and important piedmont oasis towns like Samarkand, are just outside the desert area according to Köppen criteria, leaving Astrakhan (pop. 411,000 in 1970), the old Tartar port on the Volga delta and acquired by the Russians in 1556, as the largest Soviet desert town. Its Caspian sturgeon fishery and caviar factories make it unique. Bukhara, a museum town and tourist attraction because of its Muslim memorials inherited from a flourishing past, has begun to acquire industry as a result of the coming of natural gas. In contrast to the older oasis cities, there are today many entirely new Soviet towns associated with mineral and industrial development, such as Nebit Dag (oil), Shevchenko (oil), Zeravshan (gold) and Navoy (gas chemicals). They are as yet quite small.

CONTRASTING CLIMATES AND LANDSCAPES

The most widespread single Köppen climatic type in the USA is the humid temperate with hot summers (Cfa), occupying thirty-four per cent of the conterminous area; this type does occur in the USSR, but only in small areas along the Black Sea coast which total only about 0·5 per cent of Soviet territory. On the other hand, the largest single climatic type in the USSR, covering thirty-one per cent of the country, is the humid continental with cool summers and cold winters (Köppen Dfc); this type does not occur at all in the conterminous USA but only in Alaska. In area, therefore, these two types and the ensuing land-scapes may be taken as most typical of their respective countries. The contrast between them is some measure of the difference between the physical and human geography of the two states.

From the examples taken from the central part of each of these nationally dominant climatic types (Table 4.4) it can be seen that the American station receives twice as much moisture as the Soviet station, and that its mean annual temperature is also twice as high; but the temperature difference is much greater in winter (46°F) than in summer (17·5°F). There is a great contrast in the degree of uniformity within each type. The large area of the United States to which the Köppen label Cfa applies, in reality includes regions with very different climatic conditions, and well illustrates the weakness of the Köppen classification. It would be difficult to convince the winter traveller arriving at Houston, Texas, having flown in from a snow-bound New York, that he had re-mained within one climatic type. But the vast Soviet Dfc area, extending from Finland to eastern Siberia in a broad and widening belt, does have a common stamp; and although winters get colder eastwards, they are already cold enough in the west for this change to be one of degree rather than of kind. The traveller who flew in winter from one end to the other, would find no such transformation as the one flying from New York to Houston.

The natural vegetation of the south-eastern United States was a broad-leaved deciduous trees with oak and hickory plentiful, and with magnolia and other subtropical trees in the south; pines flourish on the sandier areas and there are swamps and swamp forests along the coasts and in the Mississippi flood plain. Throughout northern Russia and western and central Siberia, on the other hand, the great *tayga* forest of needle-leaved coniferous trees, with a fringe of birch along the northern and southern margins, spreads over almost the whole territory. In the American area the forest has largely been cleared and its place taken by agriculture, arranged latitudinally in the long-familiar belts, in

TABLE 4.4 SELECTED CLIMATIC PARTICULARS OF NASHVILLE
AND SURGUT

Station	Nashville, Tennessee	Surgut, W. Siberia
Köppen climatic type	Cfa	Dfc
Position	36·07N, 86·41W	61·15N, 73·30E
Height above sea level	177 m (581 ft)	43 m (141 ft)
Annual precipitation	1,147 mm (41·2 in)	484 mm (19 in)
Wettest month	January: 139 mm (5·5 in)	August: 68 mm (2·7 in)
Driest month	August: 73 mm (2·9 in)	February: 17 mm (0·7 in)
Mean annual temperature	15·6°C (60°F)	−2·7°C (27°F)
Mean temp. of warmest month	26·8°C (80°F)	17·0°C (62·5°F)
Mean temp. of coldest month	4·4°C (40°F)	−21·0°C (−6°F)

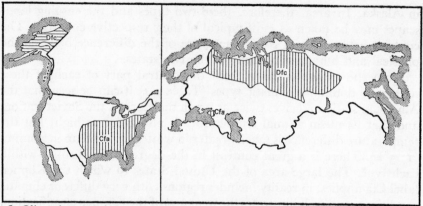

16. Climatic types important in one country only

which one crop predominates, though not to the exclusion of others. The whole region is agricultural, except for urban and mining areas, the Appalachian and Ozark uplands, still in forest, the many smaller woodlands, and the swamps and forests of the lower-lying coastal areas.

In the Soviet area the forest continues to dominate the landscape almost everywhere, although it is interrupted by great swamps in western Siberia, and its nature changes from mainly spruce in the west to chiefly larch in the east. The trees get sparser and shorter towards the tundra zone on the north, and almost the whole region has permanently frozen ground, only the surface thawing in summer, at which season the air above the ill-drained swamp is filled with mosquitoes, midges and flies. Agriculture is limited to the southern margins, except near some of the Arctic towns where costly enterprises rely on artificial heating of the air or the soil to raise crops. Despite the intensification of human activity in the Soviet period – new lumber camps, mines, railways, pipelines, power stations, towns – its manifestations are everywhere dwarfed by the great northern forest which surrounds and engulfs everything.

The American area, being almost wholly farmed, is settled throughout and, in addition, holds most of the country's urban areas. It also has its largest coalfields, oilfields and gasfields, most of its primary and secondary iron and steel industry, and almost all its textile manufacturing. It includes the greater part of the Mississippi and Ohio waterways and the major seaports of the country. The Soviet area has only sporadic settlement, large areas being entirely unpeopled, and very few towns. None the less, it too contains the country's largest coal resources, oilfields and gasfields, and a great variety of other valuable minerals, including those of the Urals. For just as the American Köppen Cfa area includes the Appalachians, except for their northernmost part, so the Soviet Dfc area includes the Urals, except for their southern extension.

5 Natural Resources

A resource is some aspect of the natural environment that can be used by man to his advantage. Whether the occurrence of a physical commodity or natural process is a resource or not depends therefore on the state of knowledge of the men in whose possession it lies. Uranium did not become a significant resource until the discovery of nuclear fission. As technology advances, some materials lose their resource value because they cease to be needed, while others may acquire resource status for the first time.

Natural resources may be classified according to whether they originate in the lithosphere, the hydrosphere, the atmosphere or the biosphere. In the first category come those attributable to geology and to physiographic relief, i.e. minerals and most sources of fuel and power. The hydrosphere, consisting of the water bodies, is a source of salts and tidal power as well as an aid to transport. From the atmosphere come the climatic resources of warmth and moisture, as well as wind as a source of power. Connected with the biosphere are those derived from the flora and fauna – timber, furs, fish, etc. In addition, there are composite resources obtained from more than one division of the natural habitat – notably the soil, in the formation of which geological structure, climate and natural vegetation all play a part. Resources may also be classified according to the sector of the economy in which they are used, i.e. agriculture, mining and manufacturing, transport, and such tertiary activities as recreation.

RESOURCES FROM THE LITHOSPHERE AND HYDROSPHERE

Because of similarities in their geological structure and physiographic relief, the resources which the two superpowers derive from the lithosphere are in many ways comparable in kind though not in quantity. That those of the USSR are on the whole greater is explained mainly by its much larger size. The mineral wealth of the USA is not only less abundant but lacks the universality of the Soviet resources. Thus, although the USA has more production firsts in the world ranking shown in Table 5.1 (eighteen as against ten), there are also eight

TABLE 5.1   SUMMARY OF WORLD RANK IN PRODUCTION OF
IMPORTANT MINERALS 1968[1]

	USA	USSR
1st:	Petroleum, natural gas, uranium, cadmium, copper, magnesium, molybdenum, titanium, vanadium, barite, china clay, diatomite, feldspar, gypsum, nitrogen compounds, phosphate, salt, sulphur	Coal, peat, chromite, iron, lead, magnesite, manganese, platinum, mica, potash
2nd:	Coal, iron, talc	Petroleum, natural gas, uranium, beryllium, cadmium, copper, gold, magnesium, nickel, titanium, tungsten, vanadium, zinc, asbestos, diamonds, diatomite, feldspar, fluorspar, phosphate, sulphur
3rd:	Tungsten, zinc, potash	Bauxite, mercury, molybdenum, silver, china clay, graphite, nitrogen compounds, salt, talc

important minerals for which American domestic supplies are almost totally lacking. Further, there are only eleven minerals listed in Tables 5.2, 5.3 and 5.4 for which 100 per cent American sufficiency is recorded, compared with forty-three for the USSR. The other countries of the surrounding oceanic 'rimland' are individually quite unable to match the riches of the Soviet 'heartland', but some of them are well endowed in one or other mineral for which they have become suppliers to the rest of the non-communist world, including the United States, e.g. Malayan tin, Indian manganese, Arabian oil, Turkish chromite, Portuguese tungsten (Appendix B).

As the geological exploration of the USSR progresses and prospecting is pursued, new and exciting discoveries are constantly being made. Thus estimated reserves are nearly always underestimates, liable to continual upward revision. Yet already the USSR has sufficient resources in almost all industrially needed materials for a long time to come, and large surpluses to spare of many commodities. The United States, on the

TABLE 5.2   RELATIVE SELF-SUFFICIENCY IN THE OUTPUT
OF FUELS 1968[2]

Fuel	Self-sufficiency (percentage)		Share of world output (percentage)		World rank	
	USA	USSR	USA	USSR	USA	USSR
Coal	100+	100+	19	23	2	1
Petroleum	88	100+	24	16	1	2
Natural gas	96	100+	62	19	1	2
Peat	68	100+	1	99	4	1
Uranium	95	100	38	31	1	2

other hand, already fully mapped and explored mineralogically, is experiencing growing shortages and becoming increasingly dependent on outside sources for a widening range of important minerals. This dependency is not so serious as it appears statistically, because the two

TABLE 5.3 RELATIVE SELF-SUFFICIENCY IN THE OUTPUT OF METALS 1968[3]

Mineral	Self-sufficiency (percentage)		Share of world output (percentage)		World rank	
	USA	USSR	USA	USSR	USA	USSR
Antimony	72	100†	1	10	12	4
Bauxite*	12	86	4	12	10	3
Beryllium*	2	100	3	22	6	2
Bismuth*	4	90	16	4	5	7
Cadmium*	80	100†	34	16	1	2
Chromite*	0	100†	0	35	—	1
Cobalt*	0	100†	0	7	—	5
Columbium*	0	100	0	n.a.	—	n.a.
Copper*	75	100†	19	14	1	2
Gold	23	100†	3	13	4	2
Iron	65	100†	13	22	2	1
Lead*	33	100†	11	14	4	1
Magnesium*	100†	100†	48	23	1	2
Magnesite	54	100†	1	30	9	1
Manganese*	<1	100†	<1	44	31	1
Mercury*	38	100†	11	15	4	3
Molybdenum	100†	100	71	12	1	3
Nickel*	11	100†	3	21	5	2
Platinum group*	1	100†	<1	59	6	1
Rare earths*	n.a.	100†	n.a.	n.a.	n.a.	n.a.
Silver	23	100	12	12	5	3
Tantalum*	0	100	0	n.a.	—	n.a.
Tin*	0	80	0	11	—	4
Titanium*	70	100	25	17	1	2
Thorium*	n.a.	n.a.	n.a.	n.a.	n.a.	n.a.
Tungsten*	90	100‡	15	19	3	2
Vanadium*	100‡	100†	53	n.a.	1	2
Zinc*	38	100†	9	11	3	2
Zirconium*	65	100	n.a.	n.a.	n.a.	n.a.

* Listed by US Defense Production Act as 'strategic and critical material' and stock-piled.
† Exports.
‡ Small or occasional imports.
N.a. = not available.

main sources of foreign imports of minerals are the adjacent North American land areas of Canada and Mexico. If North America is taken as a whole the comparison with the USSR is less unfavourable.

In examining Tables 5.2, 5.3 and 5.4 certain considerations should be borne in mind. The American domestic consumption of any mineral is normally much greater than the Russian, so that it is possible for the

USA, though producing more of a given commodity than the USSR, to be forced to import; on the other hand the USSR may be self-sufficient or in surplus with a much smaller domestic production. The USA sometimes imports a raw material, not because it is unable to produce enough of it within its own borders but because foreign prices are lower. Thus the index of self-sufficiency shown in the tables is not always a true one. Self-sufficiency has, in any case, been calculated only on a natural resource basis, i.e. the relation of domestic mine production to consumption, but often – especially with metals – there are other secondary

TABLE 5.4 RELATIVE POSITION IN THE PRODUCTION OF NON-METALLIC MINERALS 1968[4]

Mineral	Self-sufficiency (percentage)		Share of world output (percentage)		World rank	
	USA	USSR	USA	USSR	USA	USSR
Asbestos*	15	100†	4	29	5	2
Barite	71	63	24	7	1	5
China clay	100‡	100†	35	16	1	3
Diamonds	0	100	0	22	—	2
Diatomite	100†	100	42	27	1	2
Feldspar*	100‡	100	33	12	1	2
Fluorspar*	19	80	8	12	7	2
Graphite*	1	100†	1	20	16	3
Gypsum	63	100†	19	10	1	5
Mica*	<1	99	<1	23	20	1
Nitrogen compounds	100†	100	28	13	1	3
Phosphate	100†	100†	45	22	1	2
Potash	64	100†	16	20	3	1
Salt	94	100†	33	9	1	3
Sulphur	100†	100†	34	12	1	2
Talc, etc.	100†	100†	20	8	2	3

For symbols, see Table 5.3

and recovery sources, e.g. scrap, which give a considerably larger degree of self-sufficiency. And because of the greater manufacturing production of the USA and its longer history of industrialisation, its secondary sources of reclaimable metals are very much greater than those available to the USSR. In most cases the serious American lack of sufficiency is more apparent than real because of the huge stockpiles that have been accumulated in essential minerals.

When Soviet production of a mineral is less than that of the USA this is often because of a smaller demand. Were this demand to expand, greater reserves are normally there to permit a larger production than the American eventually. As with the USA, Soviet imports of a mineral do not necessarily mean lack of resources, but the reason is different,

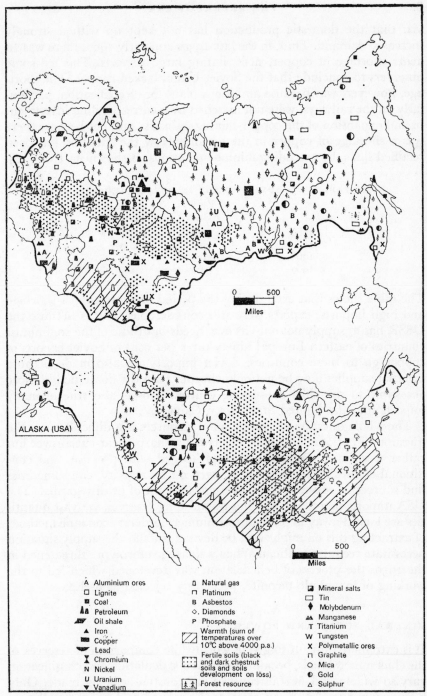

Ā Aluminium ores
☐ Lignite
▨ Coal
Ḁ₳ Petroleum
⚒ Oil shale
▲ Iron
▨ Copper
◡ Lead
Ⅹ Chromium
N Nickel
U Uranium
▼ Vanadium

◻ Natural gas
⊓ Platinum
B Asbestos
◇ Diamonds
P Phosphate
◢ Warmth (sum of temperatures over 10°C above 4000 p.a.)
░ Fertile soils (black and dark chestnut soils and soils development on löss)
🌲 Forest resource

▨ Mineral salts
☐ Tin
◆ Molybdenum
⋀ Manganese
T Titanium
W Tungsten
X Polymetallic ores
⊓ Graphite
O Mica
◐ Gold
△ Sulphur

17. Resources

viz. that the domestic production has not kept up with a strongly increased demand. Thus, in the late 1950s and early 1960s there was an acute shortage of copper, necessitating large imports. This led some observers to conclude that the Soviet Union lacked copper. The shortage, however, was because ambitious plans for electrification, particularly on the railways, were not matched by a corresponding investment in and expansion of the copper-mining industry, and not because there was a shortage of copper in the ground. How the situation has been rectified since, by extending mining operations, is shown in Table 5.5.

TABLE 5.5 SOVIET TRADE IN COPPER 1962–7[5]
('ooos of tons)

	Exports	Imports
1962	71·0	106·4
1963	72·0	88·0
1966	120·1	7·4
1967	94·0	1·4

The table shows that even during the period of acute copper shortage and high imports, exports were still considerable. This is because the USSR has to supply not only its own needs but those of the communist countries of eastern Europe: ninety-three per cent of Soviet exports of copper go to these countries. Soviet imports are also made because external supplies may be not only cheaper than the domestic but more accessible to the chief consuming centres. This is also true of many imports into the United States from Canada.

The whole question of evaluation of resources is a difficult one: 'the question of national adequacy elicits not a sharp, clear-cut answer but rather a series of equivocal answers hedged with premises and conditional clauses'.[6] Technology, spurred on by scarcity, can sometimes find sources or substitutes hitherto not thought of or disregarded. The USA imports petroleum and has diminishing reserves, yet vast quantities are locked away in oil shales within her borders: economic methods of extracting this oil might well be devised, should the supply situation necessitate recourse to them. When a shortage of iron ore threatened in the 1950s the process of beneficiation was developed which led to the working of low-grade taconite, previously rejected as useless.

MINERAL FUELS AND POWER

It is extremely difficult to give a worthwhile comparison of reserves of the chief mineral fuels, because methods of calculation and classification vary so widely and new discoveries are constantly being made. Only a few years ago, American reserves of coal, oil and gas were all con-

TABLE 5.6   ESTIMATED RESERVES OF MAJOR FUELS AND OF
HYDRO-ELECTRIC POTENTIAL[7]
(*percentage of world total*)

	Coal	Petroleum	Natural gas	Hydro-electricity
USA	15	6	11	4
USSR	62	11	12	17

sidered greatly superior to those of Russia, but this was because the American resource was fully explored while much of the Soviet wealth went unsuspected. The 1960s witnessed the discovery of one vast Soviet oil or gas field after another, and in 1970 *World Oil* placed Soviet reserves ahead in both fuels.[8] Further discoveries in Siberia and Alaska are likely to increase the known reserves of both countries. Comparison of their resources for nuclear energy is ruled out by the secrecy maintained by the USSR on the subject, but both countries seem adequately supplied with uranium.

When one turns to actual production the United States still leads in the output of all forms of energy except coal (Table 5.7). When comparing these figures it has to be remembered that Soviet consumption is much less than American. Even when the obligation to supply the communist countries of eastern Europe is allowed for, the needs of the USSR remain well below those of the USA. Thus, from her smaller production of petroleum the Soviet Union was able to export nearly 80 million tons in 1967, whereas the much larger American production had to be supplemented by imports of about 130 million tons a year.

TABLE 5.7   PRODUCTION OF ENERGY 1969–70[9]

	Coal* (mlns of metric tons)	Petroleum (mlns of metric tons)	Natural gas (blns of cubic metres)	Hydro-electricity (blns of kwh)
USA	539 (1969)	534 (1970)	660 (1969)	268 (1969)
USSR	624 (1970)	353 (1970)	200 (1970)	115 (1969)

* Anthracite, bituminous coal and lignite.

The widespread use of oil in motor transport and domestic heating in the United States is a major reason for this difference. As for electricity, it has been estimated that the average American household consumes seven times as much as its Soviet equivalent.[10]

In both countries hydro-electric power contributed about seventeen per cent of the total electricity supply, which in 1969 amounted to 1552 billion kwh in the USA and to 689 billion in the USSR. But although Soviet production is less, it is generated in larger units, including the largest hydro-electric stations in the world. This is in part because of the suspicion with which federal activity in the industrial field has been regarded in the United States where it has often been branded as socialism. Hence much of the generating capacity has been provided by private companies which do not have the resources to build plant of the largest scale. The largest-capacity stations in the USA are all federally owned, and although the federal hydro-electric stations number only eleven per cent of the total, they have over forty per cent

TABLE 5.8 USSR: LARGEST HYDRO-ELECTRIC POWER STATIONS
(capacity in millions of kw)

Shushenskoye (Yenisey R., Siberia)	6·4*
Krasnoyarsk (Yenisey R., Siberia)	6·0
Bratsk (Angara R., Siberia)	4·6
Ust Ilim (Angara R., Siberia)	4·5*
Boguchansk (Angara R., Siberia)	4·0*
Nurek (Vakhsh R., Central Asia)	2·7*
Volgograd (Volga R., Russia)	2·3
Kuybyshev (Volga R., Russia)	2·1

* Under construction in 1971.

of the capacity. Physical conditions more favourable to the construction of huge products are another reason for the larger scale of modern Soviet hydro-electric development. The United States Federal Power Commission is, however, reconstructing and enlarging some of its older stations and building new ones, and the largest American hydro-electric installations will eventually be as shown in Table 5.9.

TABLE 5.9 USA: LARGEST HYDRO-ELECTRIC POWER STATIONS[11]
(capacity in millions of kw)

Grand Coulee (Columbia R.)	5·5*
John Day (Columbia R.)	2·7*
R. Moses Niagara (Niagara R.)	2·0
The Dalles (Columbia R.)	1·8*
Chief Joseph (Columbia R.)	1·7
McNary (Columbia R.)	1·4
Hoover (Colorado R.)	1·3

* Ultimate capacity.

In nuclear power the United States is forging ahead to a commanding world position. In 1966 her civilian nuclear generating capacity was only 1·9 million kw, an amount not much more than that of the Soviet Union and less than that of the United Kingdom.[12] Since then there has been remarkable expansion and capacity now in use or under construction totals 32 mln kw. In the 1970s the United States will have forty-two nuclear power stations. Ten of the new stations will have ultimate capacities over a million kw: the largest are shown in Table 5.10. Little is known in detail of the Soviet nuclear programme. There

TABLE 5.10 USA: NUCLEAR POWER STATIONS WITH
CAPACITY OVER TWO MILLION KW[13]

Location	Capacity (mln kw)	Initial operation
Decatur, Ala	3·2	1970–2
Seneca, S.C.	2·5	1970–3
Peach Bottom, Pa	2·1	1970–2
Salem, N.J.	2·1	1971–2
Zion, Ill.	2·1	1972–3

are two medium-sized stations, one at Voronezh in southern Russia (present capacity, 0·6 mln kw) and the other in the Urals at Beloyarsk (0·3 mln kw), and several smaller ones in the remote regions of the Far North, where other forms of energy are unobtainable. Kosygin in 1971 said that

> During the coming five years we shall launch a broad programme for the building of atomic power stations, chiefly in the European part of the country, where fuel resources are limited. This programme envisages the commissioning over the next 10–12 years of atomic power stations with a total capacity of 30 million kw.

He added that 'we could not start such a programme during the last five-year period because the engineering industry was not then prepared for the manufacture of the necessary equipment'.[14] There seems little doubt that, in terms of actual construction of stations and production of nuclear power, the United States has a strong lead.

Despite the building of spectacular hydro-electric and nuclear power stations and the increased use of oil and gas as fuels, the bulk of the greatly increased electricity output envisaged for the 1970s is expected to come from thermal stations using coal. As a result coal production in both superpowers is expected to continue to rise fast. In the USA, where it increased from 298 million metric tons in 1960 to 539 million in 1969, it has been suggested that it could reach 800 million tons by 1980. Even greater rates of expansion are forecast for the USSR.

The USSR is unique in its large-scale use of peat as a fuel in the generation of thermal electricity. The low-lying, ill-drained nature of so much of the country gives it immense reserves. Both superpowers have tidal power projects: the USA in the far north-western corner of the country, at Passamaquoddy Bay on the coast of Maine, where the Bay of Fundy tides are extremely high; and the USSR on the shores of the White Sea. The Soviet Union also has a geothermal station in Kamchatka which uses boiling water from natural geysers.

Because the swing to oil and gas came twenty years later in the USSR than in the USA there is a considerable difference in the relative

D

TABLE 5.11   OUTPUT OF ENERGY BY MINERAL FUELS 1969[15]
(*percentages*)

	Coal	*Petroleum*	*Natural gas*	*Others*
USA	21·5	41·3	37·2	0·0
USSR	38·2	40·9	18·7	2·2

importance of the various mineral fuels, as shown in Table 5.11. The greatest discrepancy is in the use of natural gas, but the gap here is narrowing rapidly – the contribution of gas in the USSR in 1960 was only eight per cent; in 1970 it was nineteen per cent.

In 1969 and 1970 a new situation developed in the United States. This was a shortage of energy which began to interfere with the flow of industrial production and the comfort of domestic life. Gas and electricity were the energy sources most seriously affected. So rapid has been the rise in gas consumption that the once huge reserves are being rapidly run down, and the business world was shocked to learn that 'the gas industry is about to run short of its raw material'.[16] Specially equipped ships are already being built to carry liquefied gas from Algeria to the eastern seaboard to alleviate this new famine.[17] But this expedient, apart from seriously raising the cost of the fuel, will increase America's dependence on overseas sources for vital commodities, and so aggravate her vulnerability to submarine warfare.

The electricity shortage has arisen because, with the multiplication of demand-stimulating gadgets and playthings, the construction of power stations cannot keep pace with the demand. Colour television sets consume more electricity than black and white, and the arrival of the electric carving knife is just one more addition to the constantly swelling appetite for power. Although the USA has plenty of coal to supply the great number of new power stations needed to satisfy the demand, and although she will also be able to expand the output of nuclear energy, the growing concern about pollution is likely to arouse hostility to their expanded use on a large scale. Gas is the fuel favoured on environmental grounds, but gas is the energy source for which the supply outlook in America is bleakest.

Despite its larger reserves and smaller consumption the Soviet Union is not entirely trouble-free in this respect. The problem is a shortage of pipe, the more severely felt because the major sources of oil and gas are far from the main markets. The steel industry, hard pressed by insistent demands from many directions, cannot provide all the pipe needed to enable the conversion of the Soviet economy to oil and gas to go forward as fast as planned. Maladministration has aggravated the situation, particularly the failure to co-ordinate the throughput of trunk lines with the capacity of their tributary branches, and to provide enough compressors and pumping stations.[18]

Other Minerals

Table 5.3 makes it clear that the USA has serious deficiencies in most metals, and that in consequence they have to be stockpiled. Vanadium, molybdenum and titanium are the chief exceptions. Iron ore and the ferro-alloy metals (bismuth, chromite, cobalt, columbium and tantalum, manganese, molybdenum, nickel, tungsten and vanadium) are raw materials for the all-important steel industry. As this industry is called upon to produce steels to meet ever-rising degrees of hardness and resistance to heat, speed, friction, tension and impact, so the skilled use of alloys becomes more vital. Bismuth and columbium, of little importance a few years ago, are increasingly used in electronics, nuclear reactors and space vehicles.

Other metals called to the fore by the ever more exacting demands of modern technology are beryllium, magnesium and the platinum group. The United States government financially assists exploration for beryllium within the country. Its importance may be gathered from a single sentence in an official publication: 'defense agencies and the National Aeronautics and Space Administration continued to delve deeper into the technology of beryllium for possible larger use of the metal in high-speed aircraft, missiles, and space craft'.[19] The situation with the platinum group is an extreme instance of the difference between the two states: America consumes and Russia supplies over half the world production. Of the non-minerals, fluorspar, graphite and mica have all become increasingly essential to modern industrial and military requirements.

RESOURCES FROM THE ATMOSPHERE

In atmospheric warmth and moisture, both vital for success in agriculture, the United States is far better endowed than the Soviet Union. The more southerly latitudes of the former, as well as its greater proximity to the oceans, guarantee higher annual temperatures and less severe winters. Field has shown that whereas eighty per cent of Soviet cropland falls within the 'least productive thermal zone', the proportion for the United States is only nineteen per cent. On the other hand the United States has thirty-two per cent of its cropland in the most favourable thermal zone, the Soviet Union only four per cent.[20] This superior American endowment of warmth, although of principal significance for agriculture, is valuable in other ways, providing, for instance, better living conditions and recreational opportunities.

Fig. 18 gives a rough guide to the difference in the amount of summer warmth in the two countries. The average monthly mean temperatures

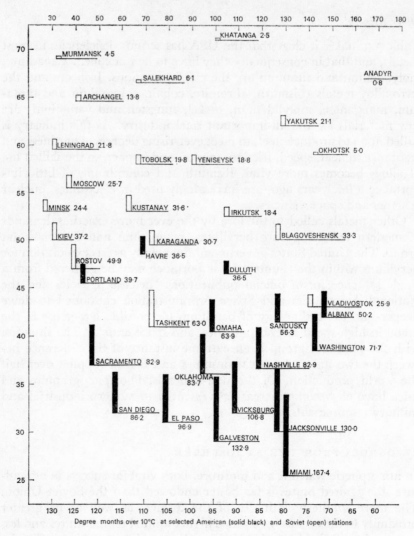

18. Accumulated warmth: degree–months over 10°C at selected places

above 10°C (50°F) have been added together for a representative selection of places in each. These have been spaced vertically according to latitude, and horizontally to show their approximate longitudinal or west–east relationship.[21]

The USSR is also unfavourably placed in regard to agricultural moisture. Its continental position means a low rainfall generally and a more restricted water supply: it has no extensive humid areas corresponding to the American east, south-east and north-west, regions into which moist oceanic air is drawn without impediment. Only a relatively small district in the Caucasus near the Black Sea coast experiences heavy rainfall. As a result, the average annual precipitation over the United States (782 mm) is much larger than that for the Soviet Union (490 mm).[22] Because the much greater precipitation falling over the USA is offset to some extent by the greater evaporation caused by higher temperatures, the contrast is lessened, but even so, the fact remains that moisture deficiency limits agricultural productivity in only one-third of American arable land, whereas in the USSR the proportion is nearer two-thirds.[23]

TABLE 5.12 DESALTING PLANTS 1969[24]
(capacity in thousands of gallons per day; Soviet plants are shown in italics)

Plant	Location	Capacity
Shevchenko III	Caspian Sea	31,700*
Shevchenko II	Caspian Sea	3,600
Key West	Florida	2,620
San Diego II	California	2,600
Texas City	Texas	2,160
Clairton	Pennsylvania	1,440
Shevchenko I	Caspian Sea	1,320
Siesta Key	Florida	1,200*
Freeport	Texas	1,000
Roswell	New Mexico	1,000
San Diego I	California	1,000

* Under construction in 1969.

Water use is not confined to agriculture, however. Dense urban and industrial concentrations consume enormous and growing quantities of relatively pure water and return it in a polluted state to the natural environment. Not only the arid and semi-arid areas of the United States but the densely peopled areas of the north-east, where the annual rainfall is abundant, are constantly threatened by water shortage. And water is the one mineral resource for which there is no substitute. Although hitherto most water-deficient areas have been supplied by transporting water from areas with a surplus by means of aqueduct or irrigation canal, increasing use is being made of desalting plants to distil sea and other saline water. The larger of these are shown in Table 5.12.

The American installations are to be found on the Atlantic, Gulf and Pacific coasts, as well as in the arid south-west. The three Soviet plants are all at Shevchenko, the centre of an expanding oil-producing region on the Caspian Sea. The new plant at Shevchenko will be, on completion, far and away the biggest desalting plant in the world, the present largest being Terneuzen in the Netherlands (7,650 thousand gallons per day).

RESOURCES FROM THE BIOSPHERE

There are three main resources arising from natural vegetation and wild life, and these differ greatly in importance. They are timber, fish and furs.

Timber

Because of its vast extent within the latitudes of 50° and 60°N, the Soviet Union has the largest forested area in the world, amounting to nearly three times the woodland extent of the USA. The volume of timber reserves is estimated as follows: USSR, 2,650 billion cubic feet; USA, 628 billion cubic feet. There is, however, an important difference in the composition of the forest reserves: in the USSR only sixteen per cent is composed of hardwood species, whereas in the USA the percentage is thirty-one – yet another result of more southerly position.

For practical purposes the discrepancy between the two reserves is not so great. The American forests are much more accessible to the densely peopled areas and chief markets of the country, but the greater part of the Soviet reserve is in remote parts of Siberia. In 1965 the area west of the Urals consumed fifty-two per cent of Soviet timber but produced only seventeen per cent, the remainder having to be transported over immense distances.[25] The United States can also call upon the large Canadian forest reserve, estimated at 611 billion cubic feet.

The gap between the actual timber production of the two countries is much smaller than that between their reserves. In 1963 the total cut amounted to twelve billion cubic feet in the USSR and to ten billion in the USA. But there are big differences in the utilisation of the wood cut. A large proportion of the Soviet output – twenty-eight per cent – is burnt as fuel as against only five per cent in America.

Fisheries

The United States, which lies close to the important fishing grounds of the Atlantic–Gulf of St Lawrence area and the North Pacific shore, had a larger total catch than the USSR until recent years. But whereas, during the 1960s, American catches showed a downward tendency, the Soviet fish harvest expanded rapidly, placing Russia far ahead of America (Table 5.13). Only Peru and Japan now catch more fish than the Soviet Union. The rapid Soviet progress has resulted from heavy government investment in modern trawlers and factory ships, a policy not unconnected with the failure of Soviet agriculture to feed the country's population adequately. Modern factory ships of the *Spassk* class process 100 tons of frozen fish and 120 tons of fish meal a day, as well as canning another 50 tons. The trawler fleet is being replaced by new refrigerated diesel-electric vessels. The private operators of other nations find it difficult to compete with this state-aided application of up-to-date but costly technology.

TABLE 5.13   FISH CATCH 1940–68[26]
(*thousands of metric tons*)

	USA	USSR
1940	1,827	1,404
1950	2,205	1,755
1960	2,224	3,541
1961	2,335	3,724
1962	2,409	4,168
1963	2,181	4,681
1964	2,043	5,171
1965	2,140	5,774
1966	1,965	6,093
1967	1,824	6,538
1968	1,941	6,784

Furs

Because of her more northerly latitude and possession of the world's greatest belt of boreal forest, the Soviet Union has an unrivalled fur resource. The corresponding environment in North America is wholly in Canada. However, the expansion of fur farming has greatly reduced the importance of naturally-bred furs. Furs earned only 0·5 per cent of the value of Russian exports in 1968.

SOILS

In the soil resource the position of the two countries is rather different. The USSR has half as much again of the rich prairie/steppe black-earth type of soil. But because of the warmth and moisture conditions already discussed, she is not able to make as full use of this soil as America can. Further the more northerly situation of the USSR means that a far larger part of the country was covered with ice in the Ice Age. As a result of this glaciation much good soil has been rendered unusable by being piled up into morainic heaps, mixed with huge boulders or ruined by bad drainage.

ANTI-RESOURCES

The natural environment has both positive and negative aspects with regard to man. The resources which invite development are the positive aspect; the obstacles which hinder it constitute the negative side, and can conveniently be termed anti-resources, as they oppose the development of the resources in various ways. Fig. 19 shows that the United States is but lightly afflicted with anti-resources whereas over much of the USSR they form a formidable combination, increasing the difficulty and raising the cost of almost all human activities. The term 'anti-resource' is not absolute. Few natural phenomena or environmental conditions are wholly favourable or wholly hostile to man, and what is favourable in one human culture may be unfavourable in another. The saying that 'it's an ill wind that blows nobody good' is apposite here. In most instances, however, a natural condition is clearly, on balance, either desirable or undesirable as an adjunct to human activity.

Many of the anti-resources from which the Soviet Union suffers are a direct consequence of its interior or 'heartland' global position. This gives it the unfavourable characteristics of a continental climate to an extreme degree: severe winter temperatures with heavy snowfall and blizzards; killing night frosts occurring late in spring and early in autumn, so that the growing season is short and uncertain; the abrupt transition from the winter season, when all moisture is held frozen, to the free-running water of summer – the sudden release of snow melt and thaw water results in floods and a heavy loss of soil through erosion; a low total average annual precipitation, arising in part from the fact that the country is ringed round with mountains, high plateaus and frozen sea, and which falls largely in destructive summer thunderstorms and hailstorms; hot scorching winds which leave whole regions dusty and parched behind them.

The United States, although suffering much less from the hostile aspects of a continental climate, does not go scot-free. The interior has an annual visitation by the dreaded tornado, while in autumn ferocious hurricanes lash the coasts of the south-east. The incidence of tornadoes is getting worse. Fortunately loss of life has not risen in proportion owing to improved forecasting and precautionary measures. Floods are probably more destructive in the United States because the flooding rivers there flow through more densely-settled valleys; they cause hundreds of millions of dollars' worth of damage each year. In the period 1951–60, 1,385 Americans were killed by tornadoes, 780 by floods and 923 by hurricanes.[27]

Past climates have left their legacy of anti-resources through the process of glaciation. Land covered by ice sheets during the last great ice age, which ended about ten thousand years ago, has been particularly adversely affected in many ways. Over some areas the soil has been removed, leaving naked, ice-carved, ice-grooved rock; over others the material thus removed has been deposited in haphazard heaps of a useless mixture of boulders, gravel, sand and clay; elsewhere, although a tolerable soil-covering has survived, its economic use in agriculture has long been made difficult or impossible by a scattering of giant boulders. Modern techniques have at last made possible their removal, as powerful tractors can drag them off the fields, but this, like other measures designed to overcome anti-resources, is expensive. Glaciation also disturbed and blocked the natural drainage system that had taken aeons to form, leading to widespread swamp formation and a profusion of lakes, large and small. The United States, because of its more southerly and more oceanic position, has far less glaciated land than the USSR. In the latter country this amounts to over a third of its vast territory; in the United States only the northernmost margins and the more mountainous areas have suffered.

Severe cold is an anti-resource because when the ground is frozen, cultivation cannot take place and animals have to be housed indoors and stall-fed. Water transport ceases and industrial processes using water have to be sheltered and heated. Special lubrication problems are met as temperatures drop, and constructional materials, normally strong, become fragile at extremely low temperatures. Costly heating of buildings is also required for human comfort. The attendant snowfall disrupts transport and damages communications including overhead cables. Almost the whole of the USSR has at least three months with average mean temperatures below freezing point, and only the southern fringes escape a lengthy period of frost. But only one-third of the United States falls within this category. Although navigation ceases on the Great Lakes for a period, most of the Mississippi waterway remains navigable throughout the winter. With regard to the sea the relative position of the USSR is even worse than on land. Whereas all the coasts of the USA remain permanently open, the whole coastline of the USSR is impeded or imperilled by ice. However, shipping – aided by icebreakers in the worst seasons – can normally use the ports of Odessa on the Black Sea, Vladivostok and Nakhodka on the Pacific, and Murmansk on the Arctic shore. But the winter closing of the Baltic Sea is a serious disadvantage because of its proximity to and links with the more highly developed parts of the country, and because of the access it provides to Russia's chief trading partners.

About half of the Soviet Union – but none of the conterminous United States – suffers from permafrost, a condition in which the ground beneath the immediate surface remains frozen even throughout

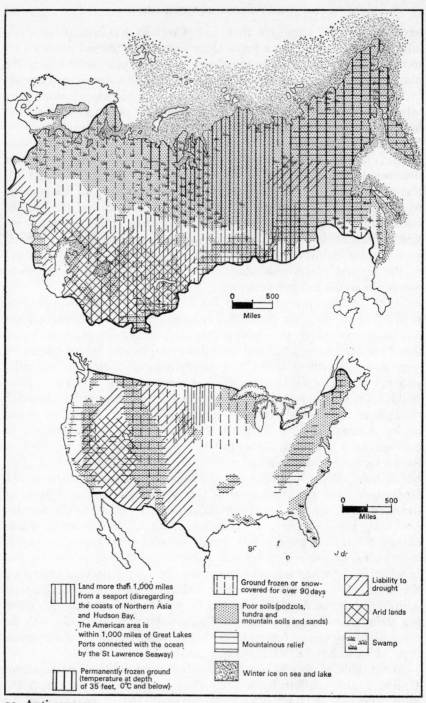

19. Anti-resources

the summer. At that season the uppermost layers thaw, but the abundant water derived from this thaw, from snow melt and from rain, is unable to drain downwards because of the frozen ground beneath. Except where slopes are steep enough to provide drainage, swamp conditions are therefore characteristic of the warmer season and make any form of surface movement exceedingly difficult. Wood-built settlements find themselves almost floating in a sea of mud, and the iron-hard resistance presented by the frozen ground beneath prevents the pile-driving necessary for more substantial buildings. Mining activities are confronted with a similar problem. However, where precipitation is very low, as in the arid basin of the Lena in eastern Siberia, the permafrost can actually be an advantage. The summer thaw precedes the downward penetration of a crop's roots, thus providing moisture that would not otherwise be available. As summer temperatures are relatively high here, agriculture is thus rendered possible in an arid region.

Except in parts of Alaska the United States does not experience a long dark winter night during which artificial light is essential at all times for the performance of most human activities. But over a third of Soviet territory lies north of the sixtieth parallel and experiences a prolonged period of darkness, while in the regions north of the Arctic Circle there is no daylight at all in mid-winter. Yet several large Russian towns are found in this zone of winter darkness, notably Archangel (pop. in 1970, 343,000), Murmansk (309,000) and Norilsk (136,000): at Norilsk there is no daylight for 47 days and snow lies on the ground for 250 days of each year. On the very border of this same zone of darkness lies the great city of Leningrad (3,950,000) which suffers a gloomy daytime twilight for several weeks of each year. The prolonged absence of sunlight can have serious effects upon health, to which may be added the depressing psychological effects of continual darkness. The cost of lighting urban centres in this zone has to be added to that of heating them, and electricity-generating stations – isolated by distance from any grid – have to be built to a capacity equal to the unusually high seasonal demand. The corresponding absence of total darkness at mid-summer offers no compensating advantage in this respect.

Ill-drained ground is a widespread Soviet anti-resource which is of limited extent in the USA. The swampy areas of the USSR are very inimical to human activity throughout the summer season, as movement across them is impossible by conventional means of land transport, and clouds of mosquitoes make life unbearable. The West Siberian plain, the largest area of nearly level land in the world, occupying a million square miles east of the Ural mountains, consists almost entirely of a vast swamp, frozen in winter but impassable in summer. As it is now the scene of extensive oil and gas workings, this handicap is being keenly felt, along with the concomitant plagues of mosquitoes which reduce the productivity of labour in summer by between thirty and fifty per cent.

Most of the northern and eastern parts of the Soviet Union have poor soils, either because of mountainous terrain or because precipitation exceeds evaporation to such an extent that the predominantly downward movement of moisture through the soil leaches out the soluble plant food; and the cool damp conditions of much of the Soviet territory slow down the chemical and biological soil-forming processes. In the warmer, drier parts of the country high concentrations of salt on the surface, notably in the *solonchak* soil, are also unpropitious for agriculture. Here again America, though possessing areas with podzolic and saline soils, has them to a considerably less extent.

Although Russia is often thought of as a monotonously flat country, mountainous terrain comprises nearly a quarter of the area of the USSR. It occupies a similar proportion of the United States, but the Soviet mountain ranges, because of their more northerly latitude, and because increased altitude produces a sharp drop in temperature, are much bleaker and less hospitable to man than those of America. Even the southernmost mountains of the USSR, the high Pamirs, carry some of the largest glaciers in the world.

Both countries have arid areas where agriculture can be carried on only with irrigation, and a yet larger area in which farming is periodically imperilled by drought. The Soviet Union is worse off again in this respect, because almost all her warm land suffers from drought, whereas in America aridity is a problem only in the west. Rostov-on-Don in southern Russia provides an example of the Russian predicament. From averaged statistics it would appear to have an excellent climate for agriculture, but the unreliability of its rainfall is such that utter crop failure may occur through drought. For the years 1956, 1957 and 1958 its annual precipitation was 30 inches, 23 inches and 27 inches, but in 1959 it was only 3 inches![28] Unreliability of rainfall may also afflict parts of the United States, but American records for places similar in the average to Rostov show nothing approaching the disastrous experience of the Russian area.

Distance from the open sea is a disadvantage from which a vast proportion of the Soviet territory suffers, but as Fig. 19 shows, only a very small area of the USA is more than a thousand miles from the sea. Even that limited area is close to the Great Lakes, which are linked to the ocean by the St Lawrence seaway. Distance from seaports is an antiresource because it hinders participation in overseas trade and because the movement of bulky goods by sea is so much cheaper than by vehicular transport on land. The United States derives immense economic benefit from its ability to move goods in bulk by sea from the Atlantic via the Panama Canal to the Pacific shores and vice versa, instead of having to transport them overland. For the Soviet Union the only sea alternatives to overland transport from the Baltic or Black Sea regions to the Pacific are either the impracticably long voyage via the Cape (if the Suez Canal is closed) or, for a short period only each year, the difficult, dangerous and costly Northern Sea Route. The Soviet disadvantage in this respect is worsened because her shores are, in any case, almost all ice-fringed in winter and access to them is usually controlled by foreign and potentially hostile powers.

Much has been made of the fact that the serious disadvantages imposed by the natural environment can be increasingly nullified or mitigated by modern technology. Advances in scientific knowledge and industrial techniques have made it possible to drive piles into the permafrost by using steam jets, to protect whole settlements from the extreme cold by erecting plastic domes over them, to illuminate the winter night by generating abundant electricity, to combat the infertility of soils with mineral fertiliser, to overcome aridity with irrigation, to drain swamps and so forth. In both countries justifiable pride is felt at the triumphs over nature implicit in this progress. This is especially so in the Soviet Union where the challenge of the natural environment is much greater and the sense of achievement at successfully wrestling with it therefore much deeper.

If the greater cost to Russia of fighting winter were to be calculated, it alone would represent an immense millstone around the Soviet neck in its economic competition with the United States, where the same problem, though serious, is not of such magnitude. Building is now an all-season activity in the USSR, but winter costs are from ten to thirty per cent higher than at other seasons. Keeping railway lines open costs 26 million roubles a year, clearing highways another 17 million, and this does not include the removal of snow from urban streets.[29] There is also a wide range of increased industrial costs arising from the severe winter.

In short all such technological achievements are expensive. They do not abolish the anti-resources but merely convert them into money terms. They have to be paid for, and the labour and capital devoted to them have to be diverted from other uses. Given equivalent resources and national incomes, this means that the country with the greater burden of anti-resources will have less to spend on other calls upon its finances, whether those of the armed forces, of industry, or of the private consumer. In the USSR the greater burden of anti-resources is likely, therefore, to mean a lower material level of living than that of the USA, at least until its greater resources have been developed sufficiently to compensate. But these greater resources are limited to forests and to minerals, and the inadequacy of resources for agriculture may check the speed of such compensating progress.

The burden of anti-resources is not entirely a physical one, but also human and psychological. The early Soviet development of mining and industry in the remote and inhospitable northern and eastern parts of the USSR was carried out by compulsion, just as it had been before the Revolution. But compulsion will not work where skill and ingenuity are needed, as they increasingly are in modern industry and technology. Incentives must be used instead. Higher wages and other benefits have to be paid in order to encourage migration to the north and east, but these still further raise the cost of overcoming the anti-resources of a harsh climate.

The adverse natural environment of the USSR presents, therefore, a dilemma to Soviet power. Either its conquest must be paid for with a reduced level of living, which could cause dangerous discontents. Or, as in tsarist times, little attempt could be made to develop the country's northern and eastern regions, reliance being placed on overseas trade. This remedy would, however, bring into play Russia's unfavourable position in regard to the sea, and could lead again to backwardness and poverty; it would expose her to the threat of blockade in times of international tension by the powers controlling the seas leading to her ports.

It is not easy for the Communist party to persuade those Soviet citizens who are aware of the gap between their material standard of life and that of the Americans, that this gap is a necessity if the USSR is to continue to exploit its own resources in the face of hostile natural conditions, and that the country must, if it is to retain its independence and ultimately to flourish, pursue the struggle without abatement. It is all too easy to assume that conditions are easier in the USA for purely social and political considerations, and that if the high cost of developing resources and countering anti-resources in Russia ceased to be paid, the ordinary citizen could benefit from an increase in consumer goods. This would prove a fallacy in the long run. The Americans, in their benign natural surroundings, can afford many freedoms which have to be denied – at least temporarily – to the Russians who in a sense, are constantly at war.

6 The Economy:
I – Direction and Motivation

A country's economy is the mechanism by which goods and services of material value are produced and disposed of. In this chapter and the next certain aspects of this mechanism will be considered, namely direction and decision-making, the motivation of the decision makers, the organisation of the economy and, finally, output or product, its disposal, and its relation to demand.

DIRECTION AND DECISION-MAKING

It is often stated that whereas the USA is a market economy, the USSR is a command economy, implying that the free operation of the laws of supply and demand govern the American system, but that the Soviet economy is controlled by directives from above. It is also said that in the USA the 'consumer is king', directing the economy from the demand side by indicating his wants and preferences through his purchasing power: 'the buyers tell the sellers what they want and the sellers in turn tell the producers'.[1] However, a growing area of the American economy no longer operates under freely-operating market laws but is subject instead, like the Soviet economy, to planning. This is that part of the economy which is in the hands of the large corporations: 'the initiative in deciding what is to be produced comes not from the sovereign consumer ... it comes from the great producing organisation'.[2] The two thousand largest corporations, all with assets of over a hundred million dollars, accounted in 1966 for over sixty per cent of total corporation assets, leaving the remainder – under forty per cent – to be shared among over one and a half million smaller companies. The 216 largest had thirty-four per cent of the total assets and over eighty per cent of total sales.[3] Many important industries are largely in the control of a very small number of big corporations. More than half the motor vehicles, motor tyres, iron and steel, aircraft, aircraft engines and parts, photographic equipment, aluminium, cigarettes, metal cans, telephones, soap and detergents were produced by four companies or fewer in each industry.

The big corporations do not leave those branches of production for which they are responsible to the unpredictable and uncontrollable forces of the market, but seek to subject them to management and planning. Their great power enables them to set prices, to create and stimulate demand, to control the supply of raw and semi-finished materials or of components and accessories, to acquire capital without recourse to the money market, to finance their own research, and – in conjunction with the unions and professional associations – to determine the rates of pay for labour and skill. Because all American newspapers, magazines, and radio and television companies are heavily dependent upon advertising revenue, the views of these business concerns must be borne in mind in the presentation of news and features: they thus affect the evolution and nature of society. Through grants and research assignments they harness university scholars, and through generous contributions to party funds, by persuasive lobbying and in many other ways, they influence politicians and policies.

Such functions in the USSR are discharged, in the main, by the state and the Party, not by the individual enterprises. Hence the real contrast is not so much one between a market economy and a planned economy, but between an American economy which is largely and increasingly planned by giant industrial corporations, and a Soviet one which is almost wholly planned by the organs of the Soviet state and the Communist party.

Power in the big American corporation does not lie, as in the old-fashioned entrepreneurial company, with one man, nor even a small handful of men, but with interdependent groups who make their decisions in committees. These groups, which are necessary for the development, production and marketing of modern goods, are managerial, technical, sales, research, etc.; they include 'all who bring specialised knowledge, talent or experience to group decision making'.[4] In the Soviet Union such specialist functions are exercised by very similar groups within or attached to the industrial ministries. The leadership and the planning authorities in the Soviet Union are as dependent upon these technical staffs for information and advice, for innovations and policy alternatives, as are the heads of the large corporations in the United States.

Traditionally, business in America is associated with an almost fanatical opposition to state intervention and control, and above all to state enterprise. The United States stands alone among the political democracies of the West in having no significant socialist party and no nationalised industries. President Roosevelt's attempts to extend the activities of the federal government were bitterly contested. This attitude now, however, is held – lip-service apart – only by that small and diminishing part of the American economy which is in the hands of the entrepreneurial firm – or private enterprise proper.

The predominant sector of the American economy which is directed by the large corporation is in fact closely linked with the state, which is its chief customer. Most of the bigger corporations do substantial business with the government, and for many companies federal contracts exceed all other sales. Such sales have the advantage that they are usually on a costs-plus-profit basis and the contracts are often long-term, giving in-built stability. In 1930 only about ten per cent of the national income was spent by government; by 1950 this had risen to twenty per cent, and in 1968 it was over thirty per cent. Hence the lobbying and other activities directed towards securing government business form a vital part of the sales promotion programme of most large corporations, and far from feeling hostility to government interest in the economy, as the old-fashioned entrepreneur would have done, the executive of the modern corporation is more likely to welcome and promote it. A great advantage of this government interest is that it is accompanied by a willingness to invest public funds in technological research. As most government spending is in the military and space sphere, most subsidised research is carried on in these fields, but the results are often of service to the wider civilian economy.

The state also provides valuable assistance to the corporate business world by regulating demand through its fiscal policy: government 'as the largest single revenue receiver and spender in the nation, is . . . in a strategic position to raise or lower aggregate demand in the economy'.[5] The discharge of this function means that big business can plan ahead without the fear of any such catastrophic fall in demand as occurred in the 1930s.

The tendency in the American economy is therefore to substitute for a large body of individual consumers, freely exercising their choice in the spending of their money, and on the supply side, a number of entrepreneurs seeking to make profits by producing what the consumers want with as little government interference as possible, a quite different system. In this new state of affairs, government takes an ever larger share of the individual consumer's income in the form of taxation and deals directly with the corporations. Although the government buys mainly military supplies, these are not only a matter of aircraft and ships, ordnance and weapons systems but also of the wherewithal to clothe, feed and otherwise equip armed forces numbering three million: its effects are thus widely diffused throughout the economy. The government also finances the space programme and – not only at federal but also at State and city level – gives out contracts for the provision of roads, schools, housing and other purposes. Nor do the smaller companies, many of which are still run by old-time entrepreneurs, escape the effects of this change. For they depend more and more on sub-contracting to the big corporations and less and less on direct inter-change with the consumer.

This means that the contrast between the economies of the two super-powers is less strong than would at first appear. In both there is a close and intimate relationship between the state and the firm. But in the Soviet Union this relationship is not only very much closer, but the state completely dominates the firm; whereas in the United States, not only is the relationship less intimate but there is evidence of overweening influence by the big corporation over the state, or what Galbraith calls 'the accommodation of the state to the needs of the mature corporation'.[6] But there are signs of convergence of the two economies in this respect, however wide the gap between them may now appear to be. While in the USA, the state and the big corporation move closer together, in the USSR recent reforms have given the individual firms more freedom from state control and more say in matters of production policy and technological advance.

Just as the economic power exercised by the large American cor-poration is not wholly in the hands of the chiefs at the top but extends down into the various groupings of experts whose knowledge and advice is essential to the company's policies and plans, so the economic power of the state lies not so much with the government leaders as in the com-mittees of specialist bureaucrats upon whom those leaders rely for information and guidance. As the growing complexity of technology strengthens the bureaucracy, it weakens the power of the legislature correspondingly. Decisions are taken, often jointly, by technical officials of government and of industry. It follows that participation in this process 'is the key to power'.[7]

In the Soviet Union decisions on matters requiring technical know-ledge, as do almost all facets of an advanced economy, have inevitably to be reached by a similar process. But whereas this power in the USA is divided between the corporations and the government bureaucracy, with the corporations providing the initiative, in the USSR it is divided between the Communist party and the state bureaucracy, with the Party acting as prodder and invigilator. In the Soviet Union, of course, the Supreme Soviet, the legislative body, has even less say than Congress in matters already decided on by the experts and bureaucrats.

Both Marx and the classical economists regarded the holders of capital as possessing power in the capitalist economy: 'in the assumption that power belongs as a matter of course to capital, all economists are Marxists'.[8] But, as is widely recognised, shareholders or stockholders have generally no say whatever in the policy of the big corporation.

Capital has given way to technological knowledge in modern advanced economies as the source of power.[9] Use of the terms 'capitalist' and 'socialist' to distinguish America and Russia implies a much deeper gulf between the two superpowers than in fact exists. Although the organisation of their economies differs widely, in each the power of economic decision-making and policy-formulation lies largely with a new class of men and women skilled in administration, management, technology or science.

It must not be supposed that in either country this class is homogeneous in composition or unanimous in view. Differing backgrounds, interests and viewpoints mean that sometimes the leadership in both countries has to make a choice between alternatives, both of which are strongly supported among the influential bureaucracy and technocracy. Examples are the controversy in the USA as whether or not to deploy an anti-ballistic missile system, and in the USSR, whether or not to build more gigantic hydro-electric stations.

A fundamental difference between power and decision-making in the two economies remains. This is their concentration in the Soviet Union and their diffusion in the USA. When one says that economic power in the Soviet Union is shared between the Communist party and the government apparatus one is speaking of but two highly centralised institutions with a common head; but when one adds that in the United States economic power is shared between the large corporation and the state, one is speaking, as far as the corporations are concerned, of numerous firms, each with its own organisation, its own policies and plans, and making its own decisions. A mistake made by the Communist party is total or macro-economic in its effect, whereas a mistake made by a single American firm is limited or micro-economic in its impact. Another consequence of this difference is that a member of the monolithic Soviet organisation has no escape if he does not like its aims or methods, whereas a manager or technocrat in the United States has alternatives available. In short he has more freedom.

The spread of economic power among many corporations, with usually more than one competing in each industry, even when there are only two or three as in the motor industry, gives a degree of competition absent from the Soviet system. And while it is true that the big corporation has succeeded in eliminating price from competition, preventing prices from becoming the plaything of market forces, competition still exists in other respects: the modern corporation entrepreneur 'advertises and merchandises his product with even greater energy and aggressiveness for not being allowed to cut prices. And for the same reason he remodels, repackages and, on occasion, seeks to improve his product in order to entice customers from his rivals.'[10] The existence of competing firms, even when they have become mature corporations, still means that the inefficient may founder or be taken over. On the other hand, there are many indications from the USSR of the problem of controlling a vast economy from a centralised organisation. It seems that the Communist party is hoping that in the 1970s 'there will be sufficient digital computers to automate decision-making' and that it will therefore be able to 'maintain a central monopoly of economic knowledge, while still administering from the centre a vast and complex mechanism'.[11]

Various constraints exist upon the use of economic power. Some of these are ideological or psychological. In the USSR the necessity to subscribe to the Marxist view that value is created by labour has prevented the operation of an efficient pricing system based on scarcity values. Thus it has been said that, although the Soviet system is based on planning, 'the practice of planning calls for theoretical guidance which Marxist value theory is incapable of providing'.[12] Likewise modern economic analysis and linear programming, now extensively used by American corporations in their own planning, were for long criticised in the USSR as too closely related to Western and non-Marxist notions of marginalism, and therefore rejected. On the other hand, when the forgotten facts that input–output analysis had been developed in the Soviet Union in the 1920s, and that linear programming also was a Soviet invention (having been conceived in the 1930s by Kantorovich) were rediscovered, opposition to their use in the Soviet economy abated considerably.[13]

Although the big American companies use these advanced mathematical techniques, there is powerful opposition to their application to the economy as a whole, on the ideological grounds that they would facilitate the socialist regimentation and control of the economy. As a result, in America 'this fundamental work has now come to a complete standstill because of lack of financial and organisational support'.[14] Meanwhile, the Soviet Union, as a result of its recent conversion, is forging ahead. The old capitalist ideology, in the form of devotion to the ideal of free competition, finds continued expression in such American legislation as the anti-trust laws, and although their enforcement is half-hearted and does little to hamper the more powerful corporations, it impedes the rationalisation of the economy as a whole.

Limitations upon the unbridled use of economic power operate internally from public opinion, and externally from foreign trade, the pressures exerted by foreign powers, and the exigencies of the international situation. Public opinion in the Soviet Union has led to a greater diversion of resources into consumer goods than would have probably been the case otherwise, while in America public opinion about pollution has led to more expenditure by big business upon its prevention than would have been the case without such concern. Foreign trade is a much more important factor in the USA than in the USSR where its size and composition is closely controlled. Those who exercise economic power in the United States have no such tight control over the level of imports and exports, yet these can greatly affect the nature and degree of economic activity. Pressure can be brought upon government to raise tariffs or lower quotas, but in the Western world such actions are usually matters for negotiation with other countries rather than for unilateral action.

The USSR is more vulnerable to international crises. The United States, with its vast and not fully used industrial capacity, can welcome on economic grounds further shipments of arms to Israel, but the Soviet Union can only increase its shipments to Arab countries by diverting scarce and already fully committed resources from other sectors of the economy. The Soviet Union is also subject to embargoes by the United States and its allies, which deny access through trade to a long list of of goods dubbed 'strategic'. It can be argued, however, that these embargoes have helped the Soviet economy in the long run by forcing it to become self-reliant in sectors in which otherwise it may have remained dependent on imports: 'from a strictly economic point of view, what we have in essence done, as a result of our strategic trade controls, is to prepare the Soviet Union for a total embargo ... they have developed those substitutes which are necessary to make them completely self-sufficient'.[15]

MOTIVATION

Those possessing economic power will attempt to direct the economy according to policies which accord with their objectives. These in relation to the USA and USSR are sometimes put simply as the maximisation of profit on the one hand and the aggrandisement of state power on the other. This is a great oversimplification. For the diminishing part of the American economy that is still run by classical-style entrepreneurs, maximum profits are doubtless the prime goal; but in the growing world of the large corporation, where power is diffused among those holding the top executive and managerial positions and the technical and scientific brains that advise them, motivation is more complex. Therefore if we are 'to know how and to what ends we are governed it is necessary to know the goals of the techno-structure'.[16] This class seems more concerned with a secure level of earnings than with the maximum profit which the shareholders would prefer. Large American corporations use funds in many ways which might not be

justified if profit were the sole motive: in adding to their reserves, in
enhancing their prestige, in creating a certain 'image' of themselves, in
taking over other companies, in placating organised labour with increased wages and fringe benefits, in furthering cultural and political
campaigns, and above all in promoting growth – even though it may
be profitless growth. Growth – expanding production, enlarging assets,
increasing sales – that is the chief aim of the modern corporation, and
it has also become the dominant overall objective of all national
economies. These are now universally judged by the rate of growth of
their national product, and growth is assumed to be a desirable end in
itself: 'the belief that increased production is a worthy social goal is
very nearly absolute'.[17] The executive–technical class looks to growth
not only because of any increased earnings it may bring but because
there is a sense of satisfaction in working for a growing company,
and because such expansion 'means more jobs with more responsibility
and hence more promotion and more compensation'.[18]

Contraction must be avoided at all costs. Whereas in the old entrepreneurial company a decision to cut down meant dismissing part of the
wage-earning labour force and had little effect upon management,
contraction in the modern corporation is likely to involve a contraction
in the executive–technocrat group itself. Even unremunerative expansion is therefore to be preferred to contraction or merely standing
still.[19] The elimination of fluctuations in demand is almost as important
as avoidance of contraction or stagnation, since they complicate planning. Such goals bring the American corporation and government
together, for the state also wishes for growth so as to promote full employment and it hopes to avoid recessions which interfere with its own
planning. Growth is powerfully aided by technological advance because
of the obsolescence it brings to existing types of goods, but technological
research is costly and risky and could end in disaster for the individual
corporation. Thus technological advance is another goal of the great
corporation, provided it can secure it at the taxpayers' expense.

In so far as American foreign policy is to maintain a 'free world' –
free that is of communist control, and to resist, if need be, by force of
arms, any communist encroachment, it accords with the interests and
goals of the world of big business. For the United States is becoming
increasingly dependent upon imported resources, and it is vital to her
economy that she retain access to these. Also the big American corporations are becoming multi-national and their branches or subsidiaries are spreading into most non-communist countries. There is no
room for this promising field of expansion in the communist world, any
extension of which is so much territory lost to potential American
growth.

In the USSR the powerful managerial–technocrat class will share many of the aspirations of the American technostructure. It will tend to put its own security and specialist interests foremost, and seek to persuade the socialist bureaucracy, its nominal masters, that all is well, while pursuing its own aims, just as the same class in America will dress up a report to the capitalist stockholders, the legal owners, to reassure them that everything is being done to make the company profitable.

In the USSR growth is proclaimed as the prime objective of the economy, and the percentile rate of growth is the main preoccupation of everyone from Party and government leaders to workshop foremen. For a time, during Khrushchev's rule, when growth was so rapid that there seemed a real prospect of overtaking the United States in industrial production, this achievement was also proclaimed to be a goal. An important difference, however, is that the Soviet Union is concerned mainly with a growth in production. The unsatisfied demand is so great that there is no need to stimulate it; industrial capacity is fully employed. In the United States, on the other hand, where industrial capacity is underemployed, the main need is to stimulate demand so that production can be increased to meet it. There is therefore in the USSR less need for technological advance to foster demand by making existing goods obsolete. On the contrary, maximum growth in output can usually be achieved fastest by sticking to the bulk production of existing types and models. Only when technology will help improve productive efficiency or capacity, instead of stimulating demand, will it be welcome. And not always then, as the introduction of even the most useful innovations of this kind will cause an interruption in production and a decline in output in the short run.

One motive shared by both the large American corporation and its much smaller and less powerful Russian counterpart – the individual Soviet enterprise, is a desire for autonomy, for freedom from interference. This is of much greater importance to the American firm as it cannot plan smoothly for its goal of security and growth if it is to be subject to interference, whether from shareholders wishing to make it more profitable or from government departments attempting to regulate it. The former have been rendered harmless by reducing their annual company meeting to an impressive but meaningless ritual, and the latter by keeping up the old entrepreneur's battle-cry against state interference. The main means by which the corporation in America has secured autonomy is through financial independence, i.e. by placing in reserve a far greater share of profits than the shareholders would like. Instead therefore of having to go to the market for capital and in so doing submitting its policies, plans and prospects to the investor, it is increasingly self-financing.

As most of the planning for the Soviet firm is already performed by state bodies, its need for autonomy is much smaller. Neverthless the managers and technicians of such firms have, ever since they were free to do so, made it clear that the tight and inflexible bureaucratic controls to which they have been subject, are hostile to enterprise and efficiency. The cautious reforms of the late 1960s have all been in the direction of increasing the autonomy of the Soviet firm.

The rigidity of the Soviet system of centralised controls need not be so bad in practice as it appears on paper, if the manager of a firm is clever. A skilful manager can win a surprising measure of freedom of action by establishing good relations with the local state and Party officials whose job it is to control and supervise him.

Although the class of managers and cognate officials with whom they have to deal in their daily lives is clearly a potent force in the USSR, its power is weakened by being diffused. That of the Communist party, the official monopolist of power, is concentrated very much in the top leadership, which sets targets, dictates policies and creates and dissolves organisations and institutions. Its motivation is obviously important and may be said to include the following objectives: to keep the Soviet state internationally strong, militarily invincible, economically self-sufficient and politically under the control of the Party; to raise living standards to such a point as not only to give satisfaction to Soviet citizens but also to advertise to the world the superiority of the system; in so doing to overtake the United States; and finally, to institute communism as a society in which the needs of all will be met from abundant productivity, irrespective of the value of the contribution they are able to make to it.

There are some who maintain that the main purpose of the Soviet leadership is to perpetuate the dictatorship, and to use this supreme power for the continued expansion of heavy industry, at the expense of the consumer, and as a basis for aggressive military strength. The promises of increased consumer satisfaction they dismiss as a cynical bait calculated to keep up morale. There are, however, substantial reasons why the steady improvement of the material level of living until 'true communism' is reached should be taken as a genuine goal of the Party. One such reason is that there is no alternative open to them other than a steady improvement in living conditions. The Soviet people have been promised this improvement emphatically and continually. Were it to be denied now, the brute force and terror of Stalin's reign would have to be reintroduced to secure compliance. But such a return, although it might gain compliance, would forfeit co-operation, and the Communist party could not advance the economy under modern conditions without such co-operation: 'Soviet leaders know better than ever before that their future depends upon the degree to which they can satisfy their people's demands'.[20] Khrushchev realised that disappointment here could undermine the régime: 'if the socialist system gives a person fewer economic and spiritual goods than the capitalist system, certain people are going to think it over and say: "Why the devil did we substitute one for the other?" '[21] A good performance in this field is essential also if other communist countries are to be kept willingly within the socialist camp, and if uncommitted ones are to be impressed and attracted.

The Party leaders may, however, well be sincere because 'for the true Bolshevik, belief in this utopia is not a dogma. It is the force that drives him not only to personal sacrifice but to the imposition of sacrifice on others . . . It has provided the Bolshevik with the simplicity of a single and known goal.'[22] Whether this is so or not the facts speak for themselves. There is no doubt about the rising standard of living in the USSR, and all the indications are that the main preoccupation of the leaders is to increase its rate of growth. Stalin's five-year plans gave the consumers what little was left after production targets for heavy industry were met, but there was a change in 1961. This had the effect of switching 'the final objective from production (through accumulation) to consumption (by postulating an end of plan pattern and size of consumption)'.[23] The only conclusion one can reasonably draw is that 'the present Soviet leadership is not only taking this craving for material improvement into account, it is encouraging it and to some extent catering to it'.[24]

One Soviet goal which was made much of by Khrushchev but is seldom heard now, was that of overtaking the United States in the near future. The draft programme of the Communist party, adopted by the 22nd Party Congress in 1961, included the following paragraph: 'in the current decade (1961–70) the Soviet Union, in creating the material and technical basis of communism, will surpass the strongest and richest capitalist country, the USA, in production per head of population'.[25] By 1970 the USSR had not passed the USA in total production, let alone *per capita* output, and was in fact no nearer doing so in 1970 than in 1960. This has been to some extent due to expansion of American production to meet the needs of the Vietnamese war and the Middle Eastern crisis. As the industrial plant and labour force in the USA were underemployed in 1960, the additional commitments assumed by America in these international conflicts could be met from surplus capacity. But Soviet capacity was fully taken up: the necessity to aid and arm North Vietnam and the Arab countries could not therefore be met in addition to civilian production and consumption, but only instead of it. When making one of his many promises to overtake the capitalist world, Khrushchev did say that it would happen only 'if the imperialists do not stick their pigs' snouts into our socialist garden', by which he meant presumably, 'if we are not forced to divert more productive capacity into armaments'.[26]

Economists often speak of consumers as being sovereign in what they assume to be a market economy, but a preponderant and growing part of the American economy is 'planned' by the large corporations, and this planning includes deciding what the consumers will or should want and then persuading them to buy it. But none the less the American consumer has an overflowing abundance and a bewildering choice of goods which he is being constantly wooed to buy. What is his motivation? According to Vance Packard in *The Hidden Persuaders* it is becoming less and less a genuine motivation from within and more and more a manipulation from without, while the same author in his *The Status Seekers* shows that a main objective in the purchase of many goods is to gain status and compete socially.[27]

Whether or not American consumers are 'sovereign', there is little doubt that 'sovereign consumers would not choose the paths of growth chosen by Soviet rulers'.[28] They would unquestionably choose a greater profusion and range of better-quality goods, and this motivation would arise from genuine need and the unstimulated desire for a better life, not from needs implanted by psychologists at the behest of the producers.

7 The Economy: II – Organisation

An economy may be viewed as the application of skills, labour and inanimate energy through equipment to resources (raw or semi-finished, domestic or imported), with the help of services (construction, transport, commerce, finance, education and research) to the requirements of a market or a plan, to achieve an output of goods and services to satisfy a demand (domestic and foreign). Such a process needs organisation and administration. The key phrase in the above definition for this comparison is 'according to a market or plan'. It has already been stated that the oft-asserted contrast between the USA and the USSR as that between a market economy and a planned economy is too simple, since the American economy contains a growing element of planning.

Planning in the USSR is both macro-economic and micro-economic and embraces almost the whole economy. The only sectors not planned are the private allotments of collective farms, the produce of which can be sold at urban markets at uncontrolled prices, and the activities of a small number of self-employed persons, speculators and black marketeers. There are also the *tolkachi* who act as unofficial intermediaries between the managements or various enterprises, and are used because of the slow and cumbersome nature of the official channels. The detailed plans are annual, the so-called five-year plans being general programmes and declarations of intent.

The planning is done in two stages. In the first, requirements move downwards from the top. The Council of Ministers communicates to the State Economic Agency (Gosplan) the policy and preferences of the leadership, for instance for more emphasis on motor-car production. A provisional annual plan is then drawn up giving the targets for the various ministries and so on down through the subordinate levels of the bureaucracy until it reaches the actual producing firms. At each level the aggregate totals set in the provisional plan are subdivided until, at the end of the chain, the individual factory manager knows his provisional target. The next stage, of information moving upwards, now begins. The plant manager states the output he can achieve and the inputs of capital and labour he will need; these data are collated as they move up through the organisations to ministry level and finally to Gosplan, which attempts to reconcile the outputs desired with the inputs available, and the end result is the Annual Plan for the Development of the National Economy of the USSR. In this the inputs claimed as necessary by the individual ministries and the individual firms are reduced, thus putting pressure on the producers to achieve greater output with lesser inputs.[1]

In the USA, because of political ideology and economic mythology, there is psychological and emotional hostility to the idea of planning and to the regulation, control and interference it implies.[2] This has prevented the development of macro-economic planning by the federal government, while the growth of micro-economic planning by the corporations, which is veiled in industrial secrecy, has developed largely unnoticed. Nevertheless, the federal government does some macro-economic planning through its fiscal and monetary powers, mainly in an attempt to raise employment or check inflation. This is because the great depression of the 1930s opened the door to the theories of Keynes who, on the grounds that 'the world will not much longer tolerate the unemployment which, apart from brief intervals of excitement, is associated . . . with present-day capitalistic individualism', concluded that: 'the State will have to exercise a guiding influence on the propensity to consume partly through its scheme of taxation, partly by fixing the rate of interest, and partly, perhaps, in other ways'. But he was careful to add that 'beyond this no obvious case is made out for a system of State Socialism which would embrace most of the economic life of the community', and went on to assert: 'if the State is able to determine the aggregate amount of resources devoted to augmenting the instruments and the basic reward to those who own them, it will have accomplished all that is necessary'.[3]

The big American corporation has to plan ahead because the development, production and marketing of a new product is, owing to growing technological complexity, a long-drawn-out business and too expensive to be left to chance. The various stages in the process require the co-operation of numerous groups, each expert in their own speciality, and the successful integration of their efforts can only be obtained through planning. In contrast to the limited and hamstrung government planning, American corporations use, in conjunction with computers, elaborate mathematical–economic tools such as input–output analysis and linear programming, to plan production to a greater degree of refinement than the Soviets themselves have been able to achieve.[4] In fact such planning has gone to extreme lengths in the USA and there is some reaction against it: 'the most important business decisions cannot be reduced to neat mathematical terms'.[5] Another important way in which the large American corporation has transferred parts of the market economy to its own planned control is through vertical integration: 'the planning unit takes over the source of supply or the outlet; a transaction that is subject to bargaining over prices and amounts is thus replaced with a transfer within the planning unit'.[6]

Soviet planning is faced with enormous difficulties and seemingly insoluble problems. As the products required from the economy become more variegated and more intricate, the need for transactions between industries grows rapidly; but the planning system is based on a division into separate industries, each with its own ministry and bureaucracy. The director of the computer centre of the USSR Academy of Sciences has been quoted as saying that 'in a growing economy the number of linkages and ties increases as the square of the number of separate elements, and the difficulty of plan optimisation increases even faster – as the cube of the growing number of elements'.[7] Difficulty also arises from the fact that the number of available resources steadily increases and the techniques for extracting and utilising them become more elaborate; at the same time the number of claimants for these resources multiplies. How can their allocation be optimally and scientifically governed, other than by a return to a market-governed price system? Even Prime Minister Kosygin has said that 'no one, not even the chairman of Gosplan himself, could say whether the new plans being worked out at the time really did provide for the proper proportions among sectors of the economy'.[8]

There are admitted defects in the Soviet planning system. Reliance on an annual plan is inadequate in view of the needs of present technology.[9] The primitive system of 'balances' upon which the plans are based – balancing the planned demand for goods to accord with the planned output and balancing the planned flow of funds to consumers with the value of the goods and services available – does not always work out as well in practice as on paper: surpluses develop here and shortages there. As the planning becomes more complicated, so it takes longer, and individual enterprises are left waiting for their targets after the planned year has begun.[10] Even when plans are rushed out they are often incomplete through lack of time, or inaccurate through hasty preparation, and the work of enterprises is then further complicated by receiving corrections and adjustments. In Orenburg oblast 'during the first nine months of 1969 almost half the plants in the oblast had their sales plan changed, and one in five had it changed three times, some up to six times'.[11]

A whole host of evils, too long to list, is associated with bureaucratic overcentralisation and red tape. Enterprises are sometimes required to send in their detailed input needs before they have been given the output plan to which the inputs have to be related.[12] The overall plan has been condemned as less 'macro-economic' than it would first appear, being rather the ill-coordinated aggregation of a series of micro-economic plans drawn up by different experts in separate ministries.[13] These deficiencies result in the low quality of many goods. Other factors contribute to low standards of workmanship, such as the emphasis on physical output rather than quality in the plans, frustrating delivery delays and 'storming' – the tendency to take things easy until the final date for fulfilling the plan approaches, and then to make a desperate rush to complete the target on time.

The Soviet economy would also appear to be seriously infected with such diseases as nepotism and favouritism, bribery and corruption, swindling and embezzlement, and in one year alone only those thefts from state enterprises that were the subject of prosecution amounted to 56 million roubles. Various kinds of falsification of information and gerrymandering of accounts are also rife.[14]

The problems of the American economy are of a different kind. If many of those in Russia stem from too much control and regulation, from overcentralisation and the smothering of individual initiative, American difficulties are often attributable to lack of co-ordination and absence of discipline, to the want of an overall economic policy or the means to effect it. The difference is mainly macro-economic. There is less contrast than one might suppose between say the motor industry in the two superpowers. In the Soviet Union the industry is under the control of one government department. In the United States it is almost monopolised by three corporations but in many senses they may be viewed as one. They design and manufacture a similar range of models, make almost identical annual changes of style, and set comparable prices. But whereas the automotive industry in the USSR is subject to bureaucratic control from without, the motor industry in the USA is not – except in specific instances such as legislation requiring safety or anti-pollution devices. In America the management and the unions between them fix wages and in the light of this the corporations fix prices. In Russia the state fixes both wages and prices.

This fundamental difference explains the present American economic dilemma, which is the occurrence of recession and high unemployment simultaneously with inflation and rising prices. Inflating the economy by the state through demand-stimulating fiscal and monetary policies no longer arrests the growth of unemployment, and raising unemployment by cutting demand no longer stops inflation. The view of Keynes and his disciples who have advised successive governments since the war, that such fiscal and monetary controls are 'all that is necessary',[15] no longer seems tenable. This is largely a result of the freedom of corporations and unions to fix prices and wages irrespective of government policy and regardless of the economic situation of the country.

The pattern of the wages–costs–prices spiral is a familiar one and hardly likely to tempt the USSR to lose faith in its macro-economic planning. Under threat of strike action or as the result of a strike, a new contract is negotiated between management and the union, under which higher wages are paid. Prices are then raised to cover the costs of the strike, if there was one, and to meet the higher wages bill. Because of the growing cost of labour more automation will be used, and unemployment will be aggravated. Because of the higher prices production may have to be cut, especially if imports now become more competitive, likewise adding to unemployment. For both the corporations and those workers still in employ, whose gains are eroded by the rising prices, what remains is 'profitless prosperity'. The uncontrolled accommodation of the big corporations to the interests of their own technocrats and their own section of organised labour, regardless of the welfare of the United States economy as a whole, is a situation the government appears only to be able to meet with exhortation or meaningless threats of unenforceable legislation.

Another significant factor in the rapid inflation bedevilling the American economy has been the rising tide of unproductive military and space expenditure, and particularly of the vast sums appropriated for war in South-East Asia. Thus military crises affect America in a different way from Russia. The supply of arms to North Vietnam is a problem for the Soviet Union because it involves cutting back some other essential sector. The war in Vietnam for the United States has meant vastly increasing the money supply without any corresponding increase in productivity, thus bringing about rapid inflation and contributing towards the balance of payments deficit. The latter, another worsening problem for America's economy, reached $12 billion in 1970 and her chief creditors – notably West Germany – were in a position to bankrupt her if they chose to demand conversion of their dollar credits into gold.

The American economy, unlike the Soviet system, is liable to be affected by the electoral calculations of politicians. At the beginning of 1971, the Nixon administration made it clear that it was about to switch from its policy of curbing inflation to one of going all out to achieve a higher level of employment. The President himself said, 'I am now a Keynesian.' It was generally accepted that this change was made because the President knew that he would face defeat at the end of 1972 unless unemployment had been reduced by then to a low level. In adopting this pattern of 'squeeze' and deflation in the two years of office following his election, followed by reflation in the two years preceding his hoped-for re-election, he was following a procedure that has become familiar in the political democracies of the West.

If Western economists are at a loss to solve the American economic dilemma, their Russian counterparts have urged positive reforms for the Soviet system. Some of these have been adopted since 1965 by the Brezhnev–Kosygin administration. There is disagreement, however, as to whether the reforms already put into effect are far-reaching enough to resolve the ills of the Soviet economy. The most important of these reforms were those proposed in 1962 by Liberman, some of which were introduced on an experimental basis in a few enterprises under Khrushchev. They have now been extended to most parts of the economy. Under the new dispensation, plans for industrial firms and collective farms are to be more stable – normally for five years instead of one; sales and profitability are to be the chief indicators of success rather than volume of output; individual enterprises are to have more control over the composition of outputs and inputs, i.e. over what they make and what they make it with; enterprises are now required to pay interest on their fixed and working capital; and firms can now retain a large share of all profits over ten per cent and use them for a variety of purposes: to pay into the wages fund for additional bonuses – although the resultant rise in wages must not exceed the growth in productivity; for worker housing and other welfare needs; for new capacity and technical improvements; and for investment. This means that Soviet individual factory managements now have more freedom and a wider range of responsibility than most plant managers operating within a large American corporation. A similar freedom and encouragement to experiment was given to the collective farm managements in the late 1960s.

Another reform which has spread since 1964 has been the amalgamation of previously distinct enterprises, corresponding usually to a single factory or works, into large firms: 'the aim is to economize on managerial costs, to form units large enough so that specialized technical and other personnel can profitably be employed, and to increase efficiency by having each of the small sub-units in the large "firm" specialize in one or another aspect of the productive process'.[16] This, of course, brings the Soviet firm much closer to the American corporation in its structure.

The 'economic reform' has now been extended up from the individual enterprise to the ministries and *glavki*, which are the regional administrative bodies coming, in the hierarchy, between the ministries and the enterprises. This extension began in 1970 with the Ministry of Apparatus, Automation and Control Systems Manufacture and the *Glavmosavtotrans* (the Moscow Motor Transport Board). Hitherto such bureaucratic bodies have themselves had little more responsibility than the enterprises had before the reform. Their function was to pass directives downwards and information upwards to the state planners, and to hand subsidies down from and profits up to the state budget. According to the Soviet economist Birman, 'the still occurring red tape and formalities in the work of economic bodies is explained to a large extent by their lack of material responsibility for the work of subordinate enterprises'. Under the reform they are to be made responsible for the profits and losses of their own industries and 'the state budget will discontinue entirely all types of financing in this sector'. And for the first time, 'the money that is not spent by the end of the year will not be taken away from the Ministry, but will remain at its disposal for future use'. If they need more money they will have to make their industries more efficient, using the new freedoms to plan, research and expand that they have now been given.[17]

Reforms, however, do not always bring the promised results, and there have been some difficulties and not a little disillusion with the working of the new methods. Many Soviet enterprises, including five per cent of shops and twenty-nine per cent of public catering services, make losses because of prices or charges fixed at a low level for social reasons; they cannot therefore share in the incentive schemes, for however hard they try, they will never be able to make the minimum ten per cent profit. There is evidence that many managers of factories and chairmen of collective farms do not want the new wide responsibilities, but prefer to be told precisely what to do, and corresponding to this is an unwillingness of bureaucrats and party functionaries to give up their control: 'often planning and supervisory authorities have informally, but nonetheless effectively, frustrated the attempts of enterprise directors to exercise choice even within the ostensible limits'.[18]

Probably the chief obstacle to the success of the reforms is the absence of a plentiful and varied array of tempting consumer goods to make higher earnings worth while. As it is, the chief result of profit distribution among the workers has been to swell the deposits in the savings banks, despite a rate of interest of only two per cent. In 1968 such deposits rose by twenty per cent, and in 1969 by seventeen per cent, to a total of some forty million roubles – double the amount in 1966.[19] Meanwhile factories continue to produce unwanted consumer goods, so that instead of the money and goods exchanging, each accumulates in its respective dead end – the banks and the warehouses.

An important new trend in the Soviet economy is the application of mathematical–economic techniques, such as input–output analysis and linear programming on a vast macro-economic scale, hampered only by the shortage in numbers and inadequacy of performance of the

E

present output of computers. An American authority on input–output analysis testifies that

> The recent Soviet *ex post* table for 1966 is by far the most ambitious and impressive accomplishment of Soviet statistical and research agencies in the field of input–output analysis. Should all planned phases of the work be completed, the 1966 Soviet table could probably compete for the title of the world's most comprehensive and versatile set of input–output data.[20]

In short, techniques designed and developed in the West as ideal instruments for the guidance of an economy as a whole, and which could be used with beneficial effect in the American economy, are not being used there above corporation level. Instead it is the Soviet-planned economy that is beginning to reap the benefit.

Although it is usual to associate the Soviet system with hordes of officials, such comparison as can be made appears to suggest that American industry is more bureaucratic. In most big American corporations the number of office workers has increased much more rapidly in recent years than the number of productive workers in the factories. In fact, well over a quarter of the industrial labour force consists of white-collar workers in America, but only some fifteen per cent in the Soviet Union. The surprising conclusion to be drawn is that 'whatever problems are created for Russian industry through the Soviet system of central planning – and certainly they are multitudinous – the creation of an enormous bureaucracy, gobbling up Soviet manpower, does not seem to be one of these difficulties'.[21]

PRICE

Prices are obviously a vital part of the economic mechanism. If they are too high, goods will remain unsold; if they are too low, shortages will develop. In a purely market economy prices will be set at a level which brings about an equilibrium between supply and demand. In a planned economy an attempt will be made to make the aggregate price of the goods to be disposed of correspond to the volume of purchasing power available through wages and salaries, less the amount desired for savings. Before the 'reform' all Soviet prices, except those charged in collective farm markets and on the black market, and fees for a certain amount of private practice by professional men, were fixed according to state lists. These official Soviet-listed prices have remained remarkably stable for fifteen years or more, unlike American prices which have moved steadily upwards: consumer prices in the USA rose by twenty per cent in the decade 1958–68.[22]

Soviet prices are based on the average costs of production, to which fixed rates of profit and turnover tax are added. When all prices were centrally fixed the profit rate was a modest and fairly standard one. Now that enterprises have been given a strong motive to make a profit and some latitude in price fixing, they have tended to overcharge, as instanced in these examples given by the chairman of the state committee on prices:

Quite recently we had to rap the Udarnitsa chocolate factory in Moscow for mulcting customers of 193,000 roubles by costing the carton of one brand at 11 kopeks although in fact it only cost seven. Again, we had to confiscate 90,000 roubles excess profits made by the Saratov Gas Appliances Company, which had, we discovered, fixed the price of one item to allow a profit five times as large as could possibly be justified. In fact, during 1969, the State Committee had to confiscate three million roubles of unwarranted profits derived from inflated prices.[23]

Demand is not normally a criterion in setting prices which are often too low, and long queues result. Many prices, for example of children's clothes, apartment rents, utility charges, canteen meals, are under-priced for social reasons. An attempt is now being made to use prices to increase efficiency and technical progress: 'this can be done, in the first place, by making regular price cuts on obsolescent and, even more, out-dated items, so that it is no longer worth a factory's while to go on producing them'.[24]

In the large corporation sector of the United States economy the fixing of prices is not so different. They too are based on a costs-plus-profit basis. Although open collusion in prices is illegal the corporations normally have a tacit understanding to keep their prices in line.[25] Because of rising costs and the successive negotiation of new contracts with unions, each embodying an increase in wages and benefits, these prices almost invariably rise periodically. But because there is more retail freedom in the USA, retailers and agents may lower the manufacturers' prices considerably to clear stocks. Agriculture is the main sector of the American economy where prices still fluctuate according to supply and demand, and here, despite the general fall in the value of the dollar, prices of some farm products have failed to rise during the past decade.

Taxation

In the USA personal taxation in 1967 amounted to $133 billion or about one quarter of personal incomes. In the USSR, in the same year, personal taxation amounted to 49·4 billion roubles or about forty per cent of personal incomes.[26] Thus, although the total amount of taxes levied was much less in the USSR, because of the smaller aggregate personal income of that country, these taxes represented a higher share of that income. But real income in the USSR is rising faster than the rate of taxation and faster than real income in the USA.

There is a difference in the nature of the taxation. In the USA just over half of all personal taxation is income tax, the rest being made up of property tax and sales tax. But in the USSR taxation is preponderantly indirect, eighty per cent coming from the turnover tax. In addition to personal taxation, American corporations paid $36·2 billion in tax in 1967, while Soviet state enterprises paid 41·8 billion roubles out of their profits to the state treasury.

OUTPUT, DISPOSAL AND DEMAND

Gross National Product

The term most commonly used by Western economists to denote the total production of goods and services by an economy is the gross national product (GNP), 'gross' because it does not make allowance for depreciation which is difficult to calculate accurately and comparatively. A comparison of American and Soviet GNPs is exceedingly hard to make since there is no really satisfactory way of relating the dollar and the rouble. An American estimate gives the Russian GNP as 32·1 per cent of the American in 1950, 36·5 per cent in 1955, 44·6 per cent in 1960 and 46·7 per cent in 1964. A 1969 estimate puts it at fifty per cent, with the American total at $932 billion and the Soviet at $466 billion. But the American figure is exaggerated by inflation. In terms of 1964 dollars, the Soviet percentage would be fifty-three per cent, and in terms of 1958 dollars, fifty-six per cent of the United States total. In *per capita* terms, because of the larger Soviet population, the figures are even less favourable to the USSR.[27]

Gross national product, calculated in the standard way, does not offer a fair comparison between the output of the two countries. The American total contains many significant items which do not occur in the USSR because the system does not require them, and which would be considered totally unnecessary and unproductive, and therefore irrelevant to the economy's output. Thus in the USA there are many more financial and commercial intermediaries, and a vast apparatus of business advertising, insurance and litigation, all of which swell the gross national product. Nor does the GNP give any indication of the quality, performance and usefulness of the output. It is therefore of very limited value as an index of industrial power or military strength. The level of the GNP is important, however, as a morale factor in each country, since so much publicity is given, both at home and abroad, to its comparative level and growth, and it affects the way in which non-aligned and backward countries regard the success of the rival systems:

> The spectacle of a Soviet economy successfully pursuing rapid economic growth with a sense of utmost urgency is bound to hold strong attractions for the less developed countries and would lend conviction to the Soviet claim that, in the age of industrialism its own style of planned economy is superior to the market economy of the West and that its example constitutes a relevant model of economic development for all of the underdeveloped world.[28]

During the 1950s the growth rate of the Soviet GNP was about double that of the American (seven per cent to 3·5 per cent per annum), a rate fast enough to make catching up seem feasible within a decade or two. But in the 1960s the Soviet growth rate slackened to an average of only four per cent, not greatly ahead of the American average of 3·2 per cent.[29] This margin is too small to enable the Soviet Union ever to overtake the United States. Soviet productivity was slowed down in the 1960s by a labour shortage induced by the low birth rate during the 1941–5 war, by reductions in the length of the working week, and by the dislocations caused by introducing new technologies. The American national product was stimulated, on the other hand, by the demands of the war in South-East Asia and the space race. On 15 December 1970, according to Department of Commerce computers, the American GNP reached a trillion dollars, and the event was celebrated at a function attended by President Nixon. However, as the chief contribution to this achievement had been that of inflation rather than real growth, the rejoicing was restrained. The year 1970 in the USSR recorded a high growth reminiscent of the 1950s – 8·5 per cent according to a United Nations survey, compared with less than five per cent in 1969.[30]

If the gross national product is looked at from the point of view of the part of the economy from which it is derived (Table 7.1), it may be observed that, while the proportion originating in industry (i.e. mining

TABLE 7.1 GROSS NATIONAL PRODUCT BY ORIGINATING
SECTOR 1963–4[31]
(*percentage of total*)

	USA (1963)	USSR (1964)
Agriculture	4·1	25·2
Industry	32·3	33·9
Construction	5·0	9·2
Transport and communications	6·0	9·7
Commerce	16·2	5·3
Services	36·0	16·5

and manufacturing) is about the same in both – roughly one-third – the remainder of the American product comes largely from commerce and services, whereas agriculture, construction and transport are more important on the Soviet side.

Disposal by end product

As Table 7.2 shows, a much larger proportion of the American GNP goes to the personal consumption of goods and services, although the discrepancy between the two countries is much less for food and clothing

TABLE 7.2   GROSS NATIONAL PRODUCT BY DISPOSAL 1964[32]
(*percentage*)

	USA	USSR
Personal consumption	63·4	46·5
Investment	14·9	30·5
Government (incl. military)	20·4	23·0
Net exports	1·3	—

than for consumer's goods, housing and personal services. On the other hand, twice as much of the Soviet GNP in percentage terms (but a similar amount in absolute terms) is invested. The purpose of the large Soviet investment is, of course, to speed up the growth of the economy and is made possible by the restriction of consumption. The nature of Soviet investment differs greatly from that of the United States as may be seen from Table 7.3. These data, though somewhat old, show that a much larger share of Soviet investment – sixty-three per cent as against thirty-nine per cent – is productive and adds directly to the strength of the economy.

A large proportion of the national product of each country allocated to government use is military, and this amounted in both cases to between nine and twelve per cent in the 1960s. But in absolute terms, United States military expenditure is much larger, partly because of greater commitments but also because of higher costs. The expense of

TABLE 7.3   COMPARATIVE COMPOSITION OF CAPITAL
INVESTMENT[33]
(*percentages*)

	USA (1958–63 av.)	USSR (1959–64 av.)
Agriculture	4·7	15·8
Industry	19·2	34·0
Energy	7·4	4·2
Transport and communications	7·8	9·7
Housing	30·8	19·9
Other	30·0	16·5

supplying, equipping and paying an American soldier is much greater than the similar cost of a Russian soldier; and it is likely, in view of the great cost of lobbying for defence contracts in Washington, and the high profits made by United States corporations supplying the military, that the defence rouble goes further than the defence dollar. An official American source gave American military expenditure in 1968 as $79·6 billion, that of the USSR as $39·8 billion.[34]

Part of the national product is exported from each country abroad, but as such exports are nearly balanced by imports, the net effect in value terms is negligible. Exports from the USA in 1968 were four per cent of the GNP, while those from the USSR were about two per cent.

Demand

The purpose of production is to meet and satisfy demand. The volume of demand in the USA is affected by government monetary and fiscal policies, by the velocity of the circulation of money, by the pricing policies of the big corporations, by the wages policies of the trade unions, by the savings and investment policies of companies and individuals, and, in the market section of the economy, by the volume of supply operating through prices. In the USSR the volume of demand is controlled by the state through the amount of purchasing power made available through salaries and wages, through direct and indirect taxation, and through the socialisation of many services. In the USA the composition of demand is affected by the type of goods available, the advertising campaigns of the companies, and the personal choice of the consumer. In the USSR the composition of demand is determined by the goods available: there is little advertising and the wishes of the consumer have much less effect.

Demand comes from three main groups: from domestic personal consumers, from foreign importers and from the government, mainly for military purposes. Not only is the total volume of domestic consumption much higher in the USA than in the USSR, despite the smaller population, but the range and quality of goods is greater. Many consumers' goods and services which are abundantly available in the USA are either non-existent or extremely scarce in the USSR. Many such goods and services, however, would be thought frivolous or socially undesirable in the USSR. As for quality, the new economic reforms, by making profitability rather than total output the index of a Russian firm's progress, have already greatly improved this, and very often the difference between Soviet and American quality is a matter of packaging, presentation and finish rather than basic durability and reliability. The unpretentious but robust Russian motor car is as efficient and long-lived as its glossy stylish counterpart. Nor does the Soviet firm have the incentive to incorporate in its products the 'built-in obsolescence' familiar to American consumers.

A big difference is noticeable in the method of acquiring expensive consumer durables. In the USA these are usually bought on credit and in 1970 American consumers owed $120 billion: four-fifths of this huge debt was on account of automobile purchases.[35] In addition, their homes carried a mortgage debt of $150 billion (excluding farm mortgages) giving a total indebtedness of $270 billion or $1,300 for each man, woman and child in the country. In the Soviet Union, on the other hand, although credit schemes have been available for the purchase of durables since 1959 and limited mortgage facilities are available for house purchase, they are not yet significant, and such goods have therefore to be saved for.[36]

Large stocks of unsold and unsaleable goods in Soviet shops alongside queues for scarce goods in great demand are quoted as evidence of the subordinate position of the Russian consumer, compared with his American counterpart, and despite the economic reforms, the quantity of unsold goods continued to rise in 1966–8.[37] However, it could be queried whether Americans would have freely chosen to buy many of the goods they actually bought, had they not been persuaded to do so by advertising. One of the more noticeable differences between the 'typical' American and Russian male is that the former has become increasingly anointed, scented and deodorised, and this has undoubtedly been brought about by the skilful use of advertising to create a hitherto unsuspected want – by suggesting that scented men are more attractive to women. One advertisement for a man's scent reads 'Women like it. Because it doesn't smell like the stuff they wear'; another asserts of its 'after-shave' that 'its subtle, masculine aroma makes women behave outrageously. They invent the wildest excuses just to be near you' and that its deodorant is 'the male way to keep cool on tough assignments'; one should 'try the whole arsenal' for 'each gives you the license to kill . . . women'. The American consumer cannot open his morning mail, read his newspaper, listen to his radio, watch his television or drive along the road without repeated and seductive appeals to buy which have been scientifically designed by psychologists to overcome any resistance he may feel. All the wooing and flattery of the consumer implicit in American advertising may make him feel like a 'king', but in reality he is being controlled, though without any physical compulsion: 'the management to which we are subject is not onerous. It works not on the body but on the mind.' But management there nonetheless is and its object has been described as to 'develop the kind of man the goals of the industrial system require – one that works reliably because he is always in need of more'.[38] Estimated expenditure on advertising in the United States in 1970 totalled $20 billion. Even the pharmaceutical industry spends more on advertising than it does on research.[39] The Soviet consumer escapes this psychological pressure; his conscious needs are far fewer, and despite a narrower range of goods available to him and their inferior quality, he may yet feel no more dissatisfied than his American counterpart, and he may well suffer less emotionally. For 'we can only guess at the tensions and anxieties generated by this relentless pursuit of the emblems of success in our society'.[40]

Standard of Living

The personal consumption of goods and services is referred to as the standard or level of living and this depends upon the relationship between personal incomes and the cost of living as well as upon the availability of such goods and services. Exactitude is impossible in comparing the superpowers here because there is no satisfactory way of converting dollars into roubles and vice versa: such comparisons as may be drawn must be regarded as general and inconclusive.

Personal incomes are, on an average, much higher in the United States. There they formed in 1968 sixty-five per cent of the national income compared with under forty per cent of the much smaller national income of the USSR. This would give the average American wage or salary earner an annual income between three and four times that of his Russian counterpart. This does not give a true comparison, however, because of the higher share of the American's income which goes to direct taxation, insurance, medical care, transportation and housing (Table 7.4). If these inevitable outlays are deducted, the American citizen is left with only forty-six per cent of his income for the purchase of goods and services, whereas in Russia he can dispose of ninety per cent. When this is taken into account, the real average personal income of the Soviet worker is over half that of the American employee.

TABLE 7.4   ESTIMATED EXPENDITURE OF AVERAGE INCOME 1965[41]
(percentages)

	USA	USSR
Direct taxation	12	2
Social insurance	4	0
Rent and communal services	19	5
Medical care and education	6	0
Transportation	13	3

Cost of living is difficult to relate to these incomes. While on the one hand Soviet citizens pay a higher rate of indirect taxation, raising the costs of many goods, notably adult clothing and some foodstuffs well above the American level, other prices are subsidised, bringing them below American equivalents. But the real factor operating to keep the cost of living down in the Soviet Union compared with the United States is the fact that many goods and services on offer in America are not freely available in Russia; they cannot be bought because they are not to be had, and therefore cannot figure in a cost-of-living index.

Average incomes are of little value unless the actual distribution is taken into account. This is much more uneven in the USA where the top ten per cent of the population by income receives about thirty times as much as the bottom ten per cent; in the USSR the top ten per cent receives only between three and four times as much as the bottom ten per cent.[42] The USSR has no millionaires, not to mention billionaires, and the absence of inherited wealth, large holdings of stocks and shares, capital gains, big business deals and large-scale organised corruption and crime, militate against the acquisition of large sums of money by individuals. In the USSR there are few salaries above 300 roubles a month. Most managerial salaries fall in the 200- to 300-rouble bracket, while the minimum wage established in 1968 is 60 roubles.[43]

The result of this difference is that there is both more real affluence and more real poverty in the United States. According to Michael Harrington, besides the 'familiar America', which is celebrated in speeches and advertised on television and in the magazines 'and which has the highest mass standard of living the world has ever known', there is also 'the other America' in which forty to fifty million people are hungry or poorly nourished on cheap foods and 'without adequate housing and education and medical care'.[44]

In the USSR the poor people are mostly in the rural areas, although even here the gap between them and urban dwellers has slowly narrowed since Stalin's death in 1953. The rural surcharge, which made the cost of living higher in the countryside, was abolished in 1965. At first sight, Russian peasants look more poverty-stricken than the American poor. This is because their clothing is often worn, old and ragged, a reflection both of the high cost of clothing in the USSR and the rural population's lack of concern for appearances. On the other hand, 'America has the best-dressed poverty in the world . . . It is much easier in the United States to be decently dressed than it is to be decently housed, fed or doctored.'[45]

8 Factors of Production:
Labour, Capital and Management

Traditionally the factors of production were considered to be land, capital and labour. Land was an obvious factor in the age of agriculture, but its significance is much less in an industrial economy. The land on which a factory is erected plays a wholly passive role, and in the USSR until recently it was totally ignored as a factor, since not even rent was paid for it. Modern economists sometimes substitute 'natural resources' for 'land', which widens the concept considerably. Land is fixed and cannot be imported or exported, but natural resources can be brought in from other countries; land can be used as it is, resources have to be developed. It is more common today to confine attention to capital and labour, although management is often regarded as a third factor. Education and technology also qualify in some classifications, but education may be regarded as an aspect of labour, and technology as an aspect of capital. Education improves the quality of the labour force and technology increases the productivity of capital.

LABOUR

As one would expect from its greater population, the Soviet labour force is larger than the American: 109 million in 1969 as against 77 million. In age distribution, the United States has a relatively small work force aged between thirty and forty-five, owing to the shortfall of births during the great economic depression, while the Soviet Union has an exceptionally small group aged twenty-five to thirty because of the deficit of births during the 1941–5 war. By sex, women formed thirty-seven per cent of the American labour force in 1969, but made up fifty per cent of the Soviet total. By occupation, the main differences are that America has over half its labour force in commerce, the service functions and government, while Russia still has a large work force employed in agriculture (Table 8·1).

There is little difference between the average hours worked in each

country. The length of the working week in 1968 was given officially as
37·8 hours in the USA and 40·1 hours in the USSR. In America the
figure is affected by varying demand and rises and falls from year to
year, although with a general trend downwards. In the USSR it remains more constant, being governed by the application of a standard
working week to almost the whole economy. This official length was
reduced in 1957 from 47 to 41 hours. Some branches of Soviet industry
work less because of the nature of their working conditions: in coal
mining the average is 38 hours. In America there is much greater
diversity, with metal miners averaging 43·5 hours and building workers
only 36 hours. The shortest hours are worked in the USA in the retail
trade and in the USSR in education.[2]

TABLE 8.1   EMPLOYMENT BY ECONOMIC SECTOR 1969[1]
(*percentage of total employment in each country*)

	USA	USSR
Agriculture	4·6	24·8
Industry	27·1	28·9
Construction	4·4	6·1
Transport and communications	5·0	8·3
Commerce	19·1	6·7
Services and government	35·6	22·2
Military	4·2	3·0

The difference in the productivity of the two labour forces is much
greater than that between the number of hours worked. Soviet GNP
per person employed, as a percentage of the American, was put at only
thirty-two per cent in 1962: in other words a dollar's worth of GNP
required 3·14 times as much labour input in the USSR. There are
several reasons why productivity per man is less in the Soviet Union.
There is much concealed unemployment. Although officially it does not
exist in the USSR, there are inevitably periods when workers are kept
on the payroll of an enterprise even though no work for them is available. In the absence of the pressure of increasing wage costs, Soviet
industry does not strive as effectively as American to make the most
efficient use of its labour. And as, in industry as a whole, there is less
mechanisation and less automation, more labour is required. Furthermore the physical anti-resources – especially the severe winter climate –
of the USSR inevitably reduce productivity, especially in agriculture.

It may be that deteriorating labour relations in the USA will reduce
productivity there at a time when the economic reforms are increasing
it in the USSR. The American motor industry in particular has begun
to suffer seriously from deteriorating conditions on the shop floor:

For management, the truly dismaying evidence about new worker
attitudes is found in job performance. Absenteeism has risen sharply;

in fact it has doubled after the past ten years at General Motors and at Ford, with the sharpest climb last year . . . five per cent of General Motors' hourly workers are missing from work without explanation every day . . . Tardiness has increased, making it even more difficult to start up the production lines promptly when a shift begins. Complaints about quality are up sharply . . . There is more turnover . . . The quit rate at Ford last year was 25·2 per cent. Some assembly-line workers are so turned off, managers report with astonishment, that they just walk away in mid-shift and don't even come back to get their pay for the time they have worked.[3]

Average remuneration in the United States, at $5,300 (less income tax, insurance, etc.) in 1967 is at any realistic dollar–rouble conversion rate above the 1,236 roubles of the Soviet worker. But the latter's outlays on rent, rates, heat, light and medical care, items which consume a major part of the American wage-earner's income, are negligible. Furthermore, differentials between groups of workers are greater in the USA, and whereas in that country clerical workers receive more than manual, in the USSR manual workers get more on the average than clerical.[4] Within employment categories, however, there is a much greater differential in the USSR, where individual workers can greatly enlarge their earnings through bonus and incentive schemes. In the USA the 'union rate' and the fact that such bonuses as are given are distributed at a fixed proportion, militate against such great differences between people doing the same kind of work.

The difference between workers in town and country and on and off farms is great in both countries. In the USA in 1967 farm workers received only a quarter of the average employed male's remuneration; only the unemployed, a large low-income category not to be found in the USSR, suffered comparable poverty.[5] In the USSR the gap is being narrowed, but in the USA it is increasing. Between 1947 and 1968 the American farm worker's wage dropped from a third to a quarter of the national figure, but in the same period the Russian peasant has gained a guaranteed wage, lower taxes, higher procurement prices and pension rights. As for the differences in remuneration between male and female, this is negligible in the USSR, but in America men on an average get more than twice as much as women.

Wage rates are differently based in each country. In America they are compounded of social tradition, the prosperity or otherwise of the industry, union pressure, scarcity or over-abundance in the supply, and the degree of education or training required. In Russia they are the result of a deliberate attempt to determine the 'socialist value of labour': this attempts to take into the account the importance of the industry to the economy, the geographical situation of the enterprise (with higher rates and benefits in the harsher parts of the territory), the working conditions (with higher rates where these are particularly unpleasant) and the educational or technical qualifications needed. Such considerations establish the 'norm', over which considerable increases may be earned by greater productivity.

Motivation is not wholly a matter of pay. Other factors are involved – security of employment, status in society, interest in the job, prospects of advancement, conditions of work, geographical location and other environmental considerations; and the weight accorded to each factor varies from individual to individual. Remuneration is not normally the sole motive, but where the nature of the job leaves it the only possible one, as in certain types of labouring or assembly line work, discontent and strife are at their greatest. Although there are powerful and independent trade unions in the United States, there is more actual participation in management, production and innovation by Soviet workers. Unions are strong in America, whereas they are branches of the administration in Russia; but this does not mean that the ordinary worker is more influential in the former. American trade union bosses are often liable to act despotically and corruptly, and although they have succeeded in enhancing the workers' pay and material working conditions, they have done nothing to implicate him in the industrial process as an interested and creative participant. Rather they have bred in him distrust and hostility towards management, producing a kind of permanent 'cold war' in industry.

In the USSR, on the other hand, because the state desires above all else increased productivity and because it needs to exploit to the full the creative and productive resources of the labour force, the trade union movement is used to implicate the worker as much as possible in the productive process as a willing and cooperative agent.

With regard to the degree of employment of the labour force, it can be generally said that the USSR suffers from shortage, the USA from surplus. The shortage in the USSR is particularly severely felt in the northern and eastern regions of the country where conditions are harsh, but also in the great industrial city of Leningrad where the birth rate is low and where, because of the northerly location, there is not a dense rural population in the surrounding countryside from which to draw. There is, however, a 'concealed' labour surplus in Soviet agriculture – concealed because agricultural tasks and income can often be shared out between a large family living and working together, in a way that would not be possible for factory workers living in towns.

In the USA, where in the 1960s unemployment fluctuated between three and seven per cent of the labour force, the unemployed were mainly unskilled manual workers, especially Negroes. At the same time there was an acute shortage of people with trained skills and educational qualifications. American unemployment results mainly from techno-logical advance: this makes unskilled labour redundant, either by rendering a whole industry obsolescent or by substituting mechanisation and automation for human labour. Between 1960 and 1968 the number of railway workers in the United States fell from 885,000 to 663,000, and the number of coal-miners from 165,000 to 120,000, even though the production of coal increased steadily throughout the period. But unemployed railroad workers and coal-miners could not fill the vacan-cies in the kind of industries that were growing and needing labour. They had become in fact, especially in the case of older men, unemployable.

Employment is largely bound up with the mobility of labour. This mobility may be either horizontal, involving movement from place to place, or vertical, implying transfer from one kind of job to another. The USSR suffers to some degree from the horizontal or geographical im-mobility of labour. A strong love of one's locality, close ties with rela-tives, friends and neighbours, transport difficulties and, until 1969, the absence of any kind of labour exchange, have all contributed to this. The development of the natural resources of the country, which are mostly in the east, requires some shift thither of the working population, who are mainly in the west. Since the Soviet government gave up its powers to direct labour in the late 1950s, it has tried to attract labour to newly developing areas by financial and other incentives, but with only partial success.[6] On the other hand, not only is the rural population of Soviet Central Asia growing faster than is economically necessary but workers from central Russia have begun to migrate there, attracted by the warmth of the climate and the availability of subtropical fruits and other inducements.[7] This is mobility, but mobility in the wrong direction from the economic point of view.

In the USA the labour force has long been the most mobile in the world, and men think little of moving from say New England to California to take up a job. About one-fifth of the population changes house every year, and although much of this movement is confined to to the same locality, some thirteen million people move annually from one county to another, implying a change of job location. But the high degree of mobility in America does little more to solve the problem of high unemployment than the low degree of it in Russia helps with the labour shortage there. The unemployable middle-aged Pennsylvanian or West Virginian coal-miner will be no more likely to find work if he goes to Florida or California.

Vertical mobility – the change from one kind of job to another to meet the changing requirements of the economy caused by advancing technology – appears to be greater in the Soviet Union, because of the more ambitious systems of technical education for people already at work. A much larger proportion of the Soviet labour force undergoes such training on a day-release or evening class basis, because this educational side has been built into the Soviet industrial system by the state. In America participation in such schemes is left more to voluntary individual or corporate enterprise. The United States relies heavily on imports of trained skills from all parts of the non-communist world and is thus relieved to some extent of the necessity to provide such training: the Soviet Union has inevitably much more limited recourse to this source of supply.

Education

Labour must today be regarded qualitatively rather than quantitatively. It is no longer so much a matter of how many 'hands' are available for employment as how many trained brains. Consequently the quality of education is of growing significance to any assessment of the human resource.

Viewed purely from the scholastic and the economically utilitarian viewpoints, the quality of Soviet education is greatly superior to the American at all levels up to post-graduate. The gap is apparent from the difference in the difficulty of the work done in school at equivalent ages.[8] This state of affairs has been ascribed to a variety of causes. Soviet youth is more strongly motivated. There is in the community as a whole a deeply ingrained respect for learning which contrasts with the anti-intellectualism of American public attitudes. In the Soviet Union a higher education is the only way out of the working class, whereas in the United States there are many non-academic avenues to greater wealth and independence. Furthermore, in Russia there is no easy way to an academic qualification, while 'a college diploma can always be obtained somewhere in the United States, with very little effort or ability, by just about anyone who can pay the tuition and write a semi-literate paragraph'.[9] But the Russian student cannot buy his way into college:

> If the Soviet student wants a college diploma very badly, he has to work hard to gain admission to be graduated. The very intensity of the drive for education, and the competition of many applicants for the limited number of admissions, permits the high schools and colleges to maintain high standards of performance . . . The consequence is that the typical Soviet student works harder than the typical American student.[10]

Another cause of discrepancy is the differing purpose of education in each country. Although one of the aims of the Soviet system remains to inculcate loyalty and devotion to the communist philosophy and an ungrudging acceptance of the leadership of the Communist party, it remains fundamentally practical and closely related to the economic tasks of the state. In the USA the aims of education have never been primarily academic. The system was evolved with the main purpose of developing a sense of identity among diverse immigrant groups, and ever since, 'life-adjustment' rather than scholarship has motivated the educational theorists who have guided the American schools. It has sometimes seemed as if the concern was rather to amuse the untalented majority than to train the gifted few: 'we wanted every child to be happy and contented and to have a feeling of success, and we thought this could best be assured by de-emphasizing standards, competition and grades, by broadening the curriculum, and by eliminating the distinction between curricular and extra-curricular activities'.[11]

Both countries spend a similar amount on education, but this amounts to less than four per cent of the United States gross national product, but nearly seven per cent that of the USSR.[12] This is an index of the greater value attached to education by the Soviet state and society. Americans spend more on advertising, holidays and travel, sport, tobacco, alcohol or gambling than on books, whereas in the USSR expenditure on books exceeds that on any such item.[13]

The historical achievement of each system has been different. The United States has succeeded in producing an all-English-speaking society from a population of recently diverse national origin. The Soviet Union has established literacy among a population only a quarter of whom were literate before the Revolution; but for a large proportion of the population, the native non-Russian tongue is used as the language of instruction. Russian is, however, learned as a second language in the schools of the non-Russian peoples.

In both countries there are regional differences in opportunity. Members of the various Soviet non-Russian-speaking nationalities are handicapped in that they must learn and use Russian if they are to have full access to the more responsible positions. In the United States, because of the local financing of education, those living in poor States have less opportunity than those residing in the richer areas. The poor wherever they are – and this includes most Negroes – may have to forgo higher education in the United States for financial reasons. This is less likely to happen in the Soviet Union, as students who are accepted qualify for a state grant. In both countries rural areas are handicapped – by the dispersed nature of the population in America and by poor communications in the Soviet Union – making the provision of higher education particularly difficult. The USSR is much worse off in this respect because it has such a large proportion of its population living in the countryside. On the other hand, female talent is under-used in the United States, so that in many branches of higher learning the students are almost wholly male. In the Soviet Union opportunity between the sexes is much more nearly equal.

One might ask how, if the difference in educational standards is so great, the United States has been able to achieve so much in industrial, military and space technology. The answer is simply that America can afford the luxury of non-academic education because she is wealthy enough to hire trained talent elsewhere. Without foreign brains, there would have been very few American technological firsts – the A-bomb, the H-bomb, jet aircraft, missiles and their propellents, spacecraft, the moon landing and many other dramatic achievements were all highly dependent for their success upon the contribution of scientists imported from abroad.

In America all the States except Mississippi and South Carolina have compulsory education. This is usually for a ten-year period, from six to sixteen, but laws vary from State to State in the length of schooling required and in the latitude permitted in deviating from it. In the USSR compulsory seven-year education was introduced in the towns in 1930–4, and extended to the whole country after the war. Between 1952 and 1956 compulsory ten-year education was introduced into the towns and is expected to become universal in the 1970s. When this has been achieved the number of pupils in Grades 9–12, at present far below the American total, will become more comparable to it (Table 8.2). The pupil–teacher ratio is slightly lower in the schools of the Soviet Union, being nineteen to one as against twenty-one to one in the United States.

In both countries the single-category, non-selective school is the rule, although in Russia there are special language schools to which talented children may be assigned and in which much of the instruction is in a foreign language; and also special schools for children gifted in mathematics or music. In addition, in the Soviet Union there are vocational secondary schools whither children destined for some calling needing early specialised training go, after leaving primary school.

Eighteen per cent of American elementary schools and fourteen per cent of secondary schools are private or run by some non-public body, notably the Roman Catholic church. In higher education two-thirds of the colleges are independent of the state. In the USSR, of course, all schools and colleges are public. Many of the private schools in America are boarding schools and the Soviet Union also has boarding schools to which more and more children are being sent for various reasons: because they are orphaned, because their parents live in rural districts far from a secondary school, because their parents live a nomadic life, or because – for some other reason – it is considered advisable for the welfare of the children. At the end of 1968 there were 1,600,000 pupils in Soviet boarding schools.

The American universities and institutions of higher learning turn out rather more graduates at first-degree level (671,591 as against 510,600 in 1968), but the proportion of Soviet graduates in science and technology is much greater. Engineering, for instance, gets only five and a half per cent of America's graduates, but in the USSR the proportion in 1968 was about forty per cent![14] All higher education is provided free by the state in the USSR and students receive a grant of thirty-three roubles a month. In America most students have to 'put themselves through college', financing their education from their parents, from their vacation earnings or from their wives' or husbands' earnings.

TABLE 8.2 NUMBER OF STUDENTS IN SCHOOLS AND
COLLEGES 1968–70
(*millions*)

	USA (1968)	USSR (1970)
Elementary (Grades 1–8)	33·8	41·9
Secondary (Grades 9–12)	14·1	11·9
Higher	6·8	4·6

CAPITAL

Labour works to transform materials into desired goods through capital, mainly in the form of industrial buildings and machinery. The most obvious difference between the capital equipment in the two superpowers is its ownership. In the United States capital is owned and directed almost wholly by private corporations and individuals. In the Soviet Union it is owned and directed wholly by public institutions: industrial equipment is the property of the state itself, but collective farm buildings and machinery and the premises and tools of certain *artels* will be owned by the collective or *artel*. Lack of information makes it impossible to compare the volume of capital equipment, but the Russian total may be estimated at about one half the American. However, whereas Soviet plant is always working at full capacity, under chronic conditions of overstrain and shortage, there is always an excess capacity in the United States. Even in 1968, the year in which the demands for military equipment for Vietnam were running at their highest level, this excess capacity was sixteen per cent.[15]

Because of its more rapid growth, and owing to the fact that most equipment in the western parts of the country occupied by the Germans had to be replaced after the war, Soviet fixed capital is younger than

American. It also has a longer average life, partly because of the faster rate of technological change in the USA and partly because obsolescence is not outlawed by competition as it is in America, where a plant that failed to modernise would be eliminated by its rivals. However, in sectors of the Soviet economy which enjoy a high investment priority there is little difference between the service life of capital assets in the two countries: for hydro-turbines and metallurgical plant it is the same. But in the production of consumer goods, which have enjoyed a much lower priority in Russia, the service life is much longer in that country. The average life there of textile machinery is fifty years compared with only fifteen to twenty-five years in America.[16]

Generally speaking, plant in the USSR takes longer to erect and install, is of inferior quality, and works less efficiently than in the United States. Brezhnev complained to the 24th Congress of the CPSU in 1971 that 'the number of unfinished projects grows' and that 'the quality of construction remains poor'.[17] It has been stated that, because of the high rate of breakdown, 'equipment maintenance and repair workers constitute by far the largest single skill category of workers in the USSR economy', that a sizeable 'portion of the economy's equipment stock does not work because it is out of order or being repaired', and that 'some portion does not work because it is of the wrong type for the purposes of the plants in which it happens to be placed'.[18] Too much importance, however, should not be accorded to such statements. Because criticism of the working of the economy is actively encouraged in the USSR as a spur to efficiency and a counterweight to bureaucratic smugness, journals are filled with complaints of malfunctioning. In the general and trade publications of the USA, partly because one of their functions is to advertise equipment and not to denigrate it, very little attention is paid to defects and breakdowns.

The higher rate of fixed capital formation in the USSR has resulted not merely from increased investment. In many sectors of the economy there has simply been an increase in the volume of plant of a standard type, without modification or improvement. In the USA, on the contrary, more investment goes to replacing obsolescent equipment and less to enlarging existing equipment.

Technology

Just as the effectiveness of labour is improved by education, so that of capital is increased by technology. In each case knowledge is applied to the factor of production to increase its productivity. Labour is made more aware and more skilled; equipment becomes more complex.

Technology has two sides: research, in which new developments are evolved and tested; and application, in which they are tried out in industry and, if successful, adopted. In the United States the research is mainly carried out by the corporations and sometimes for government. Since the corporations are autonomous and largely self-financing, the transition from research to application is a relatively easy one administratively. In the USSR research is mainly the function of the Academy of Sciences and its various institutes, whereas the application of resulting new technology is a matter for the government departments of the various ministries. This means that it is much more difficult administratively for the scientific discovery to be translated into practical application. In 1967 the 'scientific production centre' was introduced as an experiment to solve this problem. These organisations are research centres to which large industrial enterprises are attached. They have full autonomy, liberal budgets and a generous provision of automated control systems and computers. This form of co-ordination has an advantage over that implicit in the American corporation, in that it is the scientists and technologists who direct the centre, not accountants, managers or company directors. The results of this experiment are said to have 'justified the most optimistic forecasts'.[19]

Hitherto, over the economy as a whole, the USA has been much more successful with technological advance. Where competing companies strive to outpace each other with something new to attract the customer, there is a strong incentive to innovate. On the other hand, Russian firms have had more disincentive than incentive to modernise. The introduction of new equipment and new methods is certain to delay fulfilment of the plan, upon which achievement the salary and career of the manager depend, and at the same time to introduce a host of new problems. New equipment is likely to have teething troubles which are not easily dealt with in the Soviet system.

In many sectors of Soviet industry the level of technology is twenty or twenty-five years behind that of the United States. Often the gap is even greater, especially in certain types of consumer goods. But in some fields, notably military, aeronautic and space, the USSR is equal to or ahead of America. Soviet technology lost ten years as a result of the war and Stalin's lack of interest in new techniques. Wartime destruction gave a great opportunity for modernisation, as it did in Germany and Japan. But whereas in those two countries the industrial plant was rebuilt along the most modern lines, Soviet manufacturing equipment, as rebuilt by 1950, differed little in technological level from 1940.

Whereas American industry moves forward technologically as a whole, certain sectors only of the Soviet economy – because special attention has been directed towards them – leap forward dramatically from their previous backwardness to a position close to that of the

United States. This has happened with hydro-electric power; with many forms of transport – e.g. nuclear ships, aircraft, railways, pipe-lines, hydrofoils; with synthetic fibres; and more recently, with watches and cameras. The production and use of computers has been an example of technological disparity between the two countries (Table 8.3). Some attempt is being made to remedy this deficiency and contracts have been placed with foreign firms to supply business machines, but it will be some time yet before this serious gap is narrowed significantly.

TABLE 8.3 PRODUCTION OF COMPUTERS BY VALUE 1960–5[20]
(*US production 1960 = 100*)

	USA	USSR
1960	100	9
1965	251	32

The Soviet Union is often a borrower of technology rather than an innovator, and in recent years it has been more and more ready to encourage foreign firms to come in and build modern plant, especially in the chemical industry. Technological co-operation is given high priority in discussions with those advanced capitalist countries with which the USSR has succeeded in improving relations. The Soviet moon vehicle *Lunokhod I* which travelled on the moon's surface in November 1970 incorporated some French equipment. Also in 1970 the Soviet Ministry of Iron and Steel agreed on a plan of joint research with a Swedish group into the development of special tube steels. The USA is more of an innovator and less of a borrower, although her techno-logical advance is greatly aided by imported brains. Commercial com-petition and trade secrecy hamper technological co-operation, even with allied countries, for American multi-national companies rely upon their technological lead to compete with native firms.

The USSR, because of its present relatively backward position, has more opportunity to make technological growth in the future. Because science plays a more important part in its educational system, and because the number of scientists, engineers and technicians in its population is far greater than in the USA, it would seem to stand the better chance to move ahead of that country into new realms of technological progress, if the rigidities and bottlenecks of the bureaucratic system of state con-trol could be removed. It is very difficult to get a new idea or invention adopted in the USSR. Thus in 1962 the Byelorussian Institute of Heat Exchange developed a greatly improved method for the high-speed, non-oxidising heating of metals. But 'as a result of red tape and argu-ments about who should finance research and application' the new method was not introduced until 1969.[21] As in tsarist times ideas originating in Russia have been taken over and developed in Western countries, especially in the United States.[22]

Whatever the future, the technological race means that, in each superpower, a vast proportion of the richest natural resources, and of the best human brains and skills, will be devoted to spheres of activity which do little or nothing to alleviate the problems of poverty and deprivation which, in differing degrees, afflict a large proportion of the population in both. In neither have the people at large had any say in the choice between technological and sociological advance.

MANAGEMENT

Management is often treated as a factor of production because it directs the inter-relationship between labour and capital. Although theoretically management is part of 'labour', the gulf between management and (the rest of) labour is so great that they are often regarded as the 'two sides' of industry, and hostile, conflicting sides at that.[23]

American managers differ markedly from their Soviet counterparts in background and training. They are more often the sons of middle- or upper-class families, they have little or no shop floor experience and often no knowledge of the 'working class'. Increasingly they are college graduates, but whether they have studied 'business administration' at college or not, their training is most often in personnel management, sales technique or finance. They are often accountants. In the USSR managers in industry are almost always college graduates in engineering.[24] Only recently has it been recognised that they need specialist training for their job.

In the USA industrial management has to compete for brains with the better-paid professions and services – with medicine, law, advertising, finance and commerce. This wide array of alternatives may account for American complaints that there is an inhibiting shortage of good managerial talent. In the USSR highly paid competition for brains is narrower and comes only from education, science and the Party.[25]

The managers of the two countries, in their training and experience, become proficient in different ways which reflect differences in the two economies and societies. The Russian manager fully understands the technical and production side of his firm, and he soon acquires experience in procurement; but marketing and finance are foreign to him. Yet it is these two aspects of business that come first in the American manager's priorities, and he probably relies wholly upon others for technological information. Both groups, however, are 'organisation men' in that their whole lives are closely bound up with the firms for which they work. In the USSR the manager 'is inured and sagaciously adapted to the directive system', and in both societies 'he surrenders to organisation because organisation does more for him than he can do for himself'. For 'organisations seem to develop "organisation man" types, whether the organisation happens to be communist or capitalist'.[26]

The pressures on the managers of both countries are great: 'in both countries it is a career accompanied by long hours and a high ulcer rate'.[27] But the pressures are probably greater in the Soviet Union because, there, not only are the consequences of failure more drastic but the manager is exposed to the vigilant observation of numerous individuals and institutions who are encouraged to keep an eye upon his performance, and to report and publicise his shortcomings. By contrast, the American manager works in relative privacy as far as government official, private consumer, newspaper editor and ordinary worker are concerned. The nature of their problem differs. Pushing up sales and dealing with the unions are the chief worries for American management; procurement of supplies and holding on to scarce labour in conditions of full employment are the real problems of the Soviet manager.

In both societies the managerial class is relatively well off financially. Although Soviet managers' salaries are closer to the wages of the workers whose activities they direct, they are able to earn large incentive bonuses. These may amount to over half of their basic income in heavy industry and to a quarter of it in light industry.[28] The American manager – unless he is also a director or stockowner – relies more completely on his salary.

In both economies the divorce between ownership and management means that managers may sometimes have interests of their own which conflict with those of the formal owners. In the USA the stockholders, who are the owners, want maximum dividends; in the USSR the state, which is the owner, requires the maximum production consistent with maintenance of quality. However, in each case, management tends to regard the enterprise as its own and to resent intrusion. In the USA, where the shareholders are normally passive and the political climate is against government interference, management has much less of a problem in this respect than in the USSR, where the glare of unwelcome publicity may come from many directions. The Russian executive is uneasily aware that

any government official can at any time demand to examine any aspect of the firm's operations he wishes to, that at any time he can be called on the carpet by the local party boss to explain a charge made by an irate customer, that any member of his staff (perhaps bucking for his job) can write a letter to *Pravda* exposing him for having made an irregular deal on some supplies, that any scatter-

brained worker who wants to 'get his picture in the papers' can rise
at a public meeting that the director is obliged to attend, and compel
the director to explain why he hasn't yet installed the new assembly
line.[29]

Although legislation in the USA is continually expanding the sphere
of government activity, and firms have to yield more and more information about their activities, they remain 'private' and very little is
known about their internal affairs. Blanks in published American industrial production statistics abound to the chagrin of the research worker,
and are footnoted as 'withheld to avoid disclosing individual company
confidential data'. The Liberman reforms in the USSR have gone some
way to give the Soviet manager more control over the planning of his
production, but he remains mercilessly exposed to investigation and
inquisition.

The Soviet manager tries to protect himself against such prying into
his firm's affairs by seeking the co-operation of those whose business it is
to watch him. These include the firm's accountant, who is independent
of the management, the local Party secretary, the officials of the
Ministry of Finance, of the State Bank, of the planning organisation, of
the statistical bureau, and of his own ministry, the trade union chairman
and the local newspaper editor. As they are local people and are as
interested as he is in making a good impression upon their superiors, this
co-operation may be forthcoming.[30]

In both countries the motives in resisting outside control may include
the desire for greater security and greater financial rewards. In the
USA the corporation executives 'even if they own a large block of stock,
can serve their own pockets better by profits at the expense of the company than by making profits for it'.[31] In the USSR the large bonuses,
although intended to increase efficiency and production, lead instead
to practices inimical to the interests of the state. In order to fulfil the
plan and thus earn his bonus the Soviet manager may resort to a variety
of expedients, evasions and illegal acts. A planned economy is utterly
dependent upon an upward flow of accurate information, yet the
temptation for the Soviet executive to falsify and mislead is very strong.
He may underestimate his plant's productive capacity in the hope that
his target will be set the lower. Production figures can also be falsified
by borrowing from the next month, or the target can be met by
sacrificing quality and the needs of the consumer, and turning out
useless 'plan fodder'.

Another form of insurance which, though in the Soviet manager's
own interest, is against that of the state, is the over-ordering of supplies
or their diversion to his firm by irregular means. Procurement is the

Soviet manager's greatest problem because almost everything is scarce and quality needs careful watching. But a factory manager who succeeds in getting more than he needs dislocates the economy because it happens at someone else's expense. The practice of employing *tolkachi* or travelling buyers who, operating outside the official system, use their valuable knowledge of the supply situation to oblige their patrons, likewise could play havoc with orderly planning, if at all widespread.[32]

The Soviet executive, in order to reach his target and thereby earn his bonus, may be tempted to misappropriate funds, to the detriment of the overall objectives of the state. Thus he may be tempted to raid the workers' housing fund or materials allocated for domestic housing, in order to build an extension to his factory so as to increase output. To do this he would have to rely upon *semyestvennost* or the 'family togetherness' of the local bigwigs to see him through.[33]

Because the Soviet system encourages exposure and criticism of its executives from all quarters in order to reinforce the socialist ethic and state law, the pathology of the Soviet economy tends to loom large in the Soviet press and likewise in foreign appraisals based upon this source. In the absence of reliable data it is impossible to say whether it looms too large, although this seems probable. One must also beware of assuming that there are no shady expedients, clever evasions and illegal acts in American management, because of lack of publicity about them: 'large sectors of the enterprise's internal operations are protected from the eyes of curious outsiders'.[34] There are obviously cases in which the management acts in its own rather than in the stockholders' interest, as when it fails to liquidate parts of the business which are unprofitable, or uses profits for expansion regardless of likely profitability, in order to feel the satisfaction of growth. Illegality and irregularity are probably less frequent in America than in Russia because there are far fewer laws and rules affecting the enterprise to be broken.[35]

Perhaps the most important result of the different positions in which they find themselves is that, with his greater privacy of operation and security of tenure, the American executive can plan well ahead. His Russian counterpart has his attention constantly focused on the end of the month and the end of the year. Immediate success is imperative, even though it may not be to the ultimate benefit of the concern. He knows that at any time his own failure or another's intrigue could bring about his dismissal, so he tends to live for the present. This again may paint too dark a picture, but it seems likely that 'bonuses, promotions and demotions all follow one another too quickly to allow any but the most secure or idealistic Soviet manager to give full weight to the long-run implications of his decisions'.[36]

9 Agriculture

Agriculture consists of the application of labour and capital to land in order to produce human and animal foodstuffs and industrial raw materials. How this is done depends upon the organisation of agriculture and especially upon how policy decisions are made and by whom.

POLICY AND ORGANISATION

There is an immense difference between the agricultural policy-making and organisation of the two superpowers. In the United States there are some three million farmers (owners, partners and tenants) who, although they are mostly organised in co-operatives for purposes of marketing their produce and buying their supplies, make individual policy decisions about farming. In the Soviet Union, on the other hand, there is but one major policy-making authority – the Communist party working through the ministry of agriculture and down through the Republican, regional and local executives to the managers of the state and collective farms.

There are qualifications to be made to these general statements. Policy decisions by American farmers are influenced by government price supports, acreage quotas and the state of the market. Big agricultural corporations play an increasing role in some regions. These buy or rent farmland over as extensive an area as possible and, following the onset of spring, move up from the south across the country with their machines and gangs of hired labour, for ploughing and sowing; in the fall they do the same for harvesting. Large vertically-integrated companies often engage in the whole agricultural process, from production of machinery and fertilisers to the marketing of the crop.

On the other hand, there is an important private sector in Soviet agriculture. Besides the 12,000 state farms (average size, 60,000 acres – the average size of the American farm is 369 acres) and the 36,000 collective farms (average size, 15,000 acres), there are the smallholdings belonging to the individual farm households. These average little more than an acre, but there are nearly fifteen million of them and they produce thirteen per cent by value of market produce. Their small size, however, limits their scope to the production of vegetables, poultry and eggs, although the peasants often contrive to keep cattle and pigs as well.

The motivation of agricultural policy is quite different in the two countries. In America agricultural policy is controlled by the market, by profitability, by the conditions of world trade, subsidies, prices and surpluses. In Russia it is governed by the state's determination to be self-sufficient, by communist doctrine, and by the ever-pressing demand from a population increasing rapidly in numbers and purchasing power for more food. In the case of the individual farmers, the motivation in America is one of high incentive and a high degree of personal interest, although the 'sidewalk farmer', who has rented his land to a corporation and lives in the town, no longer has much interest in his farm as such. In the USSR, except on the private plots, interest is low. The bureaucratic system of control over every aspect of the farmer's work inevitably stifles it, and for this reason the collectives have been encouraged recently to do more planning on their own account.

LABOUR

Agricultural policy is put into effect through the application of capital equipment to land by means of labour. Here again the contrast between the USA and the USSR is great. The farm population of the former in 1970 was only ten million or a mere five per cent of the total, while in the Soviet Union it numbered forty-eight million or twenty per cent of the total. In each case there has been a rapid decline over the past few decades. If the numbers actually working on the land are taken the difference is yet greater – about two and a half million in the USA and forty million in the USSR. For whereas in America farm work is largely confined to able-bodied males, in the USSR it is the lot of most of the farm population, men and women, young and old. It has even been suggested that at times of extreme urgency – at harvest time, for instance – the number actually working on Soviet farms may double from forty million to eighty million, the extra reserves coming from the towns, universities and colleges, and from the army.[1]

One reason for the much greater farm population in the USSR is the fact that the towns, though expanding rapidly, cannot absorb any more newcomers from the countryside than they are already doing. There is, for instance, a greater farm population in White Russia than would be justified by modern agricultural practice, yet the Republic's towns cannot take any more migrants from the countryside. It is, however, unlikely that the Soviet farm labour force could ever be reduced to the American level because the long harsh winter necessitates the concentration of agricultural tasks within a short period. This requires a larger total labour force than if work could be more evenly spread over the whole year, as in much of the United States. In some areas of the USA, however, notably in the fruit-growing districts of Florida and California, work is also concentrated heavily in a peak period, and the resulting temporary and seasonal demand for extra labour is met both by internal migration and by immigration from Mexico and the West Indies.

It is because so much labour, though needed in the brief summer, remains idle throughout the winter that Soviet policy has been to amalgamate collective farms (*kolkhozy*) into single giant units. In 1938 there were about 250,000 with an average size of 1,000 acres, nearly three times the size of the average American farm. There are now only 36,000 with an average area of 15,000 acres. As the farms have been combined into larger units, so one village becomes the administrative centre while the others are left to decay. The idea is that this one centre should develop into a small town, an *agrogorodok*, with modern housing, schools, theatres, hospitals and all urban amenities. With the population so concentrated, factories can be built to employ the farm population during the winter. This process has already begun on a large scale in Orel *oblast* or county, south of Moscow. The existing villages, 4,168 in number, are to be replaced by 960 larger centres over the next fifteen years.[2] A new *agrogorodok* has been built in the Kirov collective farm in Moscow *oblast*. It is connected by new surfaced roads to the nearest town, to a railway station and to the various parts of the far-flung *kolkhoz*. It has a rope works and is developing other industries.[3] The new rural industries will be mainly food-processing and other light industries working up the local farm produce. This is a return to a pre-revolutionary practice that prevailed for much the same climatic reason. In 1914 seventy per cent of all factory workers were outside the towns and a contemporary writer wrote that 'Russian capitalism goes from the town to the country, and there builds its palatial factories besides the humble *izba* of the *mujik*'.[4]

The farm labour forces of the two states differ greatly in composition by sex and age. In America farm workers are mostly male, though there has been a rise recently in the amount of female labour, which at peak periods may account for a third of the total. These women are, however, usually migrant or seasonal workers, and the female share of the permanent labour force is small. In the USSR, on the other hand, mainly as a result of the decimation of the male population during the war, farm workers are predominantly female: sixty-five per cent in 1950 and sixty per cent in 1962. The situation is moving towards a more even balance.

Turning to age, there is a strong tendency in the USSR for the young to migrate, leaving the aged behind on the farms. Thus a quarter of the labour force is probably now composed of old-age pensioners. The extent of the flight of the middle or 'able-bodied' age group (men of 16–59 and women of 16–54) in some areas is shown by the figures for able-bodied farm workers in Pskov *oblast*: there were 200,000 in 1957 but only 110,000 in 1964.[5] In America, on the other hand, it is the older man who retires to the town, after selling his farm, handing it over to his sons or renting it to a corporation. There has, however, been a progressive but less pronounced ageing of the farm operators in the United States, the average age rising from forty-eight in 1940 to fifty-one in 1960.[6] But this slow advance of the age of the farmers is offset by the youthful nature of much of the hired labour, in which students and young immigrants are prominent.

It is not easy to distinguish the quality of labour in the two countries, because there are so many unmeasurable factors and regional variations. In health and strength the older sector of the Soviet farm population has inevitably suffered from the stresses and deprivations of living through periods of war, revolution, terror and famine, but in formal education and innate skills there is no reason to think that the average Russian would lag behind the average American. The illiterate, superstitious *muzhik* characteristic of old Russia has almost disappeared and his place has been taken by a farm worker who has been to school, is familiar with machinery, and aware of the world around him to some extent through his television set. But whereas the American farmer, living in a highly competitive world, is compelled to be not only a good businessman, but also knowledgeable and up-to-date in such matters as machinery, fertilisers, new breeds and varieties, the Soviet farmer has little initiative in these matters. The thinking is done for him and the decisions taken elsewhere.

Although the American farmer enjoys greater freedom, his material rewards are not so much greater as might be expected. The big money is made by the large corporations and amalgamated farms, not by the small family farmer whose returns are often pitifully low and who is often saddled with heavy mortgage payments. In the American South much of the farm population is Negro, with an income well below that of neighbouring whites. The gap is widening, and according to a recent report 'the outlook is for little if any improvement in the poverty level of Negroes'.[7] The prospect for the Soviet peasant is more hopeful. Collective farmers have had notoriously low incomes in the past but these are now moving upwards.

Until 1965 *kolkhozniki* were paid on the basis of the amount of work done, calculated as 'labour days', and payment was made – in cash or in kind – after the harvest. In 1966 a system of guaranteed minimum wages, paid monthly, was introduced, funds being advanced where necessary by the state bank. The *kolkhoznik* also has income in kind from his private allotment and, when he is able to sell his produce in an urban market, in money also; in America many farm workers supplement their wages from other jobs. Rural poverty in the United States is particularly severe among migrant farm labour. An increasing part of the American farm labour force is migratory, and recruited for movement across the country with the ploughing, sowing or harvesting. Labourers travel distances of up to two thousand miles during the year, from their first to their last work location, living while away from home – if any – in labour camps.[8] They are often accompanied by women and children and their low wages result in real hardship.

Regional differences are great in both countries. In America only in the large highly-capitalised farms are returns high; in many types of farm in many parts of the country very little is left for the farmer himself after he has paid all his expenses. There are also considerable differences in collective farm income between different parts of the USSR. Incomes are very low on the overcrowded marginal lands of western and northern Russia and even in parts of the Ukraine, but they are high in the Far East and on the irrigated cotton-growing areas of Central Asia. High returns from this type of land are a feature common to both the USA and the USSR.

Nevertheless, there can be little doubt that at present the average material level of living is higher on the American farm. But many American farmsteads suffer from the isolation imposed by past methods of land division whereby, over much of the country, the land was granted in blocks, each of which originally constituted a separate farm with its own isolated homestead. Despite modern communications, the loneliness of living apart in this way constitutes a real hardship to many people and has undoubtedly been a cause of rural depopulation. Russian farmers, on the other hand, live in large villages where mutual comfort and consolation and an intense degree of social intercourse is part and parcel of everyday life. The many communal institutions provided increasingly on the collective farms – clubs, schools, kindergartens, etc., are another aspect of Soviet rural life. How Russians value the intimate society of the village was shown in the years immediately before the Revolution when the Russian statesman, Stolypin, attempted to set up a class of independent freehold farmers on the American pattern. This was done in the belief that they would provide a bulwark against the subversion and discontent that flourished in the communally organised villages. Peasants were encouraged to consolidate their scattered holdings into compact farms and to build their own separate isolated farmhouses thereupon. Opposition to the scheme was strong, especially among the women, who were unwilling to forgo the social life of the village for the loneliness of the homestead.[9]

CAPITAL

The capital of agriculture consists of the existing stocks of machinery, feeding stuffs, fertilisers, fuel, livestock and other commodities present on the land, and the buildings in which they are housed. This capital is being constantly depleted by use and depreciation, but also replenished by capital inputs and by investment in agriculture.

Here, as so often, the standard comparison applies: the American stock of capital is greater than the Russian, but the latter is increasing at a faster rate. This can be seen in regard to the most important aspect of capital investment, farm machinery (Table 9.1). Sufficient machinery

TABLE 9.1   SIZE OF THE MACHINERY PARK 1950–69[10]
(thousands)

	USA		USSR	
	1950	1969	1950	1969
Tractors	3,394	4,810	595	1,908
Combines	714	850	211	605
Trucks	2,207	3,160	283	1,153

in good repair is vital to the progress of Soviet agriculture. Because the growing season is short there is little margin for safety. The ability to sow or harvest a crop with the maximum possible speed can make a great difference in yield in Soviet climatic conditions. Khrushchev's placing of the emphasis in capital investment on fertiliser production and other costly programmes at the expense of machinery has been criticised by experts as an important factor in slowing down the progress of Soviet agriculture in recent years. There is evidence that much machinery is not available to Soviet farmers for lack of repair facilities. This is a situation also ascribable to Khrushchev who in 1958 disbanded the specialist machine tractor stations, handing the machinery over to the collective farmers who were often not equipped to maintain it.

Soviet expenditure on agriculture has expanded much more rapidly than American, especially when allowance is made for monetary inflation in the USA (Table 9.2). In relation to total national investment, spending on agriculture in the USSR amounts to about eighteen per cent of the whole as against a mere five per cent in the USA. There can

TABLE 9.2   INVESTMENT IN AGRICULTURE 1950–69[11]
(billions of dollars or roubles)

	USA	USSR
1950	4·8	1·6
1960	4·6	4·9
1965	7·9	8·7
1969	9·4	11·9

be little doubt that Soviet agriculture is the most expensive in the world, and a high price has to be paid for the determination to feed 250 million people from the country's own resources, despite a natural environment mostly hostile to farming.

NATURAL RESOURCES FOR AGRICULTURE

To produce crops and livestock derivatives, agricultural labour and capital have to work with the natural conditions of warmth, moisture and soil. The relative position in regard to these has already been considered in Chapter 5. The effect of the USSR's poorer endowment in resources for agriculture has been summed up as follows by Field: 'given equal technology and capital inputs the Soviet Union can never hope to achieve . . . an average level of productivity from its cropland resource approaching that of the United States'.[12] Attention here will be confined to man's attempts to exploit and improve these resources.

Warmth and sunshine

Lying, except for Alaska, wholly south of the fiftieth parallel, the United States, seldom finds lack of warmth and sunshine a prohibiting factor. On the other hand, a great extent of the USSR has insufficient warmth for any kind of agriculture, and often, where there is enough statistically, late spring and early autumn frosts prevent its practical use. However, in some parts of the Soviet North there are large urban populations with difficult communications with the rest of the country, and great effort and expense are devoted to providing them with fresh vegetables and dairy produce by artificially heating the air in hot-houses and the soil by means of electrodes in the ground. Buildings to accommodate livestock indoors are also part of the equipment of the northern state farms attached to such centres as the Arctic mining town of Norilsk and the saw-milling town of Igarka. Much research has been devoted to finding frost-resistant varieties of plants and varieties with short growing seasons so that the limits of agriculture can be extended.

Moisture

Man can correct moisture deficiency by works of irrigation, and moisture surplus by drainage. In both of these ameliorating activities the United States leads, although rapid progress has been made in the Soviet Union, especially under the 1966–70 five-year plan. In America there are nearly seventeen million hectares of irrigated land compared with twelve million in the Soviet Union. These figures are not, however,

F

strictly comparable: nearly half the American total is made up of supplementary sprinkler irrigation whereas the Soviet total is mostly canal irrigation and confined to arid lands. Only about sixty per cent of American irrigation is in the arid districts of the west. Hitherto, most Soviet irrigated land has been devoted to cotton and fruit, but the present extension is being applied to rice, and several new state farms have been established for the growth of this crop on newly-levelled and irrigated lands. The Soviet Army has played a large part in the necessary levelling and other preparatory work for this rice-growing campaign. In 1970 the USSR grew over a million tons of rice, mostly from newly-irrigated lands along the lower Dnieper, Volga, Kuban and Amu Darya rivers and in the arid lands of Kazkhstan. In 1960 the harvest was only 190,000 tons. The United States harvested a record total of four million tons of rice in 1967, about half from naturally-watered land in Arkansas and Louisiana and about half from irrigated land in California and Texas.

In drainage the United States is far ahead with nearly seventy million hectares of artificially drained land. In Russia there were only about six million hectares drained by the time of the Revolution, to which the Soviets had added another twelve million by 1970. Again there is a difference in the nature and scale. Most American drainage has been done by private farmers to improve land which was not entirely useless. The new Soviet drainage schemes, involving huge capital expenditure by the state, are designed to drain previously unusable marshes, such as those of the Povolzhe and the Meshchera, and convert them into dairy farms and market gardens.

An unwelcome form of moisture that does much damage to crops is hail. The Soviet Union claims to have gone a long way to defeat this crop-flattening menace with its anti-hail service. Clouds likely to precipitate hail are detected by radar and then seeded with lead iodide and other agents discharged into them by rocket missiles. It has been asserted that hail damage has been reduced by two-thirds. Hail does serious harm also to the crops of the United States, where insurance against it forms an additional expense. Three States – North Dakota, Colorado and Montana – have hail departments which also provide insurance. Losses paid by insurance, which amounted to $81 million in 1962 – a bad year – cover only a fraction of the actual damage sustained.[13]

Soil

Soil is being constantly formed by natural processes but cultivation methods often lead to its loss by erosion and to the depletion of its fertility. Massive use of artificial fertilisers is the modern remedy, and

whatever the long-term results of this upon soil structure and the nutri-
tional value of the resulting food production, artificial fertilisation,
correctly applied, certainly results in extraordinary increases in yield.
In its use the United States has been a pioneer and the Soviet Union
a laggard, but the great fertiliser drive instituted by Khrushchev has
enabled Russia to overtake America in the amount applied (Table 9.3).
But there remains a big gap between the American situation, with
numerous varieties of well-packed high-grade fertiliser, available when
and as wanted, and that existing in Russia where the product is seldom

TABLE 9.3   CONSUMPTION OF ARTIFICIAL FERTILISERS 1950–70[14]
(millions of tons)

	USA	USSR
1950	20	5
1960	24	11
1965	33	31
1970	38*	55

* 1969.

properly stored or transported: there are vast losses from exposure to
the weather, and the farmers have little say in when they will receive
fertiliser, how much they will get and of what kind. Nevertheless, the
results of the Soviet fertiliser drive, though not commensurate with the
physical increase in production, are already improving yields, notably
of cotton.

THE AREA OF CROPLAND

The size of the cultivated area and the numbers of livestock are obvious
factors in productivity, and greater quantities can compensate for lower
yields, and vice versa. Over the last twenty years the American cropland, once larger than the Russian, has declined in area while the
Soviet has increased to become considerably more extensive. The
American acreage reached its peak in 1944 (162 million hectares) as a
result of wartime demand for agricultural products. It has declined

TABLE 9.4   AREA OF CROPLAND 1950–69[15]
(millions of hectares)

	USA	USSR
1950	155·4	146·3
1960	142·4	203·0
1969	121·6	208·6

since mainly because agricultural surpluses have depressed prices and
much marginal land has gone out of cultivation, but also because of
urban expansion and opencast (strip) mining.[16] The Soviet cropland

area reached a maximum of 218·5 million hectares in 1963 as a result
of Khrushchev's great campaign to plough up the semi-arid 'virgin and
idle lands' of southern Siberia and northern Kazakhstan. Between sixty
and seventy million more hectares were ploughed up in ten years, bringing
the Russian total from somewhat less than the American to its present
level of over fifty per cent higher.

CROP PRODUCTION

In both countries about half the sown area is devoted to grain, but
whereas in 1968 the United States produced 228 million tons from
64 million hectares, the Soviet Union harvested only 170 million tons
from 122 million hectares. Because of climatic unreliability there is a
much greater variation in the Soviet total from year to year. In 1963 it
was only 107 million tons and in 1965 only 121 million; but in 1966 it
was 171 million and in 1970 the record total of 186 million tons was
claimed. Some Western experts do not accept the Soviet figures and
give considerably lower estimates. There is a considerable difference in
the composition of the grain harvest of the two states. Well over half the
American total is made up of maize (corn), whereas a similar proportion
of the Russian production is of wheat. Barley and rye are more important in the USSR, oats and grain sorghum in the USA (Table 9.5).

TABLE 9.5   COMPOSITION OF THE GRAIN CROP 1967[17]
(*percentages*)

USA		USSR	
Maize	59	Wheat	52
Wheat	19	Barley	17
Oats	8	Rye	9
Grain sorghum	7	Oats	8
Barley	4	Maize	6
Rice	2	Millet	2
Rye	1	Buckwheat	1
		Rice	1
		Others	4

In non-grain crops the preponderance of Soviet production is overwhelming in potatoes and sugar beet, but the United States is able to
grow sugar cane on the Gulf coast and in Florida. Sugar beet production
is one of the most successful branches of Soviet agriculture. With the
shift of grain growing to the newly-ploughed lands of northern
Kazakhstan, much good land in the Ukraine became available for this
crop. Between 1950 and 1960 the sown area doubled from 1·3 million
hectares to 3 million, and production rose from 21 million tons to
58 million. Production in 1968 was 94 million tons, compared with an

TABLE 9.6 PRODUCTION OF CROPS 1969[18]
(*millions of tons*)

	USA	USSR
All grain	202	162
Wheat	40	80
Maize	116	12
Barley	8	25*
Oats	14	12*
Rye	1	11
Grain sorghum	19	0
Rice	4	1
Millet	0	3
Potatoes	13	92
Vegetables	19	19
Cotton	2	2
Sugar beet	24	71
Sugar cane	20	0
Soya beans	30	1
Sunflower seeds	0	6
Hay and green fodder	114	89*

* 1967.

American total of 22 million tons. The yield per hectare is still higher, however, in the United States (Table 9.6).

Cotton is another crop in which Soviet agriculture has had some success, catching up with the United States, so long the world's leading producer (Table 9.7). American cotton production reached its peak (4·3 million tons) as long ago as 1926, and since then has oscillated, but with more downs than ups. In yield per hectare the USSR also claims first place.

TABLE 9.7 COTTON LINT PRODUCTION 1950–69[19]
(*millions of short tons*)

	USA	USSR
1955	3·53	1·47
1960	3·43	1·64
1967	1·70	2·25
1968	2·63	2·26
1969	2·16	2·16
1970		2·61

LIVESTOCK

In quantities of livestock the main difference is the larger number of cows and sheep in the USSR, a result in the main of rapid shrinkage of the American herd (Table 9.8). The number of milch cows in the USA dropped from twenty million to fifteen million between 1960 and 1968, and the number of sheep from twenty-nine million to nineteen million. American sheep farmers have been making heavy losses in recent years. But livestock are more productive in America, as can be seen by

TABLE 9.8   NUMBER OF LIVESTOCK 1970
(*millions*)

	USA	USSR
Cattle	112·3	95·2
Milk cows	13·4	40·5
Sheep	17·6	130·7
Pigs	56·7	56·1
Poultry	438·7*	590·3

* Chickens and turkeys only.

relating the production of livestock products (Table 9.9) to the numbers given in Table 9.8. Meat is the main livestock product in America, while dairy produce is more important in Russia.

AGRICULTURE AND IDEOLOGY

In neither superpower is agriculture healthy, and its sickness in each case is to a great extent attributable to ideological causes.[20] In both countries, if economic and technical considerations alone were taken into account, the agricultural problem might well be solved, but so strong is the belief that agriculture should have a certain type of structure, that this form of organisation is persisted in and subsidised, at great cost but with continuing failure.

TABLE 9.9   LIVESTOCK PRODUCTS 1969
(*millions of tons*)

	USA	USSR
Meat	15·9	11·8
Milk	52·3	81·5
Butter	0·5	1·2*
Cheese	0·9	0·4*
Eggs	68·9	37·2

* 1967.

In America the trouble lies in the romantic belief that the small, independent, individualistic farmer is an essential and desirable part of the American way of life, and that his survival must be safeguarded. President Eisenhower expressed this feeling when he said, 'in America agriculture is more than an industry; it is a way of life. Throughout our history the family farm has given strength and vitality to our entire social order. We must keep it healthy and vigorous.' Such sentiments are strengthened by the fact that so many Americans, even though they live in cities, are the sons and grandsons of farmers, and have a nostalgic and sympathetic attitude towards them.[21] Aided by the fact that in many States the electoral districts are so demarcated as to favour the rural voter, large subsidies to agriculture have become a regular feature of the United States budget. But these payments fail to rescue the small, individual farmer from penury and debt: his basic problem is low prices caused by huge surpluses. Instead such money benefits the large, highly capitalised and often company-run farm, enabling it to invest further in fertilisers and machinery, thus swelling yields. These increased yields have the effect that, although the subsidies to agriculture are often made conditional upon reducing acreage, the total production continues to rise, even though it comes from smaller areas. Consequently surpluses grow and prices continue depressed below the level at which the small family farmer can prosper.

In the Soviet Union, where the problem is insufficiency rather than overabundance, the doctrinaire insistence on the collective farm, i.e. upon a communistic agricultural structure, prevents farmers from working wholeheartedly and efficiently to raise production because it does not give enough play to individual interest and initiative. And just as the glorified but scarcely viable small American family farmer is undermined by the larger, corporate and highly-capitalised unit, so the Soviet collective farm is undermined by the coexisting system of private allotments, to which the collective farmers devote much of their zeal.

CONCLUSION

A comparative study has been made of agriculture in those parts of the USA and USSR which have a certain similarity in climate and soil.[22] In these comparable areas it appears that the United States has more fallow and more natural pasture but a smaller proportion in crops. There is more diversity in the Soviet crop pattern, with a greater emphasis on industrial crops such as sunflowers and sugar beet and, of course, much less maize (corn). There are more livestock in the USSR. In the USA the emphasis is mainly on beef cattle, except in the forested north, where dairying becomes more significant. In the USSR dairying is prominent in all the compared regions.

As one proceeds from the more arid to the moister lands in the United States there is a pronounced increase in fodder crops, because of the economic attraction of rearing beef cattle where conditions permit, but in the USSR it is the industrial crops that increase with the same progression from arid steppe to forest region. Yields behave in a rather peculiar fashion. In the drier lands they are comparable, but as one moves into areas with a positive moisture balance, they increase much faster in America than in the Soviet Union; thus, in the needleleaf forest belt, average yields of oats are four times as great in the American region and the average milk yield is half as big again as the Russian. The reason for this probably lies in the fact that in the cooler, moister parts

of the United States there has been a flight from the land, leaving only
the best and most productive lands in cultivation. In Russia, however,
although some land has gone out of cultivation in the *tayga* forest and
northern mixed forest zone, a much larger proportion of the cultivated
land is poor and marginal, reducing the average yields.

In view of the adverse natural conditions against which it has to
struggle, the productivity of Soviet agriculture seems remarkable, the
volume of production falling not so far short of that in the more favoured
United States. The reason for this lies partly in the fact that American
agriculture is restrained from reaching its full capacity by several
factors: food surpluses, high costs, foreign competition, quotas and
restrictions, the flight of men – and women – from the land. Without
government support to the tune of $4 or $5 billion a year, it would
contract to a far greater extent than it already has done. In 1968
American agriculture recouped only seventy-three per cent of its costs,
government deficiency payments and subsidies making up the balance.
Soviet agriculture is even more heavily subsidised, in order to reach
national self-sufficiency in food for a population of 250 million in a predominantly cool northerly country. Contributions from the state budget
rose from a total of thirty-five billion roubles in the ten years 1946–55
to sixty-two billion in 1956–65. In the 1971–5 five-year plan the amount
is set at 129 billion roubles compared with seventy-one billion in
1966–70.[23]

Despite the reforms instituted in agriculture in 1965, Brezhnev's
speech at the plenary meeting of the Party's central committee in
November 1968 made it clear that all was still not well with Soviet
agriculture. Much progress in yields and production had been made in
some areas but various shortcomings remained, and the goals being set
for the 1966–70 five-year plan were not being reached. The reason for
this was that 'far from all collective farms are conducting their affairs in
an efficient way'. Certain regions were mentioned as failing in cereal
production. The state was providing more machinery, but sometimes to
little purpose: 'we cannot fail to draw attention to the fact that on a
number of collective and state farms poor use is still being made of
tractors, combine harvesters and other machines'.[24] The old problem of
misuse of funds, particularly in local collective farm bureaucracies
instead of in the field, was still present: 'huge resources are being ex-
pended on the upkeep of the administrative and managerial apparatus,
and extravagance is permitted in the amounts paid out to some office
workers. We can scarcely reconcile ourselves to practices of this kind.'
Most serious of all, money appropriated for agriculture was being
diverted to other uses. Brezhnev gave as examples the diversion of three
million roubles from funds intended for agriculture in Azerbaydzhan

towards building the underground railway in the Republic's capital of Baku, and 'in Moldavia, too, of the resources destined for agriculture, attempts were made to hand over 2,900,000 roubles for the reconstruction of a railway line, trying to justify this, incidentally, by the fact that the railway would be running through rural localities. A very dubious argument!'

The environmental factor should never be forgotten, however. The great bulk of Russia's cropland lies well to the north of the latitude of the United States, and much of it is of such poor quality that it would have been abandoned long ago by American farmers: 'much land now tilled is as poor as the abandoned farmland of the Appalachian mountains or the Dust Bowl in the United States'.[25] The most remarkable fact about Soviet agriculture could be that it is so productive in the face of such hostile conditions: 'when we consider the USSR's adverse natural endowment, we can see that the Soviet collective farm is not quite as inefficient as is often supposed'.[26]

The general impression that Soviet agriculture is a failure is strengthened by the attention which the leadership constantly devotes to its shortcomings. It would be much easier and cheaper for Russia to import much of her food requirement, but any such dependency on foreign trade would be fatal to the country's independence, given its landlocked position and the control of all access from the oceans by hostile powers. It is expecting a great deal from an environment comparable to that of Canada and Scandinavia that it should provide a fast-growing population of some 250 million with a well-balanced diet.

Most of the troubles of American agriculture arise from its high costs and serious dependence on the world market. The United States is the largest exporter of agricultural produce and her exports amount to one-fifth of the world total, but this high-cost industry with large surpluses has difficulty, not only in holding its foreign markets but in defending its home market. That it is enabled to do so is the result of the huge subsidy it receives from the government. Thus the American agricultural problem is quite a different one from that of the Soviet Union, but it exists none the less and is reflected in widespread rural poverty.

10 Manufacturing Industry

Industry takes various raw and unfinished materials and transforms them into manufactured goods. These are then available for further use in production (producers' or capital goods) or as consumer end products (consumers' goods). This transformation is effected with power-driven machinery, and consequently draws upon sources of energy as well as upon materials for processing. The existence of these energy sources and materials within the bounds of a state constitutes its resource base, which is made up of materials and fuels together with other sources of power, actual and potential, such as falling water, ebbing and flowing tides, winds and the sun. Fuels and raw materials are animal, vegetable or mineral. Before the industrial revolution they were almost wholly animal or vegetable, and drawn from both wild and domesticated animals, from natural and artificial vegetation, but now they are preponderantly mineral. Animal and vegetable products – hides and skins, oils and starches, fibres and timbers are, of course, still used in industry, but to a diminishing extent as substitutes of mineral origin replace them. These resources have been surveyed in Chapter 5 and it seems reasonable to conclude that the mineral resource base of the USSR, taken as a whole, in the light of its larger area and existing geological knowledge, is at least twice as extensive as that of the United States. Its narrower agricultural base is to some degree compensated for by its wider forest resource.

EXTRACTIVE OR PREPARATORY INDUSTRY

Minerals in the ground, trees in the forest, fibres on the plant are not immediately available for manufacturing. The minerals need mining, smelting or concentrating, the trees need felling and preparing, the fibres have to be separated from the plant. Since the bulk output of timber, technical crops, fuels and minerals in both countries is approximately similar, though with Soviet output rising at a faster tempo, it is likely that the volume of preparatory plant is roughly equivalent in both countries.

An industrial country is not, however, entirely dependent upon its own resource base, which can be supplemented by imports. The United States adds to its indigenous supplies of fuel and materials imports of a net value (i.e. after subtracting exports) of some $2 billion. The Soviet Union, on the other hand, produces more fuels and raw materials than its own industries can consume and, accordingly, has net exports of some $3 billion.

CAPITAL PLANT AND EQUIPMENT

Industry transforms raw and unfinished materials by the use of equipment in works and machinery in factories. This industrial plant forms on the surface of the earth the geographical expression of industry. In the absence of information about its volume within the two superpowers, that of the USSR can be estimated to be about fifty per cent of the American total. There are three important differences between the two: first, the Soviet plant is growing at a faster rate than the American; second, a greater proportion of Soviet equipment is concerned with basic, heavy industry; and third, Soviet plant is worked to full capacity while the American is chronically underemployed.

THE LABOUR FORCE

The smaller quantity of Soviet industrial plant holds a larger labour force than that of the United States. This results from several factors – the low efficiency of some sectors of Soviet industry, the less advanced techniques employed, the necessity to combat extreme weather conditions, the larger proportion of women engaged, the official absence of unemployment in the USSR, and the shorter working week. Soviet labour works shorter hours than in any other advanced industrial country, but the increased leisure resulting from the standard application of the five-day week seems to have been a mixed blessing, resulting apparently in more drunkenness rather than in more chess and museum visiting, with adverse rather than beneficial effects on productivity. Figures for the industrial labour force are given in Table 10.1. They include both mining and manufacturing. The Soviet statistics do not distinguish between them, but as it is known that almost a million people are employed in the Soviet coal-mining industry, it is likely that for mining as a whole the total is about three million – six times the

TABLE 10.1 THE INDUSTRIAL LABOUR FORCE 1969[1]
(*millions*)

	USA	USSR
Employed in industry	20·1	31·2
Engaged in production	14·7	25·1

TABLE 10.2 EMPLOYMENT BY INDUSTRY 1969[2]
(thousands)

	USA	USSR
Coal mining	136	972
Ferrous metallurgy	878	1,126
Machine-building and metal-working	7,534	8,969
Chemicals and petrochemicals	1,233	1,218
Pulp and paper	716	214
Building materials	661	1,646
Food processing	1,794	2,373
Textiles and clothing	2,405	4,204

American figure of half a million. This is an index of the extent to which American mining has been mechanised. Where comparable figures are available for individual industries they are given in Table 10.2. The rapid expansion of industry in the USSR has resulted in a chronic shortage of skilled workers, and much of the low quality or poor finish sometimes observed in Soviet manufactures comes from the use of semi-skilled labour.

INDUSTRIAL PRODUCTION

In 1969 the Soviet statistical bureau estimated that the value of Soviet industrial production in terms of that of the United States was 'about seventy per cent' compared with 'under thirty per cent' in 1950.[3] The greater rate of Soviet growth is shown in Table 10.3, from which it may be noted that this growth slowed down in the 1960s compared with the 1950s. Many Western economists do not accept the Soviet growth estimates but there is not enough evidence to prove or disprove them.

Qualitatively and technologically Soviet equipment and output are inferior to American in many branches of industry, and the range of product is much narrower:

The machine-building industry has still not been able to produce a respectable line of agricultural machines. When the time came to build plants for plastics and synthetic fibers, Soviet industry had neither the know-how, designs, equipment or materials for the job.

TABLE 10.3 GROWTH OF INDUSTRIAL PRODUCTION BY
VALUE 1950–70[4]

	(1950 = 100)			(1965 = 100)	
	USA	USSR		USA	USSR
1950	100	100	1965	100	100
1960	145	308	1966	109	109
1965	191	470	1967	110	113
1966	208	508	1968	116	129
1967	211	562	1969	121	138
1968	221	608	1970	121	149
1969	230	651			
1970	230	705			

The Soviet-built plants have experienced inordinate delays in construction and in achieving capacity output after completion. The growth of these modern chemicals has depended in large part on imported plants. The machine tool industry, which has outproduced all others in the world in the number of machine tools, is not able to equip a modern automobile plant.[5]

But, as Nove has pointed out, the assumption that poor quality is a characteristic of Soviet production 'needs to be carefully qualified', and he goes on to warn against making too much of Soviet self-criticism: 'an outburst of criticism directed at some sector is not necessarily proof that it is peculiarly defective, or that its efficiency has declined; the reason may be a decision to launch a campaign to improve it, or possibly even a desire to discredit the minister in charge'.[6] Defects in American goods get little publicity and the efforts of consumer associations are dwarfed by the great volume of laudatory advertising. However, recently the consumer movement in the United States has gathered pace, and as it makes its voice heard there is more revelation of 'things that don't work: lawnmowers that won't cut grass, or television sets that burst into flames'.[7]

In 1969, in an attempt to improve quality, the Soviets introduced the State Mark of Quality, something comparable to America's *Good Housekeeping*'s Seal of Approval. To qualify, the producer has to satisfy 'a special commission made up of experts from various branches of industry and headed, as a rule, by an eminent scientist', and the commission's decision has to be unanimous.[8] Since its introduction the mark has been awarded to over two thousand manufactured items, including turbines, diesel locomotives and engines, lorries, cranes, excavators, watches, television and wireless sets, refrigerators, textiles, articles of clothing and many foodstuffs.

ORGANISATION AND POLICY

As in agriculture, labour and capital in industry do not operate of themselves but need to be organised for production, and those at the head of organisation must formulate plans according to policies. In the United States most industrial production is in the hands of corporations or companies who use privately-subscribed capital, bank loans and withheld profits to acquire their plant and equipment. A main objective is to make a profit from which to reimburse their directors, pay salaries and wages to their labour force, finance the modernisation and expansion of their plant, and distribute interest to their creditors and dividend to their shareholders. They strive, in competition with other companies in the same field, to win government contracts by various forms of lobbying and to woo the consumer by persuasive advertising. They finance research, not only in their own establishments but also in universities and institutes. Some of them are so large that their turnover exceeds the national income of many countries. They carry out their business in their own way with little government control or interference.

The situation in Russia is, of course, very different. The state planners of Gosplan draw up a programme for a whole industry. The ministry for that industry elaborates this and allocates quotas to the various works or factories for fulfilment. Yet, despite this bureaucratic system, the local factory manager has surprising scope for initiative. He can and does concern himself, in association with the trade unions, with the feeding, housing, holidays and general welfare of his workers. He has to face the often appalling problems of finding reliable sources for the supply of materials of adequate quality, but his overriding task is to reach the planned production targets set for him.

Most Soviet industry now works under the 'new economic reform' whereby individual enterprises are encouraged to make a profit by allowing them to dispose of some of it themselves in bonuses and other benefits. This means more attention to quality, as the factory turning out the best goods is the most likely to get orders. One of the first applications of this system was in the watch-making factories of Uglich, north of Moscow. Within a few months the town became prosperous and a shortage of consumer goods in the shops soon developed; workers began to apply for permits to build their own private houses with their high earnings. The quality of the watches, previously deplorably low when the only need was to fulfil a quantitative quota, rose sharply to a level competitive with the best foreign products.

The Liberman incentive system, by raising not only the quality of the goods but also the income of the workers, has created some fresh problems. When there is more money to spend the demand for consumer goods rises and the limited supply becomes even more inadequate, resulting in discontent and public pressure for more resources to be diverted to their production. In the absence of such goods highly-paid workers turn to food, thus worsening the agricultural crisis, or to drink, thus aggravating a social problem.

DISTRIBUTION OF MANUFACTURING

Manufacturing differs from agriculture, forestry, mining and other primary industries in that it does not have to be carried on at the source of its materials. There is a choice of locations. It may be located near the source of power. When the source of power is bulky, as with coal, or difficult to transport, as with electricity, an industry is likely to locate nearby if its demands for power are heavy. In both countries the principal concentration of heavy industry is on a coalfield – the northern Appalachian coalfield in the United States and the Donbass or Ukrainian coalfield in the USSR.

As materials and fuels can both be imported, seaports make convenient industrial centres, having the added advantage that they are also favourably placed for exports. The landlocked 'heartland' position of the USSR militates against this type of location. Nevertheless, Russia has in Leningrad one major seaport industrial centre with other large concentrations at Riga, Odessa and Rostov. However, if the first twelve Soviet manufacturing cities are taken, Leningrad is the only seaport among them. But in the United States most of the large industrial centres are at seaports or at Great Lakes ports connected with the sea.

Other possible locations for manufacturing are where skilled labour is available and at the point of demand for the product. These tend to overlap because large concentrations of population will normally possess both accumulations of skilled labour and high potential demand. The environmental factor plays an increasingly important part here. The more skilled the labour the more difficult it is to compel it to move: unskilled manual labour can be moved and its effort extorted under compulsion, but skill is likely to vanish in such circumstances. Because of the reluctance of skilled labour to leave the old western towns, such as Moscow, Kiev and Kharkov, for harsh and forbidding Siberian surroundings, the Soviets have had to perpetuate the concentration of high-quality engineering industries in these older centres.[9] In the United States the congenial climates of Florida, California and Arizona have been a factor in the attraction of high-value manufacturing, since employers know that they have a better chance of attracting scarce skills to these regions.

The size and shape of a country have important bearings on industrial location. The United States is small and compact enough to allow regional specialisation, i.e. the concentration of an activity in the area economically best suited to it, with the transport of the product thence to all other parts of the country. This necessitates an efficient and pervasive transportation network, but America has fully developed this along with the rest of her economy. As a result a remarkable degree of the country's manufacturing is found in the north-east. In the Soviet Union, on the other hand, the immense size and elongated shape of the state make such specialisation economically prohibitive because of the physical strain that would be placed on the transport system and the high freight-moving costs that would be incurred. For a variety of reasons Russia's transport network has always been more skeletal than America's. Thus, in the United States, ninety per cent of steel-making capacity is concentrated within a radius of 250 miles of Pittsburgh and at Chicago, i.e. in the Great Lakes–Atlantic region of the north-east. The remaining ten per cent is scattered among nine or ten works in the south and west, most of which were built during wartime by the US government for strategic reasons. In the Soviet Union, by contrast, there is no one dominant region. Forty-two per cent of Soviet steel is made in the Donbass–Dnieper region of the Ukraine, thirty-two per cent in the Ural region a thousand miles farther north-east, and six per cent on the Kuzbass coalfield in Siberia, 1,200 miles east of the Urals.

The metal-working and machine-building industry in the United States shows almost the same degree of concentration in the north-east as the iron and steel industry, although there are important outliers on the Pacific coast. In the USSR this branch of manufacturing is more widely spread throughout Russia and along the Trans-Siberian railway in Siberia, with outliers in Central Asia and the Far East.

The large volume of military spending has a strong influence on the distribution of industry in the United States. When it is mainly spent on the needs of conventional war, as during the Korean and Vietnamese wars, it reinforces the concentration in the older established areas of the north-east and mid-west, areas where heavy ordnance and armoured vehicles are manufactured. But when it is primarily spent on so-called sophisticated weaponry (missiles, nuclear warheads, electronic devices, nuclear submarines, supersonic aircraft), as was the case in the 'cold war', the impact is felt chiefly in the newer industrial districts of the south and west as well as in parts of New England (Table 10.4).

TABLE 10.4   USA: GEOGRAPHICAL DISTRIBUTION OF
MILITARY SPENDING 1952–66[10]
(*percentage distribution*)

	Korean War (1952)	Cold War (1962)	Vietnam War (1966)
North East and Mid-West	67·4	48·9	52·4
South and West	32·6	51·1	47·6

In the USSR there is much less regional specialisation of military production. Factories seem to be allocated to individual towns rather than to individual districts, and these towns are selected according to their position in relation to labour supply, growth potential, energy availability and transport facility. Except for heavy industries like primary metallurgy and petrochemicals, very little in the way of a regional pattern emerges. In so far as there is a concentration of military industries, it would appear to be focused on the Urals, a region from which foreigners are excluded and the one over which the American U2 high-altitude photographic reconnaissance plane was shot down in 1960. There are also armament industries at Gorkiy on the Volga, and on the Donbass coalfield in the Ukraine.

Trends in the geographical location of industrial growth show a certain similarity. In both countries the fastest developing areas are generally along the southern margins. In the USA growth is greatest in the south-east; in the USSR it is fastest in the south-west, in certain areas of the southern borderland, but also in the west and along the Baltic coast. In each case more favourable climate and a greater reserve of potential labour supply in agriculture are powerful factors encouraging a southerly movement of industry.

If the absolute rather than proportionate increases in manufacturing are considered, however, in both countries, these are overwhelmingly in the older established areas – in the American north-east and in the four major industrial areas of the Soviet Union: the central (Moscow) district, the Ukraine, the Urals and West Siberia. But the dominance of these areas, although still very great, is slowly lessening. Between 1958 and 1967 the value added by manufacturing in the north-east of the United States declined from sixty-one per cent of the national total to fifty-eight per cent, but the south increased its share from twenty to twenty-three per cent.

In the USSR the dramatic increase of manufacturing in Siberia that characterised the Stalinist period of industrialisation has slowed down, and most new manufacturing is now located in the western, south-western and southern districts (Table 10.5). But resource development, especially of fuel and power, is proceeding at an accelerating rate in the eastern regions of the USSR, and growing quantities of coal, petroleum, natural gas and electric power are now moving westwards from the great Eurasian heartland to the manufacturing industries of the west (Table 10.6). This is mainly because increased capacity and improved

TABLE 10.5 USSR: SHARE OF THE EASTERN REGIONS IN THE OUTPUT OF CERTAIN MANUFACTURES 1940–69[11]
(*percentages*)

Industry	1940	1960	1969
Pig iron	28·5	40·0	37·4
Steel	32·3	43·2	42·0
Machine tools	7·1	19·9	18·5
Tractors	27·1	21·0	19·3
Synthetic fibre	—	20·4	16·5
Fertilisers	31·5	40·6	29·7
Paper	19·7	29·6	29·0

Commodity	1940	1960	1969
Coal	35·9	47·4	51·1
Petroleum	11·5	26·7	34·3
Natural gas	1·0	6·5	29·6
Electricity (capacity)	23·5	37·7	42·7

equipment in railway haulage (especially electrification), pipelines and electrical transmission have made it more feasible to shift vast quantities of power and other commodities over long distances, so that it is now less necessary to bring reluctant workers into the uncongenial Siberian environment.

IRON AND STEEL

The iron and steel industry is the basis of a country's industrialisation. Russian production of steel has risen steadily at an average of four or five million tons a year for the past twenty years, and the only interruption to the upward trend during the Soviet period was occasioned by the 1941–5 war. American production, by contrast, moves up and down according to periodic changes in civilian and military demand, though showing a general upward tendency (Table 10.7). Another important distinction is that American output is always well below capacity, whereas Soviet production runs to the limit of capacity. Soviet production of 116 million tons in 1970 was not far off the American output of 117 million tons. But the United States also has net imports amounting to about fourteen million tons, the USSR net exports of some seven million tons, so that although the production of the two countries is similar, the American consumption of steel is much greater. The USSR has all the raw materials for the industry within its borders, but the USA imports large quantities of iron ore and a wide range of ferro-alloys.

Soviet steel output contains a much larger proportion of heavier goods than the American: nearly forty per cent is made up of sections compared with just about a quarter in the USA, and the weight of castings is five times as high. On the other hand, American output of flat-rolled products is, at thirty-four per cent of the total production, double the Soviet proportion of seventeen per cent.[13] These differences are largely due to the contrasting natures of the demand. The largest consumer in the United States, taking about a fifth of the output, is the motor-car industry, but the chief users of Soviet steel are the oil and the

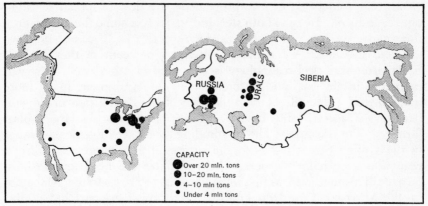

20. Integrated steel works

gas industries – for the growing network of wide-diameter pipelines – and the heavy engineering industries.

The difference in the economic systems also has its effect on the structure of the Soviet output. The setting of planned tonnage targets and the inordinate importance attached to their achievement, have meant that the steel industry, which itself has little responsibility for marketing, tends to make its products heavier than need be. On the other hand, the American industry, under commercial pressures, cannot afford to waste material and in any case has to achieve products as light as possible, consistent with strength, in order to compete with lightweight materials such as aluminium and plastics. Similar conditions affect quality and range. The American industry, to remain competitive, has to offer the widest range of high-quality steels; but the emphasis on weight in the Soviet industry militates against improvements in both quality and range.[15]

The Soviet system likewise works against the rapid adoption of technological innovations, as their introduction is likely to interrupt production. Thus, although the Soviet steel industry has pioneered various processes such as oxygen furnaces, continuous steel casting and

TABLE 10.7 PRODUCTION OF STEEL 1913–70[14]
(millions of metric tons)

	USA	USSR		USA	USSR
1913	31·2	4·3	1945	72·3	12·3
1917	44·9	3·1	1950	87·8	27·3
1921	20·1	0·2	1955	106·2	45·3
1929	55·6	4·7	1960	90·0	65·3
1932	13·9	5·9	1965	119·2	91·0
1937	51·3	17·7	1970	116·6	116·0
1940	60·8	18·3	1975		142·0*

* Planned target.

electro-slag remelting, such improvements are slow to spread through-out the industry. In 1960 both steel industries had some four per cent of their capacity in oxygen furnaces; by 1970 this had become fifty-two per cent in the USA but only twenty-two per cent in the USSR.[16] Soviet iron and steel technology is advanced in other ways, however, especially in the size and automation of the equipment in its more modern works. The fifteenth anniversary of the Revolution in November 1967 was celebrated by the opening of the world's largest blast furnace in the Ukraine.[17] The outstanding recent technological advance in the United States has been the successful application of a direct-reduction iron-making process which obviates the need for the blast furnace. This method was first introduced in 1968 at Mobile, Alabama, by the McWane Cast Iron Pipe Co.[18] Although a somewhat similar process was earlier discovered in the USSR, its inventors were not able to persuade the ministry of the ferrous metallurgical industry to develop it.

MACHINE-BUILDING AND METAL-WORKING

Most of the steel produced in each country goes into the engineering industries, the quantitative and qualitative levels of which are all-important to a nation's industrial and military stature. The normal quantitative comparison applies to most branches of this vital industry – an American lead of diminishing proportions, although the Russians now produce more machine tools. Qualitatively the situation is less clear. An American study has shown that, generally, the United States is well ahead in the application of most important technological inno-vations, for instance in the increased use of metal-forming relative to metal-working machinery and, within the field of metal-cutting, in the use of numerically (tape) controlled machine tools. Yet there are areas, such as electrical and electro-chemical methods of machining, in which the Soviet Union is ahead of the United States: 'the data bearing on the overall level of technology used in the Soviet metal-working sector relative to the US level seem to indicate a bizarre mélange of backward-ness, modernity, and in certain respects even superiority.'[19]

In the automotive industry, however, the gap is of quite abnormal size, reflecting the relative unimportance of road transport in the Soviet economy (Table 10.8). In addition, America had a net import of more than two million foreign vehicles – a number far greater in itself than the whole Russian production. Against this laggard position in motor production must be set a higher Soviet production of railway locomotives and rolling stock and of river shipping. A steep increase in the production of cars and lorries is contemplated during the 1971–5

TABLE 10.8 PRODUCTION OF MOTOR VEHICLES 1970[20]
(*thousands*)

	USA	USSR
All vehicles	8,239	916
Private cars and taxis	6,547	344
Lorries (trucks) and buses	1,692	572

plan, by the end of which car production alone is expected to be 1,200,000.

The Soviet automotive industry does not reflect the concentration of American production at one centre, Detroit. Vehicles are made at several places, some of them great distances apart. They are all over-shadowed by the large plant erected and equipped by Fiat at Tolyatti on the Volga for the manufacture of private cars, and by the giant new lorry works under construction at Chelniy on the Kama.

ALUMINIUM

The United States, with a production of well over three million tons, and the Soviet Union, with an estimated output of well over a million tons, are the world's largest producers of aluminium metal. The disparity in their consumption is larger than the difference in the quantity produced suggests, for the United States imports another one and a half million tons, mainly from Canada, whereas the Soviet Union exports about 400,000 tons of its production. Many of the uses which make aluminium such a widely-used metal in America – lorry trailer bodies, car engines, containers, wrapping materials, etc. – are of little significance in the Soviet Union. During the 1960s the aluminium smelting and fabricating industry grew very rapidly in the United States, doubling its output, but growth in Russia has been slower.

In both countries the smelters are normally located near a source of cheap and abundant electricity supply, but they are also found at points of bauxite mining or import. In the USA there are twenty-one smelters with a plant capacity of over 100,000 short tons, but only seven in the USSR, but the Soviet Union has the largest single smelter, located appropriately near the world's largest hydro-electric power station at Krasnoyarsk on the Yenisey river in Siberia (Table 10.9).[21] As the table shows, the biggest American smelters are in the north-west, where imported bauxite has to travel short distances only to the great hydro-electric power stations of the Columbia river, and near the Gulf of Mexico, where Caribbean bauxite can be conveniently brought to power generated from local natural gas. In the USSR most of the

TABLE 10.9 LARGEST ALUMINIUM SMELTERS BY CAPACITY 1968[22]
(thousands of short tons)

USA		USSR	
Bellingham, Wash.	270	Krasnoyarsk, East Siberia	276
Chalmette, La	260	Irkutsk, East Siberia	220
Hannibal, Ohio	240	Novokuznetsk, West Siberia	176
Rockdale, Texas	225	Bratsk, East Siberia	165
Mead, Wash.	206	Kamensk-Uralskiy, Urals	149
Listerhill, Ala	194	Bogoslovsk, Urals	154
Longview, Wash.	176	Volgograd, River Volga	138

biggest smelters are either near the large Siberian or Volga hydro-
electric power stations, or close to bauxite mines in the Urals.

Neither superpower is self-sufficient in aluminium ore. American
aluminium is derived wholly from bauxite, four-fifths of which is
imported. The USSR uses domestic supplies of bauxite, nepheline and
alunite as ores, but also imports bauxite and alumina (aluminium oxide
extracted from bauxite) amounting to about one-fifth of its alumina
consumption.

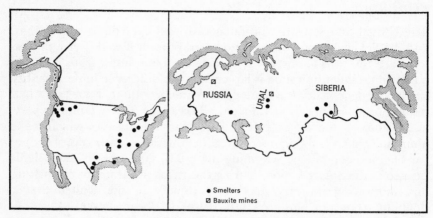

21. Aluminium smelters with capacity over 100,000 short tons

CHEMICALS

During the 1960s the emphasis of Soviet industrial investment was
shifted to the chemical industry, a backward branch of the economy
which lagged far behind the West. Production of fertilisers, plastics and
synthetic fibres was previously almost non-existent. The shift from coal
to oil, which led to a large increase in oil-refining capacity, has provided the opportunity for the expansion of the petro-chemical industry,
and complete factories have been purchased abroad. During the six
years from 1963 to 1969 the British companies, Imperial Chemical

Industries and Simon Carves, supplied and collaborated in the erection and equipment of four polythene factories which have been built at Kazan, Ufa, Polotsk and Sumgait. Even so, the Soviet Union's capacity for producing low-density polythene is estimated at only about 200,000 tons compared with almost two million tons in the USA.

Although the output of synthetic resins and plastics grows rapidly in the USSR, it continues to expand in the USA, with the result that Soviet production is normally equivalent to the American level of from fifteen to twenty years earlier. In 1968 the value of output from the Soviet chemical industry, at $15·8 billion, was well behind the $52·8 billion value of production in America.

WOOD PRODUCTS INDUSTRY

The United States demand for paper and board is stimulated by the existence of large newspapers carrying a heavy load of advertising, by an abundance of widely-read magazines of all kinds, and by the multifarious needs of the packaging industry. Such requirements in the Soviet Union are much more modest, and to an American production of paper and board almost four times that of the Russian, must be added large imports from Canada. However, the USSR has the resources and the potential demand for extremely rapid growth.

CONSTRUCTION MATERIALS

This is one of the few major industries in which the Soviet Union has already passed the United States, although if the latter country were to embark upon a really serious programme of urban renewal, she might regain her former lead. Soviet output of cement overtook the American in 1964 and is now well ahead of it, while the lead in the production of bricks, glass, etc., is even greater. This not only reflects the rapid pace of industrial expansion in the USSR but is also the result of housing the growing urban population in large apartment blocks, whereas much American domestic housing continues to be in frame houses built of lumber.

TEXTILES AND CLOTHING

The chief contrast between the textile and clothing industries lies in the differing importance of man-made fibres. These account for well over half the material used by American industry, but for not much more than a sixth of the fibre consumption of the Soviet Union. Further, the non-cellulosic man-made fibres have long since outdistanced rayon in

America, but in Russia rayon still predominates. The fibre situation in the USSR today is somewhat similar to that prevailing in the United States in 1955 when man-made fibres were much less prominent, and three times as much rayon was produced as nylon. The greater importance of linen and wool in the USSR may also be noted (Table 10.10).

TABLE 10.10   CONSUMPTION OF FIBRES 1955–68[23]
(thousands of tons)

	USA		USSR
	1955	*1968*	*1968*
Cotton	1,972	1,871	2,036
Wool	186	83	302
Flax	4	2	250
Rayon and acetate	654	731	424
Non-cellulosic (nylon, etc.)	202	1,760	130

Much more of the man-made fibre produced in the United States is used outside the textile industry, especially for tyre manufacture, leaving production of cloth roughly similar in amount in the two countries. But whereas the textile and clothing industries of the USA employ only two and a quarter million people, those of the USSR give occupation to over four million, suggesting much lower labour productivity in the USSR.

A similar concentration of the textile industry to that in Russia's Moscow region was at one time found in New England, but the American textile industry has now largely migrated to the southern Atlantic and Appalachian States. Japanese and other foreign imports have slowed the growth of the American industry, especially in woollens, but Soviet textile imports are balanced by exports of a similar value.

11 Transport

The extent and density of the network of a nation's transport system, together with the frequency and efficiency of the service it provides, will determine to what degree people and goods are able to move swiftly and cheaply from one part of the country to another. These considerations will also affect the location of economic activity: the less developed the transport system the narrower will be the choice of suitable sites. Industrialisation relies in large measure upon large-scale operation; this in turn necessitates the concentration of a high degree of the industrial activity at one spot; such a measure of regional specialisation can, however, only be achieved if the transport facilities exist to assemble the required materials and to distribute the finished product.

FREIGHT

The total movement of goods and people within a state can be gauged by multiplying the bulk moved by the distance travelled. This gives an estimated volume of total freight transportation for each country as follows: USA– 2,771 billion ton–km (1969), USSR– 3,014 billion ton–km (1970).[1] Soviet inter-city freight turnover is therefore well above that of the USA, a remarkable fact when the much greater American agricultural and industrial productivity is considered.

Levels of economic development and productivity are not, however, the only factors influencing the transport turnover of a state. The size and shape of its territory, and the geographical distribution of its population, industry and sources of raw materials and fuel are also important. It is obvious that if these are located close together, less transport will be required than if they are far apart. The concentration of population, industry and such important commodities as coal and iron ore in the north-east of the United States, contrasts with their more scattered distribution in the USSR. Furthermore, the maritime situation of several major American centres of industry and population, and the large part played by imports and exports in their economies, diminish the need for inland transport.

Soviet movement of goods is not only high in proportion to the level of economic development and productivity but is growing faster than the gross national product. This rose two and a half times between 1950 and 1965 but freight traffic rose three and a half times. On the other hand, United States freight traffic has grown less than industrial output since the 1941–5 war.[2] The more highly developed economy of the USA has a greater share of high value/low bulk production and requires, proportionately, less transportation.

The volume and direction of transported goods and passengers are inevitably affected by the physical plant available. Because in the United States the number of vehicles and the length of railways, roads and pipelines is much greater than in the Soviet Union, and the network denser, there is little physical restraint upon traffic. The volume of traffic in the Soviet Union would undoubtedly be greater if there were more vehicles to carry it and more roads and railways for them to run upon. As it is, American equipment is under-used but the Soviet plant is worked to and beyond its full capacity. And the flow of freight and passengers in the USSR is heavily concentrated along a few main arteries whereas in the United States it is more widely diffused.

It is often said that the USA has a system in which the different forms of transport compete with each other, and that the USSR has a unified system. But while it is true that the user has little choice, the Soviet system can hardly be called unified. Rail, river and marine transport come under different ministries, pipelines are operated by the oil and gas industries, and lorry (truck) transport is in the hands of the local and regional authorities. As a result, the co-ordination of their activities is difficult and there is far less mixture of mode of transport than is desirable. For example, because of administrative difficulties a consignment is more likely to take an all-rail or an all-water route, even though a mixed rail–water route might be more economical.

The division of the total volume of freight and passengers among the various forms of transport is shown in Table 11.1. Sea transport is not included for lack of comparable statistics.

TABLE 11.1   INTER-CITY MOVEMENT OF FREIGHT ACCORDING
TO MODE OF TRANSPORT 1969–70[3]
(*percentages*)

USA (1969)		USSR (1970)	
Rail	41	Rail	83
Pipeline	22	Pipeline	9
Motor vehicle	21	Waterway	6
Waterway	16	Motor vehicle	2
Air	0*	Air	0*

* The overall share of air freight is negligible, amounting to 0·17 per cent in the USA and 0·07 per cent in the USSR.

PASSENGER TRANSPORT

If the total freight turnover in the two superpowers is roughly equal, there is no such similarity in inter-city passenger movement. Because of the great mobility which the private car gives to Americans, they – in 1968 – travelled 1,739 billion passenger-kilometres compared with only 297 billion by Soviet citizens.[4] But Soviet passenger turnover increased five times in the 1950–68 period while the American just doubled. Table 11.2 shows that increased travel by air and bus in the USSR has lessened the great preponderance of rail travel. This remains, none the less, far and away the chief means of passenger movement in the USSR and contrasts strikingly with its almost total disappearance in the USA. The latter phenomenon results as much from the desire of the railways

TABLE 11.2 INTER-CITY MOVEMENT OF PASSENGERS BY MODE
OF TRANSPORT 1968[5]
(*percentages: 1950 figure in brackets*)

USA		USSR	
Private automobile	86·7 (86·2)	Rail	63·6 (92·7)
Air	9·4 (2·0)	Air	20·9 (1·7)
Bus	2·4 (5·2)	Bus	13·7 (1·9)
Rail	1·2 (6·4)	Waterway	1·8 (3·7)
Waterway	0·3 (0·2)	Private automobile	0·0* (0·0)

* There are no Soviet data under this head but the amount is almost certainly below a tenth of one per cent.

there to rid themselves of their loss-making passenger obligations as from decreasing demand. Not only have the schedules been reduced to such a degree that it is not easy to find a train at a convenient time – if there is one at all – but the companies have resorted to all kinds of tricks to shake off or scare away traffic, so that they can go to the Interstate Commerce Commission and apply for permission to abandon statutory services on the ground that they are underpatronised. Such means include withdrawal of sleeping cars and refreshment facilities on long runs, neglect of lavatories, removing baggage lockers from stations, leaving information requests unanswered, scheduling trains to leave or arrive in the small hours of the morning and ensuring that trains do not connect. The number of American inter-city passenger trains dropped from 1,400 in 1958 to 488 in 1970.[6] In the USSR, on the other hand, passenger train services continue to improve in speed, frequency and comfort, as well as in the number of passenger-miles travelled (despite a fall in the percentage proportion). Turnover doubled between 1957 and 1967.

RAILWAY TRANSPORT

The much greater importance of rail transport in the USSR appears clearly in Tables 11.1 and 11.2, and this despite the greater route length in America. In 1968 this was 334,800 km compared with 133,600 km in the Soviet Union. And whereas the length of American railways is declining with the closure of uneconomic lines, and is now only eighty-nine per cent of the 1940 figure, that of the USSR has grown continuously since the Revolution. New lines under construction at present include one across the swamps of West Siberia from Tyumen on the Trans-Siberian railway to the new oilfield town of Surgut. This new line is part of a projected railway which will run between 250 and 430 miles north of the existing Trans-Siberian, and which will shorten the distance from the Urals to the Soviet Far East by some 650 miles. It will not only open up new districts to mineral exploitation but will be more secure from the threat of Chinese interference.

There are several reasons for the overwhelming predominance of the railway in the Soviet transportation system. Physical conditions favour the construction of railways rather than roads over most of the settled parts of the country, where gradients are slight, but where winter frosts break up the roads. Inheriting from the pre-revolutionary period a fairly extensive rail system but only the sketchiest of road networks, the Soviets concentrated their efforts upon the former. But social conditions are even more important. In Western countries where private car ownership is widespread, there is an insistent demand for a good, modern and pervasive road network, and a willingness to pay for it. The cost of building and maintaining roads is spread over almost the whole population, and the road hauliers usually pay far less than their share, whether on a mileage or an actual physical damage basis. According to recent research by the US Army Corps of Engineers, the damage inflicted upon a road surface varies as the cube of the load on the tyre. This means that an average lorry or truck may destroy a road at five hundred times the rate of a private car while paying only about one-fifth of the tax per ton mile.[7] In a country like the USSR, with but few roads and private automobiles, almost the whole cost of building and maintaining roads and running trucks upon them would fall upon the state, and comparative costs show this to be quite out of the question economically on any but the shortest distances (Table 11.3).

The turnover on the Soviet railways is almost double that on the American, despite a route mileage of a little more than a third. This means that in 1968 each route kilometre of railway in the USSR was responsible for seventeen ton–kilometres of freight turnover, compared with under four ton–kilometres in the United States. It represents a

TABLE 11.3 SOVIET ESTIMATE OF AVERAGE COST OF
VARIOUS MODES OF TRANSPORT[8]
(*kopeks per ton–kilometre*)

Oil pipeline	1·00
Sea	1·36
Rail	2·32
River	2·42
Motor	56·86
Air	170·30

highly intensive use of the available equipment, and it was only approached in America in the war years of 1943 and 1944. A very rapid turn-around is a striking aspect of this efficiency. Freight car turn-around time, about fifteen days on the American system, is less than six in the Soviet Union.[9] This intensification of rail haulage yields great savings: the railways now make a substantial profit and their contribution to the state budget is between three and four times the annual investment in them.

The Soviet customer has a very different standard of service from that received by his American counterpart. Consignments have to be ready at any hour of the day or night, to secure a constant flow of traffic. As a member of the United States Congress said in 1959, 'theirs is an austerity form of transportation, even in the industrial sector'. But even when allowance is made for this, the outstanding success of the Soviet railways makes nonsense of the view often expressed in the West, that this form of transport is obsolete: 'nothing would be further from the truth. Where water carriers or pipe lines cannot serve, railroads have an unchallengeable ability to move mass freight over long distances at low cost.'[10]

Both countries have witnessed a technological revolution in their railway systems during the last twenty years, but with different motives. In the USA modernisation was intended to arrest the decline in traffic by increasing competitiveness through lowering costs, not entirely without success. Between 1945 and 1961 the freight turnover on American railways fell steadily, but between 1961 and 1968 it increased every year except 1967. In the USSR, on the other hand, improvements have been designed to cope with increasing demands rather than to arrest falling ones. Electrification and dieselisation have resulted in greater frequency, load and speed of trains. The VL80-K electric locomotive is a 8,700-hp unit which, it is claimed, can pull a train of up to 10,000 tons at seventy miles per hour. The importance of the Soviet rail system is now such that it carries nearly half the world's rail traffic.

In most aspects of modernisation the USA has been five to ten years ahead of the USSR. Thus steam departed from the American railroads almost completely during the 1950s. In the Soviet Union the demise of steam belongs to the 1960s, but whereas in America it was wholly replaced by diesel–electric power, in the USSR electrification is more important. This emphasis on electrification may have been in part due to the technological difficulties of building good diesel locomotives, as well as to the recent availability of large quantities of cheap electricity – the result of the coming into operation of large new power stations. However, electrification is in any case best suited for a rail system so intensively used as is the Soviet. In the use of containers on flat cars, obviating the necessity for piece-by-piece loading and unloading, the USA is ahead; but in the adoption of automatic block signalling and automation in control, the USSR is making fast progress. The substitution of four-axle freight cars for the old, standard small two-axle wagons has proceeded rapidly, and six-axle freight cars have been introduced for the moving of heavy goods such as iron ore. The Russian retention of some small two-axle cars is not a measure of backwardness: as the railways carry many small and light consignments that in the West would normally go by road, these wagons are adequate for the purpose.

Although the USA is far ahead of the USSR in the adoption of containers on the high seas, the Soviet Union is a pioneer in the application of the 'land-bridge' by rail idea. Although the American railways have been hopeful for some years that they might be able to benefit from the transport of containerised cargoes across the country from coast to coast *en route* between Europe and the Pacific world, their financial difficulties and disorganisation have prevented real progress. Furthermore, container ships plying from the Pacific ports of the United States have been monopolised by military supplies for south-east Asia, thereby obstructing the growth of containerised commercial traffic. The unified, efficient and highly profitable Soviet railway system, on the other hand, has been able to put a Eurasian land-bridge into effect. Under an agreement with Japanese interests and the European Inter-Container Company the container carriage of freight began in late 1971. Japanese goods travel from the Niigata container terminal to the Soviet Pacific port of Nakhodka. Thence they are carried in fifty-car trains, each carrying a hundred containers. At Brest on the western frontier of the USSR they are taken on to trains of the European Inter-Container Company. A saving of twenty per cent over the all-sea route is estimated.[11]

MOTOR TRANSPORT

The development of motor transport in the USSR is severely inhibited by the relative scarcity of roads (Table 11.4) as well as by the much lower output of motor vehicles. In the United States almost all motor transport is road-bound, but in the USSR much of it takes place off roads – on farm tracks, on desert trails and, in winter, on frozen river roads.

The stock of vehicles available for use is also very much smaller in the USSR. An estimated total of about three million lorries (trucks) is increasing only slowly because new production does little more than offset depreciation. The USA had over seventeen million trucks in 1970. With passenger cars the difference is much greater. If all the auto-mobiles produced in the Soviet Union since 1950 (and very few indeed were produced before that date) were still on the road, the total stock

TABLE 11.4   TOTAL ROAD LENGTH 1968[12]
(kilometres)

	USA	USSR
All roads	5,919,000	456,000
Surfaced roads	4,640,000	177,000

would have been only two and a half million in 1967 and it was almost certainly much less. In fact, an American estimate put the total stock of passenger cars at under a million in 1964, only half of them in private ownership.[13] This compares with eighty-seven million cars on American roads in 1969, sixty-two per cent of which were under five years old. The visitor to the larger cities of Russia does not realise the immensity of the gulf, because the Soviet stock of automobiles is concentrated on the streets of these towns, especially Moscow. It is not, therefore surprising to find that the gap between the two countries in passenger turnover is even greater than that in freight (Table 11.5).

TABLE 11.5   INTER-CITY MOTOR TRANSPORT TURNOVER 1968–70[14]

	USA	USSR
Freight (billions of ton–km)	574	64
Passengers (billions of passenger–km)	1,549	41

Reasons for the contrast include the lesser cost of the intensively used railways in the USSR and the more advanced state of the American economy. Road transport becomes more necessary when industry is dispersed and there is a large production of consumer goods to be widely distributed among the population as a whole, than when the main need is to move bulky industrial goods from one major centre to another. As for private automobiles Khrushchev's policy (1954–64) was not to encourage individual ownership but instead to further the use of taxis and car pools. When he was in San Francisco and saw the volume of car traffic, most cars holding only the driver on his way from work, Khrushchev said, 'We do not want such extravagance.' Later he stated, 'We will make more rational use of automobiles than the Americans do. We will develop public taxi pools on an even broader scale; people will get cars from them for necessary trips.'[15]

In 1959 Professor Holland Hunter expressed doubt whether the Soviet people would be content, as their standards of living rose, to accept this restriction upon their car-owning and car-using habits.[16] He was proved right. The post-Khrushchev rulers decided on much greater passenger automobile production and agreed that Soviet citizens were entitled, as their incomes and standards rise, to own and operate private cars. Kosygin, after Khrushchev's fall, spoke scathingly of the earlier policy:

> You remember how sedulously the idea was propagated among us that our country did not need a large output of private cars. Everybody was expected to use buses. Everything possible was done to deny even managers of large factories and establishments the right to have a car. As a result, many managers had to use lorries!

Any attempt to catch up with the USA in the foreseeable future is, however, out of the question, as the diversion of resources needed, not only to produce the cars and lorries (trucks) but to build a road network and equip it with service stations, would be enormous. Yet the 1971-5 plan envisages a large increase in the output of private cars and

> the western 'irrationality' that Khrushchev feared may yet invade Soviet society . . . Moscow traffic is getting congested, even though there are at present only 71,000 private cars in the city . . . It is not obvious to me that the USSR would welcome the attendant traffic jams, smog, injuries and fatalities, and landscape disfigurations which have confronted North America, Western Europe, and Japan. Perhaps the USSR will develop a compromise solution that avoids the worst evils of the automobile age. As between an automobile-dominated and a State-dominated society, the disadvantages are perhaps arguable.[17]

Since this was written many more Americans have become hostile to the domination of their country by the automobile in its present form.

On the other hand, it can be argued that, particularly on the freight side, a considerable development of road transport is necessary if the Soviet economy is to make progress in consumer satisfaction. Factories manufacturing consumer goods need to be more widely dispersed than the centres of heavy industry which, hitherto, it has been the main function of the Soviet transport system to satisfy. Nor could such goods be widely diffused among the population without road transport.

Agriculture has been particularly handicapped by the utter absence of good rural roads. Over most of Russia the growing season is perilously short and much of the harvest is often lost because it either fails to ripen or, having ripened, cannot be garnered before being damaged by rain, frost or snow. In the absence of a surfaced rural road system, machinery and supplies cannot be brought up and farm work cannot begin until the ground has dried out firm enough to take heavy lorries and tractors. Likewise, as soon as the autumn rains begin to turn the surface into mud, all mechanical and vehicular activity must perforce come to a stop. These autumnal rains and the resulting quagmires saved Moscow from the German advance in late 1941, but they have lost many a good harvest before and since. A good rural road system would make possible the prolongation of the effective farm year at both ends of the season, but to create such a road system would be enormously expensive, especially in the adverse physical conditions prevailing. As it is, many rural areas, far removed from any railway or surfaced road, are forced to depend upon shallow streams for their annual supply of bulky goods. These rivulets may only be navigable for the two or three weeks during which they are swollen by the spring snow melt. Yet such waterways were estimated to have carried eighteen million tons of oil, fertilisers, farm machinery, foodstuffs and other goods in 1969, and 300 million cubic feet of timber besides.[18] A special passenger-carrying hovercraft has been designed to navigate over these and other such shallow waterways.

INLAND WATERWAYS

These are more important in America than in Russia, which is not surprising when it is remembered that Russian rivers are navigable for only six to eight months a year, and that they do not link important centres of heavy industry in the same way as do the Great Lakes and Ohio waterways in the United States. In the United States forty per cent of waterway traffic is carried on the Great Lakes and another thirty-five per cent on the Mississippi system (mainly on the Ohio section) which, like the Great Lakes, serves the north-eastern manufacturing region. In the USSR fifty per cent of waterway traffic is on the Volga–Kama system. There is a difference in the composition of the cargoes. It is building materials and timber rather than coal and ore that dominate Soviet waterway traffic.

American inland waterway freight turnover has doubled since 1945, but the Russian total has increased sevenfold. Yet it is still only thirty-five per cent of the American figure. In view of their present-day diminished importance in the Soviet transport picture as a whole, the attention devoted to the waterways is somewhat surprising. They are

G

distinguished by the modernity of the craft using them. Large new 10,000-ton and 5,000-ton motor vessels are being built for use on the Volga and the Siberian rivers, while passenger hovercraft and hydro-foils are increasingly seen.

AIR TRANSPORT

The two superpowers stand alone in the mileage of their internal scheduled air routes and in the number of passengers flown. The USSR is still behind the USA in volume of freight and number of passengers, but advancing rapidly. The details are given in Table 11.6. It is

TABLE 11.6 DOMESTIC AIRLINE DATA 1968[19]

	USA	USSR
Route length (thousands of km)	188	221
Cargo (millions of ton–km)	3,105	1,803
Passengers carried (millions)	146	61
Passenger–km flown (billions)	141	62

interesting to note that, despite the difference in size of the two countries, the average domestic distance flown is roughly the same – 920 km in the USA and 1,016 in the USSR. The location of most of the largest American cities on the Atlantic, Pacific and Gulf coasts means that a relatively large number of passengers cross the whole length or breadth of the country. In Russia, by contrast, the number making the long flight from western centres to the relatively small Pacific city of Vladivostok is much less.

The very rapid development of air transport in both countries may be seen from Table 11.7. However, if present trends continue it will be the 1980s before the USSR catches up with the USA in the number of passengers flown. But the Soviet Union is already ahead in some aspects of aircraft design and production, thanks largely to the work of four men, Antonov, Ilyushin, Mikoyan and Tupolev, the initial letters of whose names, AN, IL, MI and TU, appear on most aircraft in the service of Aeroflot and on many in the Air Force. They are the Soviet equivalents of Boeing, Douglas, Lockheed and Martin. The TU-144,

TABLE 11.7 GROWTH OF DOMESTIC PASSENGER AIR TRANSPORT 1950–69[20]

	Route length (thousands of km)		Number of passengers carried (millions)	
	USA	USSR	USA	USSR
1950	124	108	17	2
1960	163	134	56	16
1969	210	240	154	68

the world's first supersonic passenger air liner, test-flown on 31 December 1968, has a range of 4,000 miles, a ceiling of 65,000 feet and a take-off distance of only 2,000 yards. Mikoyan has designed not only military aeroplanes – including the famous MIGs – but a whole breed of helicopters.

Lacking the magnificent network of surface communications which characterises the USA, and possessing vast tracts of forest, swamp and mountain which present formidable difficulties to land transport, Soviet Russia has paid special attention to the problems of carrying heavy loads by air. Aircraft and helicopters have been designed specially for weight-lifting, notably the AN-22 which carried a record-breaking eighty-eight tons to a height of twenty thousand feet at the Paris Air Show in 1966. This world record was taken away by America's Lockheed C-5A in 1968. Much Russian interest is also being shown in the use of dirigible airships, while hovercraft are used to transport heavy drilling equipment to the oilfield in the West Siberian swampland.[21]

ELECTRICITY TRANSMISSION LINES

The whole eastern half of the United States is covered by a very fine net of interconnected transmission lines. Another similar net follows the Pacific coast. The western interior contains two or three grids of a more open nature. Ten years ago there were few long-distance transmission lines at all in the USSR, except for a few converging on Moscow and for smaller, independent systems in the industrial areas of the Ukraine and the Urals. There was no grid. The size of the country and the immense distances involved meant that a national grid could only be evolved by improvements in the technique of long-distance transmission. Here Soviet technology has risen to the occasion, enabling the 1960s to see rapid advance with large systems of interconnected lines. The whole of Russia (i.e. the Soviet Union west of the Urals) is now covered by a single grid. The 1970s will see these systems themselves joined together by long-distance trunk power lines of very high voltage, a process begun in the 1966–70 five-year plan. This achievement has been made possible by the development and installation of super-high-tension steel–aluminium lines. The use of DC current, although involving expensive transformation, enables cheaper cable to be used and makes for increased safety and control. Under the 1971–5 plan a one-and-a-half-million-volt line is being constructed from a group of large new thermal power stations on the Kazakh coalfield at Ekibastuz to central Russia, a distance of 1,800 miles. Such lengths and voltages are unequalled elsewhere in the world, but nowhere else are they so necessary. They provide yet another instance in which Soviet determination to triumph over an 'anti-resource' – in this case distance – has succeeded. The gains will be immense because peak demand varies latitudinally with the variation in the length of day, and longitudinally with the eleven time zones into which the country is divided. Separate isolated stations or systems are forced to work beneath capacity for much of the time. The USA has long enjoyed the benefits of a fully integrated grid system, but has little need for transmission lines of great length and very high voltage because normally power can be used near the generating site.

PIPELINES

The United States has long possessed an intricate and widespread system of privately-owned oil and gas pipelines, mostly of small diameter. In the USSR the pipeline has been mainly a new feature, introduced in the 1960s with the discovery and development of new oil and gas fields, but it is now the Soviet transportation medium with the fastest growth rate: in 1965 oil pipelines alone overtook both motor transport and waterway transport on a ton–kilometre basis.

TABLE 11.8 PIPELINES 1968[22]

	Petroleum		Natural gas	
	USA	USSR	USA	USSR
Length (thousands of km)	269	34	468*	56
Throughput (millions of tons)	1,014	301		
Throughput (billions of cubic metres)			462	146

* Transmission only (i.e. excluding gathering and distribution).

The American pipeline systems are extensive collecting, transporting and distributing networks, with many times the mileage of the Soviet lines which are, for the most part, long-distance trunk lines carrying oil and gas direct from the producing field to the consuming region. The Russian pipelines, though less extensive, are of greater diameter, and consequently their throughput per mile is much greater.

COASTWISE TRANSPORT

In both countries some goods (passengers only to a slight degree) are moved from one part of the country to another by sea, but to a far greater extent in the United States, where most economic activity is located within easy reach of the coasts, and where the coasts are mutually accessible by sea and at all times of the year. In the United States the movement is mostly between the Pacific and the Atlantic–Gulf coasts via the Panama Canal, and amounted in 1968 to 193 million metric tons.

In the USSR most economic activity is located at a distance from the coasts, and these are very difficult to reach, one from another. To get from the Baltic coast to that of the Black Sea by sea necessitates rounding the whole European peninsula, while to get from either of these seas to the Pacific coast involves the immense journey – with the Suez canal closed – round the Cape and across the Indian Ocean. The alternative 'northern sea route' via the Arctic coast is difficult and dangerous and only available for about four months in the year. Nevertheless, by the investment of vast sums in the building of icebreakers, the use of air navigation to reconnoitre the disposition of the ice and the construction of a series of coastal stations, the regular navigation of the 'north-east passage' was accomplished in the 1930s. Commercial convoys began to operate in 1935. The route is used to carry supplies to northern mining enterprises and, in conjunction with the great Siberian rivers, to deliver bulky freight to Siberian sites. Thus the large generators for the hydro-electric station at Krasnoyarsk were transported from Leningrad by way of the Baltic–White Sea canal, the northern sea route and the Yenisey river.

This difficult sea route between western and eastern USSR does not, however, carry enough traffic to justify its immense cost. The Trans-Siberian railway remains overwhelmingly the prime carrier of all kinds of freight between west and east, and now that a modern deep water-way system links all the seas of Russia (as opposed to Siberia), it provides the easiest way to communicate between them. In fact, the inland waterway system of Russia will now take small ocean-going vessels along its extensive improved routes. These ships are able to navigate from the Baltic Sea across Russia to the Black Sea without having to round the peninsula of Europe. New 2,000-ton motor ships, built in East German yards, are able to sail alike on rivers and the open seas, and since 1965 they have been used to establish maritime connection between internal areas of the USSR and nineteen foreign countries. The St Lawrence Seaway, a new deep waterway opened in 1959, in similar fashion allows small to medium-sized ocean vessels to reach the Great Lakes ports of the United States from the Atlantic. Regular shipping lines provide a direct freight service from Europe to Detroit and Chicago.

Until recently the United States had not been interested in such a difficult and dangerous project as a 'northern sea route' along the Arctic coast of North America, because of the relative ease with which coastwise traffic can pass through the Panama canal. The discovery of oil in Alaska has changed the situation, since the distance over which the oil would have to be carried to the east coast of the United States would be halved if it were taken eastwards through the Canadian

Arctic archipelago rather than via the Pacific coast. Accordingly, the icebreaker-tanker *Manhattan* made an experimental voyage from Prudhoe Bay in Alaska to the Atlantic seaboard in the summer of 1969.

Three-quarters of Soviet internal seaborne commerce is carried on the Caspian, Black and Azov seas, fifteen per cent on the Pacific waters of the Far East, seven per cent on the northern sea route and five per cent on the Baltic.[23] The Caspian Sea is, however, really a lake and the traffic on it, although placed in the same category as Baltic and other sea commerce by Soviet authorities, is more comparable to that of the Great Lakes than to the coastwise trade of the United States.

URBAN TRANSPORT

Most large Soviet towns have a dependable public transport (transit) system with trams (streetcars), omnibuses and trolley buses, while the largest cities all have built or are building underground railways. Yet, because of the very high density of urban population resulting from the crowding of large numbers of people in apartment blocks, long queues develop at the stops, and vehicles are usually overcrowded. In America, with much of the urban population thinly spread out in single-dwelling units, and with most families owning one or more cars, traffic congestion is endemic in the central areas and public transport has almost withered away. Where plans have been made for revived and publicly subsidised rapid transit services in American cities, they have usually been rejected. Even now that modern technology has produced turbo-trains, monorails, hoverbuses and other devices for the speedy transport of passengers through urban areas, American citizens show little interest in them, refusing to be divorced from their automobiles. Instead, their cities are coming more and more to be dominated by architectural monuments to the motor car, consisting in the main of costly freeways and flyovers. San Francisco, Philadelphia and Boston have, however, taken the initiative in building modern urban rapid rail transit systems. New forms of public urban transport are also being introduced in the USSR. Thus at Kiev the first stage of a high-speed monorail system linking the airport with the city's underground railway, opened in 1970.

12 Trade

Table 12.1 shows that American foreign trade by value is several times larger than Russian, bearing in mind the near equivalence in the official values of the dollar and the rouble (one rouble = $1.11). Complete figures for trade by weight are available only for seaborne commerce. This amounted to 457 million metric tons for America in 1968 as against 113 million tons for Russia. The large difference is not surprising: the United States has always been a leading participant in world commerce, whereas throughout the Soviet period Russia has

TABLE 12.1 FOREIGN TRADE BY VALUE 1950-69[1]

	USA (billions of dollars)			USSR (billions of roubles)		
	Total	*Exports*	*Imports*	*Total*	*Exports*	*Imports*
1950	19·9	10·8	9·1	2·9	1·6	1·3
1955	27·1	15·6	11·6	5·8	3·1	2·7
1960	35·2	20·6	14·6	10·1	5·0	5·1
1965	48·8	27·5	21·4	14·6	7·4	7·2
1969	74·1	38·0	36·1	19·8	10·5	9·3

pursued a policy of economic autarky, concentrating on the development of her own resources and relying as little as possible on the outside world. It is yet one more facet of the contrast between the global position of America as a maritime power, with easy access by several coasts to many seas and oceans, and that of Russia, so enclosed and isolated within the world island that she cannot depend upon overseas trade without jeopardising her independence. Because her way to the oceans is by landlocked, foreign-controlled seas, Russia can be easily blockaded and thus embarrassed in time of war or international tension. Such a blockade was decisive in the 1914–17 war with Germany and critical in that of 1941–5.

Although Soviet foreign trade is a mere fraction of American, it has grown at a faster rate. Much of the apparent increase in the trade of the USA shown in Table 12.1 is due to the declining value of the dollar, a consideration which does not apply so strongly to the rouble, so that it can be said that Soviet trade has multiplied over five times since 1950. The continued development of Russia's immense mineral and forest resources has produced growing exportable surpluses which have financed increased purchases abroad, an increase in trade which does nothing to weaken the economic self-sufficiency of the country. Great though the rate of growth has been, however, the gap between the two states in absolute terms has increased, even allowing for inflation.

It is clear that the Russians would like to expand foreign trade still further, but they are handicapped in two ways. Firstly, they are short of foreign exchange to purchase the type of goods they need most desperately to speed the pace of their industrial development, e.g. machine tools. It has even been suggested that they might dispose of some of their art treasures to obtain such currency: during the eighteenth, nineteenth and early twentieth centuries, the immensely wealthy monarchy and aristocracy acquired a remarkable number of European paintings and other works of art. Before the 1941–5 war twenty-one paintings in the Hermitage at Leningrad were sold for $7 million, including works by Raphael, Botticelli and Jan van Eyck.[2] It is more likely, however, that today's administration would use gold, taking advantage of the hoard built up under Stalin, when the second largest gold-producing country in the world seldom expended any in this way.

The second handicap lies in the embargo imposed by the United States upon its allies on the export to the USSR of what are listed as 'strategic goods'. This list previously included steel pipe, and the conversion of the Soviet Union's fuel basis from coal to oil and gas was delayed by the necessity of having to produce pipe at home from an already overstrained steel capacity.

In both countries exports have normally exceeded imports, but to a greater extent in the United States with its lavish foreign assistance programmes. There are important differences in the composition of these exports (Table 12.2). Machinery and industrial equipment, which are by far the main American export, take second place to fuel and metals in the Soviet Union, but in the latter country the share of exported machinery is growing.

On the import side machinery and industrial equipment form the leading import group in both countries, but they dominate Soviet imports to a far greater degree than they do American. In fact, fuels, ores, concentrates and metals were the leading American import in the early 1960s, but Japanese and other foreign imports of machines and equipment – especially cars – have grown so rapidly as to change the picture completely. Soviet imports of fuels, ores and metals declined during the 1960s, but the amount of foodstuffs bought abroad increased greatly.

Oil and oil products play a leading part in Soviet exports of minerals and amounted in 1969 to ninety-one million metric tons (89·7 million

TABLE 12.2 EXPORTS AND IMPORTS: DISTRIBUTION BY
COMMODITY GROUPS 1969[3]
(*percentages*)
Exports

	USA	USSR
Machinery, industrial and transport equipment	43·7	22·5
Fuels	3·0	15·7
Ores, concentrates and metals	8·6	19·4
Chemicals, fertilisers and synthetic rubber	10·0	3·9
Wood materials, cellulose and paper products	3·6	6·2
Textile materials	2·7	3·5
Foodstuffs	11·7	10·7
Consumers' goods	5·0	2·6
Others	11·7	15·5
	100·0	100·0

Imports

	USA	USSR
Machinery, industrial and transport equipment	27·1	37·5
Fuels	7·7	2·1
Ores, concentrates and metals	14·0	9·9
Chemicals, fertilisers and synthetic rubber	3·4	6·2
Wood materials, cellulose and paper products	7·4	2·1
Textile materials	3·5	4·3
Foodstuffs	14·7	12·9
Consumers' goods	9·9	19·0
Others	12·3	6·0
	100·0	100·0

tons when imports of 1·1 million tons have been subtracted) directed to forty-one countries, principally those listed in Table 12.3. The United States, on the other hand, is a net importer of petroleum and petroleum products to the extent of 132·6 million metric tons (1968: exports – 11·8 million tons, imports – 144·4 million tons). The principal suppliers are shown in Table 12.4.

The USSR in 1969 also exported 2·7 billion cubic metres of natural gas, mainly to Poland and Czechoslovakia. Both the total amount exported and the number of customers for Soviet natural gas are likely to increase rapidly in the near future. The pipeline which supplies eastern Europe is being extended into Austria and northern Italy, and

TABLE 12.3 PRINCIPAL IMPORTERS OF SOVIET PETROLEUM
AND PETROLEUM PRODUCTS 1969[4]
(*millions of metric tons*)

Italy	10·7	West Germany	5·8
Czechoslovakia	10·0	Cuba	5·8
East Germany	8·8	Sweden	4·7
Poland	8·2	Hungary	4·3
Finland	8·1	France	2·7
Bulgaria	6·6	Yugoslavia	2·5

TABLE 12.4 USA: PRINCIPAL SUPPLIERS OF PETROLEUM
AND PETROLEUM PRODUCTS 1968[5]
(*millions of metric tons*)

Venezuela and Caribbean	68·5
Canada	25·8
Middle East	11·2
Libya and other North African	7·6
Indonesia	3·7

an agreement to sell gas to West Germany in exchange for steel pipe was concluded in 1970. The United States, on the other hand, is a large net importer of gas, with exports (1968) of 2·7 billion cubic metres heavily outweighed by imports of 18·5 billion. As regards coal, both countries are exporters: the United States to the extent of fifty million metric tons a year (mainly to Canada, Japan and Italy) and the Soviet Union, twenty-seven million tons a year (mainly to East Germany, Bulgaria, Japan and Czechoslovakia).

The large and growing proportion of Soviet food imports reflects in part the relative weakness of agriculture within the economy and in part a rising standard of living. It consists in the main of fruit, and of subtropical and tropical produce that cannot easily be grown in the country because of climatic conditions. Imports of foodstuffs into the USA, which have declined in relative importance, consist in the first place of coffee, followed by meat and meat preparations, sugar, cocoa, fish, fruit and nuts. Despite their large imports of foodstuffs, both countries are normally considerable exporters of wheat. In 1969 the USA sent abroad over sixteen million tons, while the USSR exported six million tons. But the Soviet Union became also an importer of wheat in the 1960s, and such imports rose to large proportions after the droughts of 1963 and 1965 (Table 12.5).

TABLE 12.5 WHEAT TRADE 1960-69[6]
(*millions of metric tons*)

	USA		USSR	
	Exports	*Imports*	*Exports*	*Imports*
1962	16·3	0·1	4·7	0·0
1963	22·0	0·1	4·1	3·1
1964	18·5	0·0	2·0	7·3
1965	22·5	0·0	1·7	6·4
1966	18·1	0·0	2·8	7·6
1967	19·3	0·0	5·3	1·8
1968	14·6	0·0	4·4	1·3
1969	16·3	0·0	6·0	0·0

DIRECTION OF TRADE

By political and economic groupings

Whereas almost all American trade – ninety-nine per cent – is with other capitalist countries, only sixty-five per cent of Soviet trade is with other socialist countries, the remaining thirty-five per cent being with the capitalist world. This is a proportion that has been growing steadily over the past decade – in 1958 it was twenty-six per cent and in 1950 only nineteen per cent. This increase has mainly been with the advanced countries. The share of total Soviet trade with non-communist 'developing' countries remains fairly constant at about twelve per cent. American trade with such nations is some thirty per cent of the total, but has declined relatively, particularly with the countries of South America. Despite the 'alliance for progress' the proportion of American trade with that continent declined from fifteen per cent in 1955 to seven per cent in 1967. It is unfortunately true that the expansion of world trade is mainly between the advanced nations, and that many so-called developing countries have the greatest difficulty in enlarging their markets.

TABLE 12.6 TRADE WITH CONTINENTAL AREAS 1969[7]

(percentages)

	USA	USSR
North America	33·5	5·0
South America	7·3	0·6
Western Europe	30·4	21·7
Eastern Europe	0·6	55·6
Africa	3·3	3·8
Asia	22·4	12·9
Australasia	2·5	0·4
	100·0	100·0

By continental areas

Table 12.6 shows that each superpower has a large share of its trade with its immediate land neighbours; in other words, that propinquity is an important factor. The United States transacts about a third of her trade with other North American countries and forty-one per cent with the Western hemisphere as a whole. But Soviet trade is far more concentrated near the country's borders than is American: the USSR has fifty-five per cent of her trade with the adjacent countries of eastern Europe and ninety per cent with the Eurasian continent as a whole. This is one further aspect of the contrast between the landlocked, interior global position of the USSR and the outer, maritime location of the USA; America has the bulk of her trade with distant lands separated from her by great expanses of ocean.

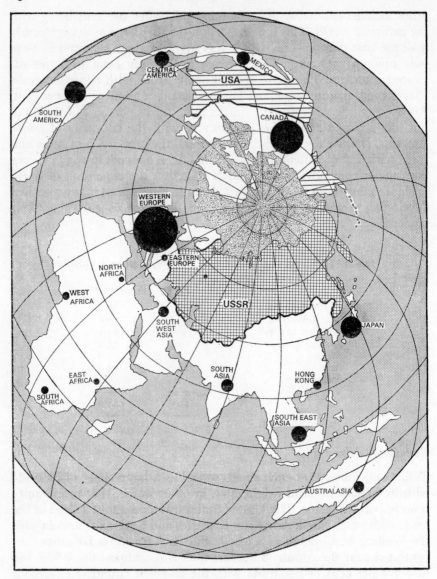

22. USA: global distribution of trade
Circles are proportionate to the total amount of trade by value (see
Tables 12.6 and 12.7)

By countries

Table 12.7 shows the principal trading partners of each country. As the Anglo-America is to some extent an economic unit, with most of the Canadian economy operating in response to stimuli from south of border, it is not surprising to find Canada in a commanding lead on the American side of the table. Before 1963 the USSR had only negligible dealings with Canada. Since then the recurrent agricultural crisis in the USSR has necessitated large purchases of grain abroad, and Canada has been the chief beneficiary. The trade is very one-sided though, with Canadian purchases from Russia almost insignificant.

TABLE 12.7 PRINCIPAL TRADING PARTNERS 1958–69[8]

USA (millions of dollars)			USSR (millions of roubles)		
	1969	*1958*		*1969*	*1958*
Canada	19,528	6,095	East Germany	3,032	1,454
Japan	8,161	1,873	Poland	2,091	578
West Germany	4,721	1,364	Czechoslovakia	2,002	863
Great Britain	4,456	1,702	Bulgaria	1,754	363
Mexico	2,479	1,342	Hungary	1,277	326
Italy	2,466	760	Rumania	833	436
France	2,038	735	Cuba	770	—
Netherlands	1,914	629	Great Britain	601	197
Venezuela	1,648	1,699	Japan	559	34
Belgium	1,644	598	Finland	501	229
Australia	1,443	284	West Germany	497	124
Brazil	1,288	1,099	Italy	494	66
Hong Kong	1,178	124	Yugoslavia	425	92
Switzerland	1,057	320	Egypt (UAR)	420	175
South Korea	990	218	France	417	151
Spain	884	372	India	354	163
India	861	519	North Korea	295	95
Sweden	832	320	Netherlands	232	67
Philippines	797	564	Mongolia	224	101
Formosa	781	113	Sweden	213	53
South Africa	748	347	Persia	196	216
Israel	586	113	North Vietnam	186	16
Colombia	543	518	United States	160	104

The countries of eastern Europe bear a somewhat similar relationship to the USSR as Canada to the USA. Their trade is dominated by the senior partner with whom their communications are principally overland. Just as Canada is economically a northern extension of the American economy, so eastern Europe is an eastward projection of the Soviet economy. But the nature of the trade is different. The more industrialised of the COMECON countries (East Germany, Czechoslovakia and Poland) send machinery and industrial equipment to Russia, while the more agricultural ones (Bulgaria, Hungary and Rumania) are suppliers of foodstuffs and livestock products. Canada's exports to the USA are quite different, consisting principally of minerals and forest products, and – since the 1965 automotive agreement – of automobiles.

Japan is well placed in both the American and Soviet lists of trading partners. She has occupied a foremost position in the American trade picture since 1950, but her importance in trade with the USSR is more recent: in 1958 she figured only twenty-fifth. She looks to both superpowers for fuel and raw materials to feed her prospering manufacturing industries and for markets in which to dispose of her inexpensive but high-quality goods. Her steel competes with the American product in California, and American affluence laps up her motor cars, motor cycles, bicycles, television sets, transistor radios, tape recorders, sewing machines, binoculars, textiles, guitars, etc. Her trade with Russia is shown in some detail in Table 12.8. This trade is growing so fast in bulky products that the port of Nakhodka, built near Vladivostok to handle it in the 1950s, is already inadequate. Work on a new port close by, Port Wrangel, was begun in 1971, and the Japanese are co-operating with the Soviet authorities in equipping it as a coal-shipping, timber-handling and container port.

TABLE 12.8 USSR: TRADE WITH JAPAN 1969[9]
(*millions of roubles*)

Exports		Imports	
Wood products	107·6	Machinery and industrial equipment	68·0
Coal and anthracite	32·0	Clothing	28·1
Raw cotton	31·5	Chemicals	23·0
Oil and oil products	22·5	Pipe	21·7
Aluminium	17·4	Woollen cloth	18·6
Pig iron	14·8	Plastics	14·5

The commercial position of Cuba *vis-à-vis* the big powers provides a graphic illustration of what can happen to the trade pattern of a small country which moves from one camp into the other (Table 12.9). In 1958 Cuba was ninth in the long and keenly contested American list of trading partners. She has since been cast out from that company as a result of the Castro revolution, but has risen to sixth in the Soviet list. The direction of her trade is now determined by the American embargo and Soviet friendship. Although adjacent to lands rich in petroleum, her oil is brought thousands of miles from Russia and, despite her proximity to the world's largest sugar importer, her sugar is carried away to the distant Soviet Union, a country self-sufficient in sugar.

TABLE 12.9 TRADE WITH CUBA 1958–69[10]

	USA (millions of dollars)	USSR (millions of roubles)
1958	1,070·2	13·9
1969	0·0	770·1

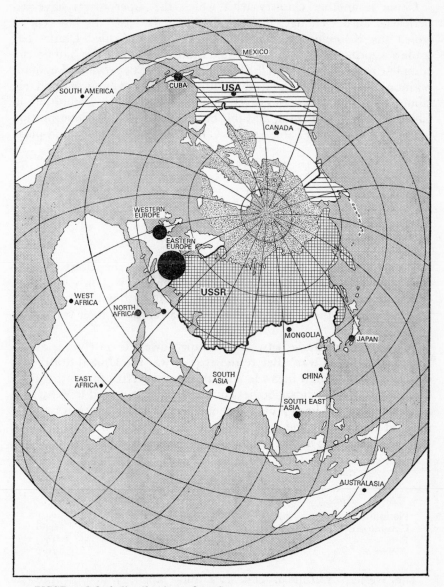

23. USSR: global distribution of trade
   Circles are proportionate to the total amount of trade by value, and are
   on the same scale as those in Fig. 22 (see Tables 12.6 and 12.7)

China is another country with which the superpowers have experienced abrupt changes in trade direction. In 1948, the last year in which the Kuomintang, under Chiang Kai-shek, ruled China, her trade was principally with the United States. By 1950 there had been a complete reversal, with the USSR holding America's previous dominant position, and American trade with mainland China completely eliminated. The 1960s, however, have seen a sharp diminution in Chinese trade with Russia, and this has accompanied the deterioration in political relations (Table 12.10). China has fallen from second place

TABLE 12.10 USSR: TRADE WITH CHINA 1960–69[11]
(millions of roubles)

1960	1,498·7	1965	375·5
1961	826·9	1966	286·6
1962	674·8	1967	96·3
1963	540·2	1968	86·4
1964	404·6	1969	51·1

to thirty-sixth in the list of countries trading with the USSR. Soviet total trade with China in 1969 (51 million roubles) was only a third of that with America (160 million roubles). But in 1970 both superpowers took steps which they hoped would lead to a revival in their trade with China.

The very small trade between the superpowers themselves is also a legacy of the 'cold war'. Before the 1941–5 war the United States was second only to Britain in trade with the Soviets. With the outbreak of the 'cold war', American–Soviet commerce almost ceased to exist, and although there has been a moderate increase in recent years, it remains small at one-fifth of one per cent of total United States trade. Table 12.11 illustrates the nature of such commerce as there is.

TABLE 12.11 USSR: TRADE WITH USA 1969[12]
(millions of roubles)

Exports		Imports	
Platinum	n.d.	Machinery, etc.	34·1
Chrome ore	8·4	Alumina	23·0
Furs	3·5	Leather, hides and skins	10·3
Tobacco	3·4	Cellulose	10·1

The western European countries and Japan, which at present monopolise Russia's trade with the advanced capitalist world, have reason to be grateful for America's reluctance to deal with the Soviet Union. The ordinary Russian's belief in the superiority of American technology and its products is so deep-rooted that an undoubted preference for American goods would exist, were they available, and the argument that Russia has nothing to offer the United States in return no longer holds, now that the Soviet Union has increasing surpluses of minerals in which the USA is deficient. Leon M. Herman is probably right when he says 'if commercial considerations were to be allowed once more to govern the flow of trade, in a setting of undisturbed political relations, the United States could be expected before very long to become a major factor in Soviet commerce with the West'.[13]

MODE OF TRANSPORT

Although it is difficult to make a comparison of the means of transport by which goods from or to the two superpowers move, owing to the incompatibility of the statistical data available, certain points can be made. Just over half by volume of Soviet trade goes by sea, and just under half by various means of overland transport.[14] Rail predominates but pipelines became important in the 1960s as a result of the building of the *Druzhba* (Friendship) oil pipeline and the *Bratsvo* (Brotherhood) gas pipeline into Europe. The *Druzhba* pipeline is being doubled. Where adjoining foreign countries have supplies of gas conveniently suited for import into the USSR, pipelines are also being built for an inward flow – e.g. one from Afghanistan, completed in 1967 and another from Persia. Soviet electricity is exported to eastern Europe by the *Mir* (Peace) power transmission line. The relatively large amount of overland transport in Soviet trade is not surprising as so much of it is with her immediate land neighbours.

Available American data are for value of trade and not weight, and are not therefore comparable, since where both overseas and overland transport is available, a shipment is likely to travel by the former if of high bulk and low value, and by the latter – or by air – if of low bulk and high value. Fifty-six per cent of American trade by value was carried by sea in 1969, eleven per cent by air and the rest over land.[15] If figures for weight were available, they would undoubtedly show a much larger proportion of goods moving by sea, while the amount moving by air would be relatively negligible.

The volume of Soviet goods exported is almost ten times as large as the amount imported. This is because exports are made up very largely of high-bulk/low-value goods while the reverse is true of imports. But American exports are much less in bulk than imports: those travelling by water in 1968 totalled 177 million metric tons as against imports of 280 million tons.[16]

Despite her possession of one of the largest merchant fleets in the world and much political and economic pressure to ensure that goods are carried in vessels of her own flag, only five per cent of American waterborne freight was carried in American ships in 1969, as against

just thirty-nine per cent in 1950. This statistical picture is unreal, however, because so much American-owned tonnage is registered – for
tax-evasion purposes – under flags of convenience, notably that of
Liberia. Table 12.12 shows that, while tonnage registered under the
American flag has declined since 1958, that of the Soviet Union has
grown very fast, mainly by the purchase of ships abroad. To some extent
the arrival of the USSR on the scene as a leading shipping power,
which has caused some trepidation in foreign mercantile circles, has
resulted from the American use of shipping embargoes as an instrument
of pressure. Because, for instance, the United States was able to persuade the shipping of non-communist countries to avoid Cuba, for fear
of reprisals in the form of exclusion from United States ports, a great

TABLE 12.12   MERCHANT SHIPPING FLEETS 1958–69[17]
(millions of gross tons)

| | 1969 | | 1958 | |
	Rank	Tonnage	Rank	Tonnage
World		211·7		118·0
Liberia	1st	29·2	3rd	10·1
Japan	2nd	24·0	5th	5·5
Great Britain	3rd	23·8	2nd	20·3
Norway	4th	19·7	4th	9·4
USA	5th	19·6	1st	25·6
USSR	6th	13·7	12th	3·0

burden was thrown upon the Soviet merchant navy. This brought home
to the USSR the importance of having her own fleet if she was to be free
to pursue her own foreign economic policy without let or hindrance,
and to come to the aid of overseas allies. This is another instance where
American action directed against the Soviet Union or other communist
states has in the long run benefited Russia, while harming America's
own friends – in this case, the great maritime nations of the Western
world. An additional reason for building and expanding her own fleet
has been the Soviet desire to save foreign currency.[18]

   A big difference between the Liberian–American merchant marines
and that of the USSR is the preponderance of oil tankers in the former
and of bulk carriers in the latter. The former is a direct result of large
American imports and coastwise shipments of petroleum, together with
the fact that big American companies dominate the world trade in oil.
As Soviet oil exports grow, the proportion of tankers in its merchant
navy, at present small, is likely to increase, but the narrow channels by
which Soviet ships have access to the open ocean will prevent Russia
from using tankers of gigantic capacity, such as are becoming normal
in the outer 'rimland' world.

'Containerisation' is playing a growing part in the movement of each superpower's trade. The idea of transporting goods in boxes of uniform size, that could be transferred from one type of carrier to another without disturbing the contents, was introduced by an American, Malcolm McLean, in the 1930s. These were not propitious times, however, and it was not until 1956 that he applied the container principle to ocean shipping. Ten years later he launched the first transatlantic container service, and McLean Sea–Land Services are still the largest container company in the world. New specially-designed ships are being built for this type of trade and container terminals have been constructed at the major ports. The Soviet Union has been slow to apply the new method to its mercantile marine, and did not begin to build container ships until 1971, when the first of a series of vessels designed to take two hundred containers was laid down at Vyborg near Leningrad. Plans for the future expansion of the merchant fleet include not only container ships but oil tankers, refrigerated vessels and timber carriers.[19]

BALANCE OF PAYMENTS

Both countries have balance of payments difficulties which differ in nature. The American problem is that, owing to military expenditure overseas, growing imports and the outward flow of investment funds, foreign claims on the dollar have grown to such a degree that they are many times the country's gold reserves. While the American difficulty is one of a surfeit of dollars, causing inflation at home and currency weakness abroad, the Soviet problem is that of finding enough dollars and other hard currencies. In order to speed up her industrial development and to make good gaps in her technology, the USSR is keen to buy industrial equipment abroad, where it is often of better quality and more advanced design than the home product. With most European countries and Japan the situation is easier, as they need Soviet raw materials, but with the United States the position is less favourable. American goods are highly prized in the Soviet Union but America does not need to buy Soviet timber, oil, gas and ore. In 1969 the USSR bought twice as much from the United States as she sold to that country. Foreign currency is also needed to buy foodstuffs so that the Soviet people may have a more varied diet, but many of the countries with the right type of food surplus are poor customers for Russian goods. Such imports may not be essential, but they are politically and socially desirable if the Russians are to have the higher standard of living they have been promised.

POLITICAL AND STRATEGIC ASPECTS OF TRADE

From the political and strategic viewpoints, the most important features of the trade pattern of the superpowers are the increasing dependence of the United States upon other countries for basic resources (Appendix B) and the growing surpluses of minerals becoming available from the USSR (Appendix C). The USA makes good its mineral deficiencies from the outer and inner circles of states which enclose the Soviet continental heartland. With nearly all of these countries the United States trades by sea, and her open coasts and ports, facing the two main oceans, facilitate this overseas commerce.

The two most important sources of mineral supply for the United States, however, are her adjacent land neighbours, Canada and Mexico. The exploitation of Canada's mineral resources is already largely in American hands, but Canada remains, none the less, a separate political state, the government of which could possibly take measures to control, restrict or even prohibit the export of certain minerals. The Americans have therefore been pressing upon Canada the need for a 'continental' policy in the development of North American resources; that is, one in which the political boundary would cease to function economically, and by which the two governments would undertake not to interfere with the free movement of minerals from one to the other. Such guaranteed access to Canada's mineral wealth would immensely strengthen America's resource position, but the objection of many Canadians to it was expressed in the words of Ottawa's minister of energy:

> It should be obvious there can be no such thing as a continental energy policy. No country can say to another 'your resources are our resources'. That's the sort of thing wars are fought about. How can anybody surrender in perpetuity a country's resources to another country?[20]

State Department officials have been quoted as regarding such attitudes as 'juvenile, even delinquent'.[21] The United States can bring powerful pressure to bear upon a recalcitrant Canada, weakened as that country is by internal divisions. The 1965 automotive agreement, which applied a 'continental' policy to the motor industry, enabling it to move its products and materials freely across the frontier, was very beneficial to Canada. The American companies found it advantageous to make more cars in Canada, and this led to a rapid expansion of the manufacturing sector of the Canadian economy. Hints were made in Washington that renewal of this agreement could be made contingent

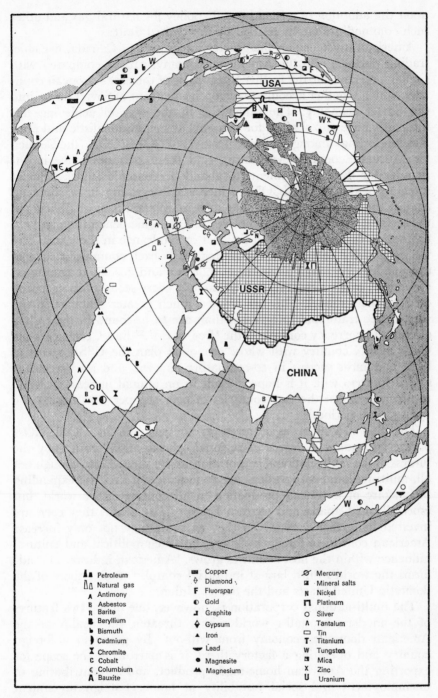

24. USA: major sources of mineral imports
Soviet mineral imports are relatively insignificant; see Appendix B

upon the adoption of a 'continental' policy for natural gas and other such commodities vitally needed by the United States.

American insistence on the greater integration of Canada, her chief trading partner, into the American economy, can be compared with similar pressures for the further integration of the east European countries, which together account for sixty-five per cent of Soviet trade, into the Soviet economy. The difficulties in the way of achieving this integration are also similar, for there are strong nationalistic and anti-Russian feelings among the lesser partners of COMECON (the Council for Mutual Economic Assistance), and these attitudes make it unpopular for their governments to abandon economic autarky. Soviet attempts within COMECON to increase integration have come up against the paradoxical truth that such integration is more difficult in the socialist than in the capitalist world. Economic penetration and co-ordination can go ahead with little let or hindrance in the latter. The USSR initially encouraged the setting up in each communist state of independent national planning authorities and insulated command economies, each attempting to develop fully every sector of its economy on the Soviet model. This has created much greater obstacles in the way of free trade and integration than are to be found in the tariffs, quotas and currency controls of the 'free world'.[22] East Germany is the COMECON country with whose economic plan the USSR seems to have had most success in co-ordinating its own, and an agreement signed in 1970 will, it is hoped, result in an annual increase in trade turnover between the two countries of over ten per cent during the 1971–5 plan period.[23]

The Soviet Union, as it attempts to persuade its COMECON partners to adopt a degree of regional specialisation, must envy the success of the multi-national corporation in the West. Most, though not all, multi-national corporations are American and they are expanding their share of industrial production in all corners of the world, but especially in Canada and western Europe. The profits they earn are invested in further growth. As they expand, they not only increase American control of foreign industry, but their political and cultural influence within the host countries grows. 'American industry abroad' forms the world's third largest industrial complex – after those of the domestic United States and the Soviet Union.

The multi-national corporation is, however, one of the two features of the modern capitalist world which threaten the health of the American domestic economy from without. By going to a foreign country and operating a factory there, it is narrowing the scope for exporting the American home-made product, and so contributing to unemployment and social instability at home. Foreign investment abroad by the multi-national corporation is also a factor in America's soaring balance-of-payments deficit. But although these companies restrain the growth of American exports, they do not diminish the volume of world trade. Thus a General Motors plant in country A may buy parts made in countries C, D and E, as well as export its finished cars to those countries.

An even greater problem for the United States domestic economy inherent in the freedom to co-ordinate and interpenetrate, which the capitalist world affords, is the threat to the domestic economy from foreign imports. During the post-war period the American tariff policy has been reasonably liberal, as it was realised that, for a variety of reasons, foreign countries must have access to the American market. It was in the interest of the United States that the states of the 'rimland' world should be as prosperous as possible and well disposed towards her. This was the surest guarantee for the containment of communism and for continued American access to the 'rimland' for resources, markets, investment and military bases. But success, especially in the case of Japan, West Germany and Italy, has been largely at the expense of the manufacturing sector of the American domestic economy, and inevitably pressures are building up inside America for more protection from foreign imports. Domestic and foreign policies are hard to reconcile in such circumstances.

Potentially, the Soviet Union, were it not for her alien political system and her state-regimented economy, would stand in a much stronger position for forging trade ties with western Europe and Japan. Unlike the USA, the USSR offers an almost unlimited market for consumer goods, a market which – again in sharp contrast to America – she will not be able herself to satisfy for many years, whatever promises the Party may make. In return, she could pay for such imports from advanced industrialised countries with a wide range of resource materials, so that the basic economic requirements for reciprocal trade on a large scale are present. Even today the great resource surpluses of the Soviet Union are making their impact felt in rising trade with Japan, West Germany and Britain, and it is inevitable that, as deposits of raw materials in the smaller and scattered areas of the islands and peninsulas of the 'rimland' world become depleted, the greater reserves of the Eurasian heartland will exert a growing centripetal pull.

Under an agreement signed in 1970 the Soviet Union will supply West Germany, over a period of twenty years, with fifty-two billion cubic metres of natural gas, starting in 1973. In return the Federal Republic undertook to send to Russia, in the period 1970–2, 1·2 million tons of steel pipe of 1·42 metre diameter. A similar arrangement was made with Italy in 1969. In March 1971 an agreement with France made provision for the supply of that country's nuclear power station at Fessenheim in Alsace with Soviet-enriched uranium. Negotiations with Japan for the joint exploitation of the great coal, oil, gas, ore and timber resources of eastern Siberia and the Far East have been going on for some time. Access to these reserves would solve Japan's raw material worries, while the Soviets would benefit, not only from the development of the Siberian regions most distant from the Russian base but also from the implication of Japan in their defence against any Chinese designs.

Already the growing exploitation of the mineral wealth of the Soviet heartland is exerting a centripetal force which is beginning to counteract the age-old centrifugal effect of ocean-borne, peripheral commerce. Undoubtedly, such great resource wealth must have momentous political and strategic significance, contrasting as it does with America's growing dependence on the outside world.

13 Population

The population of the Soviet Union in 1970 was 242 million, eighteen per cent greater than that of the USA (203 million). In 1960, when the figures were 212 and 179 million respectively, the Soviet lead was also eighteen per cent, but in 1940 the population of the USSR, within the present boundaries, was – at 194 million – forty-seven per cent greater than the 132 million of the United States. The large reduction in the gap between the two countries was mainly a result of the 1941–5 war in which some twenty million Soviet citizens died, compared with 292,000 from the United States. Further, because the large Soviet armies serving away from home separated the sexes to a high degree, the Soviet birth rate was then much lower than it would normally have been, and the infantile mortality rate was much higher because of the unfavourable conditions prevailing. The seventy thousand and more American deaths in the Korean and Vietnamese wars have had no significant impact on the population total, and statistically their effect is much less than that of motor vehicles: these have caused well over a million deaths in America since 1945.

If the total population of the USSR is greater than that of the USA, the density is higher in the latter country, amounting in 1969 to sixty-eight per square mile in the conterminous United States and to fifty-seven if Alaska and Hawaii are included. In the same year that of the Soviet Union was only twenty-eight per square mile. If the larger area of the USSR was peopled at the same density as the United States, its population would be nearly six hundred million.

In recent years the population of Russia has been growing only slightly faster than that of America, because the USSR is in a period in which there are relatively fewer potential mothers, owing to birth losses of the 1941–5 years; and in both countries the trend has been for the rate of increase to decline (Tables 13.1 and 13.2). The increases in the American total include immigration which averaged three hundred thousand a year in the 1960s. Immigration into the USSR is normally negligible, although between 1946 and 1950 over a hundred thousand Armenians are said to have returned to the Armenian SSR from their places of refuge abroad, followed by another forty thousand in the early

1960s. There is also thought to have been some migration of Uighurs from the Chinese province of Sinkiang into Kazakhstan, and Finnish building and timber workers have gone to the Soviet Union because of the labour shortage in north-western Russia.[1]

TABLE 13.1   CRUDE BIRTH, DEATH AND NATURAL GROWTH RATES
PER THOUSAND 1965-9[2]

| | USA | | | USSR | | |
	Birth rate	Death rate	Growth	Birth rate	Death rate	Growth
1965	19·5	9·4	10·1	18·4	7·3	11·1
1966	18·5	9·5	9·0	18·2	7·3	10·9
1967	17·9	9·3	8·6	17·4	7·6	9·8
1968	17·6	9·6	8·0	17·2	7·7	9·5
1969	17·7	9·5	8·2	17·0	8·1	8·9

Infantile mortality has fallen sharply in Russia and is now low in both countries (Table 13.3).

Government policy with regard to population growth is an important factor in the USSR, but much less so in the USA where individual

TABLE 13.2   ANNUAL INCREASE OF POPULATION 1965-70[3]
(millions)

	USA	USSR
1965	2·5	2·6
1966	2·3	2·6
1967	2·2	2·4
1968	2·1	2·3
1969	2·0	2·2
1970	2·1	2·2

choice operates in the light of economic circumstance, social custom and religious belief. Since 1936, in order to increase manpower for industrial and military purposes and, since the war, to make good the terrible losses suffered, the Soviet state has pursued a pro-natalist policy. Maternity benefits, child allowances for large families and taxes on the childless have been used, along with honours, such as the Order of Mother Heroine, and propaganda to stimulate a high birth rate. But in cities, where living space has been desperately scarce, and where female labour plays a vital part in the economy, a contradictory policy of

TABLE 13.3   DEATH RATE OF CHILDREN IN THEIR
FIRST YEAR PER THOUSAND LIVE BIRTHS[4]

	USA	USSR
1940	47	182
1950	29	81
1960	26	35
1967	22	26
1968	22	26
1969	21	26

encouraging the restriction of births has been followed. Legal abortion, ended by Stalin in 1936, was reintroduced in 1955, and contraceptives have been made increasingly available. As a result the urban birth rate (15·9 per thousand in 1969) is much lower than the rural (18·3 per thousand). The gap is wider than these figures, which are per thousand of the total urban or rural population, suggest, for younger people predominate in the towns, older ones in the countryside. The rural rate per thousand is higher, despite the fact that there are far fewer young women in that thousand than in an average thousand town-dwellers.

Although there is no official population policy in the USA, it has been suggested that the standards and attitudes created in America by the mass media favoured a high birth rate on economic grounds in the 1950s and early 1960s. There is much evidence for this:

'Your future is great in a growing America,' reads a so-called public service advertisement in the New York subway. 'Every day 11,000 babies are born in America. This means new business, new jobs, new opportunities.' And some weeks earlier the nation's most widely circulated weekly magazine had taken a similar tack with the cover title, 'Kids: Built-in Recession Cure – How 4,000,000 a Year Make Millions in Business.' Inside it was 'Rocketing Births: Business Bonanza'.[5]

However, by the late 1960s, with growing awareness of increasing congestion, lack of space, depletion of resources, pollution and other conservational problems, this attitude had changed. As early as 1966 *Time* magazine was hailing the fall in the birth rate as 'Welcome Decline' and noted that birth control had become more 'socially and ethically acceptable'.[6] Furthermore, government in America, as in the USSR, has now begun to concern itself with population. President Nixon has set up a 'Commission on Population Growth and the American Future' to investigate the means by which 'our nation can achieve a population level properly suited for its environmental . . . and other needs'. And for the first time Congress has voted funds to aid the spread of family planning, and for research into improved methods of birth control. Eighteen States have liberalised their abortion laws in the last few years.[7]

AGE AND SEX

The distribution of the population by age groups and sex can be readily seen from the diagrams (Fig. 25). The numbers in each five-year age group up to seventy are shown in tiers, with males on the left and females on the right. The American profile is more regular and symmetrical because calamities have interfered much less with the natural demographic progression than in Russia. Yet it does show one pronounced departure from the normal 'natural' pyramid, in which the age groups narrow from a wide base to a narrow summit. This is the 'waist' of irregularly low numbers in the age groups from twenty-five to forty-five, caused in part by the restrictions on immigration which began in 1921: immigrants were usually young people who soon started families. Then came the great economic depression which began in 1929 and continued on into the 1930s. This was the time when, in the words of a contemporary popular song, there was

> *No more money in the bank,*
> *No cute baby we can spank.*
> *What to do about it?*
> *Let's put out the light and go to sleep.*

The anti-natalist effect of the slump was prolonged by the partial separation of the sexes during the 1941–5 war. This, however, was followed by a large increase in births during the first post-war decade of peace and prosperity. But, as the narrower 'waist' moved through the main reproductive ages, the total number of births to women in these reduced age groups fell, producing the narrowing base shown in the 1970 profile. The narrowing has been accentuated by the trend towards a smaller family already observed, but it is likely to be temporary, for soon the 'wide' age groups born in the fecund post-war years will be reproductive and will probably increase the birth rate again.

The untidy ill-balanced Russian profile is the complex result of a lifetime of population catastrophes: World War One, revolution, civil war, famine, terror, World War Two. Each has not only affected the age groups in which it took place but reduced the number of births at the same time, and this smaller birth rate, by reducing the number of eventual mothers, is repeated from fifteen to thirty-five years afterwards. Thus artificially-narrowed age groups repeat themselves from generation to generation. And whereas the sex ratios in the population of the United States depart only slightly from the normal, those Russian generations which lived through the most calamitous periods (1917–25 and 1941–5) have shrivelled male components. In 1959 there were only twenty-six million men aged thirty-five and over in the Soviet Union compared with forty-seven million women, a deficit of twenty-one million. In the USA in 1960 the figures were thirty-seven and forty million respectively, a deficit of only three million males. In 1970 there was still a large excess of females in the total Soviet population, in which they totalled 130 million, or fifty-four per cent, against 111 million males or forty-six per cent.

It is noteworthy that, although the total population of the USSR exceeds that of the USA by some thirty-seven million, there were in 1970 many more Americans in the age group twenty to twenty-five than there were Soviet citizens. As this is the most important age group from the educational (post-graduate), industrial, military and demographic points of view, the significance of this fact is worth stressing. It means that in all these fields the USA has had an advantage, albeit a

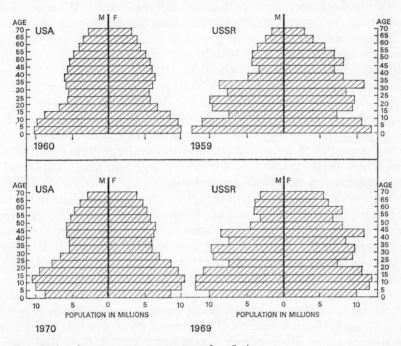

25. Population by age groups, 1959 and 1969/70
Population aged over 70 not shown

temporary one, in the greater supply of young men and women and of the human energy this greater number represents. This vital twenty to twenty-five age group was so small in the USSR because of the degree to which the wartime separation of sexes prevented births in the 1940s and also because of the high infant mortality that prevailed in those calamitous years among those who were born. The problems posed for the Soviet government by the sudden diminution in the supply of young and energetic workers, which began to make itself felt in 1963, were behind many of the difficulties and discontents that resulted in the fall of Nikita Khrushchev in 1964.

ETHNIC AND LINGUISTIC COMPOSITION

In both countries there is a large minority of non-European peoples. Of the 203 million Americans in 1970, twenty-six million or twelve per cent were non-European, mainly Negro. Of the 242 million Soviet citizens in 1970, fifty-two million or twenty-two per cent were non-European. About half of the latter are Turkic peoples inhabiting the Caucasian and Central Asian republics (Uzbeks, Tartars, Kazakhs, Turkmen, Azerbaydzhanis, Kirghiz, etc.). Although these peoples are anthropologically distinct from the Europeans, the difference is by no means so striking as that between white and black in America and presents less obstacle to racial harmony than cultural, national and other factors associated with ethnic variety. The large non-European minority in the USSR is divided among a hundred different nations and peoples, but in the USA it is almost wholly Negro. And whereas in America the Negroes do not form a majority of the population in any one State (except the District of Columbia) and exceed a quarter of the population only in five, large areas of the Soviet Union are predominantly inhabited by non-European peoples who have varying degrees of self-government.

A post-war American demographic phenomenon has been the migration of nearly four million Negroes from backward, poverty-stricken farming areas in the south-east into the towns, where they often concentrate in the decaying zone that is usually found close to the central business district. There is nothing in the USSR comparable to this Negro invasion of American cities, but instead rather a Russian movement into the towns of non-Russian areas. As a result all national Republics have Russian minorities of varying sizes, while in Kazakhstan, owing to the immigration of large numbers of Russians to cultivate the steppes under Khrushchev's 'virgin and idle lands campaign', there are more Russians than Kazakhs.

The predominating 'white' or European sections of the population of each superpower have been derived from a variety of European nationalities (Table 13.4). Whereas in the USSR these nationalities remain fairly geographically distinct, each with its own homeland and language, those of the United States have become inextricably mixed, and have often lost their separate identities, merging into one American nation. An obvious contrast between the 'white' or European peoples of each country is that those of the Soviet Union originated almost wholly in eastern Europe, those of the United States mainly from western Europe. Nevertheless, the United States has a sizeable minority of its population originating in eastern Europe.

The Soviet 'white' population is overwhelmingly Slavonic and

TABLE 13.4   NATIONAL ORIGIN OF THE WHITE POPULATION 1959-60[8]
(millions: percentages in parentheses)

USA (1960)			USSR (1959)		
British	59	(32)	Russians	115	(55)
Germans	26	(15)	Ukrainians	37	(18)
Irish	17	(10)	Belorussians	8	(4)
Italians	10	(6)	Lithuanians	2	(1)
Poles	8	(4)	Jews	2	(1)
Russians	5	(3)	Moldavians	2	(1)
Swedes	4	(2)	Germans	2	(1)
French	4	(2)	Latvians	1	(1)
Czechs	3	(2)	Poles	1	(1)
Dutch	3	(2)	Estonians	1	(1)

NOTE The USA figures for British and French origin include Canadians of those origins.

principally Russian; but no single national origin predominates in the United States, where variety is the keynote. This variety is, however, of diminished importance, because people of diverse origin have usually lost their separate cultures and languages, and have become English-speaking Americans. This is less true of those born in the United States of foreign parents (twenty-four million in 1960) and still less of those born abroad (nine million in 1960). There is nothing comparable to this 'foreign white stock' in the USSR, where immigration is almost totally unknown. On the other hand, many present Soviet citizens lived outside the pre-war borders of the USSR before 1940, when they were citizens of the independent states of Lithuania, Estonia, Latvia, or of Poland, Rumania, Finland or Czechoslovakia. They became Soviet citizens as a result of the expansion of the borders of the USSR, and in a sense might also be termed 'foreign white stock'.

RELIGION

Differences in religion between the two superpowers reflect the different origins of the population as well as the social and political system of each country. Thus, in the United States at the last available count, almost the whole population over the age of fourteen had membership of a church. But as social and even economic pressures in favour of such membership are strong, it is impossible to say what proportion of the 124 million church members were actual believers. On the other hand, in the Soviet Union, where the pressures are the other way round, the great mass of the population is not attached to any religion, although again it is not possible to say how many of these supposed atheists do not have some belief.

In the United States there are over a hundred different denominations and sects, the most numerous being the Roman Catholic church, claiming nearly fifty million members, followed by eighteen different Baptist bodies with a combined membership of twenty-five million. In the Soviet Union church membership is strongest among the old and in the Moslem republics of Central Asia. Most Russians who are religious belong to the Russian Orthodox church, but there are Roman Catholics and Protestants in the Baltic republics and other western districts previously outside the Soviet Union. There appear to have been many Baptists and Jehovah's Witness conversions of late, despite persecution, but the numbers involved are probably small, seen against the population as a whole.

GEOGRAPHICAL DISTRIBUTION

In both countries a large part of the population is concentrated in a relatively small area. In the United States in 1970, almost half was in the north-eastern manufacturing belt, in only twelve per cent of the total area of the country. In the Soviet Union, almost three-quarters of the population lived in a triangular area, with its base along the western frontier and its apex at Irkutsk (near Lake Baykal), comprising under a fifth of the total area. But density is much higher, at about 230 per square mile, in the American north-east than in the Russian triangle (100 per square mile); and outside the American zone of concentration population is more evenly spread over the rest of the country, leaving only relatively small areas of the mountainous and arid western States unsettled. In the Soviet Union most of the remaining four-fifths of the country consist of uninhabited or thinly-settled tundra, forest, desert or mountainous land; the remaining quarter of the population is crowded into three further zones of concentration –

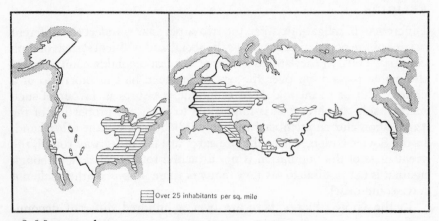

Over 25 inhabitants per sq. mile

26. Most populous areas

on both sides of the Great Caucasus mountains and in the piedmont belt of Central Asia.

There is a tendency in both countries for population to grow more rapidly in the marginal areas and least in central areas. In the United States the States with the fastest rates of growth are in the west, the south and along the eastern seaboard, while States in the interior are adding population relatively slowly or even losing it. In the Soviet Union – disregarding the vast unpopulated extent of the north-east – the fastest-growing regions are in the south, from Moldavia to Central Asia and Kazakhstan and in the Far East, while the slowest are those in the centre of Russia. There has in recent years been a drift from central Russia to the warmer and sunnier climates of Central Asia.[9] There has also been a return of Russians from the harsh northland, undoing some of the work of Stalin who, with ruthless cruelty, transplanted *kulaks* and recalcitrant peasants from the genial summer warmth of the Ukraine to new settlements in the blizzard-swept tundra.

The interior States of the USA are mainly agricultural and affected by the continued drift from the farms, but another slowly-growing or declining group of States is that on the Appalachian coalfield (Kentucky, West Virginia, Ohio) and reflects the sharp reduction in the coal-mining labour force. The central group of regions in Russia, where population is increasing slowly, include the largest industrial area of the country, but they also contain relatively dense agricultural populations from which a strong tide of emigration is flowing.

In America the new military-oriented industries and the attractive climates of the south-west and the south-east, and the persisting prosperity of the eastern seaboard continue to draw population from other regions. But in the USSR, although migration is important, the birth rate differential between the Russians and non-Russian peoples is an even stronger influence leading to the more rapid increase of population in the outer lands and especially in Soviet Central Asia.

URBAN AND RURAL

In both countries the flight from the land continues unabated, and the farms have difficulty in holding their labour. But in the United States this process has gone on longer and is further advanced. In 1970 about eighty per cent of America's population was urban or suburban, compared with fifty-six per cent in the Soviet Union. As a result, despite the larger total Soviet population, twenty-five million more Americans live in cities, towns and suburbs.

American cities are larger than those of the Soviet Union. The United States has thirty-three urban areas with a population over one

H

million, the USSR only ten; the United States has twelve over two million, the Soviet Union only two. The thirty American conurbations with a population of over a million hold over eighty million people or forty per cent of the total population. But the ten Soviet millionaire cities have a total population of only twenty-one million – a mere nine per cent of the total. In brief, four times as many Americans live in large urban areas.

Many of the large American conurbations lie close together and are becoming linked by urban sprawl into giant multi-million agglomerations known as 'megalopolises' – a word introduced by Lewis Mumford in the 1930s.[10] The larger Russian towns, on the other hand, are more compact, more concentrated and more isolated. The average distance from Moscow to the other nine millionaire cities of the USSR is 850 miles, while from Leningrad it is 1,084 miles. Moscow and the Chicago metropolitan area have similar populations, but the built-up area of the American city is twenty times as large. This is because in Moscow most of the population lives concentrated in small apartments in large buildings within easy reach of public transport, whereas in Chicago most of the inhabitants live in single dwellings, and for many of these the private car provides the only means of access. It is the ubiquitous motor car that has made possible the spread of vast urban agglomerations in America: it is its relative absence that has prevented a similar expansion in the USSR.

The relatively small number of very large cities in the Soviet Union is partly due to the strong antipathy shown by the Soviet leaders to 'overgrown' cities. There have been many regulations limiting the size of the biggest towns and many restrictions have been placed on their further growth, while nearly a thousand new towns have been established, most of them as yet small; and existing small towns have been preferred to the big centres in the allocation of new industry. But these attempts have only been partially successful, and the big city exerts its powerful attraction in the USSR as it does elsewhere. In the USA there has been no such government influence, and towns have grown according to freely-operating economic, sociological and demographic factors. As a result 'the United States is heading for a future in which most of its people will live in a dozen or so huge metropolitan complexes'.[11]

Although America has many more large cities, there is little difference between the number of towns as a whole. Thus the 1960 census gave the USA 333 places with a population of over fifty-thousand and the 1959 Soviet census gave the USSR 299.

Present trends in urban growth are illustrated by Tables 13.5 and 13.6, which show the largest absolute increases and also the more important percentage increases. The absolute increases reflect the greater American concentration of population growth in the larger metropolitan areas. It is noteworthy that ten of the twelve American conurbations listed in Table 13.5 are on the sea coast or on the Great

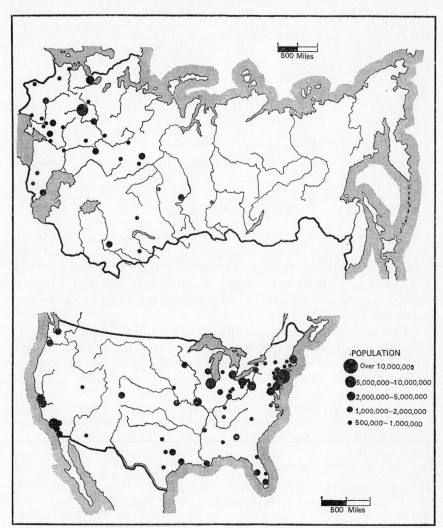

27. Urban areas, 1970

Lakes, while ten of the twelve Soviet towns are inland, and several of them over a thousand miles from the sea. The percentage increases (Table 13.6) illustrate the continued growth of great coastal agglomerations on the Pacific and Gulf coasts of the United States, and the importance of state planning on urban development in the Soviet

TABLE 13.5 URBAN AREAS WITH THE LARGEST ABSOLUTE
INCREASES OF POPULATION

(*thousands*)

USA, 1960–70		USSR, 1959–70	
Los Angeles, Calif.*	2,042	Moscow, Central Russia	1,017
New York, N.Y.–N.J.†	1,172	Leningrad, N.W. Russia	528
San Francisco, Calif.‡	884	Kiev, Ukraine	522
Chicago, Ill.–Ind.§	817	Tashkent, Central Asia	458
Washington, D.C.–Md–Va	784	Minsk, White Russia	398
Houston, Tex.	567	Baku, Transcaucasia	293
Philadelphia, Pa–N.J.	475	Novosibirsk, W. Siberia	276
Dallas, Tex.	437	Alma Ata, Central Asia	274
Atlanta, Ga	373	Kharkov, Ukraine	270
Detroit, Mich.	358	Sverdlovsk, Urals	247
Miami, Fla	333	Kuybyshev, Volga region	241
Minneapolis–St Paul, Minn.	332	Omsk, West Siberia	240

* Los Angeles, Anaheim–Santa Ana–Garden Grove and San Bernardino–
Riverside–Ontario SMAs.
† New York, Jersey City, Newark and Paterson–Clifton–Passaic SMAs.
‡ San Francisco–Oakland and San Jose SMAs.
§ Chicago and Gary–Hammond–East Chicago SMAs.

Union. Tolyatti owes its rapid rise to its selection as the site of a mammoth motor works; Lipetsk was given a large new integrated steel complex in the 1960s; Tyumen, like Houston and Dallas in the USA, is the centre of a major new oilfield development; Minsk, Ulyanovsk, Ryazan and Gomel all received several large industrial establishments under the 1966–70 five-year plan.

The towns that have grown slowest are, in both countries, mostly coal-mining or heavy industrial towns which have lost workers through mechanisation and which have no compensating service or administrative functions (Table 13.7). The inclusion of Moscow shows the

TABLE 13.6 URBAN AREAS WITH POPULATION OVER 250,000
HAVING THE LARGEST PERCENTAGE INCREASES IN POPULATION

USA, 1960–70		USSR, 1959–70	
Las Vegas, Nev.	115	Tolyatti, Volga region	247
Anaheim–Santa Ana–Garden		Frunze, Central Asia	96
Grove*	102	Lipetsk, Central Russia	85
Oxnard–Ventura, Calif.	89	Minsk, White Russia	80
Fort Lauderdale–Hollywood, Fla	86	Tyumen, West Siberia	79
San Jose, Calif.†	66	Ulyanovsk, Volga region	71
Santa Barbara, Calif.*	56	Kishinev, Moldavia	65
West Palm Beach, Fla	53	Dushanbe, Central Asia	65
Phoenix, Ariz.	46	Kherson, Ukraine	65
San Bernardino–Riverside–		Ryazan, Central Russia	64
Ontario, Calif.*	41	Gomel, White Russia	62
Houston, Texas	40		
Austin, Texas	39		

* Part of the Los Angeles conurbation.
† Part of the San Francisco conurbation.

limited value of percentage assessments of growth, since the city had by
far the largest Soviet absolute increase (Table 13.5). Deliberate
attempts have been made by the authorities to slow its growth, and no
more industry is to be developed within its boundaries. It may also be
noted that the slowest-growing Soviet towns have not declined or
stagnated to the same extent as the laggard urban areas of the United
States.

In the distribution of the larger urban agglomerations there is a
striking contrast, linked with the fundamental distinction between
Russia's heartland location in the land hemisphere, and America's more
detached position surrounded by ocean. Of the thirty-three American
standard metropolitan areas in 1970 with a population over one million,
no fewer than seventeen have a coastal location and five more are on the

TABLE 13.7   URBAN AREAS WITH POPULATION OVER 250,000
HAVING THE SMALLEST PERCENTAGE INCREASES IN POPULATION
(*percentages*)

USA, 1960–70		USSR, 1959–70	
Charleston, W. Va	−9	Prokopyevsk, West Siberia	−2
Johnstown, Pa	−6	Makayevka, Ukraine	6
Duluth–Superior, Minn.–Wis.	−4	Gorlovka, Ukraine	9
Wilkes Barre–Hazelton, Pa	−1	Nizhniy Tagil, Urals	12
Huntington–Ashland, W. Va–		Magnitogorsk, Urals	17
Ky–Ohio	−0·4	Moscow, Central Russia	17
Pittsburgh, Pa	−0·2		

Great Lakes and connected by the St Lawrence with the Atlantic. But
if the thirty-three leading Soviet cities are taken, only four are located
on the sea coast.

There are also noteworthy differences in the morphology and
general appearance of the towns of each country. With the exception
of the largest cities, with their distinctive traditional and historical role –
notably Moscow and Leningrad – and some Central Asian towns with a
predominantly Moslem architecture, the central area of the typical
Russian town tends to be rather drab, with the two-storey, painted
stucco buildings of the late tsarist period predominating. As one moves
away from the old centre the first Soviet blocks of flats, modest in height
and undistinguished in architecture, appear. And the farther one goes
out, the newer and taller these blocks become, with the veritable sky-
scrapers on the periphery. This is quite different from the American
town, with its concentrated central business district characterised by
tall blocks, and with a progressive diminution in the average height of
buildings outwards until the low and individual 'ranch-style' dwellings
– often of one storey only – of the newest and most select residential
areas are found on the fringe.

This contrast is rooted in the different economic systems. Private business develops the central areas of large American cities to provide office space for the headquarters administration of local concerns and the branch offices of national ones. But in Russia, where all economic administration is headquartered in Moscow, there is little need for office space in the normal large Soviet city. Consequently, while tertiary or service workers predominate over factory workers in most American towns, in few of which manufacturing employs more than forty per cent of the labour force, in most Soviet cities over forty per cent of employees work in factories. In brief, whereas the average share of manufacturing employment in American cities is twenty-eight per cent, in the Soviet Union the proportion is about fifty per cent.[12]

The one main point of similarity between American and Russian towns is fast disappearing. Before the 1941–5 war it could be said that a large part of the urban population lived in individual houses of wooden construction, unlike the urban populations of western Europe, whose dwellings were mainly of brick or stone. But whereas the sprawl of frame and clapboard houses continues to proliferate around American cities, the old traditional and often cunningly ornamented wooden houses of the Russian town are being systematically destroyed and the population rehoused in new blocks of steel and concrete.

Many Russian towns were reduced to rubble during the war and have been reconstructed according to master plans with handsome buildings and tree-lined avenues. The new Volgograd, which as Stalingrad was destroyed in the 1941–2 battle, is one of the most beautiful modern towns in the world. All Soviet towns, new and old alike, are distinguished by their general cleanliness, the absence of litter, the paucity of advertisements and neon signs, and by their more regular architecture. Unlike the automobile-crowded roads of American cities, Soviet streets carry mainly trolley-buses, buses, taxis and lorries (trucks), with an occasional donkey cart or hand barrow. But the number of cars is increasing.

14 Standard of Living and Way of Life

Taking the material aspects of life first and starting with the basic necessity of food, there are great differences between the two countries in the matter of diet. Americans eat more and do so from a wider variety of foods. Despite their smaller population and greater agricultural productivity, they spent over $5 million in 1969 on imported food and drink, compared with a Russian foreign food bill of just under one and a quarter million. Diet in the USSR is still largely bread-based; whereas in the USA, in common with most advanced Western countries, bread has, since the 1920s, ceased to be the 'staff of life' and assumed a relatively minor position in the national diet. Americans eat more beef, more chicken and a much wider variety of fruits and vegetables; and these are available throughout the year, and not only seasonally as in Russia. Russians eat more cabbage, more potatoes and more fish. However, according to Brezhnev, the Soviet diet is improving, with a greater consumption of meat, milk and eggs and less bread.[1]

Most American food is now processed, prepared, prepacked or precooked; it is adulterated by additives of all kinds – preservatives, emulsifiers, flavours and colours. It comes as a manufactured product and is less and less seen in its natural raw state. In the Soviet Union, however, although the canning branch of the food-processing industry is well advanced, foods are still mainly purchased in their natural condition, with all the preparation and cooking taking place in the home, the canteen or the restaurant. This practice is connected with the fact that a much larger proportion of the Soviet population is rural and lives on or close to farms, as well as with the backward state of consumer-oriented industries in the USSR compared with the USA. Foods in the Soviet Union are much more closely linked with regional produce and regional customs, whereas in the USA, although there are local specialities, a standardised diet prevails.

This difference places a heavy burden on Soviet women who, besides their employment, have to spend additional hours in the purchase and preparation of food. Unless they have access to a collective

farm market, where the farmers offer their produce for sale in open
stalls, they have to go through the cumbersome method of dealing that
is universal in the state stores: the customer first selects her purchase
and ascertains the price, then goes to the cash desk to pay and get a
receipt, after which she must return to the counter to collect the goods;
in each case she must wait her turn in what may be a long queue. Not
for Soviet women the speed and convenience of the self-service super-
market.

It may well be that the narrower range of foodstuffs available in
Russia, because they are cooked and presented with more imagination
and versatility than is possible with already processed foods, give more
flavour and enjoyment than the more varied but yet more standardised
American diet. It may also be true that the home preparation and
cooking of raw and unadulterated food gives a health advantage compensating for the defects caused by shortages in certain branches of the
diet.

The dietary needs of Americans and Russians must also be different.
Because the Soviet Union is still in the earlier throes of its industrial
revolution, with an emphasis on the construction of equipment for
heavy industry and on the rapid expansion of old towns and the building of new, and because of its much larger farm population, there are
many millions more engaged in heavy manual labour than in the USA,
where the bulk of the population is employed in relatively light tasks,
whether industrial, commercial or administrative. Such work in Russia
is almost entirely in the hands of women, who, none the less, participate
also in the heavy work of factory, farm and mine. The more severe
Soviet winter and the fact that buildings are not heated to the high
temperatures customary in the United States, also increase the relative
need of Soviet man for food, as well as the fact that he normally has no
automobile and has to walk a great deal more than his American
opposite. That a vast human effort has been sustained in these circumstances testifies to the adequacy of the Soviet diet in supplying
energy, and an American study concludes that 'the average Soviet
family – particularly the workers and students who eat their noon meal
in the factory or school restaurant or cafeteria – probably eat reasonably
well by American standards'.[2]

Restaurants in Russia are normally overcrowded and there are often
queues outside waiting to get in. Wages have risen but the supply of
consumer goods has not expanded fast enough to keep up with this
swelling purchasing power. Consequently dining out has become for
Russians the great luxury in which more and more can indulge, with
the added advantage that it lessens the burden of shopping and cooking
already alluded to. It may be that, although more Americans pick up

light snacks of the hamburger kind, when it comes to sitting down to a large meal the urban Soviet citizen is well ahead. It has been estimated that one half of the average Soviet family's income goes on food and drink, compared with the American figure of less than a quarter.[3]

Another difference between the two peoples connected with food, is that Russians appear to have no set mealtimes, but seem to be ready to eat a meal at any time of day or night, and likewise to go without food for a long time. Americans are far more regular in this respect.

As for drink, one can only make impressionistic comments, for lack of Soviet consumption data. Russians obviously drink more tea, more mineral water, and less coffee, cocoa and chocolate. Americans drink more fruit juice. In both countries consumption of spirits and beer is high, although the ubiquitous state propaganda against alcoholic drink in the Soviet Union contrasts strongly with the heavy advertising of it in America. Both countries have their local wines, with the United States also importing from Europe. The Russians, of course, have nothing to equal the vast American consumption of cola drinks, but instead have the refreshing *kvas*, a light non-alcoholic drink made from rye and barley and sold from roadside tanks.

CLOTHING

If food takes up over half a Soviet family's income, it would seem, because of the very high prices, that clothing must consume most of what remains, especially in view of the harsh climatic conditions. This is borne out by what fragmentary statistical evidence there is, viz. that expenditure on clothing is about forty-five per cent of that on food.[4] Although adult clothing is very dear, especially in relation to the Soviet wage level, hardship is alleviated by the price of children's clothing being kept low. In the United States clothing claims only ten per cent of personal consumption expenditure. The urban population in the Soviet Union is well clothed; the drabness has largely gone in the face of increased attention to design and variety, but a marked standardisation of dress still contrasts with the kaleidoscopic medley of styles found in America. Rural clothing is more often ragged and patched, and reflects the near poverty still existing in the Russian countryside.

HOUSING

In shelter there are also big differences between American and Soviet standards. Americans, on the average, have far more space – an average density of 0·63 persons per room compared with 2·3 per room in the USSR.[5] There is, in fact, a severe shortage of living space in the USSR, especially in the towns, resulting from the influx from the countryside and aggravated by the wholesale destruction of housing during the war. This has been a factor in reducing the urban birth rate, since large families cannot be reared in the small apartments that are often the only accommodation available in Soviet cities.

Urban housing differs in type and appearance. In Soviet towns, the old-style wooden houses are giving way to large municipally-owned apartment blocks, rapidly erected by cranes with prefabricated panels. But in the USA the urban sprawl is increasingly made up of privately owned single-family dwellings. In these there is an extremely wide range between the spacious, well-appointed house in an exclusive residential district and the older tumbledown shacks of a decaying area in an unsavoury part of the town. Soviet apartment houses are much more standardised and have nothing to compare with the contrast to be found in America between the expensive and luxurious apartment tenanted by the wealthy, and the filthy, crumbling tenement of the back streets.

The Soviet citizen certainly scores on grounds of cost, paying for his small apartment, and all services, no more than four or five per cent of his income, whereas the average American has to spend fourteen or fifteen per cent of his income on renting or buying his house and a like amount on household services, giving a total of thirty per cent.

In the countryside the contrasts between the two countries are less glaring. In both, wooden farmhouses are the rule. In both there are some large and comfortable houses, but there is nothing in the Soviet Union to compare with the well-appointed residences of the more prosperous farmers and ranchers of America – unless it be the country *dachas* of the party leaders. In both there are many ill-kept shacks. In America, with the disappearance of the wigwam, there is nothing like the traditional Asian *yurt* or tent in which some of the non-Russian population of Siberia and Central Asia still camp, especially in the livestock-raising districts.

SOCIAL SERVICES

All medical and dental care is free of charge without formality in the USSR, and medical staffs are attached to factories and institutions; they are preponderantly female. Rural areas suffer, however, from the unwillingness of qualified doctors to live in the villages because of the lack of amenities there. The health service cost the state nine billion roubles in 1970.[6] The free medical service, which includes treatment in hospitals and rest and recuperation in sanitoria at pleasure resorts, is organised by the various industrial undertakings and the trade unions. The sanitoria are mostly the converted mansions of wealthy pre-revolutionary aristocrats on the Black Sea coast. In certain circumstances the Soviet citizen may have to buy his own drugs.

In the United States most employees take out some form of insurance through their firms against medical expenses, although this usually leaves many items, including dental care, to be paid for privately. For the poor and uninsured, who are unable to pay doctor's fees or hospital expenses, the outlook is indeed bleak. Not until 1966 was provision made for those aged sixty-five and over, and unable to pay, to have medical care free of charge. The average share of an American's personal income to be spent on health charges is between six and seven per cent, and in 1968 the total amounted to $33 billion. In no other sphere of American life have prices risen so fast: in 1960 the cost was only $19 billion and in 1950, under $9 billion. It could be said in 1970 that 'most Americans could still be financially destroyed by a prolonged and serious illness in the family'; and that 'the most glaring shortcoming of the system is the unavailability of care to the poor, the isolated, and members of minority groups'.[7]

The Soviet Union has a system of maternity benefits and child allowances in which, in 1968, three and a half million mothers received 500 million roubles. Seen against the wage levels of the USSR the payments to mothers with large families appear generous, but people in the towns are unable to benefit because the severely limited space makes it impossible to accommodate large families. Women who are alone – unmarried, widowed or divorced – receive extra allowances.[8] In addition, nurseries and kindergartens – often attached to factories and collective farms – are provided free or at nominal charges. Family allowances as such are not paid in the United States but allowances are made for dependants against income tax. Thus, under the Revenue Act of 1964, a married couple with two children and earning $5,000 a year, paid $211 a year less tax than a childless couple earning the same amount.

Old age pensions are paid in the USSR at the age of sixty for men and fifty-five for women at a minimum rate of 30 roubles and a maximum of 120 roubles a month, except for collective farm workers whose minimum is 12 roubles and maximum 102 roubles.[9] In the United States insured men and women become eligible for social security pensions at sixty-five but they can opt for lower benefits up to three years earlier. Provision is also made for those over seventy-two who are not insured and therefore get no pension at sixty-five. These pensions, together with disability payment and medical care for the aged, cost $24·6 million in 1967.[10]

Unemployment is not a serious social problem in the USSR owing to the rapid expansion of the economy and the shortening of the working week. In the United States the percentage of the labour force unemployed fluctuates rather widely with economic conditions: it usually lies somewhere between three and six per cent. Unemployment among non-whites is more than double that among whites. Unemployment insurance is primarily a matter for the States. Maximum benefits vary from $30 to $68 a week and the period over which they can be drawn from twenty-two to thirty-nine weeks. Extra allowances are paid for dependants but, again, these vary from State to State. In addition, 'welfare' payments are now made by the federal government to those unable or unwilling to support themselves and their children.

The speed and cheapness of the administration of Soviet justice in civil cases contrasts sharply with the endless delays and mounting costs that characterise the American legal system. Court proceedings are very simple in Russia: two elected lay magistrates (people's assessors) sit with the professional judge, normally serving for two weeks, for which they get paid leave from their work; they can together outvote the judge. Counsel appear on both sides. Most civil cases coming before the Soviet courts are concerned with marriage troubles and involve disputes about maintenance, etc.

When it comes to furnishing and equipping their homes, Soviet citizens come far behind in numbers of washing machines, refrigerators, vacuum cleaners and all the other gadgets commonplace in the American home. Radios and televisions are, however, nearly universal and the number of telephones, refrigerators and vacuum cleaners is rising fast in the towns (Table 14.1). But the gap between town and country in the possession of such goods is higher than in America. Many other electrical appliances, which are becoming standard in American kitchens, are unknown or almost so in the Soviet Union.

Unlike his American counterpart the Soviet citizen is almost always dependent on public transport, which suffers from an uncomfortable degree of overcrowding; but fares are low – four kopeks for a bus ride and five for any distance on the underground railways of the larger towns. Taxis also are very cheap at 10 kopeks a kilometre (18 cents a mile). The rural resident suffers from the absence of roads, and horse-

TABLE 14.1 NUMBER OF WIRELESS RECEIVERS,
TELEVISIONS AND TELEPHONES 1969[11]
(*millions*)

	Wireless receivers	*Televisions**	*Telephones*
USA	61·1	60·3	109·3†
USSR	46·7	30·8	12·0

* Black and white only.　　† 1968.

drawn carts and sledges are still common in all rural parts of the
Soviet Union, and they often penetrate into the towns. Many collective
farmers are now acquiring motor cycles, but ownership of a private
motor car is still unusual. In contrast to the low demand made upon the
Russian purse the average American pays out thirteen per cent of his
income for transportation. In the USA seventy-nine per cent of all
families owned cars, while twenty-seven per cent owned two or more.
The percentage of families owning a car in the USSR must be a mere
fraction of one per cent.

RECREATION

The great contrast in the outdoor games played by Americans and
Russians lies in the different type of football played and watched. By
adopting association football as a national game the USSR has been
able to share a world-wide interest and to participate in contests involving most countries in the world. The American brand of football
and the national baseball game tend to isolate the United States in the
world of sport. Both countries are, however, foremost in athletics, but
as would be expected winter sports and ice hockey are more widespread
in the USSR. Artificial toboggan runs and ski lifts make up for the
failure of nature to provide adequate facilities in the flatter parts of the
country. Hunting and fishing have many eager devotees in both countries, but opportunities are more extensive in the USSR where there is
less river pollution; winter fishing through the ice is very popular on
Russian rivers and ponds. Public urban parks play a greater part in
providing recreation in Russia than they do in the United States, and
although often designated 'parks of rest and culture' they contain much
apparatus of the fairground type. It goes without saying that Russians
walk more.

The automobile gives the Americans far greater mobility, enabling
them to travel great distances from home and, at vacation time, to
travel to all parts of the country, visiting resorts, national parks and
places of historic interest. Although holidays by the sea and camping
out at beauty spots are increasing in the USSR they still have to take
place within the limits imposed by public transport. Even when people
do travel within the Soviet Union, they often cannot find hotel accommodation. The hotels seem always to be filled to capacity by members
of delegations, conferences, officials, foreign tourists and other favoured
groups. Individual travellers often have to pass the night at the railway
station. Holidays are comparable in length. The Soviet worker, like his
American counterpart, has three weeks paid holiday a year, plus eight
national holidays. They are usually arranged by the trade unions,

which also provide accommodation in the crowded Black Sea and other resorts.

A striking contrast in indoor entertainment is the broader popular support given in the Soviet Union to the theatre, ballet and opera, and the large attendance at concerts, art galleries and museums, with the cinema occupying a relatively minor role. In the United States such cultural activities tend to be the preserve of the wealthier classes upon whose patronage they are dependent for financial support. In the Soviet Union, in return for generous state subsidies, the arts are expected to foster 'socialist realism', to celebrate 'the heroic deeds of the people' and to promote 'the noble ideas of revolutionary humanism'.[12]

The circus retains a strong attraction in the USSR, which is also unique in the extent to which chess is played by all classes. The game corresponds in universality to playing cards in the United States, where bowling alleys and pool rooms are also a distinctive feature. Urban amusement arcades equipped with gaming machines and discotheques, now common in America, are absent from the USSR.

In television the contrasts are many. American television offers more variety among the competing networks, much wide-ranging and free discussion of matters of public interest and concern, but also a good deal of triviality. It tends to emphasise the more sensational events, especially those involving violence, thereby encouraging those groups and individuals who seek publicity to resort to violence. The constant interruption for advertising matter is an impediment to full enjoyment. Soviet television offers only three programmes, one of which is educational. Viewing hours are much shorter, the quality of the material much higher, and programmes are not normally interrupted. But political, social and economic questions are, as one would expect, presented to the satisfaction of the Soviet government and the Communist party, and news material is selected accordingly. Of the two general programmes, one runs from twelve noon to midnight and is largely serious in content, with news, current affairs and documentaries predominating, while the other, which operates only from 6.30 p.m. to midnight, consists of concerts, films and a children's programme.

Russians read more, and the avid eagerness for the printed word is apparent to any observer, despite the rather limited fare and the preponderance among available books and journals of social, cultural, political and technical matter. Doubtless the fact that this is the first wholly literate generation has something to do with such enthusiasm; the cheapness of Russian books is also a factor. In 1969 seventy-five thousand new books were produced in the USSR as against some thirty thousand in the USA, but the total number of copies sold is similar – about one and a half billion in each country.

LIFE IN GENERAL

The absence of political freedoms – the inability to talk politics openly, to join competing political parties, to vote, to assemble, to demonstrate – is of little concern to the ordinary Russian, who has for centuries fatalistically regarded government in the same way as the climate – harsh and unrelenting, but inevitable and immovable. Likewise, the ordinary American places such activities as sport, entertainment, television, his car and reading the comics well ahead of politics among his interests. Increasingly those Americans who have a genuine political interest appear to find the political system inadequate and frustrating, and to express their interest outside of it. Dissatisfaction and perturbation with official policy and action are widespread among intellectuals and academics.

In the Soviet Union, likewise, real discontent appears to be confined to the small minority of intellectuals whose insistence on thinking, discussing and writing freely and critically brings them into conflict with the Party. The activity and fertility of intellectual life in the Soviet Union is remarkable, even though it has often to find expression in a strong undercurrent of satire. Most intellectuals work directly or indirectly for the state, publicly serving the system they often despise while privately hating, ridiculing or merely tolerating it. Those driven to defect do so not so much from any persecution or even lack of freedom, but more from a sense of claustrophobic isolation and hopelessness – the realisation that they are a tiny minority out of sympathy with government and masses alike. American intellectuals do not suffer from this to anything like the same degree but nevertheless often feel isolated by an alliance between politicians and people. Recent years and recent problems have, however, caused the opposition to be listened to with increased tolerance and attention, and the contrast between the repetitive insistence on one dogma that characterises the Soviet press, radio and television, and the open forum which these same media now provide in the United States, for critics of all kinds, represents one of the widest gulfs between life in the two countries.

If there is less political freedom in Russia then there is more social freedom, except in the sphere of travel outside – and in some cases inside – the country. Russians know nothing of the heavy social pressures to conform and to compete which burden so many Americans. The high and ever-rising material level of living of an advanced capitalist country, combined with seductive advertising, continually creates new wants and necessities, causing discontent and unhappiness among those unable to acquire them. Neighbours are encouraged to outdo each other in the cost, splendour and modernity of the material apparatus of living, placing strains on both the successful and the less felicitous. Home, clothing and car are public badges of relative success or failure. None of these pretensions exists in Soviet society where all classes share standard apartment blocks, wear state-store overcoats and ride in public transport.

The happiness of the ordinary citizen in both countries is closely related to his conditions of work, relations with his employer, and security of employment. Here also, the ever-more refined application of economic criteria to business gives a ruthless character to this aspect of American life. Compassion among those in charge for the unfortunate often cushions the impact of the rigid Soviet economic system upon the individual, and the chaos and muddle that often exist within it allow plenty of scope for the exercise of humanity and charity as well as for idling and evasion. One cannot but agree with the conclusions of a well-informed observer that 'ordinary Russian life has more humour, toleration and social richness than exist in advanced western societies'; and that 'Russia preserves much of the simplicity, warmth and un-spoiled virtue of a pre-industrialized, pre-"Americanized" society'.[13]

Although, in contrast with the United States, the USSR is publicly a puritan country, with the exploitation and portrayal of sex almost totally absent from all forms of communication media, in private the reverse is true, with sexual relations, especially among the young, being casual, uninhibited and free from formality to a degree unknown even in the West today. The high-school 'dating' and 'petting' customs, which to some extent dictate adolescent and youthful morality in America are lacking in the Soviet Union, and young women have usually had one or more abortions before marriage. Divorce is common and increasing, and although the rate differs little from that in America, it would be much higher if related to urban population only. In the more urban districts of the USSR the rate is over four per thousand. There is little discussion of sex, public or private, and it takes its place as a normal natural function of life, to be enjoyed or suffered as the case may be.

Nevertheless, Soviet life has its darker side in the endless struggle that has to be waged against shortages, muddle, inefficiency, defective goods and bureaucratic control: the inevitable long queue that has to be stood in if anything worth while becomes available, the almost inescapable frustration in trying to make a simple telephone call or in attempting to get hold of an official whose permission is needed. How different is the American way of life where everything is done to gratify the customer! All these Russian problems of living have to be seen against the background of the harsh climate and tend to merge with it to form a mood of inescapable, predetermined doom:

Long grey months of iron cold that tax energy and nerves – it is not fair, man cannot win. When a trip out of doors is unavoidable you bundle yourself in a mountain of clothes, hunch into your collar and trudge resentfully through the beseiged city streets, conscious that this is a land where hardship is a way of life.[14]

The whole attitude to life is shaped by this mood. To quote the same observer: 'Nothing, say my friends, can be done about the weather. Or the government. Or Czechoslovakia. Or the poverty. So we busy ourselves with the little struggles and pleasures of our daily lives.'[15]

Another contrast, impossible to demonstrate statistically because of the absence of Soviet data, but apparent to anyone familiar with both countries, is that of law and order. Social cohesion seems high in Soviet Russia, and a strong popular readiness to condemn and act against anti-social behaviour is apparent. Crime is not rampant and law and order prevail except for occasional outbreaks of hooliganism and drunkenness, both rigorously punished. American society, on the other hand, is assailed by alarming increases in crime, racial conflict, hooliganism, student unrest and drug addiction. Violence is nourished by the modern glamourising of the conquest of the west, by its prominence in television, by the widespread practice of owning and using guns, and by the strains of a competitive and wholly materialistic society which appears unusually productive of psychopathic personalities. In 1969 there were almost five million serious crimes in the United States compared with two million in 1960. In the five years from 1963 to 1968 two hundred and twenty Americans died in civil commotions, a figure that pales into insignificance, however, when compared with the quarter of a million who died violent deaths in motor-vehicle accidents in the same period.

Although a relatively small number of people in the Soviet Union may live in fear of the secret police or of sudden arrest for 'anti-Soviet' activities, the vast majority of the population live in security. No doubt informers abound in all walks of life and those who wish to express strong criticism of the Party and its doings must feel under constant constraint. But in the United States fear of violence and crime has now become an ingredient in the lives of millions of city-dwellers. President Johnson spoke of the 'fear that can turn us into a nation of captives imprisoned nightly behind chained doors, double locks, barred windows. Fear that can make us afraid to walk city streets by night or public parks by day.' President Nixon has said that a 'cancerous disease of violence and terror is sweeping our country'.[16]

Crime is closely associated with taking drugs. These also do not seem to constitute a social problem in the USSR, but their abuse now constitutes a widespread evil in the United States. New York City is said to have a hundred thousand addicts and the army authorities are alarmed at the spread of addiction among troops in South East Asia, where, according to the United States command in Saigon, forty-five per cent of all soldiers have taken drugs. Because of their high cost addicts are forced to steal, thereby adding to the number of crimes.

Finally, it should be remembered that there is a great difference in both countries between life in the cities and life in the countryside. But this difference is less in America, now that rural residents have access by road to the large towns. It is impossible to generalise about rural life in the USA because of the great range of conditions between those found on a rich corn-belt farm in the Middle West and those of a poverty-stricken Negro sharecropper's hovel on a gullied farm in the old 'cotton belt'. Likewise there are great contrasts between life in an old village of primitive log houses in north-western Russia, lacking electricity, plumbing and piped water, and far from schools, shops and other amenities, and that in one of the new centralised townships which have all these services. And although some planners favour urban-type apartment houses for these new 'agrotowns', the single dwelling-house is still much in favour in the Russian countryside. Collective farmers pay about 5,000 roubles for such a house – usually in the form of a down payment of 1,000 roubles with the rest payable over five years.

15 Society

When agriculture was the major occupation and the population was mainly rural, the basic social unit in both countries was the 'extended' family. This consisted not only of the active marriage pair but included their ageing parents, their growing children and possibly also their unmarried brothers and sisters. It was an economic as well as a social unit: it worked as a team on the farm and lived as a group in the farmhouse. Other closely related families lived near by, and mutual aid and mutual visiting were frequent between them. This model was more typical, more widespread and more deeply rooted in Russia than in America, because in the United States there was more mobility, both geographically across the country and socially up and down the income scale. Such mobility weakened the large or 'extended' family and people relied more on neighbours than on relatives for mutual assistance and social contact.

The 'extended' family is now virtually extinct in the United States and in rapid decline in the USSR. It remains, however, widespread in Russia, partly because there it was traditionally a far more fundamental and persistent institution, and partly because the transference of manpower from agriculture to other activities is not nearly so advanced as in America. Its place as the basic social unit is taken, in both nations, by the marriage pair. This seeks complete independence from the parents and strives to set itself up as an autonomous and distinct residential and consumption cell. Sometimes it splits through divorce, with one or both partners joining with a third or fourth partner to form a new pair or pairs, giving rise to what has been termed 'tandem' or sequential monogamy.

The exclusion of grandparents is by no means complete, however, and the continued residence with the marriage pair of one of the grandparents only, normally a grandmother, is not uncommon. This is often a matter of finance or convenience. In both countries there are more elderly women than old men. In the USA widow relicts are often well endowed with insurance money and their contribution to the pair's income may be vital to its social progress, making possible the more rapid acquirement of status symbols – home in a select area, large car, latest appliances, etc. Where there are children the grandmother can render many welcome services in the way of infant care, shopping and looking after the house, making it possible for the wife to work and yet further augment the pair's income. This practice is even commoner in the USSR where so much time has to be spent standing in line for shopping, social services, and essential bureaucratic authorisations. The possession of a *babushka*, patient and stubborn, is an immense asset in these circumstances.

The marriage pair has not only tended to separate from the parental generation but also, though obviously to a far lesser degree, from the new and younger generation formed by its own offspring. In both countries the increasing divorce rate results in frequent separation of at least one partner from the children and, when these are placed in a foster home or institution, of both. The rise of boarding schools as a partly educational and partly social phenomenon in post-war Russia is linked with the increased number of divorces and in consequence, of unwanted children. The trend to separation is also found in the growing number of couples who postpone having children for economic, social or hedonistic reasons – through contraception in the USA and through legal abortions in the USSR. In the USA abortions are illegal in most States but there is growing pressure to change this, so that unwanted conceptions which have not been prevented by contraceptive methods can be nullified. In 1970 New York State repealed its law prohibiting abortion and substituted the most liberal law in the country, the only conditions being that the abortion be performed by a doctor with the woman's consent and within twenty-four weeks of conception. On the other hand in the USSR there is an officially-inspired campaign to popularise contraception so as to lessen the number of abortions.[1] Where the coming of children is delayed artificially in this way, it often happens that the marriage pair continues childless, and in both countries the number of children per pair is dropping. The decrease in Russia is powerfully aided by the desperate housing shortage.

Where children are born to the marriage pair, the latter takes less and less responsibility for them. This is partly a result of its own less interested and more permissive attitude, but also because the state insists on a greater degree of interference. Children are taken away for education and for their military training. In the USSR state pressures on the younger generation are much greater than in the USA. Besides compulsory schooling, children are expected to spend a great deal of their time in various youth movements. Older children are also encouraged to take part in projects in distant parts of the country, involving them in long absences from home. In America, however, many parents, unable or unwilling to entertain or cope with their offspring during the long summer holidays, pack them off to a privately-run holiday camp.

The children themselves, in both countries, now strive for independence from their parents as soon as possible, and often regard their home as a place to which they are reluctantly tied because they have nowhere else to sleep and eat. Their interests and activities soon become so incomprehensible, if not intolerable, to the parents that there is little common ground between the two generations: although sleeping under the same roof they are hardly any more an integral social unit. Often the parents are almost as anxious for their children to leave and form marriage pairs of their own as the young people themselves are eager to do. This description may seem exaggerated for typical urban American or Soviet families today, but there is no doubt that there is a trend in this direction and that therefore it may become the future pattern in both countries.

This development results from powerful social forces which are linked with rapid changes in the nature of the economy caused by the technological revolution. These forces reinforce the permanent biological factor which, through the ageing process, differentiates the interests and capabilities of infants, youths, mature adults and the aged. In the agricultural age almost all influences which guided and moulded a new generation came down vertically from the older generations, and normally such influences were exercised within the 'extended' family unit. Today the influences brought to bear on children are mostly horizontal and come in from the outside through conformity-demanding 'peer groups', and from the potent media of mass communication. Because the environmental circumstances surrounding successive generations in their formative years have differed so strikingly, each has been differently moulded at its most impressionable age from the next. People in the new industrial age, therefore, find it increasingly difficult to understand and mingle with persons of a different age, even within the same family; and urbanisation, by bringing large numbers into proximity, makes it easier to find opportunities for social intercourse within one's own age group. Rural life, especially in America, where the isolated homestead was the rule, made it much less easy to make contact outside the family circle.

In so far as urbanisation is more advanced in the USA, and the new technology more widely dispersed throughout the nation, the social splitting of families according to generations, with an unbridgeable gap between parents and children, is there more common. This process is also aided in America by the mass media, which cultivate and exaggerate the different outlooks and characteristics of the generations because they are mainly concerned with advertising commercial products, more of which will be sold if differing tastes are developed in people of different age groups.

In the USSR new technology is not so widespread, urbanisation is not so advanced, and the mass media are wholly different in character; but other powerful forces operate towards the same result. As has been seen, the housing shortage places an enormous burden on the two-generation family in the city. The attitude of the state and the Communist party is ambivalent. On the one hand they encourage the family because of its influence for social stability, but on the other hand they resent its traditional conservatism and the fact that it offers a refuge from political ideology. The temptation to reach into the family for the hearts and minds of the children is an almost irresistible one for the Party ideologues, and in so far as their efforts are successful, the family is undermined. Some dedicated Communists would like to see child-rearing taken away from the marriage pair entirely and confided wholly to the state.

Despite the tendencies noted here, many sociologists in both countries insist that the two-generation family is not a dying institution and will continue to fulfil its present functions for a long time to come.[2]

Poverty, in the absence of fully-developed social welfare services, places a great strain upon the American family in the lower income groups. It forces mothers to work even though there is no alternative care for the children, and this is particularly serious in the case of Negro communities. In 1964 about fifty-seven per cent of non-white mothers of children aged from six to seventeen were at work.[3] The position is better in the USSR because of the establishment there of a system of maternity grants, paid maternity leave, and of state factory and farm creches and nurseries, but complaints arise that there are not enough of these. Further harm is done to the Soviet family because, when both parents are working, they have to take their holidays at different times as dictated by the 'works' management.[4] Those Soviet citizens who participate in the multitudinous social, political and 'works' activities open to them or thrust upon them, have very little leisure to spend with their families. Drunkenness also appears to be a common cause of breakdown in the Soviet family.

MARRIAGE

The tendency for the extended family, stretching over generations, to be replaced as the basic social unit by the marriage pair, does not strengthen but rather weakens the institution of marriage itself. The marriage pair within the extended family was reinforced by strong and omnipresent ties with the other close relatives. But in modern urban conditions the pair no longer operates as the central focus of a larger unified family life, but tends to operate more in isolation from the rest of the family. Furthermore, the two partners in the pair usually spend most of the day apart from each other and in close contact with non-relations with whom they may become emotionally or sexually involved. Inevitably extra-marital sexual relations are commoner than in the earlier 'extended' family of the agricultural age.

Breakdown of marriage as a mutually satisfactory partnership may not immediately result in divorce, out of consideration for the children, where there are any. This is true of both countries; but in the USA legal, religious and social factors may operate to preserve the marriage to a greater degree than in the USSR. Not only does the ease and expense of obtaining divorce differ from State to State but nearly a quarter of the population belongs to the Roman Catholic church and by virtue of its faith is opposed to divorce. For many ambitious or successful people in the professional and business world, divorce may be avoided as prejudicial to their careers. In the USSR, on the other hand, apart from the Moslem world of Soviet Central Asia, not only is the religious factor of small account but there is little social or political stigma attaching to divorce. The Communist party, however, expects exemplary family behaviour from its members, and divorce could conceivably hinder a member's political progress if it revealed any disreputable or unsavoury features in his family life. But a Party member can get round this by complaining of the 'political backwardness' of his wife, and such excuses are matched in America by cases like that of the Los Angeles citizen who alleged that his wife praised the Communist party – and got his divorce.[5]

Table 15.1 shows that divorce rates have been somewhat similar in recent years. In the United States it is increasing steadily, and in 1968 over ten million Americans had been divorced, although owing to

TABLE 15.1 DIVORCE RATES PER THOUSAND OF
TOTAL POPULATION[6]

	USA	USSR
1950	2·6	0·4
1960	2·2	1·3
1965	2·5	1·6
1966	2·5	2·8
1967	2·6	2·7
1968	2·9	2·7
1969	3·3	2·7

subsequent remarriage only four million were still classified as such.[7] Among the States, Nevada, because of its easy divorce laws, had by far the highest rate (21·4 per thousand) whereas in New York State it was only 0·4. The high American figure for 1950 reflects the large number of wartime marriages which ended in divorce. On the other hand, the very low figure for 1950 in the USSR is attributed to the fact that between 1936 and 1955 Stalinist practice had made divorce very difficult to obtain in Russia.

The divorce figures for the two countries are of limited comparative value. For a variety of social, legal and practical reasons marital status matters more in the USA than in the USSR. Just as it is more essential for an American to become officially married before living with a woman and raising a family, so it is more important to secure a legal termination when the marriage no longer exists *de facto*. In the USSR, however, there is less advantage in registering a marriage and, because of the cost in fees, less incentive to official divorce. Consequently there is a large, though unknown number of *de facto* or 'common law' marriages, one or both partners to which may be officially married to someone else. The virtual ban on divorce during Stalin's tyranny was the chief cause of this practice. During that period it became part and parcel of Soviet society and continues now that the cause has been removed. Most marriages in America are still celebrated in church and accompanied by ceremonial customs, whereas in Russia they are often casual and without ceremonial or honeymoon. But recently the Soviet authorities have been trying to increase the romantic appeal of state-registered marriage by introducing some ceremonial trappings.[8]

According to some Soviet writers, the chief difference between marriage in America and Russia is that social and financial circumstances often dictate or influence choice of partner in the United States, whereas such considerations no longer apply in the Soviet Union. There is probably some truth in this in so far as the gulf between rich and poor is wider in the USA and the degree of social stratification stronger. But there is evidence that Soviet middle-class parents are just as anxious for their offspring to marry 'well' as are Americans in the same class.[9] Disregard of parental wishes is, in any case, probably increasing in both societies.

There are some important distinctions in the position of women within marriage. Although most American wives work at some time during their married lives, the average middle-class wife ceases to work when children arrive, and marriage and children are still seen as the alternative or sequel to a permanent career rather than as its accompaniment. However, the proportion of American wives who work is rising fast: from only twenty-nine per cent in 1955 it reached forty per cent in 1969.[10] But such employment is often temporary and the number of full-time permanent career wives remains small. It is still in the lower classes that working wives are commonest, and the proportion is highest of all among Negro women.

In the USSR, on the other hand, not only do most women work, irrespective of whether they are married or not but the percentage increases with education and social status. While in America the proportion of working women is highest in the lower-paid jobs (with notable exceptions such as teaching and nursing), in the USSR women form a substantial proportion of the higher administrative, professional and technical labour force. Of course, the large surplus of women in Russia is a factor in these figures, as is the fact that during the war the USSR had to depend almost entirely on women for the conduct of the whole civilian administration and economy. Nevertheless, there is also a fundamental difference in the Soviet attitude: the traditionalism, conservatism and prejudice which discriminate against female labour in the West do not operate in Russia. In 1968 the percentage of women in the labour force was fifty, but among those with a specialist education it was sixty-three.[11]

TABLE 15.2   PROPORTION OF WOMEN AS PERCENTAGE OF
THE TOTAL LABOUR FORCE[12]

	USA	USSR
1940	24	39
1945	30	56
1950	28	47
1955	31	46
1960	33	47
1965	35	49
1969	37	51

TABLE 15.3   PROPORTION OF WOMEN IN MAJOR
OCCUPATIONAL GROUPS[13]
(*percentages*)

	USA	USSR
Agriculture	16	43
Industry	26	47
Construction	5	27
Transport and communications	19	24
Trade (wholesale and retail)	66	75
Education and culture	67	72
Scientific	2	46
Health and medical	69	85
Government and administration	39	58

NOTE The groups are not strictly comparable because of differences of definition and composition.

Although Soviet women are thus fully emancipated in society and in the economy outside the home, within it they are by no means so free and independent as their American counterparts. Many observers, both domestic and foreign, have regarded the middle-class wives and mothers of America as forming a dominant matriarchy of awe-inspiring character and this has been ascribed to frontier conditions.[14] Yet in

Russian society, even in its more modern urban version, the husband still expects to be head of the house and have his wife wait on him. Although normally doing a full day's work outside the home, she still shoulders the whole burden of household tasks. Here is the greatest contrast between the position of women in the two countries. The American middle-class woman not only usually has her time at her own disposal, engaging in various voluntary social activities, but she has the aid of machinery to discharge most household tasks and may well delegate the remaining ones to her husband. The Russian woman of comparable social status works all day, and in what time is left she must perform all household tasks with little help, either mechanical or human – unless she can call in the services of a grandmother or *babushka*.[15] Boredom is the curse of the middle-class American woman's life, but the Russian woman has no time to be bored.

Pre-marital and extra-marital sex

In both countries there is now a large and growing degree of freedom from social and conventional restraint upon heterosexual relations outside of marriage. In the United States, despite the spread of contraception and the introduction of oral contraceptives, the illegitimate birth rate rose from 5·3 per cent in 1960 to 9·7 per cent in 1968. Comparable figures are not available for the USSR, but the number of unmarried mothers rose from 282,000 to 2,700,000 between 1945 and 1960. This sexual freedom is, however, more revolutionary for white Americans than for Russians, since in Russia – except among a few small sects – there was no Puritan influence such as dominated life over large parts of America in the eighteenth and nineteenth centuries. Such religious and social constraints as had been imposed by the church, the aristocracy and the bourgeoisie were ridiculed and swept away in the reaction against the old society that followed the Revolution. Stalin fostered a reaction to the early Bolshevik freedom, and a new kind of puritanism was urged upon Communists. It was no longer marriage and the family as institutions that were condemned as survivals from the old society, but their betrayal in the form of seduction, adultery, desertion and divorce.[16] Nevertheless, although Soviet sociologists, Party ideologues and others continue to speak of the need for a 'socialist morality' based on strengthening the family by adhering to the old virtues, they admit that their society is seriously lacking in these virtues.[17] It would appear to be the younger people in the USSR, as well as in the USA, who are pioneering the new move towards unrestrained freedom: 'today in Soviet Russia as in the West, the sexual revolution comes from below, not above'.[18]

In the USA this revolution is aided by the entertainments industry and the mass media of communication, which have created an atmosphere which strongly stimulates sexual desire and invites erotic experimentation among the young. There is nothing like this in the USSR, where the state control of publication and communication, of art and entertainment, imposes an extremely puritanical censorship. There sexual activity results more directly from the uninhibited biological instincts themselves. One advantage of the glare of publicity which illuminates all aspects of sex in America is that sexual education is easily obtained by young people, whereas in the USSR its dearth is lamented by sociologists and held responsible for much ignorance and anguish among young people.[19]

Material considerations have also assisted the sexual revolution among the young in America. More leisure, more money, more cars, as well as more stimulus and less restraint, have powerfully aided promiscuity and adultery. For the USSR, on the other hand, very different material causes are sometimes adduced: the housing shortage and overcrowding, the drabness of life in general, and the absence of absorbing leisure substitutes for philandering. Drunkenness and lack of parental supervision figure prominently as causes of sexual irregularity, as in almost all activities regarded as evil or undesirable by the authorities.

One great contrast remains. The law in the United States is strongly repressive and represents the views of the extreme puritanism of an older epoch. Several widespread forms of sexual activity – notably adultery and prostitution – are criminal acts in many States. In the USSR legal constraints are minimal and confined to such cases as rape and sexual assaults on children.

OTHER SOCIAL GROUPINGS

Rural and urban

For the still large but declining proportion of the Soviet population (forty-six per cent in 1970) that is classed as rural, the next important grouping beyond the family is the village. Plans to replace the scattered villages by 'agrotowns' in which the peasant families would live in flats and enjoy urban style amenities have been implemented in only a few places so far. The village never became a widespread institution in the United States. Instead farmers lived in isolated homesteads, the result of the division of the land into rectangular holdings. There was, however, the 'neighbourhood', consisting of the immediate neighbours who gave mutual aid in such communal tasks as building a log-house or husking corn, or who combined for mutual defence or to organise a church or school. But the social possibilities of the American neighbour-hood cannot be compared with those of the nucleated Russian village, where each family is intimately acquainted with and involved in the affairs of the others, and where the villagers not only meet daily but carry on much of their agricultural work in communal concert. The motor car, however, by increasing the mobility of the American farm family, greatly lessened its isolation.

Russian villages, once cut off from the rest of the world by their self-sufficiency and poor communications, are now linked to their neigh-bours by common membership of a vast collective farm covering, perhaps, 15,000 acres. Often the younger farmers have motor cycles with which they can reach a nearby town but, by and large, the rural population seldom travels beyond the limits of a collective farm.

In rural America, largely because of the automobile, the social pattern is more complex. Several neighbourhoods comprise a 'com-munity' which is usually centred on a small town. One-room country schools and small country churches have closed down and educational and religious services have been concentrated in towns. Whereas a neighbourhood might consist of between twenty and eighty families, a market-centred community might have from eighty to five-hundred families, besides the population of the town itself. During recent decades small country towns have declined. Not only has the supporting farm population drifted away, but it has been increasingly to the larger cities that the farmer and his family have gone for specialised medical care, higher education, clothing, appliances and recreation.[20]

It is doubtless easier for Americans to make the move from country to town than for Russians, for whom it means breaking the close ties of the village and losing the mutual comfort and consolation, co-operation and conviviality which village life provides. But as most urban Russians live in apartment houses and most Americans in single dwellings, some of the contrast between their rural societies is preserved. The occupiers of the flats in the Soviet apartment house, because most of these buildings have communal kitchens, bathrooms, laundries or playrooms, and because there are organised opportunities for communal dis-cussion on matters affecting their administration, may to some extent lessen the sense of loneliness experienced on becoming an urban-dweller. The American, in his individual housing unit, has much less to do with his neighbours in the city, just as in the country. Unlike his Soviet counterpart, whose movement in a large city is more restricted by the limitations of walking and public transport to one part of the town, the urban American travels relatively easily and speedily to any part of a great metropolitan region and, in consequence, is able to have friends and acquaintances on other than a neighbourhood basis.

In both countries, the place of work rivals the home as the centre where most urban life is lived, and workmates share with family members the affections, loyalties and other personal relationships of the citizen. The factory or office is more important as a social and political unit to the Soviet townsman, since much of his leisure time is spent in activities which centre upon it. For the American urban-dweller the place of work is more purely an economic unit, and his social activities are linked instead with a wide variety of voluntary organisations which normally have nothing to do with his work. And because tertiary and 'service' economic activities are so much more advanced in the United States, place of work is more likely to be a factory in the USSR and more likely to be an office in the USA. This has an added social significance in that in offices the two sexes usually intermingle to a greater degree than on the workshop floor, where one's fellow-workers are more likely to be of the same sex.

There is a great contrast between the 'rural–urban fringe', that zone in which town and country mingle on the outskirts of big cities, in the USA and the USSR. In America it is normally filled with the houses and gardens of the very wealthy, who choose to combine rural surroundings with urban amenities. But in Russia this 'fringe' is more often made up of old log-houses inhabited by families who use their location on the edge of the city to work both in town and country. The husband may work in an urban factory while the wife may be a collective farmer, or vice versa. Such a position also enables them to have a vegetable garden.[21]

Stratification and classes

Although both societies are relatively unstratified in that they do not have a rigid system of exclusive classes, there is more stratification in the USA. This is partly because wealth can be accumulated and inherited in America, leading to a far greater range of capital and income than in the Soviet Union, and partly because the USA has not experienced a social revolution comparable to that of 1917 in Russia. The 1941–5 war, because of the much greater impact it had upon Russians, forcing them into a bitter and desperate struggle for survival, dispensing personal loss without respect for social status, was also a greater leveller.

Although their boundaries are indistinct and movement between them is not only possible but frequent, distinct social classes are recognisable in the United States.[22] There is a small upper class which owns most of the wealth and includes many of the leaders in business and government. Hereditary accumulated riches enable it to perpetuate itself through the use of select preparatory schools for its offspring, followed by graduation at the superior universities of the Ivy League. Below them comes an upper middle class consisting of those highly placed in business, government and the professions: their wealth and status enable them to live a life similar in many ways to the upper class, but there are many parvenus among them. Their children or grand-children may be able to enter the upper class.

The lower middle class is made up of the better-placed white-collar workers, small businessmen, most small farmers and the more ambitious skilled workers. The home background they give their children may provide opportunities for rising to the upper middle class.

The working class is made up of semi-skilled and unskilled workers, both urban and rural, small tradesmen, and the lower ranks of those employed in service industries. This class can be divided into two: an upper section who are 'respectable' and normally in employment, and a lower division in which the unfortunate and the feckless, the sick and the destitute, the unemployed and unemployable are unhappily lumped together. It is fed by a downward drift from the social superstructure and also by immigration. In this lower division might also be included the poor farmers, mostly Negro, of the southern Appalachian region. But as their poverty is accompanied by the ownership of land (subject to mortgage), they should perhaps be regarded as a separate class, a view strengthened by the fact that they inhabit a distinct geographical area, and occupy 'the poorest, lowest, and meanest living areas of the nation by every index one can imagine'.[23]

In the USSR, in the absence of inherited wealth and social position, occupation forms the basis of stratification. There are three main divisions: first, those who work with their brains in the Party apparatus, in the state bureaucracy, in the management of industry and in the professions; second, those who work in subordinate positions in factory or office (the workers); and third, the collective farmers (the peasants). The tendency towards stratification within this main grouping is greatest among 'the workers'. This is because the demands of modern industry are replacing the simple division into skilled and unskilled by a variety of grades of skill and training. These in turn are reflected in a wider differentiation by status, privilege and income. A similar tendency is observable on the collective farm where the growing number of trained specialists differs markedly from the ordinary *kolkhoznik* in income and status.

In both countries this grading and specialisation by skill hampers social mobility, since entry into the category above is determined by education and qualification rather than by seniority. Educational level becomes the governing factor and educational opportunity the key to social equality.[24] This relatively new criterion of social position is less of a bar to social mobility in the USSR than in the USA, where the surplus labour pool gives management greater choice in choosing the trained when available and rejecting the unskilled as redundant. In the USSR the prevailing shortage of labour means that the unskilled must be trained instead of discarded, and hence the structure of adult education and industrial training is much more highly developed in that country.

That there is more equality of educational opportunity in the Soviet Union, where all higher education is free, is clear. Even Stalin's daughter 'attended an ordinary school and Moscow university with the standard maintenance grant'.[25] Nevertheless, family background, personal influence and geographical location inevitably play their part alongside native ability. Some observers make a simpler division between two classes: those who through their office or occupation in government, Party or industry enjoy high incomes and have access to special privileges, and the rest who wage the daily struggle for a share in what is left: 'a definite class society is in being and is further developing, with sharp and growing cleavages between the have-nots and the haves'.[26]

Ethnic, national and religious groups

Whereas the conscious policy of government in the United States has been to produce one nationality – American – the Soviet state is founded territorially and administratively on the recognition of different nationalities. American policy has succeeded in merging the various groups of European origin into one nation, but has failed to solve the problem of integrating white and black, so that there are in effect two nationalities: but this fact has no formal territorial, administrative, institutional or political expression.

A policy of russification and increasing discrimination against non-Russian nationalities marked the later years of the tsarist régime. This resulted in widespread support for the revolutionaries among the minorities, and non-Russians were prominent among the leading Bolsheviks. It was not surprising, therefore, that the USSR was established as a federation of republics whose basis was nationality, and that the word 'Russian' did not appear in the country's name. But just as in America the conscious policy has been to convert people of various national origins into Americans, so the attempt has been made in the Soviet Union to bring all the inhabitants of the country to think of themselves first and foremost as Soviet citizens.

The racial problem in the United States is exacerbated by the fact that formal constitutional and political equality is accompanied by social discrimination and economic inequality. The gap between the two races in such matters as levels of living, income and employment shows little sign of decreasing, a fact disguised to some extent by the growth of a Negro middle class. There is now a strong demand for educated Negroes, partly because of the proclivities of liberals among the professions in the United States, but also because with large Negro populations in the big cities, the value of Negroes in business is appreciated: 'one could be hard put to describe a person with better job opportunities than a newly-minted Negro Ph.D.'.[27] The success of the few, however, merely serves to conceal the plight of the many.

In the USSR, on the other hand, along with the territorial administrative expression of nationality, there goes a much higher degree of political, social and economic equality. For all major nationalities and linguistic groups and for many lesser ones, education is in the native language. Russian is then a compulsory second language, but this strengthens equality, as ability to speak the majority language is obviously necessary for advancement in any field beyond the local level. As a result, nowhere in the USSR does discrimination or racial tension approach the American situation, although there is some evidence that Russians would show more racial feeling if they had a large Negro minority.[28]

Russian and other Slavonic peoples preponderate in the higher levels of the Soviet economy because they have the necessary skills and initiative and are willing to migrate to remote parts of the country and assume greater responsibility. One of the disappointments of the Soviet régime has been that, despite improved educational opportunities, some of the non-Russian nationalities cling to their old rural existence and have been reluctant to go into the towns and avail themselves of technical training. As it is, not only are there not enough Russians, Ukrainians and Belorussians to go round but they are becoming more and more loath to move into the unpleasant parts of Siberia and the North, despite the attractions of higher pay and other benefits. The Soviet government, therefore, tries to involve the nationalities in economic progress.

The group in the Soviet Union against whom it is most often alleged that prejudice is felt and discrimination levelled are the Jews, and their position has been compared to that of Negroes in America. There is, however, no real comparison. Jews in the Soviet Union have shared in the general rise in the level of living and continue to occupy important posts in the bureaucracy and in the professions.[29] According to Soviet sources, Jews, although numbering only 1·1 per cent of the population, account for 14·7 per cent of Soviet doctors, 8·5 per cent of writers and journalists, 10·4 per cent of all judges and lawyers, 7·7 per cent of actors, musicians and artists, and 7·5 per cent of the scientific research workers.[30] A deputy prime minister of the USSR is a Jew, as is the well-known writer Ilya Ehrenburg. Jews are probably more prominent in Soviet sport than in that of any other country. Negroes, of course, are even more prominent in American sport, especially in athletics.

It may be fairly said that anti-semitism in the USSR is a popular sentiment rather than an institutionally fostered phenomenon.[31] The position of Jews is, however, different from that of other nationalities in some respects. Owing to the strength and influence of Jews in capitalist circles, suspicion can more easily fall upon Soviet Jews for having international connections and thence for complicity in Western espionage. Soviet involvement in the Middle East on the Arab side has increased their difficulties. The position is worst of all for orthodox Jews who strive to survive as a distinct religious and cultural entity and resist cultural integration, and it is against these that any actual persecution is directed. As in tsarist times, it is likely that local authorities may be tempted to gain popular support by encouraging – or doing little to discourage – manifestations of popular anti-semitism.

According to orthodox Jewish sources, the number of synagogues in the Soviet Union has been reduced by oppressive action to sixty-four. But the Soviet authorities put the number at a hundred and fifty, together with three hundred *minyans* or home centres of worship, and the reason for any decline is adduced as lack of demand due to the failing appeal of religion, a phenomenon not exclusive to the Jews. Instances of alleged discrimination against Jews as a religious group include the following:

Whereas other faiths are allowed token seminaries, the training of priests and ministers, the Jews are allowed none. Where other faiths have a federation which allows priests and ministers to have contact with each other in different cities, the Jews have none.

Whereas other faiths have had bibles printed, the Jews have had none.

Whereas other faiths have had permission to send representatives of their faith to world conferences, Jews have not had that opportunity.[32]

In both countries the 1941–5 war was responsible for harsh measures against ethnic minorities. In America Americans of Japanese origin were expelled from their homes in the Pacific coastal regions, and in the Soviet Union the Germans were moved from the Volga. The forced uprooting and resettlement by Stalin of such minorities as the Kalmyks

and the Chechens for supposed disloyalty after the war was an unnecessary inhumane action paralleled only by the American wars of
extermination waged against the Red Indians.

Those Americans who, through family upbringing or personal
choice, belong to a religious group or church are able to find, besides
spiritual consolation, a social milieu in which they can make contacts
outside the usual fields of family, work and neighbourhood. In many
instances the religious group, because of its tradition or dogma,
strengthens the allegiance of its members to their families and to the
social mores. Few Soviet citizens, except perhaps in the Moslem communities of Central Asia, can enjoy membership of a church without
the compensating disabilities which more than nominal participation in
its activities could bring in the form of disapproval by powerful local
communists.

ALIENATION AND CRIME

Both societies contain alienated groups. Apart from the numerous
criminal class in the USA are the various 'freaks', 'drop-outs', 'street
people' and 'hippies'. These are mostly young people who have
rejected the values of American society and sought refuge in drugs or
alternative satisfaction in idle, aimless or communal life. They are
found most frequently in California where their numbers have enabled
them to organise an alternative type of society in which regular work is
dispensed with, and they live by their wits or with the aid of friends and
sympathisers. Also a growing number of Negroes have joined militant
groups whose aim is not merely to reject society as constituted at
present but to transform some aspects of it.

A symptom of alienation is the outbreak of violence between the
guardians of established society and those alienated from it. There were
food riots in various Soviet towns in the 1960s on the occasion of
shortages or price rises, and also small demonstrations in Moscow in
recent years in support of people arrested and imprisoned for 'anti-
Soviet activities'. In America riots and demonstrations have been on a
much larger scale. The riots have been mainly by Negroes in the large
towns, and the demonstrations by students. The food riots in Russia are
said to have been 'bloodily suppressed'.[33] Four young students of Kent
State university in Ohio were shot dead by national guardsmen in a
demonstration on their own campus. The KGB still arrests political
activists opposed to the Soviet régime. After Senator Eugene McCarthy
had intervened as a candidate for nomination in the 1968 presidential
campaign as an advocate of radical policies, his headquarters were
raided by the Chicago police and national guardsmen: they beat up his

workers and sprayed nerve gas on those of his sympathisers gathered outside.[34]

An exact comparison of crime is impossible because of the lack of published data from the USSR. But both observation and probability would lead one to conclude that crime is a far more serious and prevalent social problem in the USA than in the USSR. The rate in America is 'among the highest in industrialised societies' and even juvenile crime, which has clearly caused the Soviet authorities much anxiety in recent years, is not comparable in degree between the two states.[35] This is not surprising on grounds of probability alone. Guns and cars, the two most powerful aids to the criminal in his war on society, are easily acquired in America but hard to get hold of in Russia. Organised crime in America is able to accumulate large sums of money and to corrupt and sometimes control local political machinery in ways which would be impossible in the Soviet Union.

There is a pronounced difference in the nature of crime in the two countries. In America violent crimes, especially murder, rape and armed robbery, are much more numerous than they appear to be in the USSR. In the Soviet Union the chief offences seem to be thefts of state property, peculation and embezzlement, and hooliganism.

Differences in the two societies explain much of the difference in the nature and degree of criminal activity within them. The more unequal division of wealth, reinforced by the extreme poverty of racial groups such as Negroes, Puerto Ricans and Mexicans, provides an incentive to crime in the USA which is much less in the USSR, where great private accumulations of wealth and property cannot exist. The fortunes of American millionaires are often invested in objects of gold and silver, jewellery, valuable paintings and other material possessions, as hedges against inflation. But wealth in these forms is easily stolen and relatively easily disposed of by the thieves. Shortages rather than surpluses of goods are more likely to lead to crime in the USSR. As a Soviet source puts it, 'the population is still not adequately supplied with all goods. A shortage of certain goods creates a favourable medium for speculation, abuses of office and bribe-taking.'[36]

The weakening of the family in modern urban society also contributes to crime, and the more so in the United States because this social process has gone further there than in the Soviet Union. Children brought up in broken or unhappy homes are more prone to delinquency in both societies. In the USA these are especially numerous among Negroes. Almost a quarter of married Negro women are divorced or separated from their husbands and bring up their children without the father's presence or aid. In the USSR the 1941–5 war deprived many families of the father, and these families have produced far more than their share of delinquents: one Soviet study showed that sixty-eight per cent of minors convicted of hooliganism had lost one or both their parents.[37]

Even when both parents are living amicably together, the complaint is heard in both countries that they do not always supervise their children adequately, either through absence at work or through preferring their own pleasures, or because they have neither the will to enforce parental discipline nor the conviction of its necessity.[38]

In the USA the attitude to the criminal is, in some quarters, more sympathetic and tolerant than in the USSR. Many Western liberal intellectuals see the protection and reclamation of the erring individual as more important than the safeguarding of society, and the tendency is for punishment to become more lenient and for resentment to be directed more against the law enforcers than the law breakers. In the USSR, on the other hand, state and society, governors and governed, appear united in a belief that the maintenance of law and order is paramount, and the relative freedom of Soviet society from disturbances seems to rest in part on the readiness of large numbers of the public to participate in law enforcement.

The influence upon children, adolescents and adults of the prevalence of crime and violence in material heard, read and watched, is a controversial matter; although the argument that, if the mass media of communication are successful in selling soap they are likely to be equally efficacious in promoting wrongdoing, is not easily refuted. Whereas sexual passion, crime and violence form the stock-in-trade of much American reading and viewing matter, they are almost wholly absent from the carefully selected material coming from the Soviet press and studios. Guns and war toys which are so prominent among the playthings of the American boy are not manufactured for children in the USSR. Furthermore, the United States has been at war for fifteen years out of the past thirty compared with only four years in the case of the Soviet Union.

Other aspects of American society which may stimulate a higher incidence of crime are unemployment and the strenuously competitive and acquisitive nature of the society. Some Western sociologists see delinquency in the United States merely as an exaggerated attachment to values already dominant but which 'the majority are usually too timid to express', and as an unrestrained pursuit of its goals: 'the ideal pecuniary man is like the ideal delinquent in his unscrupulous conversion of goods and services to his own ends'.[39]

Because all these allegedly crime-inducing factors are found in all Western capitalist societies, and only more so in the United States, many Soviet sociologists ascribe their own problems to survivals in their own country of such a society or to contamination through the invasion of foreign influences.[40] It must be difficult, however, at this distance in time, to substantiate the case that survivals from pre-revolutionary society are the root cause of today's social problems in the USSR, but there may be more in the claim that present Western influences have a disruptive effect. Contrasting the stimulation and excitement, real and vicarious, which American life offers, with their own dull, drab and regimented lives, many Soviet youths, if not inoculated against it by a strong dose of Communist ideology, may well find the fever contagious.[41] A Soviet writer has ascribed a measure of delinquency to 'the influence of translated foreign literature and foreign films, some of which are beautiful and touching, but in which the immature boy or girl, alas, notices only the outward form of events'.[42]

Modern Soviet sociologists, however, are increasingly ready to ascribe responsibility for social ills to defects in their own society. The shortage of many essentials and the scarcity of luxuries have already been mentioned as causes of crime, and the overcrowding of housing is also recognised by some Soviet writers as leading to trouble. Drunkenness, on the increase despite repeated government campaigns against it, is adduced as a prominent evil calling forth crime, and sixty-eight per cent of all wilful murders are attributed to it.[43] Where defects in the society are not acknowledged, it is at least admitted that crime reveals a failure to communicate that society's ideals to the individual: 'it would be a big mistake to think that the very fact of living in the land of the Soviets, in the conditions of socialist reality, presupposes a Communist world outlook in a young person'.[44]

Nevertheless, the fact remains that anti-social behaviour is a far greater problem in America than in Russia, and a recent American study ascribes this to differing experiences in early childhood – to the facts that American children are mostly bottle-fed and do not get enough affection and discipline from their parents, whereas Russian infants are breast-fed and given a stricter yet more loving upbringing.[45]

16 System, Constitution and Government

Although the governmental systems in both countries were born of revolution, each inherited much from the pre-revolutionary past. The American colonies derived from England their habits of representative government and their ideas of freedom from restraint. The only political system the Russians had experienced was one in which autocracy, orthodoxy, bureaucracy and state control were the fundamentals of government. They had no long tradition of constitutionalism, liberalism and parliamentary democracy. These concepts were essentially the habits of thought of a society in which the middle class predominated, and attempts to introduce them into Russia had failed because of the weakness of the middle class there. They were regarded with dislike as foreign importations by the tsarist aristocracy and the Marxist revolutionaries alike: the small but growing middle class was regarded with contempt by the autocracy and with hatred by the Marxists. The foreign name of 'bourgeoisie' attributed to it bespoke this dislike, and its preference for liberal, constitutional and parliamentary institutions led to their condemnation as 'bourgeois', a word normally used pejoratively. Both before and after the Revolution the Russian form of government has shown a tendency to move towards the system of a single all-powerful leader working through a cumbersome bureaucracy 'composed of individuals with little class identification'.[1]

In the presence of this centralised monopoly of power it was difficult for organised interest groups to form, even before the Revolution. The destruction of the aristocracy, the bourgeoisie, the clergy and the wealthier farmers, and the levelling down of all Soviet citizens to the category of 'workers and peasants' militated against the emergence of organised groups or classes.

In the United States there had never been a powerful concentration of government. Before independence the royal power had often been distant and ineffectual, and the governors presided over assemblies of elected merchants, lawyers and farmers who legislated much as they pleased. After the Revolution the constitution purposely made concentration of power as difficult as possible. In its absence interest groups, organised and unorganised, arose. They ranged themselves – the better to work the constitutional machinery – into two political parties, loosely enough constructed and with a sufficiently flexible ideological basis to adapt to the social and economic forces and tensions of the day. At the end of the eighteenth century these were the Republicans, representing farmers and immigrants, and the Federalists representing the established commercial classes. Successively they became, during the nineteenth century, Old Republicans and New Republicans, National Republicans and Democratic Republicans, and finally Republicans and Democrats.[2] At various times this two-party system has reflected such vague and general conflicts of interest as North versus South, West versus East, country versus town, anti-slavery versus slavery, business versus unions, as well as more specific issues such as tariffs, trusts and the role of government. In short, the parties became 'heterogeneous coalitions of interest groups and viewpoints'.[3] As if to emphasise the contrast with the Russian system American political scientists term their two parties 'bourgeois' parties.[4]

Just as there is a fundamental distinction between the aims of American and Soviet society, so the political systems are adapted to these aims. In America pursuit of self-interest is accepted as the mainspring of the economic system, whereas in the USSR state-interest dominates. The American system has therefore to provide a mechanism whereby numerous competing self-interests can compromise as far as possible, and whereby conflict is reduced to a game between two sides with the public as arbiter. An undisciplined chaos of varying self-interests cannot be expressed by a mere handful of men exercising permanent and absolute power as can the single state-interest, to which all individual self-interests must be subordinated. Thus political contest in the USA is mainly a question as to which combinations of interest groups shall prevail. In the USSR it takes the form of conflict within the leadership as to which policy best serves the state-interest.

A closely linked difference is that the Soviet system is ideological, the American non-ideological. In guiding the destinies of the Soviet state the Soviet leaders are motivated and strengthened by the Marxist–Leninist belief that they are moving with the inevitable tide of history. Although they have supplanted the Russian orthodox church and spread the new religion of communism, their insistence on ideological orthodoxy is helped by the fact that for centuries the church had combined uniformity in dogma with political subservience. The peasant bureaucrats from whom Stalin recreated the Party leadership after his purge of the original revolutionaries, 'although rejecting their peasant fathers' religiosity, were none the less predisposed toward a compliant acceptance of dogma'.[5] By working in an ideological framework the Soviet system is able to achieve more consistency, and its leaders have guidelines to follow in periods of perplexity and doubt; on the other hand, blinded by faith in their doctrine, they may continue farther along a mistaken path than would politicians more pragmatically minded. Even if they do realise that they are mistaken, it is difficult for them to change a course which they have previously justified on ideological grounds. A further advantage of an ideological system is that, in a multi-national and multi-racial state it provides a basis for unity other than domination by the most powerful group. The use of the word Soviet rather than Russian in itself removes what could be a continual irritant to the non-Russian peoples.[6]

The American system and its leaders are un-ideological or even anti-ideological; because the business of satisfying and reconciling a congeries of group and individual self-interests is a matter of practicality and pragmatism:

> Americans have often seen parties, politics and government itself as instruments to be used for individual advancement, not as means for advancing the public weal. Party organisation has provided careers for the otherwise disadvantaged, and businessmen have gone to government for special favors, grants, or protection while trumpeting loudly their aversion to government interference, welfarism and 'give-away' programs. Ideology, in short, has played little role in the activities of any of the groups involved in American politics.[7]

The nearest to which American politics become ideological is when there is a threat against certain self-interests from the government. Then 'freedom' and 'private enterprise' become rallying cries to unite all self-interests, whether it be in opposition to socialism in general or to some particular governmental enterprise such as the Tennessee Valley Authority or state medicine.

In short, there is in the USSR but a single source of political legitimacy – the Marxist–Leninist ideology as interpreted by the leaders. In the USA, by contrast, there are many founts and varying degrees of political legitimacy. Its three main sources are constitutional tradition, liberal values and popular consent, but some of these are vague terms and open to various interpretations.[8] Political parties were denounced in the early days of the young republic as 'the greatest political evil' but they have long since come to be regarded as legitimate.[9] The legitimacy of political interest groups, however, is still questioned, even though they are undeniably part of the political system.[10]

An important contrast that follows from these fundamental differences in the two systems is that, in the American, consensus of opinion is held to justify the content of policy, while in the Soviet the content of the policy elicits the consensus of opinion.[11] In other words, the bargaining that goes on between interests in the USA produces compromise policies that command wide support; whereas in the USSR, once a policy has been decided upon, support is drummed up for it.

Differences in the systems lead to differences in efficiency. In a world in which social, technological and economic changes take place rapidly it is desirable that the political system should accommodate these changes or tensions will develop. In the USA necessary progress is delayed by the separation of powers, with Congress often frustrating the Administration's desire for reform. In the USSR it is delayed by the lack of any mechanism to change the leadership, so that policies become identified with the leaders and support of the policies with loyalty to the leaders. Changes of policy to suit changes in society may have to wait for the death or deposition of the leadership, and tend therefore to be associated with intrigue and crisis. On the other hand, when a change is resolved upon at the top, it can be proclaimed as a national crusade and carried through with complete thoroughness, without the necessity for persuasion, bargaining, compromise, amendment and procedural tactics such as would delay and modify, if not almost nullify, a similar policy decision by an American president.[12]

In foreign policy the example of recent Sino-Soviet and Franco-American relationships would seem to indicate that the American system works better when differences with allies arise. But analyses of the American attitude to Cuba when a socialist revolution took place there, and of the Soviet reaction to the Hungarian revolution and Czech reforms, show that the Russian system is more effective when dealing with enemies. In the disputes with allies the militarily and economically weaker nations, France and China, resented their dependence upon what they regarded as culturally and intellectually inferior upstart powers, and began to assert their independence, resurrecting memories of their great imperial pasts. Whereas the Americans were able to adjust pragmatically to the changed situation with little permanent damage to Franco-American relations, the Soviets and Chinese had each based their stand on ideological grounds, which not only made it impossible for either to compromise or give way but imparted the ferocity of heresy-hatred to the dispute. But where a hostile movement threatened to seize control of a satellite territory, as was the case in Czechoslovakia and Hungary, the ideology of the Soviet leaders provided them with the certainty that force was justified and the confidence to use it: they were able to act with a decisive swiftness which contrasted sharply with the American hesitancy over Cuba.[13]

Both the American and Soviet systems claim to be democratic, even though the Russian pretension seems as ridiculously false to the Western political scientist as does the American claim to the Marxist. In the West democracy is regarded in terms of institutions and in communist countries more as an economic and social term. A Soviet scholar has written that 'the yardstick of genuine democracy is not so much the form of the political machinery but, chiefly and mainly, who owns the national wealth'.[14] The USA is a formal political democracy in the sense that there is a representative system, with political parties and with elections to choose between them, and that there are well-established and commonly exercised liberties of freedom of expression, assembly and demonstration. But the policy-shaping and decision-making lie within the competence of an 'establishment', and the people at large only have a choice between issues put to them, which may or may not be the issues vital to their well-being. Nor do they have any guarantee that a policy they choose at election time will in fact be carried out, nor do they have any sanction other than an adverse vote some years hence. If they reject one set of men, they can do so only by choosing another; yet they may not wish for either, and they have little or no opportunity to choose a third set who might follow policies more in tune with the popular will or in accord with the general good. Furthermore, the knowledge which they have to guide such choice as they are able to make, comes almost wholly from mass media which are strongly influenced by the governing class. But the USSR, with no choice of parties, with no liberty of political expression, with all decisions and policies made by a small power élite, and all mass media rigidly controlled by it, has no claim to be considered even a formal democracy, except on the grounds that there is a widespread popular participation in the machinery of government. Neither state has that most democratic of all political institutions, whereby an issue can be submitted to a popular vote or referendum on the demand of a section of the people themselves, and resolved by their verdict, irrespective of the opposition of government, civil service or political parties.

The United States is not an economic democracy. Economic power is wielded by the executives of great corporations and nowhere in the world are these more free of governmental control or interference and nowhere do they have a greater influence over government. The trade unions, although formally democratic in their structure, are seldom so in practice, and use their immense power almost wholly to press for increased financial rewards for their members, and in so doing often dislocate the economy by strikes, practices which hardly accord with the public good or the general will. The Soviet Union is formally an economic democracy in that the resources of the country and the means of production are owned by the state on behalf of the people, in that the exploitation of labour is only by the state for the state and not by private individuals or companies for their enrichment, and in that the profits of business are used for public purposes. It is not fully an economic democracy in the sense of worker control of industry although there is a certain measure of this, albeit small.[15] Millions of Americans are unemployed whereas the Soviet citizen has the right to paid employment, one of the few of his constitutional rights that he actually enjoys. Women have more equality of economic opportunity in the USSR than in the USA.

Both countries have elements of social democracy in their relative freedom from a formal class structure, and in the relative equality of status and opportunity which their citizens enjoy, although there is a tendency to minimise the exceptions that exist to this freedom and to this equality in both states. The USA has the advantage that more of the country's wealth is shared among the population as a whole in the form of consumer goods; on the other hand it has an extreme range of incomes, from the billionaires to the wretchedly poor. The USSR comes much closer to equality of incomes, especially as the 1960s saw a substantial increase of wages, higher pensions and lower taxes on small incomes.[16]

In so far as democracy means respect for the rights of minorities the USA is superior. In the USSR political minorities are not tolerated, religious minorities are often persecuted, and social minorities, in the sense of those who do not accept the tenets or rules of Soviet society, are rigorously isolated.

Brzezinski and Huntington, in their superb comparison of the two systems, reject the view that there is any tendency for them to converge. Instead they hold that cybernetics, by advancing the techniques of economic and social control, will make it possible in Russia to combine further economic development with the present ideological–political structure. They oppose the view that, as the Soviet economy matures, the government will become more liberal.[17] Subsequent events seem to support their judgement, and the liberalising trend introduced by Khrushchev has not been continued by his successors but, if anything, reversed. On the other hand, it can be argued that both countries are destined to become bureaucracies and to that extent will have a common system: 'whether the state be called parliamentary or totalitarian, capitalist or socialist, it is certain to be bureaucratic because the nature of the problems being handled by modern states makes them bureaucracies'.[18]

In each society there are people alienated from the system. In the USA these range from those who do not vote because of a cynical attitude to the political system, to those who militantly protest on the streets. In the USSR the lack of freedom of expression makes it impossible to arrive at a worthwhile estimate of the degree of dissent. There has been the occasional demonstration of a handful of people, often broken up by 'citizens' before the arrival of the police. More widespread appears to be a yearning among the young for the fleshpots of Western 'decadence' and a corresponding lack of interest in Marxist ideology, as well as an increase in drunkenness amongst the population as a whole. Black-marketeering, peculation and pilfering of state property also appear to be rife. Bribery and corruption of government officials appear to be common evils in both countries.

CONSTITUTION

Both superpower states have formal written constitutions which lay down rules for the distribution of governmental powers, the election or appointment to high office, the composition and functions of representative bodies and of the judiciary, and the rights of individuals. In neither case does this written constitution tell much about the political system as it exists in reality. Thus in the American constitution there is nothing about political parties, and in the Soviet constitution but one reference to the Communist party.

The American constitution was drawn up in 1787 by a convention representing the thirteen states which, as colonies, had successfully rebelled against the British crown. Its main concern was to devise a union strong enough to deal with common problems such as defence, foreign policy, trade and the native Indian, while preserving as much autonomy as possible to each of the constituent States. One reason for its failing to tell much about the present political system is that it antedated its growth. It is a relatively brief, direct and lucid document, but has been considerably amended, and the amendments are together almost as long as the original constitution. The Soviet constitution was promulgated in 1936, after the Soviet political system had been established, and its departures from reality are probably due, in the main, to Stalin's desire to present abroad a more liberal image of his country than the facts justified. It has been greatly amended but the amendments are incorporated in each new version and not added as separate articles, as are the American amendments.

The American constitution has a brief preamble stating that its aims are to 'establish justice, insure domestic tranquillity, provide for the common defense, promote the general welfare, and secure the blessings of liberty'. The Soviet constitution begins with a dozen articles which outline the economic, social and political basis of the Soviet state: it is described as a planned socialist state in which all power belongs to the workers and in which, with certain exceptions, all property is state property, and the state's aims are set forth as 'increasing the public wealth, raising the material and cultural levels of the workers, protecting the independence of the USSR and strengthening its defences'.[19]

As both countries are federations – of the fifty States of the USA and of the fifteen Republics of the USSR – each constitution distinguishes between the powers of the Union and those of the States or Republics. In both the Union is given control of foreign affairs, questions of war and peace, security, the admission of new territories, the armed forces, foreign trade, the monetary system and weights and measures. But the Soviet constitution also gives the USSR control over heavy industry, transport and communications, and the right to determine the 'basic principles' of land use, mineral exploitation, education, health, marriage and the family.

Each constitution provides for shared powers to be exercised by both the Union and its parts. In both countries these concern agriculture and industry, public works and public health. In the USA they also include the powers to borrow money, levy taxation, charter banks and establish law courts, functions reserved to the Union alone in the USSR. But Soviet Republics are given a say in the administration of fisheries, communications, geological exploration, higher education, cultural activities and defence.

There is some similarity in the powers given to the States or Republics alone. In both constitutions these include local government, education (primary and secondary only in the USSR), the maintenance of the armed forces (only the State militia in the USA), social and cultural services, and legislation and administration within these allocated spheres. In addition, the Soviet constitution gives the Republics 'the right freely to secede from the USSR' and to 'enter into direct relations with foreign states', powers explicitly denied to the American States.

Each constitution reserves powers not delegated to the Union to its federated parts. But this is largely negated in the Soviet case by the provision that 'in the event of divergence between the law of a Union Republic and the law of the Union, the Union law prevails'. In the USA such disputes go to the Supreme Court.

The American constitution places executive power in the hands of the President of the United States, and – as amended – makes provision for his eligibility, his election, his re-election, and his resignation, disability or death. The President and Vice-President are to be chosen by a majority vote of the 'electors' who are themselves to be chosen in the States by a popular vote according to the presidential candidate they are pledged to support. The Soviet constitution stipulates a collective presidency or Presidium of thirty-seven members, the chairman of which is often referred to as the President of the USSR and who acts as head of state. The Presidium is elected by the Supreme Soviet at a joint sitting of its two houses.

The President of the United States is commander-in-chief of the armed forces, has power to make treaties (with Senate approval), to appoint to the high offices of state (with Senate approval) and to initiate legislation. The Presidium of the USSR also has the power to make treaties and appoint ministers (when the Supreme Soviet is not sitting); it may also issue decrees, order mobilisation, proclaim martial law, as well as summon and dissolve the Supreme Soviet. Unlike the President, who is not responsible to any other constitutional organ, the Presidium is 'accountable to the Supreme Soviet' for all its activities.

The elective, representative and legislative bodies are the Congress of the United States and the Supreme Soviet. Each is bicameral, consisting of Senate and House of Representatives in the United States, and of the Soviet of the Union and the Soviet of the Nationalities in the USSR. In each case one of the two houses represents the constituent parts of the Union. The Senate is composed of two senators from each State; the Soviet of the Nationalities has twenty-five members from each Republic, eleven from each autonomous republic, five from each autonomous province and one from each national district. The House of Representatives and the Soviet of the Union are elected by the population as a whole, in America on the basis of one representative to about four hundred thousand people, and of one deputy to every three hundred thousand in the Soviet Union: senators and deputies to the Soviet of the Nationalities are also elected by popular vote.

Congress and the Supreme Soviet are both designated by their respective constitutions as the legislatures of their countries: 'all legislative powers herein granted shall be vested in a Congress of the United States'; 'the legislative power of the USSR is exercised exclusively by the Supreme Soviet of the USSR'. Congress is also given the rights to overrule the President's veto with a two-thirds majority, to originate money bills, to levy income tax, to raise armies and declare war, while the Supreme Soviet is declared to be 'the highest organ of state power in the USSR'. Unlike Congress, which does not choose the American administration, the Supreme Soviet 'appoints the government of the USSR, namely the Council of Ministers of the USSR', although the consent of the United States Senate is necessary for the President's cabinet appointments.

In conformity with the doctrine of 'separation of powers' the judiciary in the United States constitution is made as independent as possible of the executive (President) and the legislature (Congress), and the Supreme Court is made the arbiter of disagreements arising from the constitution. In the USSR the Supreme Court is elected by the Supreme Soviet for a period of five years but it has no power to interpret the constitution or the laws of the country: interpretations of law are handed down by the Presidium. The American constitution insists on trial by jury and the Soviet states that 'all court cases are tried with the participation of lay judges, except in cases specially provided for by law'. Only the Soviet document provides for the election of judges: the supreme courts of the Union and the Republics are elected by their supreme soviets, and in lesser localities by the local soviet or by the citizens themselves. Soviet judicial proceedings are to be carried on in the language of the local predominating nationality with interpreters available where the persons concerned do not know this language.

The American constitution makes no provision for the actual composition of the administration or 'government' of the country apart from giving the President the power to appoint 'public ministers' subject to the approval of the Senate, and insisting that 'no person holding any office under the United States, shall be a member of either house during his continuance in office'. The cabinet of departmental heads and the twelve great departments of the American administration lie outside the constitution. By contrast the Soviet constitution states that the Supreme Soviet 'appoints the government of the USSR, namely the council of ministers of the USSR' and that this council is 'the highest executive and administrative organ of state power'. It is accountable to the Supreme Soviet or the Presidium thereof, and it issues decisions and orders 'according to the laws in operation' which are 'binding throughout the territory of the USSR'. Furthermore it has the right, 'in respect of those branches of administration and economy which come within the jurisdiction of the USSR', to annul the decisions and orders of Republican and other lesser bodies.

A section of each constitution is devoted to the rights of the individual, although these rights are seen more as political and legal in the USA, more as social and economic in the USSR. Freedom of speech, of the press, and of assembly, and the inviolability of persons and their homes, subject to the law, are guaranteed by each, and the Soviet version adds freedom to associate and to make processions and demonstrations. However, these Soviet rights are stated to be 'to strengthen the socialist system', thereby excluding by implication any exercise of these rights which does not have that aim. The American document prohibits an established religion and religious tests for office, while the Soviet proclaims 'freedom of conscience, of religious worship and anti-religious propaganda'. The American citizen also has the right to keep and bear arms and to vote irrespective of race, colour and sex; he must first be indicted by a Grand Jury if accused of crime and cannot be made to incriminate himself. The Soviet citizen is given the rights to paid employment, to rest and leisure, to education, and to maintenance in old age, illness and disability; women have equal rights with men; and there is to be no discrimination on account of race or nationality. To these rights the Soviet constitution adds duties: to abide by the constitution, observe the laws, 'maintain labour discipline, to perform public duties honestly, and to respect the rules of socialist intercourse'; to safeguard state property; to perform military service and to defend the country.

Amendments to the constitution must be approved, in both countries, by not less than two-thirds of both houses of Congress or of the Supreme Soviet, but in America they must also be ratified by three-quarters of the States.

Unlike the Soviet constitution the American is fully operative with all its provisions in force, with the partial exception of Amendment XV which states that 'the rights of citizens of the United States to vote shall not be denied or abridged by the United States or by any State on account of race, color, or previous condition of servitude'. Since the 1950s, however, denial of voting rights to Negroes has diminished rapidly and successive Civil Rights Acts have 'cumulatively eliminated all but the most hard-core Southern resistance'.[20] On the other hand, several articles of the Soviet constitution are blatantly inoperative or illusory, notably the rights given to the Republics to secede, to enter into direct relations with foreign countries and to maintain their own armed forces. Nor do the freedom of speech, of the press, of assembly, of street processions and demonstrations, though guaranteed by the constitution, exist except for Communist party and other approved organisations.

The Soviet constitution is also misleading in that it asserts that the 'Union of Soviet Socialist Republics is a federal state, formed on the basis of a voluntary union of equal Soviet Socialist Republics'. The extent to which the higher central or Union executive organs of power may direct and override all the subordinate ones, whether Union or Republican, means that in effect it is a unitary state, and a highly centralised one at that. Although federalism is stronger in the United States, there is a growing consciousness there of its inadequacy in the face of modern social problems. These are usually concerned with the large urban areas, an increasing number of which overlap State boundaries.

GOVERNMENT

In both superpowers government divides into the electoral legislative part, in which elected leaders lay their policies and proposals before elected representatives who discuss them and vote upon them, and the administrative part in which, under the supreme direction of an elected leader or leaders, vast and complex bureaucracies of appointed officials, operating at the various levels of government (federal, State or Republican, local or municipal) execute and elaborate the approved policies and proposals. In each system policy originates both in the political leadership and in the administrative bureaucracy, although in the USSR the leadership is more important as a policy innovator, handing directives down to the bureaucracy, while in the USA the administrative machine is the source of more legislation, passing it up to the political leaders.[21]

One feature of the American two-party system is that the elected President, who heads the executive and administrative part of government can be, and often is, of a different party from the elected legislature; and a further complication is added when, within that legislature, one party controls the Senate and the other the House of Representatives. Such differences can block all progress on issues calling for urgent action. Domination of all offices and bodies in the Soviet Union by a single party prevents any such situation developing there, and once the party leaders have agreed on a policy, there is no further practical obstacle to its endorsement.

The electoral arrangements

The electoral machinery in both countries makes use of the secret ballot and applies the principle of universal suffrage, although many States in America deny this by applying literacy and other tests. Even today the percentage of Negroes registered to vote is under sixty in most southern States.[22] In the USSR the secret ballot is actually a disadvantage. As there is only one candidate for each place, and as voting is done by crossing out unwanted candidates, there is no point in entering the secluded booth unless one wishes to delete the name of the one candidate. To do this is to draw attention to the fact that one opposes the Party's choice. Almost all voters, therefore, drop their ballot papers straight into the box unmarked, without using the booth.[23]

The selection or nomination of candidates is a party function, and in both countries various factions and interest groups work behind the scenes to pick them. The chief difference is that in Russia one name only emerges as the 'Communist party and non-party' choice; no other candidate is possible. Nevertheless, 'an impressive number of citizens are still drawn into the nominating process' – well over a million people serve on the various electoral commissions.[24] In America a primary election is normally held in which the party's candidate is chosen by vote – either of party members only or, sometimes, by unrestricted popular vote. But candidates for the Presidency are chosen by a convention of delegates from the States. These delegates are normally chosen by the State party machine, without any reference to the rank and file membership. Only fifteen States hold primary elections in which there is a popular vote for candidates running for the nomination, but this vote is not always considered binding upon the delegates. The voting in primary elections gives some indication of how the various candidates may fare, but public opinion polls are considered to do that better. In any case, the Democratic convention of 1968 indicated that the party delegates preferred a 'safe' politician of orthodox views to a more radical choice who might possibly have brought in a larger vote. Likewise in 1964 the Republicans preferred an ultra-conservative, who seemed certain to lose, to a more liberal contender who might have stood a chance.

The legislatures

Once elected, there is all the difference in the world between the experience of a Congressman in Washington and that of a deputy to the Supreme Soviet in Moscow. The former resides in the capital for much of his time, and acts as a free and independent agent, lobbying and seeing lobbyists, taking part in debates, introducing bills – and he is well paid. The latter makes a brief visit to Moscow, usually twice a year, listens to the leaders, and is soon back home – without any pay. He has no power to initiate legislation and seldom any say in such legislation as his leaders set before him. Such debate as there is ranges 'from completely uncritical adulation of party and government policy to sharp criticism of failures in detail'.[25]

In both systems the work of committees of the legislature is more important than the formal debates, for it is here that detailed changes, often of substance, are made in bills. Congressional committees not only examine and amend bills but enquire into the performance of executive agencies. Supreme Soviet committees, surprisingly, have somewhat similar powers and functions.[26]

The executive

In the USA the executive and administrative branch of government is headed and chosen by the President, who is elected by popular vote from the two candidates chosen by the Democratic and Republican parties at their annual conventions every four years. The President chooses the heads of the great administrative departments from the top ranks of business and commerce as well as from the professional politicians and administrators, subject to the Senate's approval, but they may not be members of the legislature, i.e. of Congress.

In the USSR the executive and administrative branch is headed by the Chairman of the Council of Ministers, who is himself elected by the Supreme Soviet (the legislature) from among its members. Once elected, he forms his government – the Council of Ministers – and submits it to the Supreme Soviet for approval.[27] The Council of Ministers also includes the heads of the departments of state, but its number is swollen by *ex officio* ministers from the Republics, giving a total membership of ninety-five in 1970. This compares with only twelve departmental heads in the American cabinet, but in addition there are the heads of the numerous federal agencies whom the President can consult, as well as his own White House staff officers.

Spreading out beneath the departmental heads in both countries are the great and complex bureaucracies, organised in the various divisions, bureaus, sections, offices and 'desks' into which each department is divided. Because the Soviet bureaucracy has to administer almost all aspects of the economic and social life of the country, it is necessarily larger and more complex than its American counterpart. In the United States private corporations perform such governmental functions as health insurance, life insurance, pensions, tax collection, etc. Trade unions are also an important sphere of private government. Increasingly, however, public government has spread its supervisory powers over the private sector, with the establishment of important federal agencies such as the Federal Trade Commission, the Federal Power Commission, the Food and Drug Administration, and many others.[28] This is one of the ways in which the United States system is approaching the comprehensive Soviet state bureaucracy.

In the Soviet system there are, in effect, two parallel bureaucracies, for the Party duplicates some of the work of the state in all fields; but in the main the Party organisation is a policy-making and advisory one, while the state bureaucracy has an executive and administrative function. This may be necessary because a state bureaucracy is naturally conservative and lethargic. The Party, which contains many dynamic zealots, is needed to goad, cajole and persuade it to move along the lines of Party policy. If the criticism levelled at it in the Soviet press is to be believed, the state bureaucracy is cursed with 'chronic inefficiency, poor organisation, overplanning and overstaffing'.[29]

The patronage system whereby administrative offices, normally held in other countries by permanent officials, are distributed as party spoils after a change in administration, is a remarkable feature of American government. The tendency at federal level has been for the number of posts affected to decline, but at State level, while 'some states have developed civil services that serve loyally and impartially whatever party is in power and refrain from partisan activity; other states have an almost completely new set of employees, outside the federally protected departments, when a new party comes into power'.[30]

Participation

Active participation of the ordinary citizen in government is far more widespread in the Soviet Union, and this is one of the features which, according to Communists, makes their system democratic. Whereas under a million people work part-time in local government in the USA, there are almost two million deputies to the various soviets in the USSR, most of whom are unpaid amateurs.[31] In addition, a much greater number work unpaid and part-time in countless organisations – co-operatives, collective farms, trade unions, comrades' courts, volunteer police and fire brigades, street and house committees, parents' councils, pensions councils, women's councils, etc. A three-million strong mass organisation of volunteers known as *druzhinniki* assist the professional police in fighting crime and hooliganism.[32] These bodies are used both to provide a cheap administrative labour force, and to keep the professional administrators in touch with the thoughts and needs of ordinary people; and – as criticism of performance as opposed to policy is vigorously encouraged – they provide a check on bureaucracy. Also, participation tends to generate satisfaction. By its very comprehensiveness it involves the masses in the Soviet system and isolates the dissidents. Even allowing for overlapping membership, perhaps as many as thirty million persons are involved, and 'since most of the positions are rotated every few years there can be few Soviet adults who escape the responsibility of direct participation in government'.[33]

Participation in the USA is sometimes stimulated by a local issue when it is well publicised and when the protagonists and antagonists are active in enlisting support. Such activity is different in nature from Soviet participation, often involving matters of policy rather than the mere administration of policies already decided upon, and it has a degree of spontaneity totally lacking in the USSR. But it occurs only sporadically and much of its machinery is temporary and *ad hoc*.[34]

The contrast to participation in a system is alienation from it, but here comparison is very difficult to make for lack of data. Obviously the difference between the sixty per cent turnout at American elections and the 99·9 per cent endorsement of the Communist party in Soviet elections is little to go by. Intellectuals seem to be alienated to a degree in both societies, but much more so in the USSR where they lack freedom of discussion, expression and association except in prescribed forms. Soviet society seems more successful at the other end of the scale, remaining relatively free from 'hippies', 'dropouts' and the associated problem of drug addiction, but not from drunkenness and hooliganism.

Communication

Some degree of communication between the governors and the governed is essential in any state, even if it involves no more than the imparting of decisions, orders and prohibitions. In the USSR the mass media are used to the full to propagate communist ideology, to portray the policies and actions of Party and government in the most favourable light, and to enlist the support of the people for the measures decided upon. By contrast, political matters are not prominent in the American media because their main business is to sell advertising.[35] This entails refraining from any tedious or controversial material, and politics to the ordinary reader, listener or viewer are either one or the other. An exception to the secondary importance of political material in the mass media is the Presidential election, which because of its sporting two-sided contest, ranks more as one of the great national games than as a political event.

Although the kind of political debate that sometimes occurs on American television is absent from the Soviet mass media, public debates are often organised to sound opinion, explain official policy and allow opponents to let off steam. Newspapers open up their correspondence columns and public meetings are arranged. This was done even in Stalin's heyday, as in the controversial decision to illegalise abortion in 1936; the published draft of the law was, in *Pravda*'s words, 'being heatedly discussed by millions of people' and *Izvestiya* published numerous letters against the proposal.[36] During the public debate on the reorganisation of the machine tractor stations in 1958, there were over half a million public meetings in which three million persons took part and which nearly fifty million attended, while the newspapers published about a hundred thousand articles and letters.[37]

Communication through elected representatives has some points of similarity. American congressmen and Soviet deputies hold 'surgeries' in their constituencies at which they receive complaints about the administration and may use their rights of access to the ministries to intervene on their constituents' behalf, becoming, in American parlance, 'glorified errand boys'.[38] Not all are equally assiduous in performing this function and there are complaints in both countries of negligence. The congressman has to worry about re-election, however, and because of the looseness of party discipline in America, is more likely to be able to push the local interest irrespective of party policy. The Soviet deputy is subject to recall and this constituents' right is sometimes exercised.[39] Probably the most important aspect of communication between the Soviet legislatures and the public lies in the fact that deputies are drawn from all ranks of society, and spend most of their time at home working in ordinary jobs, where the Communist party expects them to be active in their localities as propagandists on behalf of government policy.[40] Congressmen spend much more of their time in the capital and, although they too may be derived from all walks of life, most of them are business and professional men, with lawyers predominating.

17 Parties, Politicians and Power

The representative and elective institutions provided for in the constitutions of each country would not work without political parties to activate them. Candidates have to be nominated; issues have to be formulated and policies elaborated; information or propaganda about these issues and policies has to be disseminated; sufficient interest has to be aroused among the electorate to bring people to the polling booths. The initiative in all this is provided by political parties. In any large nation there are groups and sectional interests too diverse and numerous to enter the political arena individually. Instead they act through parties staffed by professional politicians and which aim to represent as wide a range of such groups as they can. In this respect the most obvious point of contrast between the USA and the USSR is that the former is a two-party state, the latter a one-party state. The various groups and interests that seek to influence government and policy have a choice in America between the Democrat and Republican parties, but in Russia they must act through the Communist party. It follows that in America there is competition for power between the two parties, whereas in Russia the Communist party has a monopoly of it.

Political parties consist of cores of strongly motivated activists who seek power for idealistic reasons or for reasons of self-interest or from a mixture of both. They struggle among themselves to influence the policy of their party and aspire to its leadership. These activists are inevitably in contact with members of powerful groups and interests who have a stake in the shape policy may take, and often such interested persons themselves become active party members. Around these activist cores are the rank and file membership who belong to the party for a variety of reasons: because they have inherited the allegiance of their parents; because they find within it a congenial and satisfying social companionship; because its policies come closest to their ideals, convictions or self-interest; or because it gives them a feeling of participation in the affairs of the nation. Then there are those who, though not formally members, regard themselves as supporting the party and normally vote for it at elections, but play no further part in its affairs. In the United States about fourteen per cent of the adult population take a more active part in electoral politics than merely voting, whereas in the USSR only seven per cent are members of the Communist party.

The differences between the party systems of the USA and the USSR are therefore, in the main, the differences between a two-party system and a one-party system. In the former there is a choice in elections; in the second there is none, except that of crossing out the name of the Communist-endorsed candidate instead of voting for him. In the two-party system, however, the choice is often meaningless because of the difficulty of distinguishing between the consequences of electing one or other candidate. There may nor may not be clear-cut differences between platforms and promised policies; but as whichever party is successful is confronted in office with similar pressures, internal and external, and has to face identical realities, subsequent perform-ance is more likely to be guided by such pressures and realities than by election pledges. But in so far as elections to office in the two-party system may be regarded as a verdict on past performance rather than as a choice of future programmes, the choice has more value. It means that the party in power must have some regard to public opinion, although such regard will vary with the proximity of the next election.

The two-party system arouses interest in politics and national and local issues of all kinds, if only in the period immediately preceding an election. The mass of the population in large nations is apathetic to politics and the issues around which politics revolve, but the periodic concentration of all the mass media upon an election gives the people no alternative but to take notice. The two-party contest also arouses the same kind of interest and excitement as a game of football and appeals to the sporting instinct of the ordinary man; this does not happen where there are more than two parties and cannot happen where there is one. The Communist party of the Soviet Union tries to make up for this by subjecting the population to political propaganda, not only at election times but continuously, although this inevitably has the effect of producing almost total indifference.

By its very success in arousing interest the two-party system may have a divisive effect on national unity if the two parties take opposite sides on emotionally-charged issues, such as the Vietnamese war or civil rights. Such bi-polarisation is, however, quite rare in America. This is sometimes held to be because there is a consensus of opinion among the majority of Americans on the real issues, but it is more likely that it represents a consensus among those who decide which issues should be put before the electorate, i.e. among those who control the party machinery and their influential backers. The one-party system of the USSR removes any possibility of such open national division of opinion. This fact is linked with the Soviet justification of the system, namely that because in the USSR all classes and interests have been abolished save those of the workers, only one party – the party that represents the workers – is needed. The constitution defines the place of the Communist party in the state thus:

> the most active and politically conscious citizens from the ranks of the working class, working peasants and working intelligentsia voluntarily unite in the Communist party of the Soviet Union, which is the vanguard of the workers in their struggle to build a communist society, and is the guiding nucleus of all workers' organisations, public and official.[1]

In the Soviet Union an internal dispute of policy is never revealed to the people, at least not until after it has been resolved and the defeated group expelled from positions of power.

A practical advantage of the American two-party system is that no single set of politicians can expect permanent tenure of office. They are less likely therefore to become wholly professional and more likely to retain a stake in fields other than politics. When they are out of office they gain a respite from the responsibility and a rest from the labours of public office. They are enabled to travel, read, reflect and relax in a way men in power are unable to do. If they return to power they do so refreshed, and government is likely to benefit from this. In the one-party system there is no such change in prospect for the leaders, short of death or a palace revolution; and both Stalin and Khrushchev showed increasing signs of unfitness for office in the last years of their rule.

At a time when social and technological change is so rapid, a system that provides for regular changes in leadership has obvious advantages in bringing forward new and often younger men. It is difficult to see how the hierarchical system of the CPSU could bring forward a man as youthful as John Kennedy. The defeat of a party tends to discredit its leaders and when it returns to power it is likely to do so with new ones. The Soviet Union had a great opportunity to turn adversity to benefit at the end of the 1941–5 war, when much of the country lay in ruins, by rebuilding its industries according to the most advanced technology. West Germany and Japan profited by wartime destruction in this way. But the Stalinist administration reconstructed Soviet industry on pre-war lines, and the USSR had to wait until after Stalin's death in 1953 before long overdue modernisation could begin.

The contrast between the American two-party system and the Soviet one-party system is heightened by the looseness of party organisation in the United States. The Democratic and Republican parties are not centralised disciplined bodies but loose congeries of organisations which differ in structure and behaviour from State to State. Their main function is collecting financial support and nominating for office: once men have been elected on the party 'ticket' they are little subject to party control. A committee of the American Political Science Association has condemned the system in these words:

Historical and other factors have caused the American two-party system to operate as two loose associations of state and local organizations, with very little national machinery and very little national cohesion. As a result, either major party, when in power, is ill-equipped to organize its members in the legislative and the executive branches into a government held together and guided by the party programme.[2]

This is very different from the strongly-centralised, highly-disciplined CPSU, permeated by a single ideology and with an orthodoxy so rigid and so narrow as to permit not the least heresy nor the slightest deviation.

Yet in some parts of the United States there is, at local level, a sinister version of the one-party system, with party machines as powerful and relentless as the Russian Communist party, but with the leading members actuated by greed and self interest:

In blunt fact, the spoils of office are their main sustenance. It can be – according to the tolerant and perhaps honestly realistic standards of politicians – licit spoils: providing government jobs to party workers, purchasing insurance or surety bonds through political leaders who act as special agents, and awarding public work contracts to favored contractors. Or it can be the illicit spoils which flow from crime. Racketeers need the protection of policemen and public officials whose indulgence, in one way or another, has been purchased.[3]

Greed, self-interest and corruption are doubtless present in the Soviet Communist party also, and bribery and corrupt influence are too deeply rooted in the Russian bureaucratic tradition for them to be quickly eliminated. But the rigid discipline of the Party is so tight, mutual criticism and watchfulness so well developed, and the penalties for breach of the strict ethical code so severe, that where these evils flourish in the USSR, they exist rather in spite of than because of the party system.

One important consequence of the Soviet one-party system is that the political party organisation tends to duplicate and to dominate the state governmental organisation, and stresses and strains inevitably occur between them. In the American two-party system the temporary nature of any one party's tenure of power prevents it from dominating or from becoming identified or confused with government. This confusion in the USSR is such that 'it is frequently difficult to determine the division of competence between the State organ and those of the Party'.[4]

In the USSR some of the rivalry found in the USA between the two parties appears in the relationship between the Communist party organisation and the state administration; although at the top the leaders of both party and state are the same, some tend to become identified more with one interest than the other. Thus, during Stalin's long reign, the state bureaucracy 'had emerged as the dominant force on the Soviet scene' and after his death in 1953 was represented by Malenkov, who became chairman of the Council of Ministers, i.e. prime minister.[5] Khrushchev, who became general secretary of the Communist party, stood for those who were determined to reassert the primacy of the Party. The 'anti-party' group who failed in their bid to oust him in 1957 were accused of advocating the 'primacy of State organs over those of the Party'.[6] In October 1964 there appears to have been a tacit agreement between the two organisations to share power, with the Party headed by Brezhnev as first secretary and the government by Kosygin as chairman of the Council of Ministers, although the 'supremacy of the Party was stressed, and unquestioned precedence given to Brezhnev'.[7]

One may also look upon factions competing for power within the Communist party as having some resemblance to the American party system: 'the faction is the Soviet bureaucratic equivalent of the American electoral party. Both the faction and the party are groups of politicians bound together by a common interest in acquiring power or in preventing someone from getting it. They are the dynamic elements in the political system.'[8] Certainly, the changes wrought in the top levels of administration after the defeat of one faction by another bear some resemblance to the American patronage system whereby a change of party control may be followed by the replacement of a large number of the holders of civil service posts by nominees of the victorious party. Because the Republicans had been long out of office and were hungry for spoils, President Eisenhower in 1952 added 134,000 positions to the list of those which could be filled by party nominees.[9] This was almost equivalent to a Stalinist-style purge as far as the number losing their jobs was concerned.

POLITICS AND POLITICIANS

Politicians, using the word in the sense of those who, as members of political parties, operate the political system and from whom the political leaders emerge, come from very different backgrounds in the

USA and the USSR. American politicians are drawn more from the legal profession than from any other calling: in the 88th Congress (1963), sixty-six per cent of the Senate and fifty-seven per cent of the House of Representatives were lawyers, with the next group, business and banking, contributing twenty-three and thirty-one per cent respectively.[10] The legal profession has two advantages: it brings its practitioners into touch with varied interests, many of them influential and wealthy, and it can be dropped temporarily for politics and resumed again when need or opportunity arises. Higher Communist party officials, by contrast, are more often engineers by training: over forty per cent of the Party's central committee had engineering training in 1961, followed by the agricultural experts with ten per cent.[11] This reflects the technical and economic bias of the Soviet system. But the deputies elected to the Supreme Soviet come close to being a cross-section of Soviet society. Nomination tends to be given as a reward for distinguished service and is therefore widely spread throughout many occupations.[12]

Politicians on both sides tend to be generalists rather than experts, although there are exceptions when individuals come to be known as authorities on special subjects. But in both countries the average politician has to be flexible enough to accommodate as many diverse interests and pressures as possible, tactful enough to reconcile rather than exacerbate differences and adaptable to changing circumstances. He has usually moved about a great deal from place to place and from post to post, and consequently has rather loose attachments to particular regions or subjects.[13]

Significant differences between party politicians in the two countries arise from the fact that the American parties are loosely organised, undisciplined groups with distinct federal, State and local structures; these are in no way hierarchical and seldom staffed by professionals: 'the United States has industrial, administrative, military and educational bureaucracies, but it does not have a political one'.[14] The CPSU is, on the other hand, a highly-centralised, intensely hierarchical bureaucracy. A large proportion of its active members are true professionals working in the Party bureaucracy (*apparat*): at the 22nd Party Congress (1961) these *apparatchiki* made up over a quarter of the delegates and they constituted about a half of the Central Committee. At the top, in the Presidium (Politburo) and Secretariat, over eighty per cent of the party members were *apparatchiki*.[15]

For rapid advancement a young American politician needs a resounding electoral success, such as the defeat of a prominent established politician; but the young Soviet *apparatchik* needs the patronage of a highly-placed personage, not his defeat: the downfall of his patron will check his own career unless he is adroit in shifting his allegiance. Periodically, if his progress is to continue, the American politician must win votes. For his Soviet counterpart a key position in the organisation, especially one where appointments are made, is the supreme advantage, as controlling appointments is the surest means of enlisting support.

Another consequence of the structural difference of the parties is that whereas the American is dealing with equals whom he must convince or persuade, the *apparatchik* must 'please superiors and prod subordinates'.[16] Defeat, of course, brings very different results. For the American politician it means a return to his old job for a while, with the possibility of an early return to politics, depending on the degree of support he retains after his defeat and the electoral fortunes of his party. For the Soviet politician, until recently, defeat meant death or exile, and it still entails public denunciation and possible banishment from the capital; any attempt to return to political life would be extremely difficult and dangerous.

THE LEADERS

In the USA leaders come from many walks of life – the professions, business administration, the armed forces, etc., whereas in the USSR they tend to be more exclusively *apparatchiki*. Originally they were revolutionaries – men who took part in the October revolution of 1917, but few of these are active now. In the USA there is a constitutional limit on the term of a President, and congressional leaders are compelled to seek re-election. In the USSR there is no such constitutional limit.

Whereas in the USA there is always in the President one clearly designated and unrivalled leader, in the Soviet Union there appears to be an alternation between degrees of collective leadership and of personal rule, with the latter developing from the former. This can be seen by listing together the changes at the top since the Revolution (Table 17.1). The changes of President at regular four- and eight-year intervals, except where interrupted by death from natural causes or assassination, contrasts with the more irregular Soviet pattern. Of the American presidents listed, three died in office, two naturally and one assassinated; in each case the vice-president assumed the presidency as laid down in the constitution. Among the Soviet top leaders listed, Lenin and Stalin were removed from office by death from natural causes (although an earlier attempt at assassination was the cause of Lenin's death) and Beria was shot. The others were all demoted. But the arrest and shooting in 1953 of Beria, the head of Stalin's secret police, and the great reduction in the power of that iniquitous institution,

TABLE 17.1   AMERICAN AND SOVIET LEADERS SINCE 1917

1917	Wilson	Lenin
1921	Harding	
1923	Coolidge	Zinoviev–Stalin–Rykov
1929	Hoover	Stalin
1933	Roosevelt	
1945	Truman	
1953	Eisenhower	Malenkov–Beria–Molotov
		Malenkov–Molotov–Khrushchev
1955		Khrushchev–Bulganin
1957		Khrushchev
1961	Kennedy	
1963	Johnson	
1964		Brezhnev–Kosygin
1969	Nixon	

removed the element of violence, in the form of sudden arrest and physical liquidation, from the scene of top-level Soviet intrigue.[17] As far as is known, none of the leaders deposed since has suffered any harm to his person, and Khrushchev continued to live in Moscow as a private citizen after his fall.

A brief comparison of the lives and careers of President Richard Nixon and First Secretary Leonid Brezhnev may be relevant.[18] Nixon is the younger man, born in 1913, whereas Brezhnev's life began in 1906. Nixon was fifty-five when elected President but he might well have gained that office while still in his forties: President Eisenhower came close to dying or retiring on grounds of ill health during his term of office in the 1950s and Nixon as Vice-President would have succeeded him. He almost won the 1960 contest when he was forty-seven. It is difficult to see how an *apparatchik* in the Soviet bureaucracy could move up through the hierarchy fast enough to reach the summit of power in his forties. Brezhnev was fifty-eight when he succeeded Khrushchev.

Nixon was born in California and not in the North East or Middle West, the 'power centres' of the United States, from which all but three of the presidents have come during the past century. Brezhnev is not a Russian but was born in the Ukraine and owed his advancement to the favour of his Ukrainian predecessor, Khrushchev. Nixon's father was a lemon farmer who later ran a filling station and grocery shop, and although such parentage is exceptional among America's top leaders, it is representative of the massive move from country to town that has characterised twentieth-century America. Brezhnev is the son of a steelworker, and has the correct urban proletarian background for a communist leader of his generation.

Nixon studied law, and after a brilliant college career, practised in his home town of Whittier, California, in the years before the 1941–5 war. Brezhnev, after some years as a land surveyor, graduated from the

Dneprodzerzhinsk Metallurgical Institute and then worked at the local steelworks as an engineer. Whereas Nixon did not enter politics until after the war, Brezhnev, who had joined the Party in 1931, became a full-time Party official in his home town in 1938. During the war, Nixon served with the United States Navy in the South Pacific and rose to the rank of lieutenant-commander; Brezhnev acted as a political commissar in the eighteenth army on the Ukrainian front and rose to the rank of major-general.

Nixon entered politics seriously in 1945 and in 1946 was elected Republican congressman for his home district in California. He made his mark in the House Un-American Activities Committee when the former communist, Whittaker Chambers, accused Alger Hiss, a highly-placed and respected government official, of being a communist. Nixon's work on the case resulted in Hiss's conviction for perjury in 1950, and later the same year he was elected to the Senate. He was carried forward on the anti-communist tide, then flowing strongly and when he was nominated for Vice-President in 1952, General Eisenhower introduced him as 'a man who has shown statesmanlike qualities in many ways, but has a special talent and an ability to ferret out any kind of subversive influence wherever it may be found, and the strength and persistence to get rid of it'.[19] He served as Vice-President throughout the two Eisenhower terms, i.e. from 1953 to 1960. As Vice-President he travelled widely and became an authority on foreign affairs and foreign aid. In 1959 he visited the Soviet Union.

Brezhnev, after the war, served as Party first secretary at *oblast* level in the Ukraine from 1946 to 1950. From 1950 to 1952 he was first secretary of the Party central committee of the Moldavian republic, and then became head of the political administration of the Navy. Just as the Hiss case brought Nixon to the fore, Khrushchev's grandiose plan to plough up the virgin steppe of Kazakhstan and settle it with three hundred thousand farmers in order to raise grain production gave Brezhnev his chance. In February 1954 he was sent to Kazakhstan where he was successively second and first secretary of the Republic's Party central committee. In 1956 he came to Moscow as a secretary of the central committee of the CPSU, and in 1957 was promoted by Khrushchev to full membership of the Politburo. Just as Nixon was now Eisenhower's right-hand man, so Brezhnev was Khrushchev's chief lieutenant. But, unlike Nixon, he remained wholly engrossed in internal affairs and did not travel abroad.

The difference between the two systems is henceforth strongly reflected in the different courses the two men now take. Nixon in 1960 was defeated by Kennedy for the Presidency and in 1961 found himself without public office for the first time for fourteen years. He had many tempting offers to become president of a corporation, a foundation or a university, but decided to return to law practice: he joined a Los Angeles firm whose clients included many big business corporations.[20] Meanwhile, Brezhnev had become chairman of the Presidium of the Supreme Soviet, i.e. 'President' of the USSR and its nominal head of state (1960). In 1962 Richard Nixon contested the governorship of his own State of California and lost. His political career was widely assumed to be at an end. From 1963 to 1968 he was again a lawyer in private practice. Yet, although he was not nominated for President in 1964, he remained a leading political figure and increased his popularity. As urban violence grew in America, he appealed more and more strongly to the conservative middle classes as a sober-minded, realistic and capable man. This groundswell of support helped him gain the Republican nomination in 1968 and led to his election as President.

Brezhnev meanwhile continued to climb without any such vicissitudes. In 1963 he returned to the secretariat of the Central Committee of the CPSU with an unmatched background of high Party positions and administrative experience. It needed only the removal of his patron, Khrushchev, for him to move up to top place as First Secretary, while Khrushchev's other commanding position, Chairman of the Council of Ministers (Prime Minister) went to Alexei Kosygin, an authority on light industry and foreign affairs. Brezhnev himself, as a Party *apparatchik*, remains primarily concerned with the internal problems of the communist world; it is rather Kosygin, who has travelled more widely and visited the United States, who is comparable to Nixon in his broad understanding of the world as a whole.

POWER

According to the constitution, power in the United States is shared between the federal and State authorities with the federal power divided between the legislature (Congress) and the executive (President). President and Congress are independent of each other. In the USSR constitutional power is vested in the Supreme Soviet when it is sitting, otherwise in its Presidium; executive power is wielded by the Council of Ministers, which is, however, responsible to the Supreme Soviet or its Presidium.

As the election of these various constitutional bodies is organised by political parties, it is the party which exercises power when in office. The permanence of the Communist party and the absence of any competitors add strength to its hold upon the Russian governmental system, and it can be said that, within the USSR, the Communist party has a monopoly of political power. In so far as the actions of a party are determined and controlled by its leaders, it is they who wield power. The Party secretariat is the all-important body, controlling appointments and promotions, and supervising the activity of local party organisations. Its first secretaries, successively Stalin, Khrushchev and Brezhnev, have the undisputed power of patronage and are able to promote their own supporters to key positions throughout the country.[21]

For this reason the power of the top leaders in the USA is less absolute than that of the Kremlin bosses. The President's power is limited because he depends upon the co-operation of so many diverse people, groups and institutions, many of which do not come under his own jurisdiction. If his policy needs money he must persuade Congress to grant it, if it needs a treaty he must persuade Congress to ratify it, and if it needs legislation he must persuade Congress to pass it. The Congressional leaders may, in turn, be thwarted in their legislative efforts by the presidential veto – except in the unlikely event that they are strong enough to override it with a two-thirds majority. Owing to the lack of party discipline, they may well not even be able to get their legislation through their own Houses.

A Soviet leader has to win the acquiescence of only a handful of men to ensure the adoption of his policy, yet even he has to avoid action that may undermine the support on which his power rests. Khrushchev fell in 1964 because he used his power at the very top to push through measures unpopular with influential members of the Party in the Central Committee.[22] In fact, the appeals made to the Central Committee of the CPSU (or its more concise version, the Plenum) in 1957 and 1964 to decide a leadership dispute have diluted somewhat the absolutism at the top in the USSR and diffused power downwards from the Politburo to the Central Committee.[23] This has been a direct result of the agreement of the leaders in 1953, soon after Stalin's death, to curb the authority of the secret police who had previously arrested and executed any contender the top man considered a threat to his supremacy.

Because parties and party politicians have power they become inevitably the targets of pressures exerted by a variety of groups and interests; in fact the party system is often justified on the grounds that it enables some of these interests to be so modified and controlled as to be reconciled into an amalgam upon which the party can find a broad and firm enough basis of support for government.[24] The Communists have a similar view, maintaining that, in the Soviet state, the elimination of all interests save those of the workers justifies the exclusion of all other parties. Hence 'the Communist Party, the party of the working class, has today become the party of the whole Soviet people' (Communist Party rules, preamble).

K

In the United States organised pressure groups are manifold and form a complex pattern. For the most part they are private and outside the system of public government. In the USSR, because of the all-embracing nature of state and public activity and because the Communist party is the only organisation permitted to pervade such activity, most pressures must of necessity be exerted within the state system and within the Communist party.

Organised pressure groups outside government

There are several kinds of organised pressure groups in America. Some have mainly social, political, religious or ideological aims, such as the Daughters of the American Revolution, the Americans for Democratic Action, the American Civil Liberties Union, the League of Women Voters, the Zionist Organization of America, Black Power, etc. Others represent economic groups. There are the farmers' representative bodies, the business organisations, and the professional societies, notably the American Medical Association. Labour is represented by the trade unions. Trade unions also exist in the USSR, and although they are in effect an agency of the Communist party and do not bargain for wage increases nor organise strikes, they do useful work with the state bureaucracy and with factory managements for the welfare of their members; they also provide a degree of worker participation in the management of industry.[25]

All other American pressure groups are overshadowed in the power they exert, both directly and indirectly, by the great manufacturing and commercial corporations, which seem 'more like states within states than simply private businesses'.[26] Among these corporations, in recent years, as a result of the great increase in military spending, the weapon-making firms have become most prominent. Their relationship with government is particularly intimate because they depend almost wholly on Defense Department contracts for their business: 'the stake that aircraft companies, missile manufacturers, and potential suppliers of other weapons systems have in the allocation of defense contracts would be hard indeed to overestimate'.[27] This has created a complex of pressures that inevitably work, not only against each other for the allocation of contracts to one corporation rather than to another, but together for the maintenance of defence and foreign policies linked with such a high level of expenditure.[28]

Heavy industry and the armed forces also have a certain community of interest in the USSR in withstanding pressures for a greater share of national investment being diverted into agriculture and consumer goods production at their expense. The Red Army is the one important organisation outside the Communist party 'having internal cohesion, defined membership, specific interests and its own leadership'.[29] Yet although the army has undoubtedly used its influence in favour of heavy industry, the politicians have remained its masters. This was shown by the removal in 1957 of Marshal Zhukov who had tried to claim for the army more independence of the Party. His fall has been compared to President Truman's dismissal of the popular hero General MacArthur in 1951.[30]

Pressure groups in America usually operate through lobbying. Both money and votes are important weapons in the process. Politicians and political parties need money to maintain their organisations and run their campaigns, and much of this money comes from groups who wish to have influence with them.[31] In return, representatives of the donating interest may be given key posts in government agencies through the system of party patronage.[32] Some pressure groups are richer in numbers than in money and are able to use the threat of the withdrawal or transfer of electoral support.

The various interests that wish to influence policy are served by an army of lobbyists, and the larger associations have permanent offices and staffs in Washington. The lobbyists may be officials of the pressure group organisations or freelancers known to have access to or influence with legislators or administrators. They not only lobby politicians in the sense of interviewing them but argue before committees and even do research and write speeches for congressmen. They sometimes organise a barrage of letters and telegrams. There may be pecuniary ties between lobbyist and legislator or official, which may take other forms than outright bribery. Thus unconditional gifts may be made but described as contributions to campaign funds.[33] Because defence spending is now the major field of government activity, it is for military contracts that the fiercest and most costly lobbying takes place. The great corporations that depend on military orders 'imperatively need access to the officials who distribute the vital largesse' and their representation in Washington has become 'one of the capital city's major industries'.[34] Large numbers of ex-military officers work for the companies in this field.

Organised pressures within government

Although the general distinction may be made that pressures upon the party leaders in power come from mostly outside the governmental system in the USA and from within it in the USSR, it must nevertheless be recognised that there are some important sources of power within the American system. Members of Congress themselves lobby for interests

with which they are connected or with which they sympathise, as well
as for their States or districts.[35] Soviet deputies are expected to use
whatever influence they have – and this may be very little – to air the
grievances of their local districts.[36]

Within the American state apparatus powerful government departments and agencies not only urge their own policies but sometimes take
the law into their own hands. The attempted Bay of Pigs invasion of
Cuba was an instance in which the CIA 'forced policy makers, including Presidents, to accept initiatives it has devised in secret'.[37] In 1961
both Kennedy and Khrushchev were under heavy pressure from their
military staffs to resume nuclear bomb testing, as the Russian leader
admitted.[38]

Scientific experts and technocrats are inevitably exercising more
influence with government in each country, for as the politicians cannot
fully comprehend the scientific or technical aspects of many issues, they
are compelled to rely upon the advice of those who do. Such advice can
be shaped to fit the policy the experts themselves wish to implement.
Cybernetics and the application of scientific methods to social control
will still further increase the power of bureaucracy: although technologically more advanced in the USA, these methods are likely to find
fuller scope in the USSR.[39]

The power of the bureaucracies of state and Party in the USSR was
shown by Khrushchev's fall in 1964, which seems to have been a
consequence of resentment among the administrators of his reorganisation of them in 1957 and 1962. This was exceptional, however, and
pressure politics in the Soviet Union are normally a matter of competition among the various sectors of the bureaucracy for control over
the apportionment of scarce resources, i.e. for priority in the state plan.
The USSR is a state where government is concerned more with
economics than with politics, and the major domestic issues are
economic. Under Stalin heavy industry enjoyed undisputed priority,
but after his death the claims of agriculture and light industry found
powerful support, and the heavy industry interest was on the defensive.
It is even possible to link the oligarchy that assumed power after
Stalin's death in 1953 with separate interests and policies. Khrushchev
represented the Party *apparat*, Molotov the state bureaucracy, Malenkov
light industry, Kaganovich heavy industry and Beria the secret police.[40]
The others quickly agreed on the elimination of the latter, and finally,
by 1957, Khrushchev, relying on his Party organisation, had not only
secured personal supremacy for himself but had made the Party
supreme over all other interests. However, after his fall in 1964,
Kosygin, representing the state bureaucracy and light industry, is
found sharing the leadership with Party chief Brezhnev.

Unorganised pressures outside government

Unorganised pressure or power is exercised in the most general way by public opinion – the views of the 'man in the street'. All modern governments have to take this into account, and it is doubtful whether a political régime could govern a modern industrially-advanced state effectively without a broad basis of support in public opinion. In the USA, however, because of the choice available between the two parties, public opinion has to be taken into account more seriously than it does in the USSR. The development of public opinion polls makes available to American politicians statistical expressions of popular feeling on diverse issues. In Russia local communist organisations carry out soundings in their districts which, when co-ordinated at headquarters, may provide a rough equivalent.

In recent years the power of public opinion in the United States appears to have increased, forcing the politicians to act in such important matters as the war in South East Asia, pollution and car safety. In the Soviet Union the new leadership which replaced Stalin, by immediately announcing various reforms such as more consumer goods, seemed to be courting public opinion, as did Khrushchev's successors in 1964. Shortly after assuming power, they announced a programme of social reform and improved living conditions. These, and other instances, have led one authority to claim that 'public opinion is far from negligible' as a factor in Soviet politics.[41]

Broad divisions of the population into large unorganised groups with differing attitudes and interests makes a consensus of public opinion difficult to achieve on many issues. Such broad groupings in the USA are political, social, economic, religious and racial: conservative, liberal and radical; high income and low income; Protestant and Catholic, White and Negro. In the USSR likewise: Party and non-party, urban and rural, industrial and farm, official–managerial–professional–technical and workers; Russian and non-Russian. The two-party system in America gives these groups the opportunity of aligning themselves politically on different sides and competing for influence and power. In the USSR the one-party system tends to give more permanent dominance to one group as against another: thus the Communist party has been traditionally associated with urban advance and rural retardation, and more recently, perhaps, with Slavonic predominance over non-Slavonic peoples. The two-party system can also give minorities a political influence out of all proportion to their numbers: when support for the two parties is fairly divided, they hold the balance of power. Small minorities in the Soviet Union, by contrast, normally have no influence or power whatever.

K 2

It is a testimony to the value placed upon public opinion that great pains are taken to form it in both countries. The mass media are used for this and in no country are the technology and psychology of the means of persuasion more advanced than in the United States. Political parties, businesses and organisations with ends to promote spend vast sums on 'public relations campaigns' to secure a favourable public opinion. This is sometimes referred to as the 'new lobby' as against the 'old lobby' of direct intervention with legislators and administrators. Between 1948 and 1952 the American Medical Association spent over $4½ million to 'educate' the American public about the dangers of 'socialised medicine'. During a nine-month period at the height of the campaign, mail sent to congressmen swung from 2½ to 1 in favour of health insurance to 4 to 1 against.[42]

In the USSR, although in a less subtle way, the mass media are united in extolling the virtues of Soviet socialist society and of the Communist party and its policies. There is less advertising technique, no glamour, no gimmicks, but slogans in plenty, and the propaganda is much more direct and political in its nature. It is replete with the jargon and hackneyed phrases of Marxist–Leninism and probably far less effective in swaying public opinion than any American public relations campaign. Its tedium derives from its repetitiveness and from the obvious fact that it is always the same theme from the same source, whereas the fabric of American propaganda is a multicoloured cloth intricately woven with a wide variety of *motifs* from a vast range of sources.

Thus public opinion is often more a reflection of ideas supplied by those who control the media of communication, than a spontaneous reaction to information and events. But whereas in Russia the concepts and information fed to the people are all of one pattern, issue from a single source, conform to one ideology and point to a single conclusion, those supplied to the Americans are of varied origin and often of a conflicting nature. Issues are presented and publicly debated, and such arguments among the leaders give public opinion a certain degree of choice and initiative absent from the Soviet scene. Yet the basic conceptual framework of a capitalist economy and society is seldom questioned: socialist or communist criticisms have little more chance of reaching and influencing public opinion than have capitalist views on Communism in Russia. In fact, because listening to foreign radio is widespread in the Soviet Union, many Soviet citizens are subjected to more fundamental subversion than Americans. Because those who control the media are also, in the main, those who control the governmental and economic structures, or derived from the same class or community of interest, some see in both countries the existence of a 'power élite'.

In the United States the 'power élite' consists of the very wealthy and those who head the economic, political, administrative and military structures. There is much interchange between these five groups at the top level. The very wealthy are usually involved in the affairs of one or more corporations; money gives them an immense initial advantage when competing for high political office; corporation executives slide easily into government and government leaders return to business; generals and admirals move both into the corporations and into government. These interchangeable leaders derive from 'at most the upper third of the income and occupational pyramids' and for the most part they have a common social origin and formal education.[43] These factors, reinforced by psychological affinities and community of interest, form them into a well-knit ruling class, whose members are 'the more readily understood and trusted by one another'.[44]

In the USSR the 'power élite' are those who have made themselves masters of the CPSU. They are a much smaller group and their backgrounds are very different from those of their American counterparts. The older leaders, those who made their way through the rough and tumble, the danger and violence of repression, revolution, terror, purge and war, were 'tough, earthy, mobile, poorly educated'.[45] Those who have recently taken their place, though still of proletarian or peasant origin, are better educated and the products of bureaucratic order and party intrigue rather than of revolution; they are more able to communicate with the new technocrats whose co-operation is so vital to the advance of the Soviet state. Soon they will be joined by those who are themselves of middle-class origin, sons of professional men, party officials, bureaucrats, technocrats and skilled workers rather than of peasants and labourers.

By being able, when required, to show the electorate two 'faces', or offer it two choices in the form of the two political parties, the American power élite is able to accord differences within itself with such shifts in public opinion as do occur, and to this degree shares its power with the lesser politicians and the people. Unlike the Soviet party bosses it does not have an absolute monopoly of power; power is to some extent dispersed throughout the various groups making up society, but like wealth, very unequally dispersed.[46] Unlike the Soviet government, the American administration cannot be regarded simply as a power élite, and in so far as the latter exists in America, it does not have the ideological unity and political coherence, nor the sheer exclusiveness which give the top Russian leadership their unrivalled command.[47]

18 China?

A book on the superpowers can scarcely ignore China, not only because her size, her resources, her population and her ambitions give her superpower potential, but because her relationship to the two actual superpowers of today is crucial to their own future. Russia, if allied with China, not only commands the whole of the 'heartland of the world island' and its immense resources but has access to the sea on a broad and populous front. The United States, aided by an understanding with China, would be in a far stronger position to contain the Soviet Union within its landlocked prison. But an isolated China, hostile to both, poses one of the greatest questions of the time. The 1940s saw a China friendly to America. In the 1950s it was Russia's turn. The 1960s have been the decade of aggressive isolation. What do the 1970s hold in store? Certainly, in 1971 both the United States and the USSR were making it clear that they would welcome better relations with China.

The present Soviet government is paying the price for past Russian attitudes and behaviour towards China. Nineteenth-century Russia naturally wished to push her bounds as far south as possible in order to secure territory fit for agricultural settlement and a coastline free of winter ice. Between 1858 and 1860 annexations were made which brought the Russian empire south to the Amur river, and, on the Pacific coast, even farther south to Vladivostok. China today contests the Russian title to these acquisitions, but as the Siberian railway and some of the most highly-developed and densely-settled parts of Soviet Siberia and the Soviet Far East lie in them, this is a matter that the USSR could not allow to be brought in question. Furthermore, although these regions were historically part of the Chinese empire, they were not peopled by Chinese and there is no evidence that their peoples would prefer Chinese domination to that of the Russians. In the 1890s Russia, in common with the great European powers, forced further concessions upon China. Russians joined with Japanese and other 'imperialists' in the capture of Peking during the Boxer rebellion in 1900. Such incidents live on in the Chinese mind and provide a fertile seed bed for feelings hostile to Russia.

In 1945 Stalin unashamedly resumed the tsarist policy towards China by insisting on a Soviet protectorate over Outer Mongolia, the lease of the port of Dairen and the naval base of Port Arthur, and control over the Manchurian railways. The Soviet Union had thus, unlike the Western powers, carried the old imperialism towards China into the new post-war era. In 1950 Port Arthur, Dairen and control of the Manchurian railways were abandoned as part of the Friendship Treaty signed in that year with the new Communist government.

The failure of the 1950 Sino-Soviet Friendship Treaty to provide a lasting unity between the two major communist powers has been the principal setback to Russian foreign policy since the Revolution. Doubtless the Russians thought that, although China was too big and too proud to become in any sense a satellite, she would be dependent upon the USSR for technical advice, industrial equipment and modern weapons for a long time to come. Indeed, Soviet economic and military assistance were at first on a very large scale: they enabled China to participate effectively in the Korean War, to begin the process of industrial modernisation and to prepare the way for the production of nuclear weapons. In return for her aid Russia imported tungsten and other metals, and textiles. The number of Russian military and civilian technicians and advisers in China in the early 1950s was over seventy thousand. In 1960 they began to go home and a sharp deterioration in relations followed. The reasons may probably be found in some combination of the following factors: resentment by the Chinese of their dependence, Soviet refusal to help with the development of nuclear weapons, the death of the uncompromising but respected Stalin, Russian willingness to live in 'peaceful coexistence' with capitalism, the increasing use of money incentives rather than ideological inspiration in the Soviet economy, deep-rooted anti-Russian feelings dating from the annexations and forced concessions of the second half of the nineteenth century. In June 1969 Brezhnev referred to

> the persistent efforts to identify the Soviet Union with United States imperialism. What is more, the spearhead of Peking's foreign policy at the present time is aimed chiefly against the Soviet Union and other socialist countries. The Chinese leaders started by reducing to a minimum China's economic contacts with most of the socialist states and rejected political co-operation with them, and ended up with armed provocations on the Soviet frontier. Provocative calls resound from Peking, exhorting the Soviet people to 'carry out a revolution' to change the social system in our country.[1]

In China, maps showing Soviet far-eastern territory as Chinese are widely publicised, printed in newspapers, shown on cinema screens and prominent in schools. The Soviet cities of Khabarovsk and Vladivostok appear on such maps as Chinese towns, renamed Poli and Haishenwei, even though they did not exist before these lands became Russian.

The United States starts with an immense advantage in her relations with China: she did not take part in the exploitation of China when she was weak, but rather befriended her, and during the Japanese invasion of the 1930s and 1940s gave her a growing volume of material and financial aid until the downfall of the Nationalists and the flight of Chiang Kai-shek. Hostility between the two countries is therefore of recent date and, despite American military adventures in South East Asia, has perhaps not had time to become so deep-rooted as that between Russia and China.

RESOURCES

In resources for agriculture – warmth, moisture, soil – China is far more favourably endowed than the USSR and not far behind the USA; and did she but have only the population of the latter, she would have abundant food supplies for her own people and large exportable surpluses. While it is true that much of her territory is mountainous or arid, this is concentrated in the distant interior, leaving a large area, extending a thousand miles or more inland from the ocean, with a favourable combination of temperature, precipitation and soil. As this productive belt runs southwards from the fiftieth parallel and the Soviet border to the Tropic of Cancer – and beyond, it escapes the long, severe winter that afflicts most Soviet territory. Although winters are, at comparable latitudes, more severe in China than in America, summers are long and hot, and the monsoonal element in the climate ensures that rainfall comes in the warm, growing season, when it is most needed. In the south two and sometimes even three crops a year may be gathered. This broad eastern zone extends through a range of climates varied enough to make a wide variety of crops possible (Köppen types Dwb, BSk, Dwa, Cwa, Cfa, Aw, Am).

In those resources derived from natural vegetation and wild life, we meet a striking deficiency: unlike the two superpowers, China is very poorly supplied with timber. Her estimated annual cut of 36 million cubic feet amounts to only 0·4 per cent of American output and 0·3 per cent of Soviet output. On the other hand, both in the seas to which she has ready access and in her inland waters, she has the means for the establishment of a large fishery. This gives an opportunity to supplement her food supply which she has not neglected and her total catch amounts to more than six million tons or over ten per cent of the world total. She has gone much farther than any other nation in the develop-

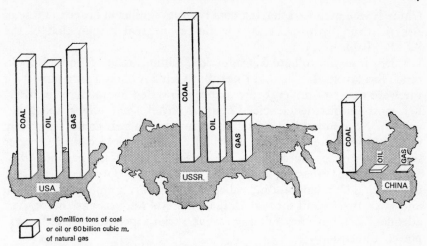

= 60 million tons of coal
or oil or 60 billion cubic m.
of natural gas

28. Comparative production of coal, oil and natural gas
The maps are on the same scale and show true relationship between the
areas of the three countries

ment of fish farming in her inland waters as well as in shallow coastal
waters. In fact, almost half of the large Chinese catch comes from her
freshwater fishery.[2]

TABLE 18.1 ESTIMATED RESERVES OF MAJOR FUELS AND
HYDRO-ELECTRIC POTENTIAL
(percentage of world total)

	Coal	Petroleum	Natural gas	Hydro
China	14	3	0·35	19
USA	15	6	11	4
USSR	62	11	12	17

In reserves of fuel and power, China appears favourably placed in
the long term. Although some estimates of her oil and gas reserves are
very low – below one per cent of world reserves as against the official
Chinese claim of three per cent – these estimates are likely to prove
too low as the work of thorough exploration gets under way. And if, as
seems likely, world supplies of oil and gas are seriously depleted during
the next three decades, possession of large coal reserves and hydro-
electric potential will become increasingly significant. In this respect

TABLE 18.2 PRODUCTION OF ENERGY RESOURCES 1968

	Coal (millions of metric tons)	Petroleum (millions of metric tons)	Natural gas (billions of cubic metres)	Hydro (billions of kwh)
China	297	16	n.a.	8 (1965)
USA	497	463	535	226
USSR	595	322	169	100

China is well endowed, having coal reserves similar in order to those of America and hydro-electric potential even greater than that of the USSR (Table 18.1).

When it comes to actual production, China's relative position looks much less favourable (Table 18.2). But China is blessed with almost all the wide range of mineral raw materials needed for modern industry, her most serious deficiencies being in nickel, gold, silver and magnesium. No doubt her production of many minerals could be greatly increased were her industry sufficiently developed to call for greater supplies. As it is, she occupies first place in the world production of antimony and tungsten, and ranks high in the output of iron ore, mercury, molybdenum, tin, asbestos, fluorspar, graphite, magnesite and salt.[3] It seems likely that China's mineral resources are more than adequate as a basis for building an industrial superstructure of 'superpower' dimensions.

China's 'anti-resources' – the physical obstacles to the development of her resources, are greater than those of the USA but not so severe as those of the USSR. Severe winters, with minimum temperatures dropping to −40°C (−40°F) are experienced in the north-east, but the USSR is far worse off in this respect. Permafrost is not a problem, but the arid area is greater than that of the USSR. China is the worst off of the three countries with respect to mountainous terrain, as not only does she have a larger area of high mountains than either of the others but about one-quarter of this highland area is made up of the 'roof of the world' – the Tibetan plateau and its mountain rim, with elevations above twelve thousand feet. A severe handicap to China, in comparison to the otherwise somewhat similarly placed United States, lies in her having only one coastline. As a result, her vast interior territory can be reached only by overland routes, which are difficult to construct because much of the surface is deeply cut by ravines and gorges.

AGRICULTURE

China's prospects for becoming a great power comparable to the USA and USSR depend upon her ability to feed her 750 million people while, at the same time, freeing an increasing proportion for work in mines, manufacturing, transportation and administration. But the policies adopted since the Communists came into power have done little to prepare China's agriculture for such a task. The course of events has been somewhat similar to that which has occurred in the Soviet Union since the Revolution. The landlord class was liquidated and the land distributed among the peasants. Then, in 1957, came collectivisation, with much the same negative effects as in Russia. The Great Leap Forward went still further, abolishing all private property, closing the free rural markets, and organising the peasants into communes which were burdened with a variety of additional tasks, such as smelting iron in small rural furnaces, road building, canal cutting and dam construction. The effects of all this interference with the traditional working of agriculture was a decline in efficiency and production which has led, since 1961, to the reintroduction of private plots and the application of incentive schemes. This has brought some recovery, but in sum there have been even more ideological interference and political mismanagement, and much less mechanisation and modernisation than in Soviet agriculture.

Nor has China been able to afford the capital investment to increase the area of cultivated land through irrigation and drainage, although, as in the USSR, the continuing crisis on the farms has led to agriculture receiving an increased share of total investment. It has been as much as the régime has been able to do to maintain existing irrigation works, especially as these had fallen into disrepair during the long years of foreign invasion and civil war that preceded the communist victory. The emphasis has therefore been placed on an increased application of chemical fertilisers and insecticides. Despite the traditional methods of returning every possible form of organic and other fertilising material to the earth, most soils lack nitrogen, and southern rice-growing soils also lack phosphorus. It is estimated that by 1966 total fertiliser production had increased from about 800,000 metric tons in 1957 to about 5,000,000 in 1966, to which may be added imports of another 3,500,000 tons. However, for a country with such population pressure upon the land such amounts are obviously inadequate.[4] The situation is even worse with mechanisation. In 1965 there were reported to be 135,000 tractors (15-hp units), compared with 4,500,000 in the USA and 1,500,000 in the Soviet Union.

China's cropland area amounts to 110 million hectares. This is about eighty per cent of America's, but much of the land in China's warm-wintered south can be double-cropped. It is little more than a half of the Soviet total, but as it is more productive, the difference in actual output is much less.

Estimates of China's total grain production vary widely, but for the most part they are pitched somewhere between the American and Soviet totals. The seriousness of the Chinese problem may be seen when it is realised that the Soviet production, probably little less than the Chinese, is barely enough to feed a population under a third the size of China's. China differs from the two superpowers in that rice is her chief cereal crop, accounting for about half the total, whereas maize and wheat dominate the American and Soviet outputs respectively. Wheat and maize are, however, both important in China: in wheat she ranks third in world order after the two superpowers, while in maize she is second, after America.[5]

Other leading food crops are soya beans, sugar cane and millet. As a grower of soya beans China is second only to the United States, but her estimated sugar production (cane and beet) compares unfavourably with the Soviet output and is well below the American. Potato production is about double the American, but amounts to only about a quarter of the Soviet total. China is also an important grower of tobacco and of tea.[6]

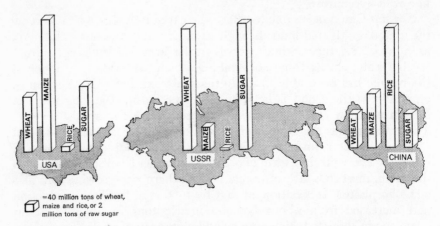

=40 million tons of wheat, maize and rice, or 2 million tons of raw sugar

29. Comparative production of wheat, maize (corn), rice and sugar
The maps are on the same scale and show true relationship between the areas of the three countries

Cotton is the leading industrial crop in all three countries. This is one of the crops in which China has been successful, and her estimated 1967 production of 6½ million bales makes her a close third to the United States figure of 7·6 million bales and the Soviet total of 9·3 million.

Up-to-date figures for livestock in China are not available but a comparison based on the late 1950s is given in Table 18.3. Although at first sight China would seem to be well placed, the fact that animals

TABLE 18.3 LIVESTOCK: WORLD PERCENTAGE AND RANK 1958–60[7]

	China	USA	USSR
Cattle	5 (5th)	11 (2nd)	8 (4th)
Pigs	33 (1st)	12 (2nd)	10 (3rd)
Sheep	6 (3rd)	3 (8th)	13 (2nd)
Goats	15 (2nd)	— —	3 (9th)

there are used to a considerable degree for transportation lowers their value as a source of food. Draft animals consume foodstuffs that might otherwise be available, directly or indirectly, for human consumption.

In conclusion it may be said that, although China's agricultural production is comparable to that of the two superpowers, the fact that her population is from three to four times greater means that its relative value to her is between one third and one quarter of theirs.

MANUFACTURING

The development of manufacturing is the clearest index to a country's economic status, and it was with this in mind that heavy industry was made the basis of the first five-year plan, which ran from 1953 to 1957. The Stalinist policy of concentrating investment on heavy industry was followed and impressive growth resulted. This rapid expansion continued during the Great Leap Forward years of 1958–60, but then fell abruptly in 1961 and 1962 as the result of the withdrawal of Soviet technical assistance and the disastrous effects upon agriculture of the

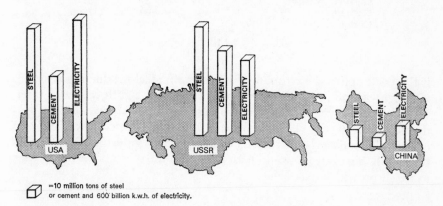

=10 million tons of steel
or cement and 600 billion k.w.h. of electricity.

30. Comparative production of steel, cement and electricity
   The maps are on the same scale and show true relationship between the areas of the three countries

Great Leap policies, especially as manufacturing was still heavily dependent upon agricultural raw materials. Since 1962, industrial production has resumed its growth, but at a slower rate than in the 1950s.

The impressive growth of the 1950s was due largely to Soviet assistance. Before the breakdown in relations in 1960, the USSR had completed about 130 of the 291 major plants she had promised to build by 1967. The Soviet Union also provided education in Russia for some 15,000 Chinese, sent 10,000 Soviet advisers and technicians to China and applied large quantities of technical information. As a direct result of this aid, China was enabled to produce such advanced goods as machine tools, electronic equipment, jet aircraft and submarines, while Soviet training in nuclear physics and the supply of nuclear reactors made possible the subsequent advance of China in this field.[8]

For lack of data it is impossible to compare total industrial production in China with that of the two superpowers. All that can be done is to make a comparison between the estimated Chinese output of certain basic products and those for the USA and USSR. This is done in Table 18.4 which leaves little doubt that, whatever its potential, China ranks at the present time only as a second-class industrial power. Even

TABLE 18.4   OUTPUT OF CERTAIN INDUSTRIAL PRODUCTS 1965[9]
(*millions of metric tons*)

	China	USA	USSR
Steel	11	118	91
Chemical fertiliser	5	36	31*
Cement	9	66	72
Cotton cloth†	4	9	9

* 1966.   † Millions of metres.

if the most optimistic estimate of her current steel production is taken, viz. eighteen million tons, this would place her eighth in world rank. It is thirty-five years since the USSR had China's present steel production, and twenty years since she had China's present production of cement. Therefore, assuming that China could industrialise as fast as the USSR has done, it would take twenty to thirty years for her output to reach present Soviet levels.

TRANSPORT

The original American colonies and old Muscovy both developed into strong powers through the exploitation of their vast and rich continental hinterlands, empires which were successfully welded on to the original 'cradle area' to form integrated economies of overwhelming strength. China likewise has her empire in the west but its exploitation cannot proceed until it is penetrated by modern forms of transport. Unlike the American West, these outer regions are not accessible to coastal shipping and the formidable anti-resources of mountainous terrain and aridity make them even more difficult to cross than much of Siberia.

The inadequacy of the Chinese transport system not only holds back the unfolding of mineral resources in the west but hinders inter-regional movement between the densely populated eastern regions. Some districts have to be denied much-needed supplies, even when these are in surplus elsewhere, either because railway transport does not exist between the deficit and surplus areas or because, where it does exist, it is too overburdened to carry an additional load.

Over half of China's transport, on a value-added basis, is still carried by the traditional methods of human and animal traction and in junks and sampans.[10] The modern sector, to which has been attributed some forty-two per cent by value added, has, none the less, expanded dramatically, and according to Yuan-Li Wu's calculations, multiplied ten times between 1950 and 1963.[11] The total volume of transportation in 1963 may be estimated at 420 billion ton–km, a figure about one-sixth only of the American and Soviet totals.

The route length of Chinese railways was about 35,000 km in 1965, having increased from about 22,000 in 1949; in addition, there has been much double-tracking.[12] Despite the building of one important main line from Shanghai to north-western China, it has been estimated that China would need another 15,000 km of route before she could make a substantial advance in her industrial production through development of her western territories. Even if this expansion were accomplished, the length of the Chinese rail system would still be less than forty per cent that of the Soviet system, and because so much of the track and rolling stock are in bad condition, the system could not be used with anything like the intensity found on the Soviet railways. Much of the Chinese system is, in fact, obsolete.

Surfaced all-weather roads in China have been estimated to have had a length of only about 80,000 km in 1949, since when they have been increased to a total of about 130,000 km, with most of the new roads in the more undeveloped parts of the country. If this latter figure is accurate, it is within reach of the Soviet total of 166,000 km, but little more than a thirtieth of the American total. The development of road transport in China is hindered by the shortage in petroleum supplies and handicapped in the developed part of the country by the absence of available land. Settlement is so crowded that roads could only be built by taking the land on which hundreds of thousands of people live and depend for their livelihood. There would appear to have been almost no construction of pipelines in China and little in the way of regular airlines. It would seem, therefore, to be reasonable to con-clude that, although a significant expansion has been made in the Chinese transport system, it remains woefully inadequate and anti-quated.

TRADE

As one would expect from a country so politically and economically isolated, the total volume of China's trade is very small and was estimated in 1966 as only worth $4·16 billion or about one-quarter of the Soviet figure.[13] The American refusal to trade with China and the embargo on the supply to her of strategic goods by America's allies have been factors in the low volume of China's trade. Imports are of grain, rubber, metals and industrial equipment; exports are of foodstuffs such as rice, soya beans and tea, and minerals such as iron ore, coal and tungsten. Recent trends include a sharp decline in trade with the USSR, an increase in trade with those communist countries which have retained friendly relations with China, notably Albania and Rumania, a significant increase in dealings with most non-communist countries, and above all with Japan.[14]

In 1959 fifty per cent of China's trade was with the USSR, but by 1967 this was down to a mere two per cent. China now looks to Japan and the industrialised countries of Europe to supply the industrial equipment that previously came from Russia, and Hong Kong fulfils a vital entrepôt position in this trade. This densely populated British colony, by spending about $500 million in China on the purchase of foodstuffs and agricultural raw materials, provides that country with a valuable source of foreign currency which it can use to buy Western goods. China and Russia began trade negotiations in 1969 with a view to improving their trade relations and in 1971 America lifted her embargo on trade with China.

Considerable Chinese imports of grain began in 1961 as a result of a domestic shortage caused by bad weather and Great Leap Forward disorganisation, and they have averaged between five and six million tons since. This is likely to increase in the future. Australia, Canada and Argentina have been the chief suppliers.[15] Cane sugar is imported from Cuba. China cannot, in fact, make economic progress without a wide range of vital imports, including foodstuffs, rubber, copper, chrome, nickel, cobalt and fertilisers. It is also likely that industrial expansion would require considerable imports of petroleum, because of China's own limited oil potential.[16]

Despite her own continuing technological dependence on foreign countries, China has attempted to act as a major advanced power by giving a great deal of assistance to 'developing' countries, especially those in Asia and Africa, where she has succeeded in staking out a sphere of influence. Between 1953 and 1965 over $2 billion have been given in grants and credits to foreign countries.[17]

POPULATION

China's population was given in the 1953 census as 584 million, after deducting Chinese living abroad and in Formosa, estimates for which were included in the census. Subsequent estimates, which have little evidence to support them, tended to put the total at about 710 million in 1966 and about 780 million in 1970. It is difficult to see how such numbers can be of any economic advantage. They may give some degree of military strength by making possible the levying of vast armies for conventional war, and they may give China some advantage in a restricted form of nuclear warfare. Such a war, whether with the United States or the Soviet Union, assuming equal casualties on both sides, could totally eliminate the populations of North America or the USSR, while still leaving between 500 and 600 million Chinese as survivors. This number would be adequate to re-colonise North America and the Soviet Union, while leaving China an optimum population for her own development. Mao Tse-tung boasted of this superiority in Moscow in 1957 when, to quote Brezhnev, 'with appalling airiness and cynicism he spoke of the possible destruction of half of mankind in the event of atomic war'.[18]

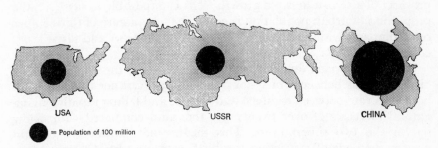

USA USSR CHINA

= Population of 100 million

31. Population related to area

China does not have the greatest density of population in the world, related to total area. In fact, the continent of Europe as a whole has a density of 240 per square mile, considerably greater than China's, and almost fifty countries are burdened with greater densities. In all other countries, however, the numbers involved are much smaller, and it is in the immensity rather than in the nature of its population problem that China is so seriously handicapped.

The contrast between the proportion of urban population of China on the one hand and of America and Russia on the other is even greater than that between the two superpowers themselves, as would be

TABLE 18.5   POPULATION, AREA AND DENSITY OF CHINA,
USA AND USSR 1970

	Population (millions)	Area (millions of sq. mi.)	Density (per sq. mi.)	Cultivated land (millions of hectares)	Density (per hectare of cultivated land)
China	780 (?)	3·7	211	110	7·1
USA	203	3·6	57	136	1·5
USSR	242	8·6	28	207	1·2

expected from the gulf that exists in industrial development. China had only thirteen per cent of her population living in towns according to the 1953 census, but since then there has been a strong tendency among the rural population to move into the cities. This has resulted not only from the increasingly desperate pressure of population upon the land but from the disorganisation and discontent caused by the foisting of political and ideological programmes upon the peasants. Because of the acute problems arising in the cities themselves from such a migration, the authorities have striven not only to hold it back but to reverse it. In this they seem to have had some success, and according to one authority 'the urban population of Mainland China is probably declining now in relative if not in absolute terms and there is no immediate prospect of a return to rapid growth'[19] It is impossible to say what the proportion of urban population is now. The 1953 figure of thirteen per cent compares with nearly eighty per cent in the USA and fifty-six per cent in the USSR.

For the last years for which data are available, the 1950s, China's birth rate was between thirty-four and thirty-seven per thousand and her death rate between eighteen and eleven, and falling rapidly, giving natural increases of over twenty per thousand compared with below ten in the two superpowers. This means that, however successful present methods of restricting the birth rate may be, China's population will inevitably grow at a much faster rate than that of either America or Russia during the next few decades, and projections give a total for 1985 of between 859 million and 1,207 million.[20] The heavy concentration of China's present population in the younger age groups – between fifty-six and fifty-nine per cent under twenty-four in 1965 – means that the proportion of young people of reproductive age is unusually large and will continue to be so for some years to come.

Neither the Soviet nor the American patterns of population distribution show any geographical concentration comparable to the crowding of almost the whole of China's vast population within the eastern half of the country. If recent experience is anything to go by, there does not seem much likelihood that China will soon witness great migrations into the interior such as have characterised the history of America and Russia, and it has been estimated that only six hundred thousand people migrated into the western territories between 1949 and 1955. Though not in itself a small number, it represents a mere fraction of the annual population growth of the country.

Migration of Chinese to the outer areas is necessary not only for their economic development, but because ethnic minorities, which represent some six per cent of the total population, tend to be located on the outer margins of the territory. In the north-west there are the Islamic Uighurs, Kazakhs and Kirghiz, Turkic peoples who, across the border in the USSR, have – in the case of the latter two – Soviet Socialist Republics of their own, where a higher degree of national autonomy and economic progress is enjoyed. Discontent and a measure of pro-Soviet feeling have characterised these regions in the past, and there was some resistance in the late 1950s to the Chinese authorities. Nevertheless, China has a great advantage over the two superpowers in the relative homogeneity of her people, ninety-four per cent of whom are Chinese.

The large numbers of Chinese living abroad, often forming influential and sometimes dominant groups in their countries of residence, give China a special position. They were estimated to amount to 16·3 million in mid-1962, with almost four million in Siam, over three million in Hong Kong, two and a half million each in Indonesia and in Malaya and over a million in Singapore.[21]

From the point of view of eventual progress, the qualities of a people are more important than absolute numbers, and few would deny that the Chinese people have the physical energies and the intellectual abilities to achieve the foremost international rank, if they could solve their problems of numbers and organisation. Talents need education, however, and although China has undoubtedly made remarkable progress in this direction, and now possesses scientists and technicians capable of designing and producing refined industrial products and nuclear weapons, the number remains relatively small. Technical and engineering personnel were estimated to be eight and a half times as numerous in 1962 as ten years before, and to amount to 1·4 million.[22] In 1965 the number of students in institutions of higher learning was put at one and a half million compared with five and a half million in the United States and nearly four million in the USSR. The education of young people was disrupted and retarded by the Cultural Revolution and this will have had an adverse effect.

The Chinese people have one of the lowest *per capita* incomes in the world – only about $100. This compares with an American figure of about $3,000. However, China is a country where the actual incomes of the majority of the people do not fall far short of the *per capita* average. In most other countries there are great inequalities in the distribution of wealth, and large numbers have actual incomes well below the average. The Maoist policy in China has been to strive for equality of income, and to this extent the *per capita* figure in China is more realistic than in, say India, where it is raised well above the average peasant level by the large fortunes of the very wealthy.

MILITARY STRENGTH

Despite her vast manpower, it is lack of modern weapons sufficient in number, range and variety that, more than anything else, disqualifies China from superpower status. But an immense effort is being made in the development of nuclear research as well as in the mass production of rifles, tanks and aircraft. Although China's regular armed forces are roughly equal in size to those of the USA and USSR – about 3·3 million – she could call upon para-military organisations with a total strength of up to two hundred million! Once the mass production of conventional weapons has made it possible to arm a mere fraction of this enormous potential, China will have such overwhelming superiority that only nuclear weapons could deter her, should she wish to move across her borders. Once she has reached nuclear parity with second-strike capability, then her conventional superiority could no longer be resisted. During the late 1960s and early 1970s reports of the testing of missiles and warheads, first of intermediate and then of continental range, have come from American sources, and President Nixon has speculated that China might be able to attack the United States with nuclear weapons during the late 1970s. The result of China's progress has been to complicate the SALT talks between Russia and America and to confuse the controversy about their further development of ABM systems.

CONCLUSION

In 1971 President Nixon put Russia and China on the same level, saying, 'There are two great powers facing us, Russia and China. They are great powers and great peoples.'[23] But in 1969 his Secretary of State had remarked that 'although we are inclined to speak of China as a great power we should remember that this power is potential more than actual. I believe there is a tendency in many quarters to build up the Chinese communists by equating their capabilities with their rhetoric.'[24] Yet it would be a mistake also to equate China's strategic strength too closely with her economic development. She has many assets, not the least being her combination of a share of the Eurasian heartland, rich in resources, with a coastline endowed with great seaports and backed by an able and industrious people. Specific economic weaknesses and general industrial backwardness have not prevented her rapid advance as a nuclear power. She does not find herself in immediate proximity to the technologically advanced and heavily armed West, as does the Soviet Union. On the contrary, she is skirted by other Asian peoples who have hitherto absorbed the full impact of American military might directed against the spread of communism. She lies close to Japan who must always be tempted by the vast Chinese market, and may therefore be relied upon as a potential source of advanced industrial goods. And because of her isolation, in part self imposed and in part imposed upon her, she did not until recently have the world responsibilities that great power brings her rivals.[25]

19 Prospect

This chapter will present a brief discussion of the superpowers' future prospects. These will depend on the successful solution of their economic and social problems, on the development of their mutual relationship, and on the evolution of their relationship with other powers, particularly China.

ECONOMIC PROBLEMS

The chief economic problems facing the USA are inflation and the underemployment of its labour force and heavy industrial plant. Monetary inflation, which stems mainly from the huge and growing volume of domestically unproductive expenditure, notably on defence, space projects and foreign aid, has weakened the dollar as an international currency and exacerbated labour and other social problems. Inflation of a different kind afflicts the Soviet economy as a result of rising incomes not being matched by an equivalent increase in the supply of desirable consumer goods. Symptoms are long queues in the shops for wanted articles, the accumulation of surplus earnings in savings accounts, or their dissipation in the high consumption of alcoholic drinks.

Underemployment of industrial capacity, both in capital equipment and in the labour force, is a malady with which the American economy has been afflicted for half a century, except for periods of war and preparation for war. A vital question is whether the problems of chronic overproduction and unemployment can be solved other than by increased government expenditure on armaments. Exporting does not seem to offer a solution. American consumer goods are designed and priced for the affluent, and so long as America's level of material living is so far in advance of that of other peoples, her goods will be beyond their reach. There are other difficulties. America's major consumer product, the large automobile, is impracticable for the city streets and narrow winding roads which characterise the countries where most of the world's population lives. American enterprise and investment abroad lessen the possibilities for American exports by producing

American goods within the countries that might otherwise import them.

The present emphasis on space research and on complex defence equipment such as the anti-ballistic missile system certainly does not point the way to a solution of the overproduction and unemployment problem. For unlike conventional war, these are not great consumers of bulky, heavy, industrial goods. They are rather consumers of skills, skills so rare that the whole 'free world' tends to be denuded of its best brains, attracted to the USA by high financial rewards and lavish research facilities.

In the Soviet Union the problem is, by contrast, one of chronic underproduction, for the Russians resemble the nineteenth-century Americans in that they still have a frontier which they are pushing eastwards into Siberia and southwards into Transcaucasia and Central Asia. They still have the dual-demand factor in their economy, having to satisfy both the normal needs of the already developed regions and also the hunger for supplies which characterises the newly-developing territories. And on top of this they have to keep pace with America in the arms race and the space race if they are to remain militarily secure and comparable in prestige.

If the Soviet gross national product is ever to equal that of the United States it must grow at a much faster rate. Such increased growth will depend upon the country's ability to make and adopt technological advances; these in turn will be governed by the presence of the necessary skills and the capacity to innovate. Since the USA is able to draw upon the brains of the whole non-communist world, it has an obvious advantage in this critical matter of skills over the USSR, whose field of recruitment is confined to its own territory. However, the competition in talent is in part a competition between educational systems and it is possible that the USSR could overcome this grave disadvantage with a superior educational system. The chief educational advantage the Soviets have probably lies in their severe selection system, resulting in an average of five applicants for every university place, so that standards are likely to be higher than in those undergraduate colleges of America in which there is virtually no selection. The Soviet system of grants, with higher rates for better performance and special scholarships for those showing first-class ability, also reflects a different attitude to education from that of the American who 'buys an education' by paying his own way. On the other hand, the Soviet strait-jacket and the stultifying effects of bureaucratic control of industry must inevitably offer a less fertile seed bed for the development of new ideas than the American scene with its restless and continuing search for technological advance and for innovations that can be put to some industrial or military use.

Certain deficiencies in American domestic supplies of vital materials for modern industry were noted in Chapter 5. These are not likely, however, to constitute an economic problem for the USA so long as she has free access to supplies in other parts of the non-communist world. Many of them come from adjacent Canada and Mexico, and stockpiles will continue to be kept as safeguards against interruption of other supplies. The situation with regard to petroleum is perhaps the most serious. Although, in the past, fresh discoveries have always increased known reserves, 'there are many indicators that the halcyon period of great oil discoveries and oil exploitation may be over'.[1] The new discoveries in Alaska may add a billion tons to American reserves, but the very fact that new exploration has moved to the Arctic, with its greater difficulties and costs, confirms the failure of the conterminous United States to offer much more in the way of large new finds.

The USSR, although with greater proven reserves and doubtless more awaiting discovery, has a production rising towards the American level. She too will face depletion eventually. If the two superpowers are to continue to use petroleum as their chief energy resource they may both, sooner or later, have to rely on Middle Eastern supplies. Because of her support of Israel the United States has forfeited the friendship of the Arab countries, while the Soviet Union has assumed the role of their protector. But both powers have large reserves of coal which could be used to generate electricity. This, supplemented by nuclear power, could take the place of oil, but such an energy revolution would require a large amount of re-equipment, especially in transport.

In both countries the basic economic problems are exacerbated by ideology. In the United States the fear of socialism has resulted in the state sector of the economy being confined almost exclusively to military and para-military fields, i.e. where it could be said that the security of the state justified it. Government has been largely shut out of the domestic field in which it could have done so much to alleviate, if not to solve, social problems, for example in urban renewal. In the USSR the adverse effect of ideology is that it militates against essential economic reforms on the grounds that they do not conform to orthodox Marxist–Leninist doctrine. Thus, although economists may argue that competition among enterprises would promote efficiency and technological innovation and that basing prices on marginal rather than basic costs would be better policy, they are condemned by conservative Party men for advocating thinly-disguised capitalism.

Nevertheless, despite these ideological barriers, it has been argued that the two economies are tending towards a similar pattern in which planning and organisation come to dominate. Galbraith maintains that this convergence 'occurs at all fundamental points'.[2] The Russian

Sakharov has also forecast a convergence of capitalism and communism by the year 2000 and the emergence of a common system. This is a view, however, that is by no means universally accepted, either in the United States or in the Soviet Union. Sakharov's views were indignantly rejected by official spokesmen in the USSR who maintain that communism and capitalism are developing in different directions, and that the struggle between the two ideologies will become sharper.[3]

SOCIAL PROBLEMS

The social well-being of a state may have greater import for its future than its economic viability and technological superiority. Here the outlook for the United States is not so promising. Law and order are becoming increasingly difficult to maintain and the wealthy in some select residential areas have had to resort to guarded fenced-in compounds. The breakdown of social cohesion may itself be the result of the very economic and technical progress on which America prides herself. Near-total urbanisation, unless carefully watched and planned, brings large concentrations of the very poor within reach of the very wealthy; it encircles the 'down-town' area of central business district, made up of banks, office blocks, luxury hotels and glittering stores, with a zone of old and decaying residential property in which ghettos form; it brings in from outside large numbers of rootless people who see the city as nothing more than a place in which to make money, legally or illegally, peacefully or violently.

The growth of 'affluence' implies competition for a constantly growing list of consumers' goods of ever-changing and increasingly advanced design. Advertising is devised to sow discontent among those who do not yet possess these goods and encourages those who do to flaunt their possession as signs of worldly success. The need for more money to acquire these goods becomes the overriding consideration in life, and the struggle for them has to be fought against the tide of inflation, ever reducing the purchasing power of incomes that do not rise commensurately. Industrial discontent, involving trade unions with employers and keeping alive the 'class struggle', leads to strikes and outbreaks of violence. Discontent, frustration, tension and conflict become endemic in such a society, and the spiritual values and social virtues upon which the cohesion of the community rests are lost and forgotten.

In the United States the situation is worsened by the fact that most of those who have moved into the decaying urban areas have been Negroes, many of whom have grievances and feel a bitterness which militant agitators have begun to exploit. The two great revolutions of

European history, the French of 1789 and the Russian of 1917, were both brought about by bringing together in one place such an explosive mixture. The monarchs wished to surround themselves with a society composed of wealthy aristocrats; but their presence created such a demand for goods and services that peasant serfs, full of hatred born of long-felt misery and oppression, moved in to the capital cities in large numbers. This concentrated dangerously in one spot feelings and emotional forces that had before been widely, thinly and innocuously spread over a whole countryside. In the United States this has happened not only in one but in most of the great conurbations and bodes ill for the future. Indeed, the greatest question mark of all which hangs over the future of the United States is whether the problem of the Negro minority can be solved and a form of civil, racial war avoided. In the USSR the white–black dichotomy is absent, and although the population is multi-racial in character, differences between the races are never so extreme as between European and Negro, and there is relatively little local admixture.

As technology develops, fresh problems confront society. The growing complexity of modern industry, based upon advancing technology, needs an élite of organisers and specialists who will be very highly paid because of the rarity of their skills; but the great mass of the population will of necessity have only monotonous or menial tasks to perform or, with the spread of automation, no function at all. Furthermore, there is a growing awareness that much more of such progress could make the environment surrounding man almost impossible to live in. These processes, all at work in American society, are not only productive of social disintegration from within, but lead to attacks on society from without. Inevitably many thoughtful or spiritually-minded people are going to revolt against the subordination of modern man to economics and technology, adding a further disruptive force.

Soviet society appears to be far more stable and there is no evidence of any breakdown of law and order. Occasional riots and disturbances do occur for varying reasons in various parts of the far-flung Soviet territory, but the attitude of the bulk of the population to such demonstrations seems to be either actively hostile or passively apathetic. Despite the autocratic form of their government and the lower level of their material standard of living, Soviet citizens seem reasonably contented and satisfied that things are getting better. When they are not so satisfied, they appear more concerned with the everyday problems of life than with protest against the society itself. Only a relatively small number of intellectuals deplore the apparent partial return of Stalinist attitudes to dissent after the brief Khrushchevian trend towards a more liberal attitude. The penalty for 'anti-soviet' activities today, however, is more likely to be removal to a mental home with release contingent upon returning to a 'saner' view, than exile and death in a labour camp.

There is a threat to Soviet power in the very differences that exist between the American and Russian ways of life. Many Soviet people have an idealised view of life in America, regarding it as the land of plenty and the country of technical superiority, probably because they have heard so much about 'catching up with America'. If the belief, false though it may be, that it is only their political system that prevents their sharing in the glittering affluence of the Western world should become widespread, then the permanence of the régime would be in danger.

Certain tendencies that characterise American society are also showing themselves in Soviet society, and although they are less pronounced they could affect the long-term prospects of communist supremacy in the country. In Russia as well as in the United States continued superpower status depends to a growing degree upon a class of indispensable specialists. The gulf between them and the Party men, with their Marxist–Leninist outlook, may well be a wide and growing one: 'increasingly the party needs the professional élite far more than the élite needs the party'.[4]

A recent phenomenon in America has been the emergence of the 'communicators' as an independent and powerful force. At first they acted merely as the servants of the sponsoring advertisers, propagating the virtues of the American world of commerce and business. But of recent years, as they have felt their influence grow, they have appeared more as the arbiters of social questions and as the critics of established institutions and values. For this they earned a sharp rebuke from Vice-President Agnew. Their attitude and the publicity they have given to protesters of all kinds, from consumers' champions like Ralph Nader to the campus 'drop-out', have contributed to another recent change in American culture – the replacement of the old, arrogant self-confidence by a puzzled diffidence in many established sectors of society such as government, the middle class and the business corporation. Together with critics and protesters of all kinds they have created in the public mind a distaste for foreign military adventures such as the war in South East Asia, a suspicion of the big corporations, especially those receiving military contracts, and awareness of the dangers of environmental pollution. They have contributed strongly to the current feeling within the United States itself as to the country's future prospects. In the USSR the 'communicators' remain firmly under the control of the Party: they have not developed as an independent group and present no danger to established values and institutions.

THE USA–USSR RELATIONSHIP

The fates of the two superpowers could be determined, not only by domestic factors, but by external forces and, in the most extreme form, by military conflict between them.

Because their foreign policies are dominated by concern over control of the peripheral areas of the 'world island' which surrounds the USSR, direct confrontation and even contact between the two superpowers are minimal. The Nixon administration's policy of 'vietnamisation', aiming at withdrawing American forces from the sensitive circumferential areas, substituting for them native personnel, and exacting from dependent states a more positive contribution to their own defence, lessens still further the likelihood of immediate superpower confrontation.

In 1971 it appeared possible that this negative relationship would give way to something more positive: that either there would be the commencement of President Nixon's 'era of negotiation', heralded by some kind of progress at the SALT talks, or a return to the 'cold war', marked by a massive increase in funds allocated to the development of strategic weapons. It is difficult not to be pessimistic. In the USA a vast industrial complex and whole regions of the country depend almost wholly upon the continued development of missiles, electronic weapons systems and other 'sophisticated' armaments. In the USSR also, a similar vested interest in this aspect of technological progress must inevitably exist. On the other hand, economic and social pressures for a more productive and beneficent allocation of resources are strong and growing in each country. In 1970 the United States government was clearly trying to hold down increases in military expenditure, and the USSR announced a decrease. In both countries there will be pressures in both directions. From the military and the industries connected with weapons production on the one side, and from those who see the need to deal with economic and social problems like poverty, level of living and aid to poorer countries on the other. The situation is complicated, especially for the Soviet Union, by the threatening attitude and growing might of China and also by the discontents of the countries of eastern Europe.

A certain amount must depend on the aims and psychology of the leaders and the peoples. If the USA insists on maintaining its predominant position in the world and is unwilling to concede parity to the USSR, then the latter will not be ready to accept this as a permanent basis for a mutual relationship. Such an American attitude is implicit in the assumption that America may ring the USSR with military bases but the USSR must not be allowed to establish a single one near the United States, and in the assertion that whereas American fleets must dominate all the oceans of the world, Soviet naval superiority must everywhere be countered, even in seas close to the Russian homeland, such as the eastern Mediterranean and the Arabian Gulf. On the other hand, if the USSR is not aiming at mere parity, but at world domination for herself, as many Americans believe, then again no permanent accommodation is possible. But while the USA predominates, 'the great unanswered question is whether the United States – either its public or its Government – is as yet genuinely prepared to share global pre-eminence with the Soviet Union'.[5]

The ideological difference is, of course, a continuing factor. Both populations have been brought up to regard the political and economic systems of the other as wholly evil, although this is something more likely to be wholeheartedly believed in the United States where the propagation of ideas and attitudes is a highly advanced science, than in the Soviet Union where propaganda remains a relatively crude and blunt weapon, as likely to induce incredulity as conviction. Many people appear to need a focus for their emotions of hatred and fear, and it often suits governments that such a focus should be in another country. For the American 'establishment' it eases the path of those implicated in the great military–industrial–administrative complex, while in the USSR it distracts attention from – and in some measure excuses – failure at home. But the real objection to Western capitalism in Soviet eyes is its growing domination by American business interests, particularly in the form of the multi-national corporation. The USSR would doubtless be readier to accept capitalist countries as neighbours and friends if it were possible for a capitalist country to be truly neutral, but states under the capitalist system are inevitably drawn into the American economic empire. Likewise, the serious aspect of Soviet communism from the American standpoint is that it offers a closed economic system from which American enterprise is excluded. Any expansion of such a system must mean a contraction in the area from which the USA could satisfy its ever-growing needs.

Thus, whereas neutral capitalist and independent communist countries could live peaceably together without undue friction, American capitalism and Soviet communism appear irreconcilable on economic grounds and armed conflict between the two cannot be ruled out.

The possibility of armed conflict

Both powers have been accused of being aggressive and bellicose. The United States maintains forces somewhat larger than Russia's and her defence budget is a great deal higher. But unlike the USSR she maintains forces in numerous countries and has treaty obligations to take part in the defence of several of them. As a result of vast government expenditure for military and para-military purposes, the manufacture of armaments has become a powerful vested interest and the industries concerned are closely linked with the armed forces, and with the defence department and the state department. Military leaders and top civil servants, with influential contacts within their departments, resign to reappear as directors of the giant corporations fulfilling defence contracts. Likewise, directors of these companies resign and reappear as powerful administrators. President Eisenhower had this interlocking of interest in mind when, in his last broadcast as President, he said:

> We have been compelled to create a permanent armaments industry of vast proportions. This conjunction of an immense military establishment and a large arms industry is new in the American experience. In the councils of government we must guard against the acquisition of unwarranted influence, whether sought or unsought, by the military–industrial complex. The potential for the disastrous rise of misplaced power exists and will persist. We must never let the weight of this combination endanger our liberties or democratic processes.

In recent years there has been a growing conviction that what Eisenhower feared has come about. On the other hand, a growing awareness of the situation has produced pressures in a contrary direction.

In the USSR, many of the motives present in the USA for an aggressive military policy are absent. The Soviet economy, unlike the American, is strained to the utmost to produce the minimum essentials for its peacetime economy. Whatever its ultimate motives may be, it has every incentive to keep expenditure on 'defence' at the lowest possible level: 'for the USSR defense outlays are onerous, and it can only gain economically from disarmament'.[6] Hence it has exercised restraint in its foreign and military policies. The main exception have been the use of Soviet forces as an umbrella under which communist régimes could establish themselves in eastern Europe during the late 1940s, pressure against West Berlin, the installation of missiles in Cuba, and the invasion of Hungary and Czechoslovakia. It has been a cardinal feature of Soviet policy, however, that those countries of eastern Europe from which the German invasion of Russia was launched should remain permanently within the socialist camp, as a necessary requirement of Soviet security, and the events of 1968 made it clear that there will be no relaxation of that policy. With Berlin and Cuba the Russians yielded rather than risk armed conflict.

Nevertheless, the Soviet Union is in possession of vast military power, comparable to that of the United States, and the men who wield this power are not open to the same degree of scrutiny as they are in the United States, where even the highest officials can be cross-examined by senators and congressmen and their dialogue published, and where the mass communications media have scant respect for the secrecy of any confidential information they may come upon. America is a very 'open' country and intelligence about it is easily obtained. The Soviet Union is a 'closed' country and little information of military or strategic interest is revealed. Although satellite reconnaissance has reduced this intelligence gap, it remains wide enough to cause concern.

Direct nuclear conflict seems unlikely between the two superpowers in the foreseeable future because of what is often called the balance of terror. In nuclear weapons both countries have 'second strike capability': if a 'first strike' were made against either of them, however destructive it might be, each has the means to reply with a 'second strike' that would effect the near-total destruction of the other side. Both countries have a proportion of their nuclear armament borne by nuclear submarines which patrol the coasts of the other and aircraft carrying nuclear bombs constantly in the air. Neither side, in these circumstances, can be expected to strike at the other except as a result of mistaken intelligence that a first strike is under way.

If nuclear war is unlikely, the possibility of a war fought with conventional forces remains, with the danger that it might escalate into some degree of nuclear conflict. This danger is in itself a restraining influence. Such conflict is most likely at those points round the world-island's periphery where communist influence is growing, despite the American 'containing ring' of client states and military bases. Another possibility is that the 'mutual deterrence' inherent in the 'balance of terror' could be upset by technological advance by one side or the other, unless there were inspectable and enforceable agreement not to make such advance. The SALT negotiations give some hope that such undertakings might be entered into.

OTHER ASPECTS OF THE SUPERPOWER RELATIONSHIP

Some believe that the chief danger to the world lies not so much in armed conflict between the two superpowers but in agreement between them. Although this may have beneficial effects, as when directed towards stabilising peace or the prevention of the proliferation of nuclear weapons, it could also be conspiratorial against the independence and freedom of smaller nations. In October 1968 four distinguished signatories wrote a letter to the London *Times* which contained the following paragraph:

We have reason to believe, on the basis of prima facie evidence, that the United States and the Soviet Union are enacting an understanding which involves the reciprocal support for the crimes of each in its agreed 'sphere of influence'. This is at the expense of the independence and self-determination of other nations, from Europe to Vietnam. The secret diplomacy of the rulers of the United States and of the Soviet Union threatens the liberty and sovereignty of men everywhere. It is essential that this identity of interests between the rulers of United States capitalism and the bureaucracy of the Soviet Union should be fully understood and opposed in the service of truth.[7]

Others will find little evidence for this point of view.

Continued tension between the great superpowers will have a harmful effect upon the smaller powers. As the arms race continues and each superpower equips itself with more advanced and more expensive weapons, so lesser powers are tempted to acquire more of these costly devices than they can afford, thus overstraining their economies and preventing any advance in their levels of living. Another adverse effect is that the best brains throughout the non-communist world are attracted to the United States. The expenditure of tens of billions of dollars on advanced weaponry and space research has created such a market for scientists and technical workers in the USA that the most able from other parts of the world are assured of jobs with much higher salaries than they could expect at home. Consequently these countries are denuded of their native talent and all, whether advanced or backward, are retarded in their economic development. Poor and backward countries also look ruefully on while vast sums that could have contributed to their own economic development are poured into the bottomless pit of military and space requirements.

The more obvious achievements of advanced technology act as advertisements for the two politico-economic systems which the superpowers represent. The early Russian successes in space added greatly to Soviet prestige, but the successful landing of men on the moon by the Americans in 1969 did as much for the United States. Future world standing will undoubtedly be determined to some extent by the course of the 'space race'. More than prestige may well be involved. The Russians refused to be deflected from their long-term plans for perfecting automatic methods of lunar exploration and for building orbiting space ships by the temptation of competing in the more sensational business of landing men on the moon. In consequence, they may be two or three years ahead in the application of technology to space and this could have great strategic value. Most American military experts are said to believe that 'the day may come when the moon has strategic value as a way station on the road to the planets, but if the Soviet Union can gain control of near space there will be no argument about the moon or the planets'.[8]

TABLE 19.7 PIONEERING ACCOMPLISHMENTS IN SPACE 1957–71

USA	USSR
	1957 First artificial satellite put into orbit (Sputnik 1). Dog carried in orbit (Sputnik 2).
1958 First American satellite in orbit (Explorer 1).	
	1959 First man-made device sent to moon (Luna 2). 1961 First man completes earth orbit (Yuri Gagarin).
1962 First American completes earth orbit (John Glenn).	
	1963 First woman in space (Valentina Tereshkova). 1964 Three men together in orbit (Voshkhod 1).
1965 First American walks in space (Edward White).	1965 First man walks in space (Alexis Leonov).
1966 Manned space craft links up with unmanned craft in earth orbit. First American spacecraft soft-lands on moon and sends back pictures (Surveyor 1).	1966 First spacecraft to soft-land on moon and send back pictures (Luna 9).
	1967 First spacecraft to land on another planet (Venus 4). Two unmanned spacecraft link up in orbit. 1968 First satellite placed in orbit round the moon (Luna 14). Animals carried round the moon and brought back to earth (Zond 5).
1968 First men circle the moon (Borman, Lovell and Anders in Apollo 8).	
1969 First men to land and walk on the moon (Armstrong and Aldrin in Apollo 11).	1969 First link-up of manned spacecraft and transfer of crew in orbit.
	1970 Cosmonauts spend 18 days in space (Nikolayev and Sevastyanov in Soyuz 9). Rock samples brought back from moon automatically (Luna 16). Moon vehicle landed on moon's surface (Lunokhod 1).
1971 First men to drive vehicle on the moon (Scott and Irwin).	1971 Spacecraft lands on Venus and transmits signals to earth (Venus 7). First orbiting space station (Salyut). First man-made capsule soft-landed on Mars.

Notes

Chapter 1 (pages 1–22)

1. A. Wegener, *The Origins of Continents and Oceans*, trans. J. Biram, introd. B. C. King (London, 1966).

2. H. J. Mackinder, *Democratic Ideals and Reality* (London, 1919).

3. Baku is on the Caspian Sea, but this is not actually a sea but an inland lake and has no water connection with the sea.

4. S. B. Cohen, *Geography and Politics in a Divided World* (New York, 1963) pp. 64–5.

5. Quoted by E. S. Virpsha in *General Military Review* (May 1968) p. 697.

6. P. Cohen, 'The erosion of surface naval power', in *Foreign Affairs*, XLIX (1971) 333.

7. E. Mazo and S. Hess, *Nixon: A Political Portrait* (New York, 1968) pp. 194–5.

8. D. J. M. Hooson, *A New Soviet Heartland?* (Princeton, 1964) p. 117.

9. From *The Military Balance*, Institute of Strategic Studies (London, 1970).

10. *Statistical Abstract of the United States 1970*, pp. 771–2.

11. L. Tansky, 'Soviet foreign aid to the less developed countries' in *New Directions in the Soviet Economy*, Joint Economic Committee, Congress of the United States (Washington, 1966) pp. 964, 974.

12. Ibid., p. 960.

13. C. Whetten, 'Empire or revolution? The dilemma of Russian policy' in *The New Middle East*, VIII (1969) 11–15.

14. Tansky, p. 965.

15. J.-J. Servan-Schreiber, *The American Challenge*, trans. R. Steel (London, 1968) p. 10.

16. *Statistical Abstract of the United States 1970*, p. 766.

17. *Financial Times* (London, 28 May 1969).

18. *The Times* (London, 24 Sep 1968).

19. D. Morrison, 'USSR and Third World: Ideal and Reality' in *Mizan* XII (1970) 15.

Chapter 2 (pages 23–38)

1. S. von Herberstein, *Rerum Moscoviticarum* (Vienna, 1549) f. XII, ii.

2. US Dept of Commerce, *Historical Statistics of the United States* (Washington, 1960) p. 42–3; V. M. Kabuzan, *Narodonaseleniye Rosii* (Moscow, 1963) pp. 159–65.

3. *Istoriya SSSR*, Akademiya Nauk SSSR: Institut Istorii (Moscow, 1968) V 229.

4. R. H. Brown, *Historical Geography of the United States* (New York, 1968) p. 121; W. H. Parker, *An Historical Geography of Russia* (London, 1968) pp. 304–8.

5. P. Dukes, *The Emergence of the Superpowers: a short comparative history of the USA and the USSR* (London, 1970) p. 34.

6. Ibid., pp. 66–7.

7. Ibid., p. 87.

8. Ibid., p. 94.

9. Ibid., p. 112.

10. Quoted in R. Hofstadter, *Ten Major Issues in American Politics* (New York, 1968) p. 252.

11. Dukes, pp. 113–14.

12. Quoted in A. J. Toynbee, *A Study of History* (Oxford 1954) VIII 139.

13. D. M. Wallace, *Russia* (London, 1905) I 205–6.

14. R. Lyall, *Travels in Russia etc.* (London, 1825) I 260.

Chapter 3 (pages 39–58)

1. *Statistical Abstract of the United States 1968* (Washington, 1968) p. 168; W. Leimbach, *Die Sowjetunion* (Stuttgart, 1950) p. 22.

2. J. Watson, *Souvenirs of a Tour in the United States of America and Canada in the Autumn of 1872* (Glasgow, 1872) pp. 57–8.

3. A. Holmes, *Principles of Physical Geology*, 2nd ed. (London, 1965) pp. 1010–11.

4. Yu. G. Saushkin *et al.* (eds), *Ekonomicheskaya Geografiya Sovetskogo Soyuza* (Moscow, 1967) p. 205; W. H. Parker, *An Historical Geography of Russia* (London, 1968) p. 119.

5. W. H. Parker, *Anglo-America* (London, 1962) p. 178; R. H. Brown, *Historical Geography of the United States* (New York, 1948) p. 200.

Chapter 4 (pages 59–76)

1. For a map of the world distribution of Köppen climatic types and a key to the code letters, see A. N. Strahler, *Physical Geography*, 3rd ed. (New York, 1969) Plate 2.

2. Data for this and subsequent climatic tables are from *World Weather Records 1951–60*, US Dept of Commerce, I *North America*, II *Europe*, III *Asia* (Washington, 1965–7).

3. W. H. Parker, *Anglo-America* (London, 1962) p. 238.

4. E. Leyzerovich, *Ekonomiko-geograficheskiye problemy osvoyeniya pustyn* (Moscow, 1968) p. 14; M. P. Petrov, *Pustyni SSSR i ikh osvoyeniye* (Moscow, 1964) p. 21.

5. Petrov, *Pustyni*, p. 23.

Chapter 5 (pages 77–98)

1. Data from *Minerals Yearbook 1968* (Washington, 1969) vols 1–2 and 4.
2. Ibid.
3. Ibid.
4. Ibid.
5. *Vneshnyaya Torgovlya SSSR za 1963g.* (Moscow, 1964) pp 28, 42; *za 1967g.* (Moscow, 1968) pp. 28, 43.
6. D. J. Patton, *The United States and World Resources* (Princeton, 1968) p. 81.
7. Compiled from various sources including *World Oil* and *The Oxford Economic Atlas of the World*, 3rd ed. (Oxford, 1965).
8. *World Oil* (Houston, Tex., 15 Aug 1970) p. 71.
9. Compiled from various sources including *Minerals Yearbook of the United States*, *World Oil*, press reports, etc.
10. E. Vennard, 'Evaluation of the Russian threat in the field of electric power' in *Comparisons of the United States and Soviet Economies (Papers)*, Joint Economic Committee, Congress of the US (Washington, 1959) p. 478.
11. *Hydroelectric Power Resources of the United States*, US Federal Power Commission (Washington, 1968) p. xviii.
12. *World Power Data 1966*, US Federal Power Commission (Washington, 1969) p. 9.
13. *Minerals Yearbook 1968*, vol. 1–2, p. 112–13.
14. In *Directives of the 24th Congress of the CPSU for the Five-Year Economic Development Plan of the USSR for 1971–75* (Moscow, 1971) p. 31.
15. Compiled from data in *Statistical Abstract of the United States 1970*, p. 506, and *Narodnoye Khozyaystvo v 1969g.*, p. 196.
16. *Fortune* (Chicago, Nov 1969).
17. *Financial Times* (London, 23 Oct 1970), p. 7.
18. *Financial Times* (London, 30 Apr 1970).
19. *Minerals Yearbook 1964*, vol. 1, p. 276.
20. N. C. Field, 'Environmental quality and land productivity: a comparison of the agricultural land base of the USSR and North America' in *Canadian Geographer*, XII (1968) 1–14.
21. Data from *World Weather Records*, US Dept of Commerce (Washington, 1965–7), I, II and IV.
22. Calculated for the USSR from data given by M. I. L'vovich in *Voprosi Geografii*, LXXIII (1968) 3–32, and for the USA from data in *World Weather Records*, I.
23. Field, p. 10.
24. *Desalting Plants Inventory*, US Dept of the Interior (Washington, 1969).
25. Yu. G. Saushkin *et al.*, *Ekonomicheskaya Geografiya Sovetskogo Soyuza* (Moscow, 1967) I 233.
26. *Stat. Abst.* 1970, p. 633; *Narodnoye Khozyaystvo SSSR v 1968g.*, p. 305.
27. *Stat. Abst.* 1968, p. 172.
28. *World Weather Records*, II 340.
29. 'Skol'ko stoit zima?' in *Sovetskiy Soyuz*, 217 (1968) 50–2.

Chapter 6 (pages 99–110)

1. S. D. Gordon, G. G. Dawson and J. Witchel, *The American Economy: Analysis and Policy* (Lexington, Mass., 1969) p. 7.
2. J. K. Galbraith, *The New Industrial State* (New York, 1968) p. 18.
3. *Stat. Abst.* 1969, p. 479.
4. Galbraith, p. 82.
5. Gordon, Dawson and Witchell, p. 329.
6. Galbraith, p. 312.
7. Galbraith, p. 320.
8. Galbraith, p. 60.
9. Galbraith, pp. 62–4.
10. Galbraith, p. 191.
11. M. Kaser, *Soviet Economics* (London, 1970) pp. 88–90.
12. R. W. Campbell, 'Marxian Analysis' in *The Soviet Economy*, ed. H. G. Shaffer (London, 1964) p. 353.
13. W. Leontiev, 'The decline and rise of Soviet economic science' in *The Soviet Economy*, ed. Shaffer, pp. 373–7.
14. Leontiev, ibid.
15. *Comparisons of the United States and Soviet Economies (Hearings)*, Joint Economic Committee, Congress of the United States (Washington, 1960) pp. 196–7.
16. Galbraith, p. 122.
17. Galbraith, p. 174.
18. Galbraith, p. 181.
19. Galbraith, pp. 182–3.
20. H. Schwartz, *The Soviet Economy since Stalin* (London, 1965) p. 241.
21. Ibid., p. 232.
22. A. S. Balinky, 'The proclaimed emergence of communism in the USSR' in *The Soviet Economy*, ed. Shaffer, pp. 107–8.
23. Kaser, pp. 119–20.
24. Balinky, p. 113.
25. Quoted in *The Soviet Economy*, ed. Shaffer, p. 82.
26. Balinky, p. 113.
27. V. Packard, *The Hidden Persuaders* (London, 1957) and *The Status Seekers* (London, 1960).
28. G. W. Nutter, 'The structure and growth of Soviet industry' in *Comparisons of the United States and Soviet Economies (Papers)*, p. 118.

Chapter 7 (pages 111–126)

1. H. S. Levine, 'Problems raised by new economic methods in the USSR', NASEES paper (Apr 1967).
2. J. K. Galbraith, *The New Industrial State* (New York, 1968) p. 34.
3. J. M. Keynes, *The General Theory of Employment, Interest and Money* (London, 1936) p. 378.

4. H. S. Levine, 'The centralized planning of supply in Soviet industry' in *Comparisons of the United States and Soviet Economies (Papers)*, Joint Economic Committee, Congress of the United States (Washington, 1959) p. 174.

5. *Fortune* (Chicago, Oct 1969) p. 127.

6. Galbraith, p. 39.

7. J. P. Hardt *et al.*, 'Institutional stagnation and changing economic strategy in the Soviet Union' in *New Directions in the Soviet Economy*, Joint Economic Committee, Congress of the United States (Washington, 1966) p. 42.

8. Ibid., p. 41.

9. *Soviet Studies Information Supplement* (Apr 1970) p. 107.

10. Levine in *Comparisons*, p. 168.

11. *Soviet Studies Information Supplement* (Apr 1970) p. 106.

12. Levine in *Comparisons*, p. 170.

13. Hardt in *New Directions*, p. 27.

14. H. Schwartz, *The Soviet Economy since Stalin* (London, 1965) p. 155.

15. Keynes, p. 378.

16. Schwartz, p. 158.

17. *Soviet News* (London, 25 Aug 1970).

18. M. Kaser, *Soviet Economics* (London, 1970) p. 103.

19. *Soviet Studies Information Supplement* (Apr 1970) p. 99.

20. V. Treml, 'A note on Soviet Input–Output Tables' in *Soviet Studies*, XXI (1969) 32.

21. D. Branick, 'Soviet–American management comparisons' in *Comparisons*, p. 146.

22. *Statistical Abstract of the United States 1969*, p. 346.

23. *Soviet Weekly* (London, 27 June 1970).

24. Ibid.

25. Galbraith, p. 205.

26. *Stat. Abst.* 1969, pp. 408, 310; *Nar. Khoz.* 1968, p. 774.

27. S. H. Cohn, 'Soviet growth retardation' in *New Directions*, p. 109.

28. H. Heymann, 'Problems of Soviet–United States comparisons' in *Comparisons*, p. 11.

29. M. Boretsky, 'Comparative progress in technology, productivity, and economic efficiency: USSR versus USA' in *New Directions*, p. 192; Kaser, p. 104.

30. *Financial Times* (London, 5 Apr 1971).

31. Cohn, p. 110.

32. Kaser, p. 203; *Stat. Abst.* 1969, p. 310.

33. Cohn, p. 118.

34. *Stat. Abst.* 1970, p. 814.

35. Ibid., p. 451.

36. Kaser, p. 128.

37. *Soviet Studies Information Supplement* (Apr 1970) p. 99.

38. Galbraith, pp. 219, 326.

39. S. D. Gordon, G. G. Dawson and J. Witchel, *The American Economy: analysis and policy* (Lexington, Mass., 1969) p. 210.

L

40. R. Lekachman, quoted in V. Packard, *The Hidden Persuaders* (London, 1960) pp. 113–14.

41. Based on table by A. Aganbegian in *The Soviet Economy*, ed. H. G. Shaffer (London, 1964) p. 281.

42. Ibid., p. 276.

43. Kaser, pp. 143–4.

44. M. Harrison, *The Other America* (Penguin: Baltimore, 1963) p. 9.

45. Ibid., p. 12.

Chapter 8 (pages 127–142)

1. Compiled from data in the *Statistical Abstract of the United States* 1970, pp. 213–22, *Narodnoye Khozyaystvo SSSR v 1969g.*, pp. 545–9, and *The Military Balance 1970–71* (London, 1970) pp. 1, 6.

2. *Stat. Abst.* 1969, pp. 217–19; *Nar. Khoz.* 1968, p. 155; 1967, pp. 663–4.

3. *Fortune* (July 1970) p. 69.

4. M. Kaser, *Soviet Economics* (London, 1970) p. 144; *Stat. Abst.* 1969, p. 327.

5. *Stat. Abst.* 1969, p. 327.

6. V. V. Pokshishevskiy, 'On basic migration patterns' in *Soviet Geography*, V (1964) no. 10, pp. 3–18.

7. V. V. Pokshishevskiy, in *Soviet News* (London, 20 Jan 1970) p. 35.

8. Evidence of this was given in *Time* (New York, 24 Dec 1956) p. 43.

9. J. S. Berliner, 'Managerial incentives and decision making' in *Comparisons of the United States and Soviet Economies (Papers)*, Joint Economic Committee, Congress of the United States (Washington, 1959) p. 350.

10. Ibid., p. 351.

11. Quoted by D. W. Humphreys, 'American self criticism' in *The Times Educational Supplement* (London, 28 Nov 1958), p. 1720.

12. W. W. Eshelman, 'Some comparisons between the Soviet and the United States economical commitment to education' in *Comparisons (Papers)* p. 511.

13. *Comparisons (Hearings)* p. 233.

14. *Stat. Abst.* 1970, p. 131; *Nar. Khoz.* 1968, p. 689.

15. *Stat. Abst.* 1970, pp. 696–7.

16. Kaser, pp. 218–19.

17. in *Report of the Central Committee of the Communist Party of the Soviet Union* (Moscow, 1971) p. 74.

18. M. Boretsky, 'Comparative progress in technology, productivity, and economic efficiency' in *New Directions in the Soviet Economy*, Joint Economic Committee, United States Congress (Washington, 1966) pp. 224–5.

19. *Soviet News* (London, 15 Sep 1970).

20. K. Miller, 'Computers in the Soviet economy' in *New Directions*, pp. 329–37.

21. A. Lykov in *Soviet Weekly* (London, 18 July 1970).

22. *The Economist* (London, 8 Feb 1969) p. 64.

23. A. Cairncross, *Introduction to Economics* (London, 1960) pp. 44–5.

24. D. Granick, 'Soviet–American management comparisons' in *Comparisons (Papers)* p. 143.

25. S. D. Gordon, G. G. Dawson and J. Witchel, *The American Economy: analysis and policy* (Lexington, Mass., 1969) p. 74; Berliner in *Comparisons (Papers)* pp. 350–3.

26. J. K. Galbraith, *The New Industrial State* (New York, 1968) p. 164; Kaser, p. 187; Berliner, p. 369.

27. Granick, p. 145.

28. Berliner, p. 346.

29. Berliner, p. 367.

30. G. Bookman, 'The split-level Soviet economy' in *Fortune* (Chicago, Oct 1961) p. 266.

31. Quoted in Berliner, p. 367.

32. Granick, p. 150; Berliner, p. 362.

33. Granick, p. 148.

34. Berliner, p. 366.

35. Berliner, p. 368.

36. Granick, p. 145.

Chapter 9 (pages 143–157)

1. D. B. Diamond, 'Trends in output, inputs and factor productivity in Soviet agriculture' in *New Directions in the Soviet Economy*, Joint Economic Committee, Congress of the United States (Washington, 1966) p. 349.

2. *Soviet News* (London, 14 Jan 1969).

3. *Soviet Studies Information Supplement* (July 1969) p. 29.

4. G. Alexinsky, *Modern Russia* (London, 1913) p. 133.

5. Ibid., p. 395.

6. E. Woytinsky, *Profile of the US Economy* (New York, 1967) pp. 201–2.

7. *Rural Poverty in the United States*, President's National Advisory Commission on Rural Poverty (Washington, 1968) p. 39.

8. Ibid., pp. 442–7.

9. W. E. Mosse, 'Stolypin's villages' in *The Slavonic and East European Review*, XLIII (1965) 257–74.

10. *Statistical Abstract of the United States* 1970, p. 590; *Narodnoye Khozyaystvo SSSR v 1969g.*, p. 389.

11. *Stat. Abst.* 1970, p. 478; *Nar. Khoz.* 1969, p. 508.

12. N. C. Field, 'Environmental quality and land productivity: a comparison of the agricultural land use of the USSR and North America' in *Canadian Geographer*, XII (1968) 11–12.

13. *Land: the Yearbook of Agriculture*, US Dept of Agriculture (Washington, 1958) p. 235; *Agricultural Statistics* 1968, US Dept of Agriculture (Washington, 1968) p. 495.

14. *Stat. Abst.* 1970, p. 590; *Nar. Khoz.* 1969, p. 151; L. Brezhnev, *Report of the Central Committee of the Communist Party of the Soviet Union* (Moscow, 1971) p. 41.

15. *Stat. Abst.* 1970, p. 607; *Nar. Khoz.* 1969, p. 308.

16. J. J. Hart, 'Loss and abandonment of cleared farm land in the eastern United States' in *Annals of the Association of American Geographers*, LVIII (1968) 417–40.

17. *Stat. Abst.* 1970, p. 605; *Nar. Khoz.* 1969, p. 309.

18. Ibid.

19. *Stat. Abst.* for various years under 'International Statistics'.

20. Z. Brzezinski and S. P. Huntington, *Political Power: USA/USSR* (New York, 1964) p. 301.

21. Ibid., pp. 315–16.

22. A. E. Granovskaya, in *Vestnik Moskovskogo Universiteta (Geografiya)* (1968) pp. 79–90.

23. V. V. Pavrov and K. N. Plotnikov, *Gosudarstvennyy Byudzhet SSSR* (Moscow, 1968) p. 213; Brezhnev, *Report*, p. 57.

24. Quoted from *Soviet News* (London, 19 Nov 1968) pp. 71–3.

25. C. D. Harris, quoted in P. Dukes, *The Emergence of the Superpowers* (London, 1970) p. 23.

26. A. Bergson, 'The great economic race: USSR vs USA' in *Comparative Economic Systems*, ed. M. J. Goldman (New York, 1964) p. 342.

Chapter 10 (pages 158–172)

1. *Statistical Abstract of the United States* 1970, p. 220; *Narodnoye Khozyaystvo SSSR v 1969g.*, pp. 165, 530.

2. *Stat. Abst.* 1970, pp. 220–2; *Nar. Khoz.* 1969, p. 165.

3. *Nar. Khoz.* 1969, p. 94.

4. Calculated from data in *Stat. Abst.* 1970, p. 696; *Nar. Khoz.* 1969, p. 144.

5. R. V. Greenslade, 'The Soviet economic system in transition' in *New Directions in the Soviet Economy*, Joint Economic Committee, Congress of the United States (Washington, 1966) p. 8.

6. Quoted by G. W. Nutter in *The Soviet Economy*, ed. H. G. Shaffer (London, 1964) p. 201.

7. *Financial Times* (London, 12 Mar 1971) p. 5.

8. *Sovetskiy Soyuz*, 249 (Moscow, 1970) 13.

9. W. H. Parker, 'The USSR moves west' in *New Scientist* (London, 21 Aug 1969) pp. 381–3.

10. *Economic Effect of Vietnam Spending*, Joint Economic Committee, Congress of the United States (Washington, 1967) I 215–16.

11. *Nar. Khoz.* 1969, pp. 160–4.

12. Ibid.

13. V. Simpson in *British Steel* (May 1970) p. 10.

14. *Stat. Abst.* 1970, p. 722; *Nar. Khoz.* 1969, p. 204.

15. Simpson, pp. 11–12.

16. Ibid.

17. Japan has since built even larger furnaces.

18. *Minerals Yearbook 1968*, US Dept of the Interior (Washington, 1969) I–II 600.

19. M. Boretsky, 'Comparative progress in technology, productivity, and

economic efficiency: USSR versus USA' in *New Directions in the Soviet Economy*, pp. 171–2.

20. *Stat. Abst.* 1971, p. 534; A. Kosygin, *Directives of the Five-Year Economic Development Plan of the USSR for 1971–75* (Moscow, 1971) p. 35.

21. There are still larger smelters, however, in Canada.

22. *Minerals Yearbook 1968*, I–II 162.

23. *Stat. Abst.* 1970, p. 713; *Nar. Khoz.* 1968, pp. 251, 285.

Chapter 11 (pages 173–186)

1. *Statistical Abstract of the United States* 1971, p. 525; *Soviet News* (16 Mar 1971) pp. 45–6. The American figure has been converted from short ton-miles to metric ton–kilometres.

2. H. Hunter, 'The Soviet transport sector' in *New Directions in the Soviet Economy*, Joint Economic Committee, Congress of the United States (Washington, 1966) p. 573.

3. *Stat. Abst.* 1971, p. 525; *Soviet News* (16 Mar 1971) pp. 45–6.

4. *Stat. Abst.* 1970, p. 535; *Nar. Khoz.* 1968, pp. 464, 476, 496, 504.

5. Ibid.

6. *Time* (New York, 5 Jan 1970).

7. W. Melville in *The Times* (London, 18 Mar 1969).

8. *Nar. Khoz.* 1967, p. 515; Yu. G. Saushkin, *Ekonomicheskaya Geografiya SSSR* (Moscow, 1967) I 355.

9. E. W. Williams, 'Some aspects of the structure and growth of Soviet transportation' in *Comparisons of the United States and Soviet Economies (Papers)* (Washington, 1959) p. 184.

10. Williams in *Comparisons*, p. 182; Hunter in *New Directions*, p. 590.

11. *Soviet News* (London, 12 Jan 1971).

12. *Stat. Abst.* 1970, p. 537; *Nar. Khoz.* 1968, p. 487.

13. Hunter in *New Directions*, p. 583.

14. *Stat. Abst.* 1970, p. 535; *Soviet News* (16 Mar 1971) pp. 45–6.

15. Hunter in *Comparisons (Hearings)* p. 90.

16. Ibid.

17. Hunter in *New Directions*, p. 588.

18. *Soviet Weekly* (London, 17 May 1969).

19. *Stat. Abst.* 1970, p. 565; *Nar. Khoz.* 1968, p. 504.

20. *Stat. Abst.* 1971, p. 556; *Nar. Khoz.* 1969, p. 486.

21. T. I. Alekseyeva, 'Dirizhabl na severe' in *Problemy Severa* (1965) IX 201–6; W. H. Parker, *The Soviet Union* (World's Landscapes: London, 1969) p. 61.

22. *Stat. Abst.* 1970, pp. 559, 515; *Nar. Khoz.* 1968, p. 486.

23. Saushkin, p. 383.

Chapter 12 (pages 187–204)

1. *Statistical Abstract of the United States* and *Vneshnyaya Torgovlya SSSR* for various years.

2. *The Times* (London, 4 June 1966).

3. *Stat. Abst.* 1970, pp. 779–83; *Vnesh. Torg.* 1969, p. 19.

4. *Vnesh. Torg.* 1969, pp. 67–8.

5. *Minerals Yearbook 1968* (Washington, 1970) I–II, pp. 12–13.

6. *Agricultural Statistics*, US Dept of Agriculture, and *Vnesh. Torg.* for various years.

7. *Stat. Abst.* 1970, pp. 788–90; *Vnesh. Torg.* 1969, pp. 11–15.

8. Ibid.

9. *Vnesh. Torg.* 1969, pp. 234–6.

10. *Stat. Abst.* 1970, p. 788; *Vnesh. Torg.* 1969, pp. 283–8.

11. *Vnesh. Torg.* 1969, p. 13.

12. Ibid., pp. 289–91.

13. In *New Directions in the Soviet Economy*, Joint Economic Committee, Congress of the United States (Washington, 1966) p. 946.

14. *Vnesh. Torg.* 1963, p. 19; *Vnesh. Torg.* 1969, p. 18.

15. *Stat. Abst.* 1970, p. 569.

16. Ibid.

17. *Stat. Abst.* 1970, pp. 829–30.

18. For a development of this point, see P. Hanson, 'The Soviet Union and world shipping' in *Soviet Studies*, XXII (July 1970) 44–60.

19. *Soviet Weekly* (London, 5 Dec 1970 and 20 Mar 1971).

20. Quoted in the *Financial Times* (London, 29 May 1970) p. 14.

21. Ibid.

22. H. Schwartz, *The Soviet Economy Since Stalin* (London, 1965) pp. 218–32.

23. *Soviet News* (London, 25 Aug 1970).

Chapter 13 (pages 205–218)

1. J. M. Stewart, *Across the Russias* (London, 1969) p. 215; *The Times* (London, 12 June 1967).

2. *Statistical Abstract of the United States* 1970 (Washington, 1970) p. 6 *Narodnoye Khozyaystvo SSSR v 1969g.* (Moscow, 1969) p. 35.

3. *Stat. Abst.* 1970, p. 5; *Nar. Khoz.* 1969, p. 7.

4. *Stat. Abst.* 1970, p. 47; *Nar. Khoz.* 1969, p. 31.

5. L. H. Day, 'The American fertility cult' in *The Population Crisis and the Use of World Resources*, ed. S. Mudd (Bloomington, Ind., 1964) pp. 231–2.

6. *Time* (New York, 6 May 1966) p. 13.

7. *Fortune* (Chicago, Feb 1971) p. 82.

8. The American figures are estimates derived from the 1920 national origin ratios adopted for the 1924 Immigration Act, modified according to annual immigration figures and data for foreign white stock in the 1960 census; the Soviet figures are from the 1959 census.

9. *Literaturnaya Gazeta* (Moscow, 11 Jan 1967).

10. L. Mumford, *The Culture of Cities* (London, n.d.) p. 223.

11. *Fortune* (Chicago, Feb 1971) p. 82.

12. C. D. Harris, *The Cities of the Soviet Union* (Chicago, 1970) pp. 69–78.

Chapter 14 (pages 219–230)

1. *Soviet News* (London, 19 Nov 1968) p. 71.
2. L. Turgeon, 'Levels of living and incentives in the Soviet and United States economies' in *Comparisons of the United States and Soviet Economies (Papers)* (Washington, 1959) p. 334.
3. Ibid., p. 333; *Statistical Abstract of the United States* 1970, p. 314.
4. Turgeon, p. 333.
5. T. Sosnovy, 'Housing conditions and urban development in the USSR' in *New Directions in the Soviet Economy*, Joint Economic Committee, Congress of the United States (Washington, 1966) p. 545.
6. I. D. Zlobina (ed.), *Gosudarstvennyy Byudzhet SSSR* (Moscow, 1970) p. 242.
7. *Fortune* (Chicago, Jan 1970) pp. 79–86.
8. V. V. Pavrov and K. N. Plotnikov, *Gosudarstvennyy Byudzhet SSSR* (Moscow, 1968), p. 337.
9. Ibid., pp. 327–40.
10. *Social Security Benefits*, US Dept of Health, Education and Welfare, Social Security Administration (Washington, 1968).
11. *Narodnoye Khozyaystvo SSSR v 1969g.*, p. 488; *Stat. Abst.* 1970, pp. 687, 493.
12. *Soviet News* (London, 22 Sep 1970) pp. 100–2.
13. *Sunday Times* (London, 19 Jan 1969) p. 50.
14. Ibid., p. 49.
15. Ibid.
16. *The Times* (London, 10 Mar 1966); *Sunday Telegraph* (London, 20 Dec 1970).

Chapter 15 (pages 231–249)

1. For a survey of recent policy in the USSR with regard to contraception, etc., see D. M. Heer, 'Abortion, contraception and population policy in the Soviet Union' in *Soviet Studies*, XVII (1965) 76.
2. R. M. Williams in *American and Soviet Society*, ed. P. Hollander (Englewood Cliffs, N.J., 1969) p. 168; P. Jouiler, ibid., p. 207.
3. D. P. Moynihan in *American and Soviet Society*, p. 292.
4. A. G. Kharchev, ibid., p. 195.
5. J. Novak, quoted by A. S. Balinsky, 'The proclaimed emergence of communism in the USSR' in *The Soviet Economy* (London, 1964) p. 121.
6. *Statistical Abstract of the United States* 1970, p. 47; *Narodnoye Khozyaystvo SSSR v 1969g.*, p. 36.
7. P. Hollander, *American and Soviet Society*, p. 166; *Stat. Abst.* 1969, p. 32.
8. *Sovetskiy Soyuz*, 241 (Moscow, 1970) pp. 10–11; Jouiler in *American and Soviet Society*, p. 211.
9. *Leninskaya Smena* (Nov 1969); Jouiler, p. 211.
10. *Stat. Abst.* 1970, p. 223.
11. *Stat. Abst.* 1970, pp. 214, 225, etc.; *Nar. Khoz.* 1968, p. 536.

12. *Nar. Khoz.* 1968, pp. 552, 693.

13. *Stat. Abst.* 1968, pp. 222, 224–5; *Nar. Khoz.* 1968, p. 552.

14. M. Mead, *Male and Female* (Pelican Books: London, 1962) p. 276; see also E. J. Dingwall, *The American Woman* (London, 1956).

15. Hollander, p. 158.

16. R. Schlesinger, *Changing Attitudes in Soviet Russia: the Family* (London, 1949) p. 343.

17. Kharchev in *American and Soviet Society*, p. 192; Geiger, ibid., p. 215.

18. Jouiler in *American and Soviet Society*, p. 210.

19. A. Vaksberg, ibid., pp. 201–2.

20. W. H. Parker, *Anglo-America* (London, 1962) p. 99.

21. Geiger in *American and Soviet Society*, pp. 213–14.

22. L. Warner, ibid., pp. 128–30.

23. M. Harrington, *The Other America* (Penguin: Baltimore, Md, 1963) pp. 48–9.

24. I. Skharatan in *American and Soviet Society*, p. 147.

25. M. Kaser, *Soviet Economics* (London, 1970) p. 71.

26. A. Parry, *The New Class Divided* (London, 1966) p. 296.

27. Moynihan in *American and Soviet Society*, p. 289.

28. Hollander, ibid., pp. 125, 284–8.

29. M. Friedberg, ibid., p. 301.

30. *Soviet Weekly* (London, 9 Jan 1971) p. 13.

31. Moynihan, p. 286.

32. Rabbi Kahane in *Anti-Semitism in the Soviet Union*, Hearings before the Committee on Un-American Activities, House of Representatives (Washington, 1969) pp. 2211, 2204–5.

33. Parry, p. 181.

34. *The Times* (London, 31 July 1968).

35. S. Wheeler in *American and Soviet Society*, p. 233; Hollander, ibid. p. 279.

36. '*Kommunist*', quoted by Hollander, p. 252.

37. Ibid., p. 250.

38. G. M. Minkovsky in *American and Soviet Society*, p. 259.

39. D. Matza and G. Sykes in *American and Soviet Society*, pp. 229, 227.

40. I. Karpets in *Sovetskiy Soyuz*, 241 (Moscow, 1970) p. 29.

41. Hollander, p. 280.

42. Vaksberg, p. 203.

43. Karpets, pp. 28–9.

44. Hollander, p. 275.

45. U. Bronfenbrenner, *Two Worlds of Childhood–USA and USSR* (London, 1972).

Chapter 16 (pages 250–266)

1. Z. Brzezinski and S. P. Huntington, *Political Power: USA/USSR* (New York, 1964) p. 172.

2. K. Lawson, *Political Parties and Democracy in the United States* (New York, 1968) pp. 29–30.

3. Brzezinski and Huntington, p. 244.

4. C. P. Magrath, E. E. Cornwell and J. S. Goodman, *The American Democracy* (London, 1969) p. 25.

5. Brzezinski and Huntington, pp. 32–3.

6. Ibid., pp. 409–10.

7. Magrath, Cornwell and Goodman, p. 25.

8. Brzezinski and Huntington, p. 45.

9. Lawson, p. 1.

10. Brzezinski and Huntington, p. 46.

11. Ibid., p. 43.

12. Ibid., pp. 230–2, 415.

13. Ibid., pp. 388–407.

14. Quoted in L. G. Churchward, *Contemporary Soviet Government* (New York, 1968) p. 262.

15. Churchward, p. 268.

16. Ibid., pp. 298–9.

17. Brzezinski and Huntington, pp. 419–33.

18. Churchward, p. 1.

19. *Konstitutsiya Soyuza Sovetskikh Sotsialisticheskikh Respublik* (Moscow, 1970) pp. 4–5 (cap. I, art. 11).

20. Magrath, Cornwell and Goodman, p. 184.

21. M. D. Irish and J. W. Prothero, *The Politics of American Democracy*, 3rd ed. (Englewood Cliffs, N.J., 1965) p. 433.

22. Magrath, Cornwell and Goodman, p. 666; for a recent examination of Soviet electoral procedures, see E. M. Jacobs, 'Soviet local elections: what they are and what they are not' in *Soviet Studies*, XXII (1970) 61–76.

23. Churchward, p. 107.

24. Brzezinski and Huntington, p. 94.

25. Churchward, p. 122.

26. J. N. Hazard, *The Soviet System of Government*, 3rd ed. (Chicago, 1964) p. 48.

27. R. Conquest, *The Soviet Political System* (New York, 1968) p. 73.

28. Irish and Prothero, p. 434.

29. Brzezinski and Huntington, p. 222.

30. V. O. Key, *Politics, Parties, and Pressure Groups*, 5th ed. (New York, 1964) p. 359.

31. Brzezinski and Huntington, p. 95.

32. Ibid., p. 101.

33. Churchward, p. 271.

34. Magrath, Cornwell and Goodman, pp. 174–81.

35. Irish and Prothero, p. 183.

36. R. Schlesinger, *The Family in the USSR* (London, 1949) pp. 251–6.

37. Churchward, p. 114.

38. Conquest, pp. 60, 62; Irish and Prothero, p. 344; Magrath, Cornwell and Goodman, p. 399.

39. Churchward, p. 109.

40. Conquest, p. 61.

Chapter 17 (pages 267–283)

1. *Konstitutsiya Soyuza Sovetskikh Sotsialisticheskikh Respublik* (Moscow, 1970) p. 28.

2. Quoted in C. P. Magrath, E. E. Cornwell and J. S. Goodman, *The American Democracy* (London, 1969) p. 260.

3. Ibid., pp. 254–5.

4. R. Conquest, *The Soviet Political System* (New York, 1968) p. 75.

5. Z. Brzezinski and S. P. Huntington, *Political Power: USA/USSR* (New York, 1964) p. 241.

6. Conquest, p. 76.

7. Ibid., p. 77.

8. Brzezinski and Huntington, pp. 235–6.

9. V. O. Key, *Politics, Parties and Pressure Groups*, 5th ed. (New York, 1964) p. 357.

10. M. D. Irish and J. W. Prothero, *The Politics of American Democracy*, 3rd ed. (Englewood Cliffs, 1965) p. 313.

11. Brzezinski and Huntington, pp. 144–6.

12. Conquest, p. 41.

13. Brzezinski and Huntington, pp. 141–3.

14. Ibid., p. 149.

15. Ibid., p. 155.

16. Ibid., p. 150.

17. Brzezinski and Huntington, p. 241; Conquest, p. 218.

18. For this idea, as for much else in this and the preceding chapter, I am indebted to Brzezinski and Huntington, pp. 163–7.

19. E. Mazo and S. Hess, *Nixon: A Political Portrait* (New York, 1968) p. 59.

20. Mazo and Hess, p. 252.

21. Conquest, p. 117.

22. Churchward, pp. 292–4.

23. Conquest, p. 112.

24. Irish and Prothero, pp. 208–9; K. Lawson, *Political Parties and Democracy in the United States* (New York, 1968) pp. 125–6; Magrath, Cornwell and Goodman, p. 228; Key, p. 167.

25. Key, pp. 63–5; Churchward, pp. 199–203.

26. C. Wright Mills, *The Power Élite* (New York, 1956) p. 124.

27. Magrath, Cornwell and Goodman, p. 344.

28. Key, pp. 83–4; V. Perlo, *Militarism and Industry* (New York, 1963) p. 160.

29. Brzezinski and Huntington, p. 198.

30. Ibid., pp. 328–49.

31. Magrath, Cornwell and Goodman, p. 301.

32. Key, p. 352.

33. Ibid., p. 138.

34. Magrath, Cornwell and Goodman, p. 344; Key, p. 84.

35. Irish and Prothero, p. 318; Key, p. 133.

36. Churchward, p. 129.

37. Magrath, Cornwell and Goodman, p. 713.

38. Ibid., p. 687.

39. Brzezinski and Huntington, p. 124.

40. Ibid., p. 241.

41. Churchward, pp. 112, 280–1.

42. Ibid., pp. 124–32.

43. Mills, p. 279; Brzezinski and Huntington, p. 134.

44. Mills, p. 296.

45. Brzezinski and Huntington, p. 415.

46. Mills, p. 170; G. W. Domhoff and H. B. Ballard, *C. Wright Mills and the Power Élite* (Boston, 1968) p. 55.

47. Mills, p. 170; Domhoff and Ballard, p. 224.

Chapter 18 (pages 284–299)

1. *Soviet News* (London, 10 June 1969) p. 128.

2. *An Economic Profile of Mainland China*, Joint Economic Committee, Congress of the United States (Washington, 1968) p. 320.

3. *Minerals Yearbook 1968*, US Dept of the Interior, Bureau of Mines (Washington, 1969–70) I–II *passim*, IV 189–200.

4. *Economic Profile*, pp. 244–6.

5. *Mainland China in the World Economy*, Joint Economic Committee, Congress of the United States (Washington, 1967) p. 41; S. H. Steinberg, ed., *The Statesman's Yearbook 1968–69*, p. 890.

6. *Agricultural Statistics 1969* (Washington, 1969) *passim*.

7. *The Shorter Oxford Economic Atlas of the World* (London, 1965) pp. 49–52.

8. *Economic Profile*, pp. 589–91.

9. For industrial production, see T. R. Tregear, *An Economic Geography of China* (London, 1970) pp. 199–230; T. Shabad in *Annals* of the American Association of Geographers, VX (1970) 807.

10. Yuan-li Wu *et al.*, *The Spatial Economy of Communist China* (New York, 1967), p. 103.

11. Ibid., p. 182.

12. Ibid., p. 107.

13. *Mainland China*, p. 4.

14. Tregear, pp. 232–40; *Economic Profile*, pp. 590–605.

15. *Economic Profile*, pp. 601–2.

16. Ibid., p. 606.

17. Ibid., pp. 589–90.

18. *Soviet News* (London, 10 June 1969) p. 128.

19. *Economic Profile*, pp. 390–1.

20. Ibid., p. 363.

21. *Statesman's Yearbook 1968–9*, p. 885.

22. *Mainland China and the World Economy*, p. 163.

23. *Financial Times* (London, 11 Mar 1971).

24. *The Times* (London, 7 Aug 1969).

25. G. E. Taylor, 'Guidelines for US policy in East Asia' in *Sino-Soviet Rivalry*, ed. C. J. Zablocki (New York, 1966) p. 200.

Chapter 19 (pages 300–311)

1. D. J. Patton, *The United States and World Resources* (Princeton, N.J., 1968) p. 50.

2. J. K. Galbraith, *The New Industrial State* (Boston, 1967) pp. 389–91.

3. *The Times* (London, 20 Aug 1968) p. 3.

4. A. Parry, *The New Class Divided* (London, 1966) p. 300.

5. David Watt in the *Financial Times* (21 Oct 1970) p. 8.

6. A. Bergson, 'The great economic race: USSR v USA' in *Comparative Economic Systems*, ed. M. I. Goldman, p. 344.

7. Bertrand Russell, Jean-Paul Sartre, Vladimir Deduer, Laurent Schwartz in *The Times* (London, 9 Oct 1968).

8. *Fortune* (Chicago, June 1962) p. 216.

Some Comparative Facts and Figures

The statistical information has normally been taken from the official sources and is of varying reliability. The date to which the information refers is given in abbreviated form in brackets: thus ('69) signifies that the item refers to 1969. The military data are from *The Military Balance 1970–1971*, Institute for Strategic Studies (London, 1970).

HISTORY	USA	USSR
Pacific coast first reached by nationals (date)	1805	1639
First trans-continental railway opened (date)	1869	1903
Revolution (date)	1775	1917
Civil war (dates)	1861–5	1917–21
Abolition of slavery/serfdom (date)	1865	1861
Outbreak of war with Japan (date)	1941	1904
Belligerent in First World War (dates)	1917–18	1914–17
Loss of life in First World War	53,402	*c.* 2 mln
Belligerent in Second World War (dates)	1941–5	1941–5
Loss of life in Second World War	291,557	*c.* 20 mln
First nuclear bomb exploded (date)	16 Jul 1945	29 Aug 1949
First thermo-nuclear bomb exploded (date)	31 Oct 1952	12 Aug 1953
First earth satellite placed in orbit (date)	1958	1957
First men landed on moon (date)	1969	—

GEOGRAPHY		
Area, gross (sq. mi)	3,702,426	8,649,490
Population (mlns)	203 ('70)	242 ('70)
Population density (per sq. mi)	57 ('70)	28 ('70)
Maximum length north–south (miles)	*c.* 1,600	*c.* 2,500
Maximum width east–west (miles)	*c.* 2,800	*c.* 5,700
Minimum length north–south (miles)	*c.* 800	*c.* 1,400
Minimum width east–west (miles)	*c.* 2,200	*c.* 4,600
Highest mountain summit	McKinley (Alaska)	Communism (Pamir Mts)
Highest mountain summit (feet a.s.l.)	20,320	24,584
Deepest depression	Death Valley (Calif.)	Karagiye Valley (Kazakhstan)
Deepest depression (feet b.s.l.)	282	433
Longest river	Mississippi–Missouri–Red Rock	Yenisey–Selenga
Longest river (miles)	3,741	3,584
Largest lake wholly within national territory	Michigan	Aral
Largest lake wholly within national territory (sq. mi)	22,178	23,924
Volcanoes, active or recently active	22	65

CLIMATE	USA	USSR
Highest recorded temperature	Death Valley (Calif.)	Termez (Turkestan)
Highest recorded temperature (°F)	134 (56·7°C)	122 (50°C)
Lowest recorded temperature	Yellowstone Park	Oymyakon (N.E. Sib.)
Lowest recorded temperature (°F)	−66 (−54·5°C)	−96 (−71°C)
Highest mean monthly temperature	Yuma (Ariz.)	Repetek (Turkestan)
Highest mean monthly temperature (°F)	94·3 (34·5°C)	90 (32°C)
Lowest mean monthly temperature	Northway (Alaska)	Verkhoyansk (N.E. Siberia)
Lowest mean monthly temperature (°F)	−22·2 (−30·2°C)	−52·5 (−46·8°C)
Wettest met. station	Tattosh Isd (Wash.)	Batumi (Georgia)
Wettest met. station (annual precipitation in inches)	79	93
Driest met. station	Yuma (Ariz.)	Turtkul (Uzbekistan)
Driest met. station (annual precipitation in inches)	3	2·4

ECONOMY: *General*		
Gross national product ($ bln)	976 ('70)	466 ('69)
GNP: proportion attributed to personal consumption	62% ('69)	46·5% ('64)
GNP: proportion attributed to investment	15% ('69)	30·5% ('64)
GNP: proportion originating in agriculture	3% ('67)	15% ('69)
GNP: proportion originating in industry	32% ('67)	67% ('69)
National income ($ bln)	801 ('70)	357 ('69)
Industrial production ($ bln)	277 ('69)	194 ('69)
Income *per capita* (dollars)	3,796 ('69)	1,485 ('69)
Personal income as proportion of national income	65% ('68)	40% ('68)
Personal taxation, total ($ bln/bln roubles)	127 ('69)	49 ('67)
Personal taxation as proportion of personal income	25% ('67)	40% ('67)

ECONOMY: *Forestry and fishing*		
Timber reserves (bln cubic ft)	628	2,650
Timber cut (bln cubic ft)	10	12
Fish catch (mln m. tons)	1,941 ('68)	6,784 ('68)

ECONOMY: *Agriculture*		
Farms, av. size of (acres)	369 ('69)	c. 15,000
Agricultural labour force (mlns)	c. 2·5	c. 40
Farm population (mlns)	10 ('70)	48 ('70)
Farm population as proportion of total population	5%	20%
Tractors, number of ('000s)	4,810 ('69)	1,908 ('69)
Combine harvesters ('000s)	850 ('69)	605 ('69)
Investment in agriculture ($ mln/mln roubles)	9·4 ('69)	11·9 ('69)
Irrigated land (mln ha)	17	12
Drained land (mln ha)	70	18
Cropland, area of (mln ha)	126·1 ('69)	208·6 ('69)

	USA	USSR
Cereals, area sown to (mln ha)	64 ('68)	122 ('68)
Grain harvest (mln m. tons)	228 ('69)	186 ('70)
Wheat harvest (mln m. tons)	40 ('69)	80 ('69)
Maize harvest (mln m. tons)	116 ('69)	12 ('69)
Barley harvest (mln m. tons)	8 ('69)	25 ('67)
Oats harvest (mln m. tons)	14 ('69)	12 ('67)
Rye harvest (mln m. tons)	1 ('69)	11 ('69)
Rice harvest (mln m. tons)	4 ('69)	1 ('70)
Potato harvest (mln m. tons)	13 ('69)	92 ('69)
Sugar beet harvest (mln m. tons)	24 ('69)	71 ('69)
Sugar cane harvest (mln m. tons)	20 ('69)	0 ('69)
Soya bean harvest (mln m. tons)	30 ('69)	
Cotton harvest (mln m. tons)	2·16 ('69)	2·61 ('70)
Cattle (mlns)	112·3 ('70)	95·2 ('70)
Cows (mlns)	13·4 ('70)	40·5 ('70)
Sheep (mlns)	17·6 ('70)	130·7 ('70)
Pigs (mlns)	56·7 ('70)	56·1 ('70)
Meat, production of (mln m. tons)	15·9 ('69)	12·3 ('70)
Milk, production of (mln m. tons)	52·3 ('69)	82·9 ('70)
Butter, production of (mln m. tons)	0·5 ('69)	1·0 ('70)

ECONOMY: *Mining and power*

	USA	USSR
Coal, share of world reserves	c. 15%	c. 62%
Coal, production of (mln m. tons)	539 ('69)	641 ('71)
Petroleum, share of world reserves	c. 6%	c. 11%
Petroleum, production of (mln m. tons)	534 ('70)	372 ('71)
Natural gas, share of world reserves	c. 11%	c. 12%
Natural gas, production (bln cubic m)	660 ('69)	200 ('70)
Hydro-electricity, share of world potential	c. 4%	c. 17%
Electricity, installed capacity (mln kw)	332 ('69)	154 ('69)
Electricity, production (bln kwh)	1,552 ('69)	800 ('71)
Electricity, proportion of production used in industry	45% ('69)	62% ('69)
Electricity, nuclear capacity, actual and planned (mln kw)	c. 42	c. 30
Energy from mineral fuels, share produced by coal	21·5% ('69)	38·2% ('69)
Energy from mineral fuels, share produced by petroleum	41·3% ('69)	40·9% ('69)
Energy from mineral fuels, share produced by natural gas	37·2% ('69)	18·7% ('69)
Iron ore production (mln long tons)	86 ('68)	203 ('71)
Copper production ('000s short tons)	1,390 ('69)	c. 880 ('67)
Lead production ('000s short tons)	458·1 ('69)	c. 441 ('67)
Zinc production ('000s short tons)	497·8 ('69)	595·2 ('68)
Tin production ('000s long tons)	0·1 ('66)	c. 26·0 ('68)
Nickel production ('000s short tons)	15·4 ('69)	c. 105·0 ('67)
Gold production (mln troy ounces)	1·733 ('69)	c. 6·040 ('68)
Silver production (mln troy ounces)	41·9 ('69)	c. 35·0 ('67)

ECONOMY: *Manufacturing*

	USA	USSR
Steel production (mln m. tons)	120 ('70)	121 ('71)
Steel production: proportion from oxygen furnaces	52% ('70)	22% ('70)
Pig iron production (mln m. tons)	81 ('68)	89 ('71)

	USA	**USSR**
Aluminium production ('000s m. tons)	3,255 ('68)	1,100 ('68)
Cement (mln m. tons)	70 ('69)	100 ('71)
Metal-cutting machine tools ('000s)	226 ('68)	205 ('69)
Metal-forming machine tools ('000s)	78 ('68)	43 ('69)
Motor vehicle production ('000s)	10,069 ('69)	1,143 ('71)
Motor vehicle production of which lorries/trucks ('000s)	1,919 ('69)	564 ('71)
Motor vehicle production of which private cars ('000s)	8,224 ('69)	529 ('71)
Tractor production ('000s)	824 ('67)	472 ('71)
Combine harvester production ('000s)	42 ('67)	102 ('71)
Locomotive production	1,610 ('67)	1,826 ('71)
Sulphuric acid production (mln m. tons)	26·1 ('69)	12·1 ('70)
Synthetic fibre ('000 m. tons)	2,520 ('69)	623 ('70)
Chemical fertiliser (mln m. tons)	37·4 ('68)	61·4 ('71)
Paper (mln m. tons)	48·7 ('69)	4·2 ('70)
Woven fabrics: all kinds (mln sq. m)	10,540 ('69)	8·9 ('70)
Leather footwear (mln pairs)	581 ('69)	676 ('70)
Television sets (mlns)	11·3 ('69)	5·8 ('71)
Wireless sets (mlns)	10·4 ('69)	8·8 ('71)
Refrigerators (mlns)	5·3 ('69)	4·1 ('70)

ECONOMY: *Transport*

	USA	**USSR**
Freight turnover (bln m. ton–km)	2,755 ('69)	3,215 ('71)
Passenger inter-city movement (bln passenger–km)	1,739 ('68)	381 ('69)
Railway route length ('000 km)	334·8 ('68)	134·6 ('69)
Rail freight turnover (bln m. ton–km)	1,130 ('69)	2,634 ('71)
Rail freight turnover as proportion of total freight turnover	41% ('69)	83% ('71)
Rail passenger inter-city movement as proportion of total passenger movement	1·1% ('69)	69% ('69)
Surfaced road length ('000 km)	4,640 ('68)	191 ('69)
Number of lorries/trucks (mlns)	17 ('70)	c. 3
Number of private cars (mlns)	90 ('70)	c. 2
Road freight turnover (bln m. ton–km)	585 ('69)	69 ('71)
Road freight turnover as proportion of total freight turnover	21% ('69)	2% ('71)
Bus passenger inter-city movement as proportion of total passenger movement	2·2% ('69)	11% ('69)
Private car passenger inter-city movement as proportion of total movement	87% ('69)	<1%
Waterway freight turnover (bln m. ton–km)	434 ('69)	184 ('71)
Airline route length ('000 km)	188 ('69)	221 ('69)
Air freight turnover (bln m. ton–km)	4·64 ('69)	1·95 ('69)
Air freight turnover as proportion of total freight turnover	0·17% ('69)	0·07% ('69)
Air passenger inter-city movement (bln passenger–km)	141 ('68)	72 ('69)
Air passenger inter-city movement as proportion of total passenger movement	9·8% ('69)	18·7% ('69)
Average passenger distance flown (km)	920 ('68)	1,052 ('69)
Oil pipeline freight turnover (bln m. ton–km)	595 ('69)	328 ('71)

	USA	USSR
Oil pipeline freight turnover as proportion of total freight turnover	22% ('69)	9% ('70)
Seaborne commerce (mln tons)	457 ('68)	149 ('69)
Merchant marine (mln gross tons)	19·6 ('69)	13·7 ('69)

ECONOMY: *Trade*

	USA	USSR
Foreign trade by value ($ bln/bln roubles)	74·1 ('69)	19·8 ('69)
Exports by value ($ bln/bln roubles)	38·0 ('69)	10·5 ('69)
Imports by value ($ bln/bln roubles)	36·1 ('69)	9·3 ('69)
Leading trade partner	Canada ('69)	East Germany ('69)

ECONOMY: *Labour force*

	USA	USSR
Labour force (mlns)	77 ('69)	109 ('69)
Women as proportion of labour force	37% ('69)	51% ('69)
Industrial labour force (mlns)	20·1 ('69)	25·1 ('69)
Proportion of labour force unemployed	5·7% ('71)	—
Average length of working week (hours)	37·8 ('68)	40·1 ('68)

SOCIETY: *Population*

	USA	USSR
Total population (mlns)	203 ('70)	242 ('70)
Birth rate per thousand of the total population	17·7 ('69)	17·0 ('69)
Infantile mortality per thousand live births	21 ('69)	26 ('69)
Death rate per thousand	9·5 ('69)	8·1 ('69)
Annual increase in population (mlns)	2·1 ('70)	2·2 ('70)
Divorce rate per thousand of the total population	8·2 ('69)	8·9 ('69)
Immigration ('000s)	359 ('69)	—
Urban population (mlns)	c. 160	136 ('70)
Urban population as proportion of total population	c. 80% ('70)	56% ('70)
Largest urban area	New York	Moscow
Largest urban area population of (mlns)	15·35	7·06
Urban areas with pop. over 1 mln	33 ('70)	10 ('70)
Population of non-European origin (mlns)	26 ('70)	52 ('70)
Population of non-European origin as proportion of total population	12% ('70)	22% ('70)

SOCIETY: *Standard of living*

	USA	USSR
Persons per room (average)	c. 0·6	c. 2·3
Families owning cars as proportion of total families	c. 80%	<1%
Wireless receivers, total numbers of (mlns)	61 ('69)	47 ('69)
Television sets, total number of (mlns)	86 ('70)	31 ('69)
Telephones, total number of (mlns)	109 ('68)	12 ('69)
New books published ('000s)	c. 30 ('69)	75 ('69)

SOCIETY: *Education*

	USA	USSR
Pupils in elementary schools: grades 1–8 (mlns)	34 ('68)	41 ('70)
Pupils in secondary schools: grades 9–12 (mlns)	14 ('68)	12 ('70)

	USA	**USSR**
Pupil–teacher ratio in schools	21·3 ('68)	19·0 ('70)
Students receiving higher education (mlns)	6·8 ('68)	4·6 ('70)
First-degree graduates ('000s)	672 ('68)	565 ('69)
First-degree graduates: proportion in engineering	5·6% ('68)	31% ('69)
First-degree graduates: proportion in law	2·5% ('68)	1·5% ('69)
First-degree graduates: proportion in education	20% ('68)	33% ('69)
First-degree graduates: proportion in economics	2·3% ('68)	11% ('69)

MILITARY

	USA	**USSR**
Total armed forces (mlns)	2·7 ('71)	c. 3·4 ('71)
Normal length of service (years)	2	2
Military estimates ($ bln)	71·8 ('70–1)	39·8 ('70)
Army: total strength (mlns)	1·363 ('70)	c. 2·0 ('70)
Marines: total strength ('000s)	294 ('70)	c. 15 ('70)
Navy: total strength ('000s)	694 ('70)	c. 475 ('70)
Aircraft carriers, number of	20 ('70)	0 ('70)
Submarines, number of	103 ('70)	370 ('70)
Submarines, nuclear-powered	44 ('70)	80 ('70)
Air force: total strength ('000s)	810 ('70)	480 ('70)
Combat aircraft, number of	c. 6,500 ('70)	c. 10,200 ('70)
Long-range bombers, number of	2,250 ('70)	420 ('70)
ICBM warheads, number of	1,054 ('71)	1,510 ('71)
IRBM and MRBM warheads	0 ('70)	700 ('70)
SLBM warheads	1,328 ('70)	440 ('71)

USA: Sources of Imports of Minerals

Note. Data mainly from *Minerals Yearbook*, US Dept of the Interior, Bureau of Mines (Washington, annual). Where a mineral is shown in capitals the country usually contributes over half of American imports; if it is written in italics, the normal contribution is between one quarter and one half; if in roman type the import is below a quarter. Minerals imported in insignificant amounts have been omitted.

Algeria: barite, liquid natural gas
Angola: columbium
Argentina: beryllium, columbium, mica
Australia: cadmium, gold, lead, magnesite, silver, tantalum, *titanium*, thorium, tungsten, ZIRCONIUM
Austria: *magnesite*, vanadium
Bahamas: salt
Belgium: *cobalt*, *diamond*, platinum
Bolivia: antimony, lead, silver, tin, tungsten, zinc
Brazil: beryllium, cobalt, COLUMBIUM, iron, *manganese*, *mica*, *tantalum*
Burundi-Rwanda: beryllium, tantalum
Canada: ASBESTOS, barite, bismuth, *cadmium*, cobalt, columbium, copper, gold, GYPSUM, IRON, *lead*, mercury, NATURAL GAS, NICKEL, PEAT, petroleum, platinum, POTASH, *salt*, *silver*, sulphur, talc, *titanium*, TUNGSTEN, ZINC, zirconium, vanadium
Ceylon: graphite, thorium
Chile: *copper*, gold, iron, manganese, silver
Columbia: platinum, petroleum
Congo: *cobalt*, columbium, manganese, tantalum
Dominica: bauxite
France: gypsum, platinum, potash, talc
Finland: asbestos
Ghana: manganese
Greece: barite, MAGNESITE
Guatemala: zinc
Guyana: bauxite
Haiti: bauxite
Honduras: antimony, lead, silver
India: beryllium, manganese, mica
Indonesia: petroleum
Ireland: barite
Italy: barite, feldspar, fluorspar, magnesite, mercury, potash, talc
Jamaica: BAUXITE, gypsum
Japan: bismuth, *cadmium*, *diamonds*, magnesite, platinum, rare-earth metals
Kuwait: petroleum
Liberia: iron
Libya: petroleum
Madagascar: beryllium, graphite, mica
Malaysia: columbium, thorium, TIN
Mexico: *antimony*, *barite*, *bismuth*, cadmium, FLUORSPAR, gold, GRAPHITE, gypsum, mercury, salt, silver, zinc

Morocco: antimony, barite, zinc
Mozambique: beryllium, columbium, mica, tantalum
Netherlands: platinum
Netherlands West Indies: petroleum, vanadium
Nicaragua: gold
Nigeria: columbium, tantalum, thorium, tin
Norway: cobalt, graphite, nickel, platinum
Persia: petroleum
Peru: barite, BISMUTH, cadmium, copper, gold, lead, mercury, silver, tungsten, zinc
Philippines: chromite, *gold*, mercury
Portugal: tungsten
Rhodesia: asbestos, chromite, tantalum
Saudi Arabia: petroleum
Sierra Leone: diamond
Siam: tantalum, tin
South Africa: *antimony*, asbestos, beryllium, *chromite*, copper, diamond, gold, manganese, mica, nickel, silver, tantalum, URANIUM, zinc
South Korea: bismuth, tungsten
Spain: columbium, fluorspar, manganese, platinum, potash, tantalum, uranium, MERCURY
Surinam: *bauxite*
Sweden: manganese, vanadium
Switzerland: platinum
Trinidad: petroleum
Tunisia: salt
Turkey: barite, chromite, magnesite
Uganda: beryllium, columbium
United Kingdom: fluorspar, kaolin, *platinum*, rare-earth metals
USSR: *chromite, platinum*, rare-earth metals
Venezuela: iron, *petroleum*
West Germany: graphite, platinum, potash, rare-earth metals, uranium, vanadium
Yugoslavia: *magnesite*, mercury
Zambia: copper

USSR: Destination of Exports of Minerals

Note. Data from *Minerals Yearbook*, US Dept of the Interior, Bureau of Mines (Washington, annual) and *Vneshnyaya Torgovlya SSSR* (Moscow, annual). Where a commodity is shown in capitals large amounts are involved; italics denote moderate movement, while small imports are shown in roman type. Very small amounts are not included. Cobalt, kaolin, mercury, platinum, tin, uranium and other minerals are also exported, but details are not available. Oil products are included with petroleum.

Afghanistan: petroleum
Austria: apatite, asbestos, chromite, coal, iron, NATURAL GAS, nitrogen compounds, petroleum, potassium salts, SULPHUR
Belgium: apatite, asbestos, coal, *magnesium*, petroleum, POTASSIUM SALTS, pyrites
Brazil: petroleum, potassium salts
Bulgaria: aluminium, apatite, ANTIMONY, ASBESTOS, *coal*, electricity, GRAPHITE, iron ore, *petroleum*, *phosphate*, *potash*, SULPHUR
Canada: magnesium
Ceylon: petroleum
China: aluminium, petroleum
Cuba: asbestos, lead, NITROGEN COMPOUNDS, *petroleum*, *phosphates*, *potassium salts*, SULPHUR
Cyprus: petroleum
Czechoslovakia: *aluminium*, apatite, *asbestos*, *chromite*, coal, COPPER, *electricity*, *graphite*, *iron*, LEAD, MANGANESE, NATURAL GAS, NITROGEN COMPOUNDS, PETROLEUM, POTASSIUM SALTS, *pyrites*, salt, SULPHUR, ZINC
Denmark: apatite, asbestos, coal, petroleum
East Germany: *aluminium*, APATITE, ASBESTOS, *cadmium*, chromite, *coal*, GRAPHITE, *iron*, LEAD, MAGNESIUM, MANGANESE, *petroleum*, PYRITES, *vanadium*, ZINC
Finland: *apatite*, asbestos, chromite, coal, electricity, gypsum, lead, *petroleum*, *potassium salts*, salt, zinc
France: ASBESTOS, *chromite*, *coal*, *manganese*, *petroleum*
Greece: petroleum
Hungary: aluminium, *apatite*, *asbestos*, chromite, coal, *copper*, cryolite, ELECTRICITY, *graphite*, *iron*, lead, magnesium, manganese, NITROGEN COMPOUNDS, *petroleum*, *phosphates*, POTASSIUM SALTS, PYRITES, salt, SULPHUR, zinc
Iceland: petroleum
India: *asbestos*, NITROGEN COMPOUNDS, petroleum, potassium salts, sulphur, zinc
Italy: asbestos, *chromite*, coal, ilmenite, iron, NATURAL GAS, PETROLEUM, potassium salts, PYRITES
Japan: *aluminium*, antimony, ASBESTOS, CHROMITE, *coal*, iron, *manganese*, *petroleum*, POTASSIUM SALTS, TALC
Mongolia: petroleum
Morocco: petroleum
Netherlands: *antimony*, *copper*, MAGNESIUM, petroleum, potassium salts, zinc
North Korea: chromite, coal, *manganese*, petroleum, potassium salts, sulphur
North Vietnam: aluminium, copper, nitrogen compounds, petroleum, pyrites
Norway: apatite, manganese, petroleum

Poland: aluminium, *apatite*, ASBESTOS, CADMIUM, *chromite*, clays, *coal*, copper, *cryolite*, *electricity*, GRAPHITE, *iron*, lead, MANGANESE, NATURAL GAS, *petroleum*

Rumania: *apatite*, *asbestos*, CHROMITE, coal, copper, cryolite, electricity, *iron*

Sudan: nitrogen compounds

Sweden: apatite, asbestos, CHROMITE, coal, manganese, *petroleum*, potassium salts, pyrites

Switzerland: asbestos, petroleum

Turkey: *nitrogen compounds*, petroleum

United Kingdom: aluminium, apatite, asbestos, chromite, *iron*, magnesium, manganese, NICKEL, POTASSIUM SALTS, pyrites, vanadium

United Arab Republic: asbestos, coal, *petroleum*, zinc

USA: CHROMITE, *platinum*, rare earths

West Berlin: asbestos

West Germany: *apatite*, ASBESTOS, cadmium, CHROMITE, copper, GRAPHITE, MAGNESIUM, manganese, NATURAL GAS*, *petroleum*, PYRITES

Yugoslavia: aluminium, *asbestos*, *coal*, cryolite, *nitrogen compounds*, *petroleum*, POTASSIUM SALTS, SULPHUR

* After opening of pipeline in 1973.

Index

abortion, 207, 232, 265
accessibility by sea, 1, 96–7
activists, 267
administrative divisions, 42–5
advertising, 124–5, 227–8, 303
affluence, 303
age groups, 207–9
agriculture, organisation of, 143–4; labour in, 130, 144–7; income in, 146–7; mechanisation of, 148; expenditure on, 148–9, 156; resources for, 87–9; production, 152–4; and ideology, 154–5; yields, 155–6; comparison of, 155–7; problems in, 156–7; environmental factor in, 157; transport and, 180–1
agrotowns, 145, 230, 239
aid, *see* foreign aid
air masses, 59–61
air transport, 182–3
aircraft carriers, 10–11
aircraft, military, 10–11
airships, 183
Alaska, history of, 29–30; position of, 39; petroleum in, 185–6, 302; transport of oil from, 185–6
alienation (social, political), 246–9, 255–6
Alpena, Mich., climate at, 65–6
aluminium industry, 169–70
American economy, the, 99–102, 103–7, 112–13, 114–16
American Medical Association, 278, 282
American Revolution, the, 31–4
anti-resources, 92–8, 128
anti-trust laws, 104
Appalachian coalfield, 54
Appalachian Mts, as barrier, 24; crossed, 24–6; structure of, 47; relief of, 53; economic development of, 53–4; compared with Urals, 53–4

Aral Sea, 57–8
area, 41
arid lands, 69–76
Armenians, 205–6
arms race, 301–10
arts, the, 226
Astrakhan, 23, 56, 74
athletics, 225, 245
atmospheric warmth, 87–8, 149
autarky, economic, 4, 33–4, 202
automobiles, 168–9, 179–80, 194, 225, 300
automotive agreement, 200–1
autonomous republics, 44

badlands, 49
balance of payments, 199
balance of terror, 309
ballistic missiles, 10
Baptists, 212
baseball, 225
bases, *see* military bases
bauxite, 79
Baykal, Lake, 58
Beria, Lavrenti, 273, 274, 280
beryllium, 87
birth-control, 206–7, 232
birth rates, 206, 208; urban, 207; rural, 207
Black Hills, 47
blast furnaces, 168
boarding-schools, 134–5, 232
books, 226
'brain drain', the, 134, 301, 310
Brezhnev, Leonid, on unfinished projects, 136; on Soviet agriculture, 156–7; on Soviet diet, 219; career, 271, 274–6; shares leadership, 280; first secretary of CPSU, 277; on Chinese policies, 285, 295
building materials industry, 171